Practical Professional Catering Manag

wkc
West Kent College

Practical Professional Catering Management

Second Edition

H. L. Cracknell, R. J. Kaufmann
and G. Nobis

First edition 1983
Reprinted seven times
Second edition 2000

Published by
MACMILLAN PRESS LTD
Houndmills, Basingstoke, Hampshire RG21 6XS
and London
Companies and representatives throughout the world

ISBN 0–333–66555–4

A catalogue record for this book is available from the British Library.

This book is printed on paper suitable for recycling and made from
fully managed and sustained forest sources.

10   9   8   7   6   5   4   3   2   1
09   08   07   06   05   04   03   02   01   00

Printed in Great Britain by
Creative Print & Design (Wales), Ebbw Vale

Dedication

Ronald Kaufmann died shortly before this book was completed. The wide knowledge and extensive experience of the industry which gave him his living are evident on every page, and this is his way of giving thanks to those he learned from and of showing the way forward to succeeding generations.

A meticulous attention to detail and an unbending aim to achieve perfection in everything he undertook ruled his life. His fastidious insistence on excellence made working with him a stimulating experience, whether on the stove or at the writing table. A joint of beef roasted by Mr Kaufmann, or any other dish he made, was unique because his inborn flair always stamped the result with his personality. So it is with this book. He will be greatly missed by his colleagues and friends.

Harry Cracknell
Gianfranco Nobis

Contents

1   **The catering and hotel industry**   1

Outline of the industry; Historical background; Tourism;
Future challenges; Challenge to restaurateurs.

2   **The catering cycle**   11

The consumer and the market; Formulation of policy;
Interpretation of demand; Convergence of facilities;
Provisioning; Production and distribution; Control of costs
and revenue; Monitoring consumer satisfaction.

3   **The consumer and the market**   16

Human needs and nourishment; Regulatory functions; The
senses; Humans and society; The market; Marketing catering
products; Feasibility studies.

4   **Formulation of policy**   26

Organisational structure; Management; Aims and objectives;
The policy; Specific policy applications; Policy procedures.

5   **Interpretation of demand**   35

The menu as a marketing tool; Gastronomic considerations;
Menu planning; The language of the menu; Menu
compilation; Daily meals; Cost distribution of menus;
Design and production of menus and wine lists.

6   **Convergence of facilities I – Planning the areas**   48

Computer-aided design; General points of planning; The
planning team; The sequence of planning; Planning strategy;
Allocation of space; Planning the areas; The function of the
kitchen and its ancillary areas.

List of plates

List of figures

Preface

We had the satisfaction of seeing the first edition of this book used widely as a textbook in catering schools and colleges in many countries. We realise that this success has been due to its practical approach to the study of catering operations and its identification as a cycle of closely related activities.

Since the book's first appearance in 1983, the catering industry has made considerable progress towards greater efficiency, much of this through technology. Managers can now keep much closer control over all aspects of their operation. This new edition aims to reflect and support these advances.

All parts of the industry have seen the need to abandon many traditional methods of operation because they no longer satisfy customers' requirements.

New technology eases many problems, but cannot completely take over the hands-on approach of management and its reliance on the social and practical skills of personnel. Customers have become more discerning about standards of food and service, whether in a work's canteen or deluxe restaurant, anywhere they are eating away from home. This requires investment in training and education, development of skills, and pride in and dedication to the work.

Research done by individuals and teams of experts has helped bring about improvements in the way the industry is run and how it is viewed by outsiders.

As a service industry, catering gives employment to a very large number of people in a wide range of jobs. The aim of this book is to make those jobs more satisfying by establishing the good practice which a dedicated workforce can carry out efficiently and enthusiastically. This new edition will give the reader an understanding of what the industry is and how it can provide worthwhile careers.

Practical Professional Catering Management was conceived as a companion volume to *Practical Professional Cookery*. Their relationship emerges in the many activities involved in the provision of food and drink. *Practical Professional Cookery* contains over 2,000 recipes and studies topics such as the new styles of cookery, ethnic dishes, nutritional aspects, and cookery methods.

The authors aim to provide readers of the two books with all the knowledge they require on the subjects of food and beverage operations.

H. L. C.
G. N.

Introduction

This book identifies the diverse activities which form the food and beverage operations of all kinds of catering businesses. It has divided the whole into eight segments and shows how they come together to form a cycle of events from start to finish.

The book demonstrates how each segment of the catering cycle interlocks with the others and how it has to be followed, consciously or not, by everyone who works in the industry. The cycle commences with the formation of a new or altered business, and goes on to show the succeeding stages. Each needs to be given deep consideration before a logical move to the next one. Each segment has to interlock with the preceding and following ones. The chapters of this book follow the sequence of activities in their logical order to encompass the relevant information.

Caterers are encouraged to introduce new ideas to attract customers into their premises, whether in the commercial or profit sector, or the welfare or cost sector. Nowadays potential customers have more time to enjoy leisure pursuits, including eating out in restaurants of all kinds. This makes them more discerning, and it is all the more necessary for caterers to acknowledge their needs positively.

The title of this book shows that it gives practical information on how to run a business that is successful because it satisfies customers' needs. The book is a store of knowledge which will help readers carry out their tasks in a thoroughly efficient way.

It will be of equal value to employees training on the job, students following courses in hospitality and catering management at colleges and universities, and caterers now holding top jobs in the industry who will find in this book new ways of thinking about the problems they may experience.

Acknowledgements

The authors and publishers would like to thank the following sources for the use of illustrations: T. S. E. Brownson, page 105; Falcon Catering Equipment, page 76; Grosvenor House Hotel, pages 8, 20; The Bath Spa Hotel, page 61; Victor Manufacturing, page 303; Viscount Catering Ltd, pages 81, 235.

Every effort has been made to trace copyright holders but if any have been inadvertently overlooked, the publishers will be pleased to make the necessary arrangements at the first opportunity.

1 The catering and hotel industry

Outline of the industry; Historical background; Tourism; Future challenges; Challenge to restaurateurs.

Providing refreshment in the form of food and drink is a very old and honourable trade, as old as civilisation itself. Its end result is almost always to increase the bodily comfort and well-being of the individual. It is therefore an extremely important aspect of today's highly organised and complex society.

The business activity which provides refreshment is carried out by the catering industry, a fairly loose term which is commonly bracketed with that of hotel-keeping. Recently the term 'hospitality industry' has been used to give a more precise image of this important section of the service industry.

The hotel and catering industry is closely associated with the tourist industry and provides food and shelter for people away from their home, on business or pleasure.

Outline of the industry

Catering is the second largest employer in the United Kingdom, providing jobs for 2.4 million people. This great industry is divided into two main sections: the commercial or profit sector, and the welfare or cost sector.

The commercial or profit sector is made up of all kinds of businesses (see Figure 1). These businesses are driven by the profit motive and by a desire to provide customers with good food and drinks at a price that ensures the profitability of the enterprise. There are more than 120,000 outlets in the commercial or profit sector, with 1.3 million full- and part-time employees (see Figure 2).

Catering establishments in the welfare or cost sector do not aim to make a profit, although they are usually expected to break even. They are often subsidised by the state or local authority. Most outlets are in the public sector such as hospitals and schools, while some are part of industry such as staff restaurants (see Figure 1). There are 82,000 outlets in the welfare or cost sector, with 1.08 million staff (see Figure 3).

Figure 1   Composition of the catering industry

COMMERCIAL OR PROFIT SECTOR	
Outlets	**Characteristics**
Hotels of all kinds	• Operates in a competitive market
Residential establishments	• Capital intensive
Café and snack bars, take-aways	• High percentage of fixed costs
Public houses serving meals	• Fluctuation of demand
Motorway service stations	• Active pricing policy
Clubs of all kinds	• Its main objective is revenue
Leisure centres	
Public schools	
Private colleges	
Catering contractors	

WELFARE OR COST SECTOR	
Outlets	**Characteristics**
Hospitals	• Usually operates for a captive market
Universities	• Infrastructure is provided
Colleges in the public sector	• Fixed cost usually absorbed by the
Schools of all levels	parent activity
Her Majesty's Forces	• Stable demand
Old people's homes	• Pricing policy may be determined by a
Staff restaurants and canteens	committee
Meals on wheels	• Its main objectives are occupancy rate
	and recovery of all costs
	• Importance of nutritional aspects

Historical background

It is often said that the past can be a mirror for the future. This short account of the history of the catering industry will show you how your predecessors faced up to and dealt with the social changes of their times.

The history of catering in all countries covers the provision of food and accommodation for people on the move. In early times people travelled for business reasons just as they do now, though in those days it was usually on the king's or government's behalf. Many people also went on pilgrimages, mainly on foot, to the shrines of saints, just as they do to the holy land or Mecca nowadays.

The first recorded institutions which provided food and shelter were in the Middle East. They were built along the caravan routes and they were called Caravanserai, inns with large courtyards for overnight stops. Thus, roads were important in the early development of the catering industry. Posting houses offered travellers food and accommodation and a change of horses. In medieval western Europe, monasteries and castles also offered hospitality to travellers, and the monks brewed good beer and cooked hearty meals for all visitors.

Local lords of the manor offered bed and board in their large country houses to travellers who could afford it, but by the middle of the sixteenth century these were in decline. Around the same time Henry VIII dissolved the monasteries. These two events boosted the importance of commercial catering establishments and, by royal edict, inns were classified and licensed.

Inns had to provide accommodation for travellers who appeared to be able and willing to pay, and to give stabling for their horses. As a result, the largest inn of each town increased in importance by taking on the business of a posting house, which was the place where mail and stage coaches stopped to let passengers eat, drink and rest while the horses were changed and mail delivered and collected.

Under King James I, who reigned from 1603 to 1625, innkeepers had to provide beds for visitors. Ale houses were also allowed to offer accommodation, but taverns could only sell liquor.

Food was plentiful for those with money and cooks commanded good salaries, but the job was not very congenial as the work had to be carried out using iron pans over an open fire that gave off dangerous fumes.

During the second half of the eighteenth century, travel by coach and horses

Figure 2   Composition of the commercial sector

Residential hotels	11.2%
Restaurants, cafés, snack bars	14.3%
Fast-food and take-away outlets	24.3%
Public house catering	32.4%
Clubs	13.9%
Catering contractors	2.1%
Holiday camps	1.7%

Kind of establishment	No. of units	No. of employees
Hotels and residential	13,644	289,200
Restaurants, cafés and snack bars	17,412	295,500
Fast-food and take-away outlets	29,569	(included above)
Public house catering	39,375	327,000
Clubs of all kinds	16,845	138,300
Catering contractors	2,546	115,700
Holiday camps	2,110	165,000*
Totals	**121,501**	**1,330,700**

* = self-employed

Source: UK government and trade reports. The figures apply to the year 1994

Figure 3   Composition of the cost sector

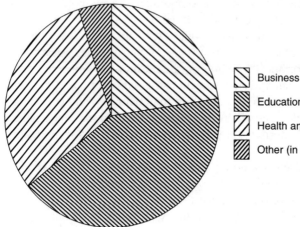

Business and industry	22.4%
Education	41.6%
Health and welfare	30.9%
Other (in MoD)	5.0%

Kind of establishment	No. of units	No. of employees
Business and industry	18,545	416,000
Education	34,370	247,800
Health and welfare	25,530	342,100
Other	4,160	73,100
Totals	**82,605**	**1,079,300**

Source: UK government and trade reports. The figures apply to the year 1994

grew alongside the growth of trade and industry. The coaching inns enjoyed good business, with an estimated 10,000 passengers being carried to and from their premises each day. Consequently the inn was the most important place in each town, and the innkeeper was a person of some eminence in the community.

Then in 1826 the first railway train ran, and soon the operating companies opened hotels at every main line terminus and buffets on many station platforms. Railway catering had a good reputation, and stage coaches and the inns where they used to stop gradually lost their importance. The first railway hotel was built at Euston Station in 1838.

The early years of the twentieth century saw the return of activity on the roads as the invention of the internal combustion engine gave people the enjoyment of motor car travel with the opportunity of stopping at inns for bed and board.

Hotels developed from inns and the growth of road travel meant that more hotels had to be built. They were needed in city centres for business people and tourists, and at resorts for holiday makers. Hotels of various standards and sizes attracted different types of customers and charged prices according to the range of services offered and any necessary amenities. Motels were built to offer a basic service without frills for motorists wishing to break long journeys. Hotel chains, some owned by airways companies, opened their own brand of hotels in capital cities across the world. Hilton, Intercontinental, Holiday Inn and Sheraton De Vere, for example, are household names in many countries. Emerging countries welcomed and assisted financially with the opening of these prestigious hotels, which gave a boost to their economy as well as providing jobs and bringing in foreign exchange from visiting tourists. New hotel companies are constantly being formed to cater for a particular market with standards and prices to match. Hotel chains are formed and grow, or are sold or taken over by another company. Established companies cannot always rely on their reputation and need to change their methods of operation according to changes in society and the prevailing financial climate.

Conrad Hilton – the first world-class hotelier

Conrad Hilton's entry to the world of catering was in 1907, when he and his brother did all the jobs involved in running an adobe house hotel, owned by his mother who did the cooking; this was in New Mexico before it had been admitted to statehood. In 1918 he was a doughboy serving under the American flag in France.

After he was demobbed, Conrad Hilton bought his first hotel in Cisco, Texas, a two-storey building called the Mobley Hotel. It was so busy that rooms were let by the 8-hour shift and not by the day, so the rooms were fully occupied for 24 hours every day. After five years of profitable ownership, he took over the Melba Hotel in Fort Worth and then the Waldorf Hotel – not the one in New York City that he later became the owner of, but a six-storey one in downtown Dallas, the city where he subsequently built a Hilton Hotel that cost $1 million.

The New York stock market crash in the 1930s meant that Hilton lost all the hotels he had built or acquired, but it was not long before he started again, firstly by leasing hotels to run and then buying them, including the well-known 450 bedroom Sir Francis Drake Hotel in San Francisco.

During the Second World War he continued to buy existing hotels and married Zsa Zsa Gabor, the film actress. Then in 1946 he founded the Hilton Hotels Corporation, with hotels all over the United States – valued at $41 million. At the same time the US State Department suggested that he establish American-operated hotels in every important city in the world, so he set up Hilton Hotels International Inc., carrying his slogan 'World Peace through inter-national trade and travel'.

The first Hilton International Hotel was the luxury Castellana Hilton in

Madrid, which was quickly followed by deluxe hotels in Baghdad, Bangkok, England, Hawaii, Tokyo, Trinidad, Rome, Sydney and Vienna – indeed every continent except Antartica. Some years later the Hilton International Group was taken over by Pan-Am Airways and then by Ladbroke's outside the USA.

Conrad Hilton, who once said his motto was 'Don't let your possessions possess you' died in 1979 at the age of 92.

César Ritz – grand hotelier

The best-known hotelkeeper of all time is without doubt César Ritz, whose name is synonymous with luxury.

Ritz was born in 1850 in a remote village in Switzerland of peasant parents. His first job was as an assistant in a hotel in the nearby town of Brieg, but after only a few weeks he was sacked for incompetence. He was so determined to make a career in hotels that he got a job in Paris during the Great Exhibition of 1867, working as a hall porter until he felt capable of waiting at table. He excelled at this and worked his way up the ladder in the best hotels in Paris then Monte Carlo, Lucerne and Vienna.

Soon Ritz earned his living as head waiter, where he could study the habits of the international jet-set of those days as he waited on emperors, kings and queens, members of government and the diplomatic corps, and moguls of every nationality. He became on intimate terms with them as he welcomed them on arrival at the best hotel in each of the fashionable resorts where they stayed during the social season. His reputation as restaurant manager was *par excellence* and he was head-hunted by Richard D'Oyly Carte, the owner of the Savoy Hotel in London, to come and rescue it from failure shortly after it opened in 1889. It had opened to great acclaim as the most luxurious hotel in Europe, but was making no profit, so Ritz was given a free hand to turn it into the successful hotel it has been ever since.

Ritz brought his own heads of department with him from Switzerland, including Auguste Escoffier who soon gained a reputation as the greatest French chef ever to work in this country. Ritz also brought elite clientele from the continent and enticed the Marlborough House 'set' of royalty to patronise the hotel. During the seven years he spent running the Savoy, Ritz also acted as consultant to many other hotel groups in Europe and the United States of America. It seemed natural that he would seek a wider field of enterprise, so he set up the Ritz Hotel Development Company. With plenty of financial backing, he built the Carlton Hotel in London, the Ritz Hotels in Paris and London, and many other luxury hotels in the world's capital cities. One of his financial supporters was Monsieur Marnier Lapastole, a wealthy vineyard owner and inventor of the liqueur Grand Marnier.

Ritz devoted all his energies to making his enterprise a success and giving his customers the very highest possible standard of hospitality. Unfortunately he had driven himself too hard, and he spent the last years of his life in a private hospital in Switzerland where he died in October 1918.

Charles Forte – a catering tycoon

The catering empire established by Charles Forte eventually became the world's largest commisariat, embracing hotels, restaurants, cafés, motorway service stations, on-location catering, airport shops and refreshment outlets, in-flight food production units, leisure complexes, entertainment centres, seaside pier amenities, central production kitchens and bakeries, and a publishing company.

Charles Forte was born in Italy in 1908 and came to England as a child where his father owned a café. He decided to follow in his father's footsteps and started work in menial jobs until he opened a milk bar in London's west end. It became so popular that he developed it into a chain. He then started to buy established businesses such as the Café Royal, Waldorf Hotel, Trust House hotel group and, later, the Lyons group of hotels. By 1993 the Forte Group ran 344 hotels in this country alone, many of them deluxe standard.

Lord Forte, as he became, passed the business to his son Rocco as chairman and chief executive, until in 1996 it was taken over by Granada in a £3.8 billion bid.

Sir Rocco Forte has since set up a new hotel group, HF Hotels, and has signed contracts with developers and investors to build a chain of 50 luxury hotels across Europe, including Great Britain.

Tourism

Tourism is the business that takes people away from their homes to other countries or parts of their own country for work, leisure, educational or health reasons. Some go to visit a shrine, or are just curious about other cultures and lifestyles and want to broaden their outlook.

Tourism is an enormous business, with a worldwide turnover of £920 billion per annum. The business is relatively young. In 1956 there were only 1 million visitors to Britain, but by 1993 this had increased 20 times, with £9,250 million being spent on food, lodgings, transportation, entertainment and shopping.

Tourism is an important source of income for many countries and provides jobs to thousands of people, not just in hotels and restaurants but in pubs, theme parks, stately homes, sports and leisure centres, and on travel. Tourism continues to grow worldwide by about 4.5 per cent per year.

Future challenges

In order to hold on to their present position in the market place, caterers have to face big challenges brought about by the great leap forward in science and technology. There are currently two main challenges: the technological revolution in communications, and the shift of economic power from Europe and the United States to the countries of East Asia.

It should be borne in mind that despite the immense growth of tourism, 40 per cent of customers are business people travelling on behalf of their firms. They can transact their business through fibre-optic communication networks, video-conferencing via satellites, and fax machines, so these facilities have to be made available. Europe's position as the world's business power house has gradually diminished, however, and the Pacific Rim countries are becoming more important. This has changed the destination of many business travellers, leaving vacant hotel rooms in Europe. Hoteliers will have to attract new kinds of tourists to fill

Plate 1   The Grosvenor House Hotel, London

their empty rooms; this may mean installing different amenities to meet the needs of a different clientele.

Customers' requirements

An ever-increasing range of commodities is transported across the world, making it possible to produce global menus. Customers hear about and see many exotic fish, fruits and vegetables and expect to be offered them properly cooked on local menus. There is an increasing demand to sample the foods of other nations. Caterers have to keep abreast of these impacts, even though they may come and go with fashion.

Customers have become increasingly health conscious and are showing an awareness of the composition of foods. Organically grown produce is widely available and should be included on menus and wine lists where there is a known demand.

Customers may have reservations about the farming of meat, poultry and fish and seek assurance of its humane treatment. Gastronomy is now a topic of interest to a wide public. Service staff must be capable of discussing it with customers wishing to improve their knowledge.

Many magazines and newspapers employ restaurant critics to evaluate restaurants for their readers. Food guidebooks give details of different eating places within regions and rate them on the quality of food, service, menu, wine list, surroundings and price. The ultimate accolade for any chef and owner is to succeed in gaining Michelin stars for their establishment. Other guidebooks award crossed-cutlery crowns, four-leaf clover marks, etc. which help gourmets decide if restaurants are worthy of their patronage.

Challenge to restaurateurs

People's disposable income has risen over the years, which allows them to spend more on leisure pursuits, holidays and meals away from home.

A measure of this prosperity is the amount of housekeeping money spent on food and drink. In mainland Europe this averages 20 per cent of family income, whereas in Britain it is diminishing as shown in Figure 4. This figure shows that expenditure on basic necessities has more than halved over 40 years, yet there has been no big increase in eating out. Restaurateurs face the problem of how to fill their dining-rooms with cash customers. They have to tempt people away from the comfort of their homes and compete with a refrigerator full of ready-made gourmet meals which cost only a fraction of the prices charged by restaurants.

It could be that companies take a too narrow view of their market. They think in terms of their product rather than the fundamental needs which they should satisfy. Customers only appreciate good food and service if it is combined with value for money and gives them total satisfaction.

Figure 4   Proportion of family income allocated to food and drink purchases in the UK

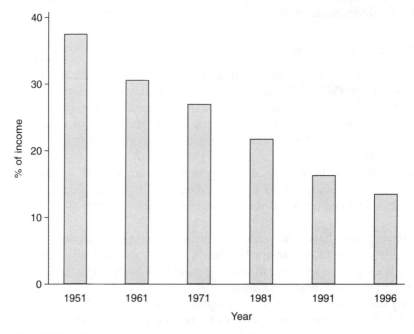

Source: Central Statistics Office

Further reading

Holloway, C. (1998) *The Business of Tourism*. Addison-Wesley

Lundberg, D. (1994) *The Hotel and Restaurant Business*, 6th edition. Van Nostrand Reinhold

Magris, M., McCreery, C. and Brighton, R. (1996) *Introduction to Catering*. Addison-Wesley

Medlik, S. (1994) *The Business of Hotels*. Butterworth-Heinemann

Mennell, S. (1995) *All Manners of Food*, 2nd edition. University of Illinois Press

Montagné, P. (1988) *Larousse Gastronomique*. Hamlyn

Tannahill, R. (1995) *Food in History*, 2nd edition. Crown Publishers

Toussaint-Samat, M. (1994) *A History of Food*. Blackwell

2 The catering cycle

The consumer and the market; Formulation of policy;
Interpretation of demand; Convergence of facilities;
Provisioning; Production and distribution; Control of costs and
revenue; Monitoring consumer satisfaction.

The catering cycle represents the sequence of activities involved in the conception and implementation of a catering operation. It helps all members of staff to see how the particular area within which they work fits with the other departments, and how each part of the cycle relies on every other part of it. The cycle continues with each new customer who comes into the establishment, and it shows how their needs should be met.

The cycle is made up of eight decision-making stages which together constitute the entire catering process (see Figure 5). Its starting point is to establish the identity of the customers and their needs. The cycle then continues through a series of closely related segments until it reaches the point where it is possible to monitor the degree of customer satisfaction achieved. After each sequence of events the cycle recommences and any alterations or improvements needed can be included in time for new customers to benefit from them. Your aim should be ultimate perfection.

The cycle defines the resources, finances, materials, manpower and machinery needed to operate the establishment.

The consumer and the market

When adapting an existing business or opening a new one, managers have to decide what type of customers they intend to attract and what sort of menu would suit them best. These decisions will be influenced by the location of the restaurant. A high-class restaurant in a first-class district contrasts with an unsophisticated café in a side street which caters for people living on the outskirts of town. Whatever the business, it is essential to anticipate the likely needs of the customers by carrying out market research (see Chapter 3).

The first stage of the catering cycle is therefore concerned with defining the customers' needs to show the potential market and indicate the required policy.

Formulation of policy

The second stage of the cycle sets out the method of operation of the business in both its internal and external dealings, based on the market analysis carried out

Figure 5   The catering cycle

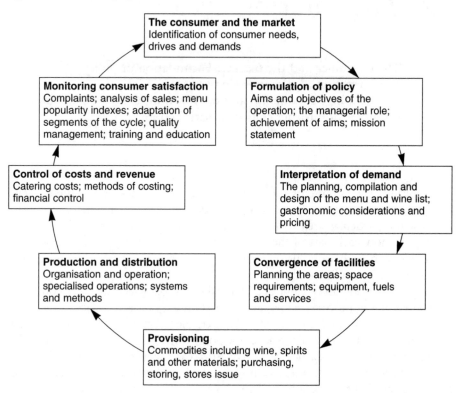

earlier. It provides purpose and cohesion to the organisation. In other words, it sets the guidelines which will govern the operation and achieve the objectives that will make it successful. The person responsible for determining the policy must be professionally qualified and well experienced, assisted by departmental heads who should contribute their expertise in drawing up a mission statement.

A mission statement is the ethos or spirit which governs the way in which a firm deals with its customers, suppliers and staff. It goes beyond practical skills to the ideas which show the public and employees that the restaurant they patronise or work for has clear objectives and is a worthwhile enterprise. For example, a firm may show commitment to the development of its staff through the Investors in People scheme.

Investors in People

The Investors in People scheme, which was developed by the Department of Education and Employment in 1991, sets 'a standard of assessing development of people and their skills as part of business strategy'. It aims to encourage the effective training of staff to help them reach their maximum potential. Management must regard it as a long-term scheme and provide the investment to support it. If implemented successfully, the scheme will increase efficiency and give staff an under-standing of each department's goals, breaking down the barriers that can arise. It will also encourage staff to be loyal to the company, result-ing in lower staff turnover and greater job satisfaction.

Interpretation of demand

In the third stage, the catering business begins to put its policies into practice. It must decide how it will satisfy the expected demand, drawing up a list of dishes and drinks which will be offered. The list of dishes will be communicated by means of a menu, which could be chalked on the window or on a blackboard in a café, or printed on a large piece of card with appropriate artwork. The menu communicates how the establishment meets its customers' demands and should also reflect the skill and professional ability of the staff. Menus and wine lists need not be pretentious, but should reflect the flair of the caterer. Full details on menus will be found in Chapter 5, and wine lists in Chapter 10.

Convergence of facilities

The fourth stage of the catering cycle transforms the perceived demand into an operational reality. This may mean erecting a purpose-built restaurant or adapting an existing one. In all cases there will be a need for specialist advice on catering equipment, layout, gas, electricity and water services, and compliance with local authority regulations. Bear in mind that technological progress in the design of kitchen equipment is continuing, and that because of the high cost of labour and energy many foodstuffs are bought in ready-prepared form. Planning must be decided in the light of these advances.

Provisioning

The fifth stage of the catering cycle relates to the purchase of commodities, all the drinks listed on the wine list, cleaning materials, small equipment and utensils, etc. A decision has to be taken on whether to keep these items in store, with the consequent tying up of capital, or whether to order as required and save the wages of storekeepers and cellar staff.

The provisions needed to fulfil the menu are dealt with in Chapter 9, and those for the wine list and bar tariff in Chapter 10.

Production and distribution

The sixth stage is the very core of the operation of every catering business. Here the raw materials are made into the dishes described on the menu and drinks are dispensed as selected from the wine list or bar tariff.

The organisation of the different parts of the catering department shows that each has a hierarchy of staff. There are several grades of personnel, each having a separate sphere of operations. Those with job titles such as head waiter, head chef and head cellarperson are the managers of specific subdepartments. In overall command of the entire food and beverage department is the catering manager, who must have a good knowledge of each subdepartment under his or her jurisdiction.

In a large company or hotel, the food and beverage manager will be responsible to a general manager. A chain of restaurants or public houses will have a senior manager at head office or regional office level who dictates the catering policy for the whole group.

Control of costs and revenue

The seventh stage of the catering cycle deals with the profitability of the business and all the incoming and outgoing cash. Several people are involved in financial control, including the restaurant cashier, barperson, sales assistant, control clerk, chief cashier and financial controller. All employees must be cost-conscious if the business is to thrive and produce good profits. Control of costs means that just the necessary number of staff are employed; there is strict supervision of deliveries, storage and usage of commodities; and no pilfering or other losses are prevalent. Wastage of energy and goods must be minimised. The day's takings must be checked against outgoings to confirm that the agreed kitchen percentage was achieved.

Monitoring consumer satisfaction

The final stage of the cycle shows how customers can be involved in measuring the performance of a business. Information may be obtained by analysing the sales of dishes, assessing plate and other waste, examining trends in consumers' eating habits, and using questionnaires to obtain knowledge of customers' backgrounds and their views on the restaurant or staff.

Quality management comes under this heading (see Chapter 17), because it means that the goods and service provided must be of the highest quality whatever the kind of catering outlet. The caterer's obligations are to provide food, drink and service of the requisite quality, governed by the prices charged, and to meet all ethical and legal requirements. Rules and procedures which monitor quality standards and safety and hygiene requirements must be implemented. Training and education (see Chapter 18) plays an important part in this.

The catering cycle is therefore an interrelated sequence of activities which are always ongoing and in a state of flux and modification. The following chapters look at each stage in more detail, and attempt to give the reader an understanding of how they are linked together to form a complete entity. It should be noted that some of the stages of the cycle have more than one chapter devoted to them.

3 The consumer and the market

Human needs and nourishment; Regulatory functions; The senses; Humans and society; The market; Marketing catering products; Feasibility studies.

When setting up a catering business of any kind, it is essential for the owner or operator to identify the kind of customers who would be most likely to use the establishment. The owner may wish to attract a particular type of clientele through the standards of food, drink and service offered, the prices charged, and the atmosphere of the dining-room.

Having settled the image for the restaurant, attracting the proposed kind of customers depends on successful marketing and building up the reputation of the business. In the past, customers showed their appreciation of good waiters or chefs by following them when they left one place to open or run another somewhere else. This happens less frequently nowadays, but it is not unknown.

Human needs and nourishment

Our needs change during our lifetime but are instinctive, such as the likes and dislikes we have of food and drink as we grow up. What we do not know instinctively is that our diet comprises a mixture of nutrients which has a great effect on our well-being. Everything we eat contains a certain quality and quantity of nutrients which, when digested in the body, help the growth and repair of body tissue. They also help transport oxygen through the body, control the metabolic rate of digestion, and create hormones and antibodies necessary for the enjoyment of good health.

All caterers, especially chefs, should have a good working knowledge of the basics of nutrition and be able to apply them whenever necessary. It is important to know how cooking affects certain nutrients. The following is a brief outline of nutritional requirements. Further information can be obtained from the books listed at the end of the chapter.

Protein

Proteins is made up of basic units called amino acids which link together in many combinations. It is vital for the growth, repair and maintenance of body tissues.

Meat and fish are particularly rich sources of protein, but it is also found in milk, eggs, bread and vegetables.

Carbohydrates

Carbohydrates are found in starchy foods such as cereals, pasta, bread, cakes, biscuits and sugar. They are the body's main source of energy. Daily requirements will therefore vary according to the activity and size of the individual.

Fats

Fats are found in foods such as butter, oil, margarine, milk, cheese, fish and meat. Fats are a good source of vitamin A and D. These are added artificially to margarine, as they are essential to health. Fats are a more concentrated form of energy than the other nutrients and a small quantity is essential in the daily diet. Unsaturated fats such as corn oil, olive oil and sunflower oil, which are liquid at room temperature, are preferable to the saturated fats found in meat and dairy products which are solid at room temperature. Saturated fats can leave fatty deposits on the walls of arteries, increasing the risk of heart failure.

Vitamins

Vitamins are of considerable nutritional importance. Vitamin A is not normally deficient in the body because it can be stored in the liver. It is connected with growth and cell linings. It is found in most animal foods and as carotene in plant foods.

The B vitamins include B1 or thiamine; B2 or riboflavin; niacin and folic acid which aren't numbered; and vitamin B6 or pyridoxine. They overlap in their values as they often occur in the same foodstuffs. They are found in meat, especially liver, fish, cereals, pulses, wholegrain rice and green vegetables. A deficiency of B vitamins can be serious. Beriberi damages the nerves and heart when there is a lack of B1; pellagra is a skin disease caused by a lack of niacin in the diet; sore lips and cracking of the skin on the corner of the mouth may derive from a shortage of vitamins B2 and B6.

Vitamin C is found only in fruits, especially berry fruits and citrus fruits, and vegetables including potatoes. It can easily be destroyed by overlong storage and overcooking. Lack of vitamin C causes a disease called scurvy, which was prevalent amongst sailors in the past who had no access to fresh fruit and vegetables.

Vitamin D is necessary for the absorption of calcium obtained in the diet, and its lack causes rickets. It is added to margarine and is found naturally in fatty fish, eggs, butter and liver, but not in many other foods.

Mineral salts

Mineral salts are needed in the diet, particularly iron, calcium, iodine, fluorine and zinc. Iron is the colouring matter in blood and a lack can cause anaemia. It is found in curry powder, baked beans, corned beef and liver. Calcium works together with vitamin D to help its absorption and is present in milk, cheese, soya beans and fish such as sardines, sprats and whitebait. A shortage of iodine can cause the growth of a goitre in the neck. It is present in soil, especially around the coast, but our main source is from fish. Fluorine helps to protect teeth from decay and in some parts of the country is added to tap water. Zinc is connected to fertility and sexual development. It is present in meat, offal and shellfish.

Water

Water is essential to all body processes. It is present in large quantities in many foods. About two-thirds of the body is water. This compound dissolves food, oxygen and wastes; makes up a large part of the blood; and helps regulate body temperature. Lack of water leads to dehydration and causes the normal body functions to stop working.

Dietary fibre

Dietary fibre is known as roughage and is found mainly in bran on the outside of cereals. It lessens the chance of constipation and has been linked with the prevention of varicose veins and diseases of the bowels.

Healthy eating

When customers read the menu on entering a restaurant, they look for dishes that they both like and think will do them good. They select food not only on price and quality, but also on its nutritional content.

It is therefore up to the caterer to ensure that each dish on the menu contains some beneficial qualities. This applies equally to institutional catering, which offers only a set meal or a very limited choice, and to lengthy à la carte menus.

A balanced meal is one that gives customers the right proportion of:

1 cereals, pulses, pastas, rice and bread products
2 fruit and vegetables
3 fish, meat and poultry
4 dairy foods including eggs and fat.

Half the day's intake should be from 1 and 2, including about 500 g of fruit and vegetables in fresh, frozen or canned form. Fish and poultry are fine, but meat should be trimmed of excess fat and preferably cooked in a minimum of fat which should not exceed 75–100 g per day for an adult.

Many customers realise that salt and sugar in excessive amounts can be detrimental to their health and are aware that hidden amounts of both are present in other foods including sauces and gravies, pastry, biscuits, and some breakfast cereals.

Regulatory functions

Our bodily functions are controlled by an area in the brain called the hypothalamus which keeps the entire organism running in a state of equilibrium known as homeostasis. Bodily needs are communicated to the hypothalamus which immediately sets out to satisfy them. Body temperature, reaction to fear, and the basic needs of eating and drinking are all controlled by the hypothalamus.

Our appetite is affected by complex feelings related to the aroma, flavour and colour of foods which will have evolved from experience and memory. In addition, our choice of food is affected by the environmental, religious and cultural factors we have grown up to accept, which mean we accept or spurn particular foods.

The senses

The five senses of hearing, sight, smell, taste and touch all contribute to a person's pleasure when eating and drinking, and these experiences can be stored in the memory to be called upon as needed. Perception refers to the way that incoming information from the senses is received, processed and given a meaning. The senses can use this internal framework to produce a state of mental arousal which motivates a person to certain goals, including the choice of food and drink.

Hunger, because it deals with a state of nutrient deficiency in the human organism, is a powerful motivating factor in eating behaviour. Hunger may be satisfied by meeting the most basic requirement of food intake. Appetite, however, is a more complex phenomenon, because the pleasure and satisfaction derived from the meal are dependent not only on the reduction of hunger, but also on the satisfaction of individual expectations which are modified by cultural upbringing, state of mind at the time the food is consumed, and the five senses. Customer satisfaction therefore involves food presentation, aroma, taste, temperature, and the harmonious balance of the immediate surroundings.

Humans and society

Humans are born with an instinct to survive, procreate, and acquire control over their environment. To achieve this, they are dependent on the collective efforts of the community in which they find themselves. They also need the stability brought about by an established order which allocates tasks to individuals in order to maintain continuity. The rewards that they receive depend on the value that society places on their role. Within this reward system, individuals are placed into certain categories and social positions.

There are various ways of grading a restaurant's customers according to their

Plate 2   A meal at the Grosvenor House Hotel, London

status. The Registrar General uses people's jobs to define their standing in society (see Figure 6). This gives a measure of their responsibility and indicates their spending power, and tastes and preferences.

Influences which affect people's preferences for a particular kind of restaurant include:

1 household circumstances such as the number and ages of people living in a family group
2 cultural and ethnic background
3 situational needs, such as where people work and if time is given for meal breaks
4 customer objectives: using the in-store restaurant when out shopping; using catering facilities at leisure or other activity centres; celebrating anniversaries or other occasions in luxurious surroundings
5 trends in eating habits such as wholefoods, healthy eating regimes, high-fibre meals, macrobiotic eating habits, and so on.

The market

The market is all the potential customers who might use a particular restaurant. The clientele of each kind of restaurant is made up of people who, in general, enjoy similar lifestyles. Information about the number of people who eat out regularly

Figure 6   The Registrar General's classification by occupational groups

Group	Occupation	Approx. % population	Preferred eating places
A	Diplomats, barristers, directors, executives, consultants, stockbrokers	3	Clubs, high-class restaurants, ethnic eating places, night-clubs, gaming clubs
B	Bank managers, doctors senior managers, accountants, producers, editors, professors	9	Medium-price restaurants, wine bars, public houses
C1	Teachers, senior technicians, computer experts, actors	18	Chinese, Indian, Italian and English restaurants, fast-food snack bars, public houses, sandwich bars
C2	Skilled manual workers	30	As for Group C1
D	Semi-skilled workers	30	Work canteens, public houses, sandwich bars, cafés, take-aways, quick-service restaurants
E	Unskilled workers	10	As for Group D

gives an indication of a nation's eating habits and economic well-being. The figures for the United Kingdom are less than half those of France and the United States.

Customer profiling

The caterer should try to find out as much as they can about the area in which the business is located, as this can help in reaching the right market. Any analysis of customers should be based on the following:

1 the socio-economic status and probable spending power of the local residents
2 customers' ages and whether the location is a retirement area or where mostly young families live
3 family background – whether eating out is a habit because not much cooking is done in the home
4 the ethnic origins of the local population
5 gender of the local population and typical marital status – families, single parents, single people, students
6 customers' self-perception – whether they are adventurous or conservative in their attitude to food.

Market research

Market research is used to evaluate business opportunities in a specific sector of the market and assist the formulation of a marketing strategy. Published data may provide figures and analysis of overall trends in the country's economic forecasts, unemployment figures, eating out statistics, average expenditure in different types of restaurants, number of foreign tourists and customer preferences. If specific information on a competitor's activities is required, it can only be obtained by commissioning an investigation by a specialist firm in this field.

Marketing catering products

Marketing is the approach that can influence consumer demand. A marketing strategy should consider place, product, price and promotion – the four Ps. Marketing will be most effective when each P is in agreement with the others. For example, the product determines the suitability of the place, which should be chosen with specific consumers in mind; the price must then be in harmony with the two Ps above, and these three combined constitute the basis for the promotional campaign.

Product

A catering product has a number of different aspects. When enjoying a meal in a luxury restaurant, the total experience includes not just the excellent meal and choice of wines, but also the decor and atmosphere of the room, pleasant waiting staff and possible live music in the background. Altogether this is quite a unique product.

Place

The product can also have an effect upon the location of any kind of restaurant, and vice versa. Choosing the right location has a lot to do with the success of an establishment. For example, a fast-food or quick-service operation should be built in a central location where there are crowds of people both day and night. This is why such places are now a feature of motorway service stations, passenger ferries and airports.

The best location for a high-class restaurant is in a select area of town, in a beauty spot, or even in a mansion or stately home where it is part of the attraction.

Any kind of restaurant has to face competition, but can draw customers in from a three-mile radius in city centres and from several miles around in suburban districts. Good value for money in meals and drinks, plus adjacent car parking are the draw. It is estimated that a 50-seater restaurant needs a surrounding population of 30,000 or more. On the other hand, a modern-style public house serving good quality food and beer which attracts everyone of 18 years and above can be successful in a surrounding area of 1,000 inhabitants.

Luncheon counters, coffee shops and snack bars usually do well at transport interchanges, cinemas and night-clubs, and in department stores and hyper-markets. High business rates may prevent their presence on the high street, but if they are good, customers will find them.

Price

The pricing policy is of enormous importance in the success or failure of every catering establishment. It does not always pay for the owner to set high prices with a view to getting rich quickly. Equally, sales campaigns and reduced prices may give customers the impression that there is a fall in business. A nearby competitor may be selling an item at a lower price. This may be because the competitor has brought the basic ingredient in bulk, or has cut the quality or quantity. Customers soon spot such moves and make up their mind about which place is best.

'Prestige pricing quality expectations' is the term given to customers' assumptions that a high price means an excellent dish. Psychological pricing is where prices are kept one pence below a round figure, say £7.99 rather than £8.

Promotion

Advertising is a mainstay of business promotion. A catering operation may decide to run a campaign to bring in more business by sending leaflets to house-holds or putting an advertisement in local newspapers and magazines. This is known as 'above the line advertising'.

'Below the line advertising' is also popular. It uses a price or other promotional inducement. For example, the bar might open with a 'Happy Hour' when cocktails and other drinks are sold two for the price of one. Offering a complementary bottle of wine to every table of four persons may encourage more people to patronise a restaurant. Some restaurants secure customer loyalty by setting up a discount card scheme for certain people, e.g. the over-60s, that operates during the early part of the evening.

Maxwell Joseph – entrepreneur unique

Sir Maxwell Joseph came into the world of hotelkeeping from a job as an estate agent when the opportunity came his way to buy the Mandeville Hotel off Oxford Street in London's West End in 1946. From this small beginning he went on to found the Grand Metropolitan Group of hotels and many other companies connected with the food business. Finally he set up the Inter-Continental Hotel group which owned 33 luxury hotels in 23 countries, of which 5 were in Great Britain.

Joseph, together with the help of Fred Kobler, a quiet, retiring man but brilliant entrepreneur, set about building the group. In quick succession he bought Mount Royal for £1 million, the Royal Palace Hotel in Kensington, St Ermin's in Westminster, and the enormous block of flats, Dolphin Square, alongside the River Thames.

By 1962 Joseph was running 16 hotels in England and 6 in Scotland, mainly by taking over unprofitable businesses. He made them profitable by employing first-class sales and marketing people to go out and sell the facilities of food and accommodation, together with banqueting and conference business.

The first purpose-built Grand Metropolitan Group hotel was the Europa in Grosvenor Square, which opened in 1964. By 1970 the group was worth £135 million and had acquired Levy and Franks, the public house chain, Berni Inns, the Mecca catering and leisure group, Express Dairies, and many others. Grand Met, as the company is known, now owns IDV which makes Smirnoff vodka, Bailey's Irish Cream, Cinzano Vermouth, Justerini and Brooks the upmarket wine merchant, and also Burger King.

Feasibility studies

At the very beginning of any catering venture, a feasibility study must be carried out to assess the project. Many people who enter the industry with the sound intention of serving their fellow men and women and making a decent living find that this is not as easy as they imagine. A feasibility study could save them from losses or even bankruptcy.

Before deciding whether to purchase or rent premises, it is essential to investigate in detail how the establishment will be run and what the likely outcome will be. Each step outlined in the catering cycle must be detailed and assessed, and revenue and expenditure must be forecast as accurately as possible. It is important to avoid a situation where it becomes necessary to lay off staff and destroy good food because a feasibility study was not carried out at the beginning. Chapter 15 shows how costs mount up and how to cover them adequately.

Further reading

Baker, M. (1996) *Marketing: An Introductory Textbook*, 6th edition. Macmillan

Buttle, F. (1986) *Hotel and Food Service Marketing*. Cassell

Coltman, M. M. (1997) *Hospitality Management Accounting*, 4th edition. John Wiley & Sons

Croft, M. J. (1994) *Market Segmentation*. International Thomson Business Press

Fox, B. A. and Cameron, A. G. (1995) *Food Science Nutrition and Health*, 6th edition. Hodder and Stoughton

Giddens, A. (1994) *Sociology*, 3rd edition. Polity Press
Middleton, V. (1994) *Marketing in Travel and Tourism*, 2nd edition. Butterworth-Heinemann
Moutinho, L. and Evans, M. (1992) *Applied Marketing Research*. Addison-Wesley
Powers, T. (1997) *Marketing Hospitality*. John Wiley

4 Formulation of policy

Organisational structure; Management; Aims and objectives; The policy; Specific policy applications; Policy procedures.

Organisational structure

In order to operate efficiently, all catering establishments must first set up a sound organisational structure, based on a strong supportive framework. It must cover every department of the business, each of which has a particular part to play and has its own specialists in charge who are skilled and experienced in that operation.

Policies have been based on organisational structure since humans first began to form into groups or societies. Each individual had a particular part to play. The formal structure had to have a clear line of authority in pyramidal shape. At the top was the chieftain, then the high-ranking officials, and lower down the burghers, while the vassals were left on the bottom rung.

Bureaucracy is a system by which officials, as a body, administer the organisation on a system of division of the workforce under a hierarchy. It can achieve a high degree of efficiency and has the following features:

- maximum specialisation
- strict job definitions stating duties, privileges and boundaries
- vertical lines of authority
- decisions taken on expert judgement based on technical knowledge
- disciplinary compliance under a supervisor's orders
- separation of policy and administration
- importance of abiding by the rules
- central authority
- horizontal management lines to be under skilled management
- continuity of people in top jobs.

Management

Managers have the responsibility of running a business in accordance with the owner's or the company's wishes. Traditionally they have not appreciated outside opinions on how this should be done. Such managers believe that trade unions and craft bodies ought not to try to influence the operation of the business for their own ends. Staff are expected to increase productivity, but without having to resort to conflict with management. This is, of course, the authoritarian approach which has led to much staff dissatisfaction. A more recent management approach takes the view that employee participation in the running of the business will help enhance their performance and lead to greater efficiency and profitability.

The catering industry follows the management practices of other industries. An example of the management structure in a large hotel is shown in Figure 7. The vertical lines represent line management and the horizontal lines staff management.

An individual owner may be a sleeping partner leaving a manager to get on with the day-to-day operation of the business – so long as the owner receives a return on the investment, the manager need not be subjected to any interference. This is fine while the business is good and the manager endeavours to maximise the hotel's potential with no specialist help needed. However, hotel groups usually find it necessary to have specialist help in areas such as finance, marketing, personnel, purchasing, training and research. In this case the management will be organised as shown in Figure 8.

The specialists will influence the freedom of the general manager to follow any personal policy or procedure. In fact, the specialists have the authority to establish any policy or procedure necessary for the efficient functioning of their area of influence. This will, of course, be applicable to all hotels or other establishments in the group. This is the only way in which the desired standards can be maintained across all branches.

Aims and objectives

The policy of a business is made up of aims and objectives. These have to be given verbally or in written form to every member of staff from manager to apprentice. These are the rules and guidelines necessary to run the business efficiently.

The **aims** are a statement of intent to achieve a stated goal over the long term. This is the philosophy or beliefs which will govern the way the business is run. It is sometimes called the mission statement, a declaration of the firm's aims as they affect customers and employees. Examples of aims could be:

- We aim to achieve a 10 per cent penetration of the market within one year.
- We intend to maintain and enhance the business through continued customer satisfaction.
- Our first priority is customer satisfaction of our products and service.
- We intend to establish ourselves as a market leader in our field.
- We take pride in the way we treat our workforce and give them just rewards for their labour.
- We dedicate our establishment to the well-being of the local community and will participate in possible social events.
- We are committed to continuous expansion while maintaining aims for the benefit of customers and staff.

Figure 7   Example of the organisational structure in a large hotel

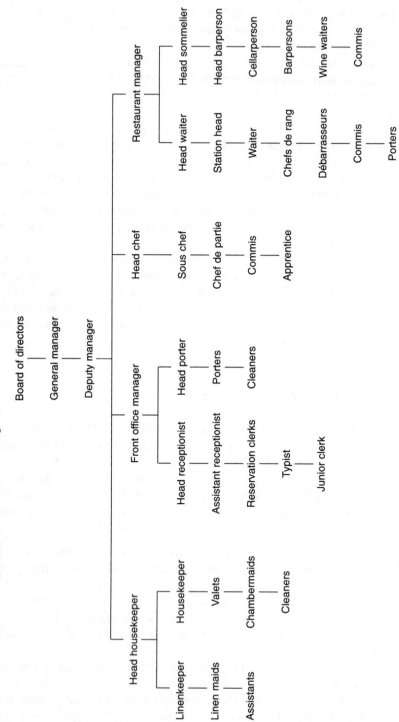

Figure 8   Staff management in a hotel group

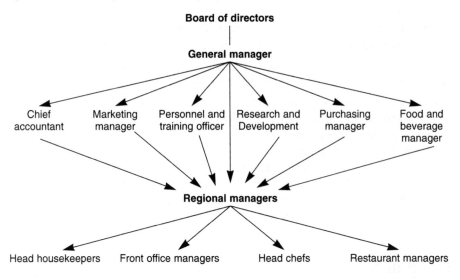

The **objectives** must be clearly spelled out and state what is expected of every employee. They should be quantifiable in terms of output, which is the number of customers served per employee. To be realistic, staff must give full cooperation to the achievement of the objectives. If necessary, on-the-job training and education must be provided to improve performance.

Objectives can be long term or short term. They can be strategic, administrative or operational. Strategic objectives are usually concerned with external rather than internal affairs, for example:

- the market segment that the organisation intends to attract and the products it intends to supply to this market
- the market positioning of the organisation so that the standard of amenities and operational concept attract a particular type of clientele
- where and how the organisation should locate its units in order to achieve the desired market penetration
- how the organisation should respond to market opportunity in a compatible sector of activities
- the form of growth envisaged by the organisation, for example by vertical integration such as the acquisition of materials and equipment supplies, or by horizontal expansion such as the absorption of competitive units in the market place.

Administrative objectives cover the following points:

- how the functions of marketing, accounting, personnel, purchasing and product design should be carried out, either at central office or at individual unit level
- the impact of technology on day-to-day operation as regards information and

communication systems; this might include a central reservations system or use of the e-mail system
- the allocation of budgets to departments that need to spend on various forms of advertising and the care and maintenance of equipment and premises.

Operational objectives are decided at department management level. They are then passed on to subordinates for implementation. They can include:

- the desired rate of occupancy and profitability
- alternative uses of areas to maximise occupancy
- maximum use of all facilities
- gain at least the minimum average spend per customer
- serve at least the minimum number of customers per service period
- meet the desired ratio of customers per meal service period
- reach the required gross profit of each department
- vary the hours of business to meet customers' demands.

The policy

The policy is a set of rules and guidelines which determines the way a business is run. To be effective, it must be simple and realistic – easy to understand and carry out by all grades of staff. The policy must include means of communication and cooperation between departments. It must give a certain amount of freedom of decision-making to departmental heads. This could include the opportunity to bring in additional business by offering discounts on drinks and meals early in the evening, discount on rooms at weekends, free children's accommodation or meals, etc. Such offers should increase the popularity and profitability of the establishment.

The framework of the policy must take into account any constraints that might infringe upon its stated aims. Figure 9 shows how external and internal factors can affect policy.

It goes without saying that the policy must include codes of conduct for every individual in the business and, stemming from that, the group itself.

A policy can be looked at from both the micro level, which is concerned with the internal factors of the business, and the macro level, which is the involvement of the business in its external affairs in society. For example, a prospectus drawn up to interest possible investors in a company will deal only with the external aims in general terms, not with the inner workings of the operation. Figure 10 demonstrates the interaction of macro level and micro level policies. The policies can be kept separate, but the principle must fuse together into a whole.

In attempting to define a policy role in an organisation, it may help if it is viewed in the context of the person actually responsible for its implementation. In any catering establishment it will be the manager of the food division or catering section who takes this responsibility, which is in effect the running of the food and beverage operation. This title may change in relation to the nature of

Figure 9 External and internal factors affecting the formulation of policies

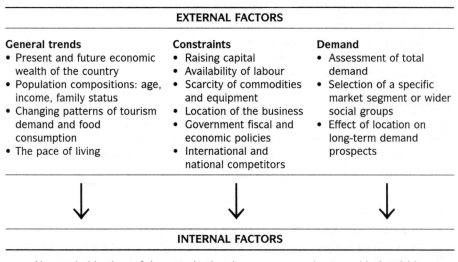

EXTERNAL FACTORS

General trends
- Present and future economic wealth of the country
- Population compositions: age, income, family status
- Changing patterns of tourism demand and food consumption
- The pace of living

Constraints
- Raising capital
- Availability of labour
- Scarcity of commodities and equipment
- Location of the business
- Government fiscal and economic policies
- International and national competitors

Demand
- Assessment of total demand
- Selection of a specific market segment or wider social groups
- Effect of location on long-term demand prospects

INTERNAL FACTORS

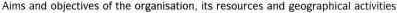

Aims and objectives of the organisation, its resources and geographical activities

Figure 10 The interaction of policies

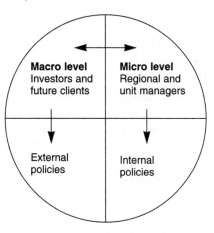

Macro level
Investors and future clients

Micro level
Regional and unit managers

External policies

Internal policies

the operation, for example director of catering for a hotel group, food and beverage manager in a hotel, bursar in a residential college, and secretary or steward in a club.

It is the manager who has the task of putting the policy, as decided by senior management, into day-to-day operation and planning the internal organisation so that the several departments under his or her control work together in close cooperation. The manager must be responsible for the design of the operational framework that supports the firm's or institution's policy decision in providing the range of products and services required, for example the range of items in the wine list. These must be at prices that the customer can afford and of a suitable quality for the money. In this way customer satisfaction will be ensured.

There are times when it may be difficult to fulfil the terms of the policy implicitly. The head chef may occasionally fail to give customers exactly what they want. For example, it may be impossible to get a particular type of meat listed on the menu, e.g. Aberdeen Angus sirloin steak; or the regional ingredients needed for a traditional pizza may not be available. Failure to stick to the standards set in your policy could lead to loss of customers. In the world of fried chicken, each franchise has its own rigid formula for preparing and cooking the pieces of chicken. Not only is each ingredient specified, but also the cooking and serving methods. All this is usually governed by illustrations which are easy to follow without the need for any deviation.

Operational decisions

The routine of daily operations is governed by the menu, whether it is a fixed or a daily one. In each case it will have been the result of market investigation to suit the expectations of the clientele. The cash taken has to keep the establishment solvent. The cost distribution of the selling price of food is as follows:

	%
Standard fixed costs	20
Labour	30
Materials (food)	33
Energy (gas, electricity)	3
Trading profit	14
Total	100

Note that in this example the basic concept only is given. Fixed costs on each cover will change in relation to turnover, but the allocation of the remaining costs should be kept constant as given in the policy document.

Specific policy applications

Policy for customers

A policy for customers should cover opening hours; handling special requests and bookings; cloakroom facilities; dealing with complaints; public relations exercises; ensurance of satisfaction regarding portion sizes and standard of service; adequacy of menus and wine lists; and methods of payment including acceptance of credit cards.

Policy for personnel

The following points need to be considered:

- Applications will be accepted from persons possessing a good knowledge of the job as advertised, taking into consideration their potential for promotion.

- Applications will be accepted from persons regardless of their colour, race, nationality, religion, gender, marital status and sexuality, provided they are eligible for employment and possess a work permit where necessary.
- A probationary period will have to be worked to show necessary competence or capability.
- A proper induction will be given to all new employees.
- A job specification will be issued showing duties, responsibilities, performance and expected behaviour.
- Performance appraisals will be explained and held at frequent intervals.
- Details of hours of duty, days off, holiday arrangements, pay and pay days, overtime, deductions and pension will be issued; reasons for dismissal will be discussed.
- Health and safety regulations, house rules, grievance procedures and trade union membership will be explained.
- A personal file will be kept for each employee, including references; an employee has the right to see the file but not the references.

Speciality policies

Each department needs a sub-policy of its own, such as a purchasing policy. This should deal with:

- the methods of purchasing for each class of goods, including perishable and non-perishable items
- contracts with nominated suppliers; not opening too many small accounts
- drawing up standard purchasing specifications for all goods, the quality in keeping with the desirable cost
- method of payment of accounts
- purchaser's discretion on carrying out the policy
- adherence to maximum and minimum stock levels; expected frequency of deliveries
- discretion in the unlikely event of disposal of surplus or outdated stock
- supervision of storekeeper, cellarperson and bartender
- recognition of the importance of adherence to purchasing policies
- obtaining maximum value for money spent in relation to gross profit
- methods of internal requisitioning of commodities
- accurate recording of sales and takings.

Operational policy

The operational policy should cover:

- consideration of customer goodwill and loyalty
- conformity to legal obligations regarding standards of hygiene and safety
- adequate supervision and regular inspection of all areas of the business
- gaining feedback from customers so as to be ready to adapt to possible changes in demand

- seeking to implement improvements by means of work and method study, and by introducing the advances being made in technological systems.

Legal policy

Many Acts of Parliament have been introduced which apply to the operation of catering establishments and it is imperative that they are understood and observed by senior management and heads of department. This will help to ensure that the business complies with all legislation which concerns its operation.

Policy procedures

To put policies into practice, it can be helpful to lay down the exact sequence of actions involved in each particular job. This can be done by studying each activity and charting the movements needed to complete it in the most efficient way. Staff must be trained or instructed to follow the step-by-step procedures. Once members of staff see that the procedures are sound and that they get the job done properly, they will soon follow them automatically.

This must cover the policy decisions for every department. Staff should be encouraged to put forward their own suggestions for possible improvements before the policies are converted into hard-and-fast rules. Each part of the catering cycle needs its own plan of action as part of the total policy; only then will every part of the operation run smoothly and efficiently to the benefit of all who are connected with the enterprise – customers, staff, management and shareholders.

Further reading

Fewer, A. and Wills, N. (1992) *Marketing*. Butterworth-Heinemann

Hales, C. (1993) *Managing through Organisation*. International Thomson Business Press

Knowles, T. (1998) *Hospitality Management*. Longman

Pettinger, R. (1994) *Introduction to Management*. Macmillan

Powers, T. (1995) *Introduction to Management in the Hospitality Industry*. John Wiley

Venison, P. (1983) *Managing Hotels*. Butterworth-Heinemann

5 Interpretation of demand

The menu as a marketing tool; Gastronomic considerations; Menu planning; The language of the menu; Menu compilation; Daily meals; Cost distribution of menus; Design and production of menus and wine lists.

This chapter shows how the theories of policy formulation are put into practice to provide customers with the kind of food and drink which suits their tastes. It covers the way in which menus have to be planned for the various sectors of the catering industry. Every catering business has to interpret the rationale for its existence in the form of lists of food and drink it will supply to customers. The list of dishes is the menu and that for drink is the wine list.

On entering a catering establishment of any kind, a customer looks at the menu to see what dishes are available and at what price, and from this information decides what to choose. A caterer views the menu as an outward expression of the business. It demonstrates how professional the people who run the business are. A menu is the 'modus operandi' of a catering business which everyone has to work from.

A menu is a marketing tool as well as a list of dishes. Its contents must show the expertise of the person who writes it as well as that of the staff who produce and serve the dishes. It must be attractive to look at, handle and read. Even if the menu itself is a blackboard fixed to the wall, it must be properly worded and legible. The menu is an aid to selling the products of the firm.

The menu as a marketing tool

Before writing any menu, the person concerned must know what market or kind of customer it is aimed at. In Chapter 3 the necessity of obtaining a clear picture of potential customers was emphasised, and now the kind of dishes they expect must be included in the menu. The menu writer has to consider three points, namely:

1 the customer's needs
2 the occasion, or why the customer is eating there
3 the customer's expectations.

These points are outlined below.

The customer's needs

It is obvious that a customer enters a restaurant to eat because he or she feels hungry, but there are also other influences. People's eating habits are ingrained from infancy and stem from factors in their background such as home, school, social class, country or region of upbringing, religion and friends. All these have some influence on acceptance of foods. The jobs that people work in, the people they mix with, the holidays they take, and the social group they consider themselves to be part of dictate the kinds of restaurants they like to patronise. It may be thought that people who have a good education or who travel abroad frequently will be more demanding and more adventurous in their eating habits than less well-educated or travelled people. However, cookery programmes on television, books and magazines on food and drink, and supermarkets make it easy for everyone to eat gourmet-standard meals at home as well as in restaurants. Menu writers must keep these facts in mind and take account of the differing needs of people of different sexes and ages. As mentioned in Chapter 3, it is also important to have a basic knowledge of the nutritional values of foods.

The occasion

The 'meal experience' is a term that sums up all the elements that go to make a meal something more important than satisfying the appetite. It includes the surroundings in which a meal is taken; the persons involved, including companions and staff; the menu and wine list; the quality of the cooking and service; the time it takes; and the feeling of money well spent. Each kind of restaurant offers a different experience and this experience should be consistent on each visit. Reputations are built on people's recommendations rather than advertising. People are happy to make a long journey to enjoy a meal in a place they have heard is worth the drive. Each restaurant is different in some way and will attract customers that suit it. Location is a factor in the popularity of a restaurant, but this does not mean that it has to be in a high-class area. A good report by a restaurant critic, mention in a restaurant guidebook, or award of Michelin stars are means of gaining a good reputation. The appointment of a well-known chef or head waiter will bring in connoisseurs of good food and drink. All these factors can add to the sense of occasion that makes a meal special.

The customer's expectations

Towards the end of the eighteenth century, a French judge, gourmet and writer, Jean-Anthelme Brillat-Savarin wrote a book called *La Physiologie du Gout*. This book is still in print and is highly regarded for its maxims on the subject of gastronomy. A well-known quote from the book is 'Tell me what you eat and I shall tell you who you are'. Caterers would do well to bear this in mind when compiling menus. It should remind them to give their customers the dishes they like and not force strange concoctions on them. It is worthwhile remembering that many people are more tolerant about their religious beliefs and politics than about their food.

Concealed gourmandising

Buntings, or Ortolans, are small birds the size of a sparrow, found anywhere between Scandinavia and the Mediterranean, including Britain. Gastronomically they are classified as game birds, although Escoffier said they were not truly of gastronomic excellence. However, he included some recipes for them in his *Guide Culinaire* and said the best way to cook them was by roasting at a high temperature for between three and five minutes only.

That was before a European Union directive made it an offence to hunt ortolans. In France it was interpreted as not being unequivocally illegal to eat them, although it is a contravention of the 5th Class under the French Rural Code which makes it an offence punishable by a heavy fine.

The effect of the EU directive has been to put ortolans on to the black market and to raise their price to almost 250 francs each. French gastronomes, especially those of Gascony, do not feel this is too high a price to pay for such a delicacy and are prepared to disguise themselves to eat them incognito.

The ritual in the best places is to eat the fattened bird, which has been boned, stuffed with foie gras and truffles and roasted, with a large table napkin placed over the guest's head and face so that nobody knows what is going on.

Gastronomic considerations

Our needs for nourishment change as we grow older and are influenced by the weather. In winter people need meals which are high in calorific value to keep the body warm. In summer light meals are appropriate and people prefer cold dishes and salads. As well as these environmental influences, people expect traditional dishes on special occasions related to their cultural and religions background. In the United Kingdom we expect to see roast turkey on the menu at Christmas, and we hope to see pancakes featured on the menu on Shrove Tuesday.

The time of day is also an important consideration. It is accepted that breakfast is a fairly light meal; lunch is slightly more substantial; and dinner is the most substantial meal and more of an 'occasion'. This ties in with the traditional sequence of courses of each meal of the day which must be kept in the proper order. There must be an orderly progression of intensity of taste sensations because any alteration to the sequence, or discordance of colour, aroma, flavour, texture or temperature, could spoil the pleasure of eating a good meal. Highly flavoured or spiced dishes eaten as a first course can stimulate the appetite but will dull the delicate flavour of the courses that follow. These aspects of gastronomy are dealt with in greater depth later in this chapter.

Menu planning

When planning to write a menu, it is necessary to consider a number of key points. First, the menu must reflect the policy of the place where it is to be used, bearing in mind the kind of customer who will order from it, the prices to be charged, and the dishes that will give customer satisfaction and the desired profit margin. Then the writer must choose the phraseology that will make the dishes more appealing. For example, instead of 'Roast beef and Yorkshire pudding', it might pay to use a few more words and describe this dish as 'Roast rib of Aberdeen Angus beef with rich gravy, Yorkshire pudding and horseradish sauce'.

The two main types of menu are Table d'Hôte and à la Carte. A Table d'Hôte menu is a set meal. Nowadays it lists a number of choices for each course rather than only one or two as used to be the case. It may consist of two, three or four courses sold at an inclusive price, or each main course may have an individual price which covers the whole meal. An à la Carte menu has a number of dishes listed under each course, with the price marked against each dish. It is usually more expensive than a Table d'Hôte menu, but customers can select only one or two dishes if they wish. There may be a minimum charge per person.

A Table d'Hôte menu should include main dishes of popular appeal that satisfy most people's tastes. These dishes are cooked in bulk to serve the estimated number of customers and must therefore keep well throughout the service period. Many foods, especially vegetables, can be cooked in batches during the two hours or more while the meal is being served. This kind of menu is widely used in both sectors of the catering industry – the cost sector as much as the profit sector – as a good way of feeding a large number of people.

An à la Carte menu has to include slightly better quality dishes than a Table d'Hôte menu. In general each dish is freshly cooked when ordered by a customer, and only a few items may be held in readiness to save a long wait. Some dishes are available for two or more people only, for example a Chateaubriand, rack of lamb, or gigot de présalé. The portions are slightly larger than for the Table d'Hôte menu.

An à la Carte menu is planned to last over a period of time and may be changed only to include seasonal commodities. A Table d'Hôte menu is written for a particular day and is sometimes included as an insert in the longer-lasting menu. Customers of quick-service restaurants choose from a set menu and their order is cooked on the à la Carte system. When planning a menu for a one-off special occasion for a large number of people, the menu writer has to use the Table d'Hôte pattern. The entire party sits down at the same time and has to eat the same food which must, of course, be of popular appeal. The only alternative would be for a vegetarian who requested a different dish from the main meat course. For a smaller party, it may be possible to offer an alternative to the first course of hors-d'oeuvre or soup. This kind of function is known as a banquet and full details of its organisation are given in Chapter 13.

The language of the menu

A menu is the means of communication between caterer and customer and therefore must be written in the language they speak and understand. The person who takes the order from a customer can discuss or explain the dishes on the menu to the person ordering them.

French is the international language of cookery and many dishes on menus all over the world are of French origin. Top hotels in many countries still use French names and terms in their menus, usually with a description written underneath each entry. This means that the menu writer must be capable of writing perfect French to ensure that genders and plurals are written correctly and that where the definite article (le, la or les) is used to prefix dish titles, as for a special banquet, there are no mistakes. It is not advisable to attempt to translate the names of foreign dishes. Customers soon learn what the names mean even if unable to pronounce them.

There are several books which give the correct spellings of dishes in international use and their contents (see 'Further reading' at the end of this chapter). These books help make life easier for people who need to write menus.

Menu compilation

After the planning stage, the menu should be carefully compiled, bearing in mind the following points:

1 the sequence of courses
2 the suitability of dishes
3 the selection of dishes and balance of the menu
4 the capabilities of the staff
5 the availability of equipment
6 the season of the year
7 the availability of resources
8 nutritional aspects.

The sequence of courses

The established order of courses of the menu should not be changed. The accepted pattern makes it easier to compile a menu of any kind, particularly a lengthy one of, say, 12 courses which a caterer is sometimes asked to prepare. The sequence for a lunch is hors-d'oeuvre, soup, farinaceous, egg, fish, entrée, relevé, roast or grill, cold buffet and salad, vegetable dish, savoury soufflé, sweet dish, cheese, dessert and coffee. These have to be grouped to provide the current requirements of three- to four-course luncheons. Groupings for a four- to five-course dinner would be from hors d'oeuvre, soup, fish, entrée, relevé, roast, cold dish, vegetable dish, sweet, savoury, cheese, dessert and coffee.

As an example, a five-course dinner could consist of soup, fish, entrée, relevé and sweet. Coffee does not really count as a course, not even if served with petits fours. Sorbet does count as a course, its real place being between the two main courses or halfway through the meal. A four-course meal does not merit a sorbet since its role is that of refreshing the palate in preparation for the next main dish. The sorbet, which is a flavoured water ice, used to be the signal to light up a cigarette such as a Balkan Sobranie; nowadays a liqueur glass of spirit such as apple brandy or Calvados is served instead of sorbet. By tradition cheese should not be included on a dinner menu; when it is included its place can be before the sweet, though traditionally it should come afterwards.

The suitability of dishes

This information shows which dishes are appropriate for the two main meals of the day.

LUNCH

Hors-d'oeuvre: grapefruit, melon, fruit juice, avocado, fruit cocktail, shellfish cocktail, smoked fish, salami, Parma ham, pâté maison, hors-d'oeuvre selection on a trolley.

Soup: the more robust broths and potages, e.g. Scotch Broth or minestrone.

Farinaceous: any kind of pasta in a sauce, the various kinds of gnocchi, and all savoury rice dishes.

Egg: any kind of hot egg dish, including omelette.

Fish: fairly simple kinds of fish and methods of cooking, not too rich or well garnished; also simple shellfish dishes.

Entrée: stew, sauté, meat pie, meat pudding, hotpot, curry, offal, rechauffé dish, bitock, burger, vol-au-vent, boiled or braised meat.

Roast: joint of beef, lamb, pork, poultry.

Grill: lamb chop and cutlet, beef steak, pork chop, mixed grill.

Cold buffet: cold joint, poultry, game pie, ham, terrine, aspic, cold fish, shellfish dish, salads.

Savoury soufflé: cheese, spinach, sweetcorn (usually instead of a sweet).

Sweet: milk pudding, steamed sponge or fruit pudding, fruit pie, flans, jelly, trifle, mousse, bavarois, compotes of fruit, fruit salad, ice-cream and ice-cream sweets.

Cheese: all varieties, served with biscuits, butter and celery.

Dessert: any kind of fresh fruit in season.

DINNER

Hors-d'oeuvre: single deluxe foods such as caviar, foie gras, oysters, smoked salmon and other smoked fish and meats, pâté, melon, seafood cocktail.

Soup: consommé, velouté, bisque, turtle.

Fish: quality fish such as sole, brill, salmon, salmon trout, turbot, lobster, scampi.

Entrée: tournedos, noisette, cutlet, escalope, supreme of chicken, magret of duck, sweetbread, timbale, mousse, vol-au-vent.

Relevé: joint of meat or game, whole poultry or game bird, saddle of lamb, braised ham, fillet of beef, cuishon of veal, haunch of venison, chicken, duck, pheasant, partridge, grouse with a good garnish, and vegetables and potato.

Roast: chicken, duck or game bird in season, served with a salad.

Cold dish: chaudfroid of chicken, foie gras, cold mousse, soufflé of chicken or ham.

Vegetable: hot asparagus, globe artichoke, corn on the cob.

Sweet: hot crêpe Suzette, pancake with fillings, hot soufflé, baked alaska, omelette soufflé, cold soufflé, bombe, parfait, biscuit glacé, coupe, fruit melba.

Savoury: flan, quiche, fondue, hot savoury soufflé, croûtes, Welsh rarebit, angels on horseback.

Dessert: fresh fruit in season, a selection of nuts.

The selection of dishes and balance of the menu

All dishes included on a menu must be suitable for the kind of customer who frequents that particular restaurant. The menu must include a good variety of dishes at prices which meet customers' expectations. When compiling a Table d'Hôte menu, the writer should endeavour to select dishes on each course which when combined into a full meal have some contrasts but unite in perfect harmony. The following components have to be balanced.

COLOUR

A pleasing blend of colours on a plate is the first thing that stimulates the appetite. Every commodity has its own natural colour when cooked: brown and red colours give a feeling of warmth; cool colours such as green and white give a sense of freshness to cold food. One colour should not predominate the plateful of food nor the whole meal. Visual appeal has a strong effect on appetite.

TEXTURE AND CONSISTENCY

It is important to include a range of textures among the foods that make a meal. This means including foods which are soft and tender as well as firm, crisp and crunchy but not tough. Chewing assists appetite by causing the saliva to flow. An all-soft diet is a dull one to the elderly as to children; on the other hand, a diet that takes a lot of chewing can be disconcerting. Shape can come under this heading, as the mouth is capable of distinguishing all the shapes into which foods are cut. For example, there is a difference between eating a shepherd's pie made from minced meat and one that is made from finely diced cooked lamb, the latter being immediately identifiable.

Consistency applies to liquids and purées. The smooth consistency of a velouté soup as against a coarse-grained peasant-style soup, or the smooth consistency of well-made mashed potato which holds its shape, are examples.

FLAVOUR AND AROMA

The four basic flavours are sour, bitter, salty and sweet, and one or more of these are present in all foods. The basic flavour of a dish comes from the main ingredient which can be enhanced or diminished by adding seasonings and flavourings but should not be entirely lost. A well-composed meal can have complementary and contrasting flavours and aromas, but there should be no repetition. After a customer has looked at the colour of the food placed on the table, it is the flavour and aroma that takes over and excites the appetite. A clean, identifiable smell is preferable to food that has been overcooked and flavoured with conflicting herbs and spices, wines and spirits.

SAUCES AND GARNISHES

A sauce can either complement a plate of food or give contrast, but should not overpower the main ingredient so as to mask its taste. A sauce can be as thin as Sauce Beurre Blanc, be of flowing or coating consistency, or be as hard as Brandy Butter. There are several methods of making sauces which should be used in a several course meal without any repetition.

A garnish is capable of adding distinction to a dish and can enlarge the portion size. A garnish can complement or give contrast to a dish though if too elaborate it can dwarf the main item and take a long time to serve, especially when using silver service at a banquet. Simplicity and appropriateness are the watchwords. A good culinary repertoire contains a long list of classical garnishes.

INGREDIENTS

There should be no repetition of any ingredient on a Table d'Hôte menu. This applies particularly to the constituents of a garnish, although potatoes, mushrooms and truffles are exempted from this unwritten rule. Care must be taken to keep the use of onion to a minimum. Fruits are used in several courses of the menu, including hors-d'oeuvre, fish, meat and sweet, but should not be used more than once in a four-course meal.

COOKING METHODS

Ideally each course of a lengthy menu should be cooked by a different method. This helps give more variety and interest to a meal, although you should avoid bizarre combinations such as boiled chicken with sauté potatoes or fried fillet of sole with mashed potatoes. Sound judgement is needed. It is acceptable to flash every dish under the salamander or in the microwave, but only to ensure it is piping hot when served.

The capabilities of the staff

A distinct level of skill on the part of kitchen and restaurant staff is required for each kind of eating establishment, and the person who writes the menus must know what the available staff are capable of. If the cooks are not very highly skilled, a complicated dish may be beyond their capabilities. This also applies to waiting staff, so the menu writer must know which NVQs the staff have acquired before beginning to compile a menu. Certainly there must be a challenge to staff to develop their potential, but not to the detraction of customer satisfaction. This does not mean that menus must be limited by the competence of the staff, but rather that the head chef will encourage them to greater things. This applies to every kind of catering establishment, in both sectors of the industry. In the cost sector, counter service staff must be capable of serving food on to plates neatly and quickly and be good at portioning; they also need a pleasant manner and should look neat in uniform.

The availability of equipment

This includes all fixed kitchen equipment, machines, utensils and serving dishes. The person writing the menu has to bear in mind what is available in the kitchen and the restaurant and how items on the menu are cooked and served. It is advisable to purchase equipment appropriate to the kind of menu in a particular establishment, or to buy equipment that is versatile in use. For example, when a restaurant switches from silver service to plate service, this usually means having to buy special plates and silver-plated covers.

The season of the year

Despite the availability of foods from around the world, a menu composer should chart the arrival of seasonal, home-grown items and be ready to add to the menu. A calendar of seasonal foods will enable publicity to be given to the arrival of new potatoes, asparagus, fresh peas, home-grown strawberries, and many other commodities. Chapter 9 gives details of the times when certain fish are at their best and when game birds are in season. New ways of cultivating foods and improved transportation have lessened the impact of the seasons, but there is still the need to observe Christmas, New Year, Easter, St Patrick's Day and many other festivals with special menus which include dishes associated with them.

The availability of resources

This concerns the sources of supply of the commodities used in the production of meals, either purchased at local markets or delivered by firms of food wholesalers to most parts of the country. Catering establishments in urban areas do not normally have any difficulty in obtaining supplies promptly, though those in more remote parts may not be so fortunate and have to forego special items because demand is low in those areas. A menu composer must resist the temptation to include dishes which use items for which there is no substitute. Supplies may be difficult to obtain because of bad weather conditions, a hold-up in transportation, or the numbers involved; for example, a game dealer may find it difficult to obtain enough grouse for a banquet of 100 people. The emergence of firms of food suppliers which deal in all commodities from distribution centres across the country has made the menu composer's life a lot easier. Their price list gives information on all the goods available, including fish, shellfish, meats, vegetables, fruit, desserts, delicatessen, cheeses and speciality provisions in wholesale packs and to specification, but even they advise giving plenty of notice for large orders of uncommon ingredients.

Nutritional aspects

The person who writes menus, whether working in the commercial or cost sector, needs a good knowledge of nutrition and should try to satisfy the customers' nutritional requirements. In some areas of cost catering, menus must supply a certain number of calories in the day's meals and the right amount of protein, fat and carbohydrate necessary to satisfy the consumers' nutritional needs (see Chapter 3). Special dietary needs must be catered for. Sometimes a customer is put on a special diet and the doctor will ask the caterer to ensure it is followed. Other constraints may be due to religious beliefs or cultural expectations.

Customers in the profit sector of catering do not normally have any nutritional requirements, but a good compiler of menus should be prepared to discuss the subject with any client wishing to do so. Table d'Hôte menus should be well balanced nutritionally.

Daily meals

The traditional daily sequence of meals in the United Kingdom is breakfast, luncheon, afternoon tea, dinner and supper. Other names used are brunch, elevenses and high tea.

English breakfast is a fairly substantial meal of two courses and several adjuncts. The first course is a choice of cereals, porridge, fruit juice and stewed fruit, with either milk or cream. The second course is chosen from fried or grilled bacon, sausage, lamb's kidney and black pudding; boiled, poached, fried or scrambled egg; poached finnon haddock or kipper; fried bread, mushrooms and tomato; cold ham; toast, croissant or brioche; butter, marmalade or jam; and tea or coffee. English breakfast is regarded by many as being one of the delights of British gastronomy. Continental breakfast consists of coffee or tea, and roll, brioche or croissant with butter and a preserve.

Luncheon is generally regarded as being less substantial than dinner with fewer courses and simpler dishes, but it can be the main meal of the day.

Afternoon tea is usually an informal meal taken sitting down in easy chairs around a small table. Freshly made tea with sugar cubes or lemon slices is accompanied by several of the following: dainty sandwiches with cucumber, egg and cheese, tomato, ham, chicken or sardine paste, or smoked salmon in brown bread; french pastries, including fruit tartlets, eclairs and choux buns; and a slice of rich fruit cake or sponge cake. During the winter, toasted muffins, crumpets or teacakes may be served. Cream teas usually consist of a pot of tea and scones spread with butter, jam and whipped or clotted cream.

High tea is a combined afternoon tea and supper meal to replace dinner for people who wish to retire to bed early or who suffer indigestion if they eat late in the evening. It is a formal meal, eaten at the table with a menu which can include a cup of tea or other hot or cold beverage, bread and butter, cake, and a hot or cold snack made from cheese, egg, fish, meat or pasta.

Dinner is the evening meal to be enjoyed after finishing work at the end of the day. This means that customers can take longer to eat it and consume it in a relaxed way. Thus the menu writer can cover a wider and better-quality list of dishes. Dinner is usually more expensive than lunch and can embrace one or two additional courses. Suitable dishes are listed on pages 40–1.

Supper can mean a sandwich or snack with a hot beverage just before going to bed, or a fairly substantial meal eaten after midnight in a night club, disco or casino. Suitable dishes for a supper menu include many of the savouries from the English and American repertoires: Club Sandwich and other toasted sandwiches, Haddock Monte Carlo, kippers, Omelette Arnold Bennett and other filled omelettes and garnished egg dishes, Chicken à la King, Lobster Newburg, and grilled steak, for example.

Meal times

Meal times which were once considered sacrosanct in the traditional pattern of English life, are fast losing their importance. This is being brought about by the accelerated pace of modern living. It has forced us to largely abandon the three daily sit-down meals of breakfast, lunch and dinner, together with a morning and afternoon break for refreshments. Instead of observing the eating habits of fixed meal times, more and more people are eating smaller snack-type meals on the job, on the move, or sitting on bar stools. Catering establishments are staying open throughout the day to suit customers who want quick and casual meals. All-day breakfasts are a common feature, the 2 p.m. and 9.30 p.m. deadlines are now open-ended and clients can obtain a set meal at any time of day, and in city centres at any time of night.

Public houses, popular restaurant chains, cafés, snack bars, motorway service stations and fast-food outlets all fulfil the needs of chance customers for impromptu meals. People enjoy eating a snack with a drink, and there is an enormous range of both hot and cold snacks available.

Cost distribution of menus

There are two ways of costing menus. In a small hotel that has a daily or weekly rate for full and half board, about one-third would be allotted for meals. The chef has to divide this sum of money between breakfast, lunch and/or dinner, then between the number of courses for either or both main meals. According to the standard rating of the hotel, lunch would be two or three courses and dinner three or four courses plus coffee. The chef would calculate the amount spent on food per person per day at approximately one-third of the third. For example, if a 3-star hotel charged £250 per week for half board, the allocation for food will be £83.30, of which almost £28 can be spent on food, which gives a food cost of £4 per person per day.

A restaurant that offers a fixed-price meal for £12.50 and has a kitchen percentage of 60 per cent will need to keep the food cost to £5, the difference of £7.50 being for the overheads of staff wages, living-in accommodation and meals on duty for staff, providing uniforms and laundering them, training programmes, welfare amenities, heating and lighting charges, upkeep of equipment, water charges, printing of menus and wine lists, table linen, value-added tax, and the net profit needed to keep the restaurant profitable.

Figure 11 shows how the food cost could be distributed between courses of a lunch and dinner menu, each having a selling price of £12.50.

Design and production of menus and wine lists

A menu is the means of communication between the menu composer, head chef, head waiter and the customer. A menu represents the business and helps establish its reputation. As discussed earlier, a menu is a marketing tool so it must be produced in a form that gives the establishment a good image. A wine list fulfils the same objective.

Figure 11   Cost distribution between courses

Dishes	3-course		4-course	
	%	Cost (£)	%	Cost (£)
Appetiser, soup, farinaceous	12	0.60	10	0.50
Egg, fish	–	–	16	0.80
Meat, poultry, game, vegetarian	45	2.25	38	1.90
Vegetables, potatoes	8	0.40	8	0.40
Sweet, cheese, savoury	25	1.25	18	0.90
Rolls, butter	6	0.30	6	0.30
Coffee	4	0.20	4	0.20
Total cost	**100**	**5.00**	**100**	**5.00**

When giving the printer guidance on the production of a menu and wine list, consider the following points:

1 the size and shape of the page and the number of pages needed
2 how the pages should be joined
3 the colour and quality of the paper or card
4 the appropriate headings or any sign or logo on the covers
5 the kind of typeface to be used and its size and colour
6 how the menu will be folded and whether a ribbon or cord is necessary to hold it together
7 whether artwork or photographs will be used
8 how long the menus and wine lists should remain in use.

A firm of printers that specialises in this kind of work will be able to advise on the design and production of menus and wine lists. Alternatively they can be produced on a word processor and printer, then laminated to keep them stiff and clean.

Further reading

Cracknell, H. and Nobis, G. (1985) *Practical Professional Gastronomy*. Macmillan*

Cracknell, H. and Nobis, G. (1989) *The New Catering Repertoire*, Volume 1. Macmillan*

Harris, P. (1992) *Profit Planning*. Butterworth-Heinemann

McVety J. and Ware J. (1989) *Fundamentals of Menu Planning*. John Wiley & Sons

Rietz, C. A. (1978) *The Master Food Guide*. AVI Publishing Company

*Out of print but available in many libraries.

6 Convergence of facilities I
Planning the areas

Computer-aided design; General points of planning; The planning team; The sequence of planning; Planning strategy; Allocation of space; Planning the areas; The function of the kitchen and its ancillary areas.

The planning of each of the areas that together form the catering department of a hotel or the entire facilities of a restaurant should be viewed over the long term to take account of possible changes in operation. Planning should allow for some flexibility of boundaries and for possible expansion or redevelopment. Problems can arise as soon as a new establishment starts trading because an oversight or fault may have a knock-on effect right through the production line.

Energy saving is an important aspect of planning, and an in-depth examination must be made of how to obtain optimum value from the use of electricity, gas and water as used for central heating, air conditioning, ventilation, lighting, power for all machinery, and energy for cooking and dishwashing. Energy-efficient measures brought into the entire operation will have a positive effect on the environment both inside and outside the establishment.

Computer-aided design

Computer-aided design (CAD) is extensively used by planners and consultants to show how the finished department will look. Many manufacturers of catering equipment supply drawings of their items in two- or three-dimensional form and to any scale, which can be placed into position on the outline plan together with the services of gas, electricity, water and the mechanical and architectural features. These can be altered and moved around on the screen to produce the ideal pattern of movement of staff, customers and goods. There is a library of some 25,000 drawings and symbols available.

Manufacturers of all kinds of catering equipment use this computer technology to design their equipment so that it will fit in with other items purchased from different sources. This new technology can provide quotations for the different firms' equipment and furnishings as well as installation costs. The resultant master plan must be submitted to the local authority planning officer, the fire officer and the local environmental health officer.

General points of planning

Ideally, the kitchen, dining-room, bars and ancillary areas should be located on the same floor so that communication between them is easy. If possible, all these departments should be on the ground floor to make movement of goods and personnel upwards or downwards unnecessary.

The dining-room should be situated next to the kitchen on the same level to avoid the need to install lifts to transport the food from the kitchen to the restaurant. Even a secondary servery between kitchen and dining-room should be avoided as it means having to employ staff to operate it and is not conducive to serving food in its best condition. Bars should be adjacent to the dining-room so that drinks required by customers do not have to be carried any distance.

Clearly it is important to identify the sequence of operations before drawing up plans. The physical layout should reflect:

1 the needs and demands of the customers
2 the policy of the firm
3 the menu and its range of products
4 the organisation of the establishment.

These four factors affect the planning needs and are the main points that have to be taken into consideration when management compiles its brief for the other specialists on the planning team.

The needs and demands of the customers

In order to identify the customers' requirements, it is important to consider their socio-economic status; their reason for visiting the establishment, whether for business or pleasure; and the changing nature of their needs at different times, such as at a business lunch or a romantic dinner.

It is clear, then, that environment and atmosphere must be considered in the planning of facilities, and that decor and layout must be flexible enough to cope with changing demands. Other factors are the number of customers expected and the time they can spend eating, which have to be reflected in the prices charged. The higher the prices charged, the better the facilities have to be; how the level of facilities is achieved is part of the organisation's policy.

The policy of the firm

This should indicate how the customers' needs are to be met in terms of satisfaction and the expected return on investment and entrepreneurial risk. The organisation will lay down guidelines and a structured framework within which consumer needs are to be met, based on the findings of a feasibility study (see Chapter 3). The policy will include specific points that affect the planning of both the food production and the food service areas. Other aspects which will influence planning include:

- the overall image of the organisation – this will affect the choice of external and internal decoration
- the expected number of customers – this affects requirements of space and interior layout and decor
- specific budgets for the various departments of the operation for purchase of equipment and furniture, and for small equipment on an annual basis
- staffing policy – this could refer to uniforms which would go well with the overall effect of the decor
- the method of food service and presentation – this has a bearing on circulation space and equipment requirements.

The menu and its range of products

The menu establishes the framework for the methods of production to be followed, and from this the range of products and the techniques of service and presentation. The more traditional the operation, the greater the space requirements for both kitchen and dining-room and the larger the amount of equipment required. Therefore, in taking the decision whether to offer a specialised à la Carte menu as against a standard Table d'Hôte one with plate service, a caterer is also making decisions about space and equipment requirements for all departments. It is obvious that the full à la Carte menu that is cooked to order requires silver service and possibly some guéridon service.

So the menu should act as the central point of planning – all too often plans are made without considering the kind of menu envisaged. When an à la Carte menu is planned, the caterer must evaluate the proportions of raw and convenience foods that will need to be purchased. This in turn will have a bearing on the number of staff required to produce the menu.

The organisation of the establishment

The planning of a department is further influenced by the envisaged organisation of the whole operation, and this naturally relates to the level of occupancy and hours of opening. The longer the opening hours and the greater the take-up of the facility, the more flexible must be the planning to cope with fluctuations in demand. For example, most restaurants close immediately after lunch and stay empty until the evening, but there may be a limited demand for a full meal service throughout the afternoon that one establishment should be willing to cater for.

Each establishment has an image of its own, be it a snack bar or ethnic restaurant, and the service offered by each is associated with a control system which covers the purchase of materials to a pattern of standardisation that governs the storage space requirements. In a large-scale kitchen the head chef can supervise the work more effectively if it is open plan, rather than a conventional set-up where responsibility is delegated to the chefs de partie.

The planning team

Planning the production and service areas of an establishment is a complex task. Its successful outcome is dependent on the skills of a group of specialists capable of evaluating the overall plan from its inception to its completion in the form of its output performance. The specialists required are normally drawn from the following three areas:

- the management team, possibly including the general manager, food and beverage manager or catering manager, the head chef, and the restaurant manager or headwaiter
- the architect and interior designer
- the catering planning adviser who will be an expert on equipment requirements and workflow.

The role of the management team is to interpret for the others on the team their understanding of the catering function as it applies to consumer requirements and operational characteristics. They also need an understanding of the principles of planning so that they can intervene when misunderstanding of their objectives is apparent.

The planning adviser uses the information that comes from these joint discussions as the basis for drawing up the plan.

The sequence of planning

The decision as to where in the sequence of operations the whole undertaking starts moving is a matter for each individual establishment. The main point is that those doing the planning must be aware of the logical sequence of activities that constitute the operation of a catering department. They should view it from a perspective that shows how each activity interlocks into a single coordinated functional operation. This sequence is common to all types of catering businesses and flows in the following manner: 1 the receipt of goods from suppliers; 2 the correct storage and control of goods; 3 the issue of these goods to 4 the preparation areas where a certain amount of processing is done before they proceed to 5 the production area which is the kitchen; 6 the distribution of prepared dishes to the servery and dining-rooms; and 7 the washing-up areas where restaurant and kitchen utensils are cleansed before going back to 8 the stowing away or custodian areas where utensils are kept in readiness for further use (see Figure 12).

Planning strategy

In planning an establishment it is often advisable to work backwards, starting not at the goods delivery bay but at the customer's entrance and the dining-room.

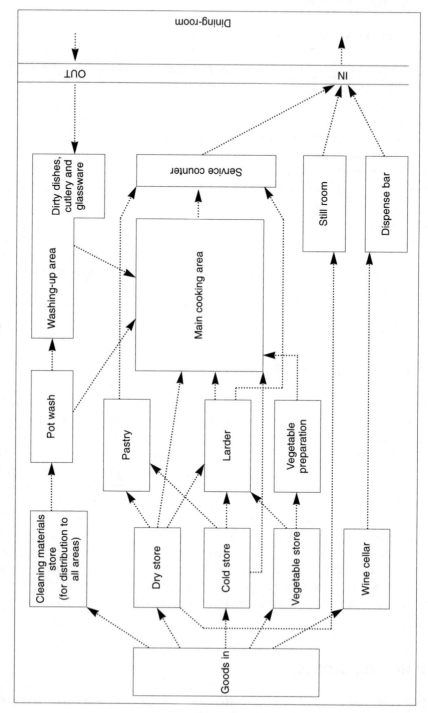

Figure 12   The functional flow of goods from the goods-in area to the dining-room

This is the first place the customer sees and, as it is also the main revenue-producing department, it is therefore the most important one. However, the dining-room cannot be planned in isolation from other areas. It is essential to know the total area available for the catering function and the approximate amount of space that is to be allocated to each component part, including bars, kitchen, still-room, stores and the other ancillary areas, in addition to the dining-room.

Where the catering operation will form part of a hotel or large business complex, the total area needed can be worked out mathematically by reference to the expected type of business, volume of customers, opening hours, and number of staff to be employed.

Where the operation will be purpose-built and the total amount of space has been decided, or where reorganisation of an existing operation is to be contained within its original boundaries, reference has to be made in the first instance to the expected or emerging type of business and its opening hours. These become the sole determinants of the volume of business and the number of staff needed to operate it.

An explanation of these factors will show how important they are in the planning process:

1 **The type of business** can range from an individually owned, seasonal, afternoon tea shop to a large hotel having many different eating and drinking outlets, several kitchens, banqueting facilities for perhaps several thousand guests, and a catering staff running into many hundreds.
2 **The volume and turnover** of business is calculated on the number of seating places in the dining-room, the average occupancy of them, the number of times each seat will be used during a meal period, and the total receipts from the sale of food and drink.
3 **The hours of business** when a dining-room is open to customers show which meals will be served, but staff will be on duty both before and after these times. This has a bearing on the number of staff required and whether they work split duties or alternate early and late shifts.
4 **The number of staff** employed has a bearing on the planning in so far as it affects the number required in a given department, as staff cannot work efficiently in a congested area. It also has an effect on the amount of space to be devoted to staff changing and amenity rooms. The specialist designer can provide the figures to be used in deciding the ratios of space.

Allocation of space

This section looks at how space is allocated for different areas within a catering establishment and how each must accommodate all its equipment, furnishing and activities. Figure 13 shows the average allocation of space within conventional catering establishments of various sizes operating a Table d'Hôte waiter service.

Figure 13   Allocation of space in catering establishments (m²)

	Number of seats				
	50	**100**	**200**	**300**	**400**
Production area					
Kitchen – including all preparation, cooking and food service areas	25	40	50	65	80
Ancillary areas					
– Stillroom	6	10	14	16	18
– Potwash	3	5	6	8	12
– Plate wash	6	10	15	16	20
Goods areas – receiving and storage	10	10	16	25	30
Total production area	*50*	*75*	*100*	*130*	*160*
Area per meal produced	*11*	*0.75*	*0.5*	*0.4*	*0.4*
Distribution area					
Dining room	80	150	260	350	440
Customer amenities – reception, bars and lounge	20	25	45	70	80
Total distribution area	*100*	*175*	*305*	*420*	*520*
Area per meal served	*2*	*1.75*	*1.5*	*1.4*	*1.3*
Other areas					
Staff facilities – changing rooms rest rooms, toilets and dining-room	14	22	36	47	60
Offices	6	7	11	16	20
Customers' cloakrooms and toilets	20	27	50	62	80
Total area	*40*	*56*	*97*	*125*	*160*
Total area of catering department	**190**	**306**	**502**	**675**	**840**
Area per customer	**3.8**	**3.06**	**2.5**	**2.25**	**2.1**

A study of ergonomics will assist in creating ideal working conditions, especially in the hot and humid atmosphere of a kitchen. Ergonomics is the study of the relationship between people at work and the surrounding environment, including the equipment they have to use. It is relevant to the chef, constantly turning from table to stove, bending to the oven and stretching to the overhead rack, and to the waiter, depositing a trayful of dishes on the sideboard, taking serving spoon and fork from the drawer, presenting and serving the dishes at table, then clearing them methodically – both doing this for several hours at a stretch. To minimise problems, it is important to consider the needs of the staff. Work bases should be the right height – 850–900 mm for females and 900–950 mm for males on average. Work benches should provide a working space of 1,200 mm.

Dining-room, dispense bar and cellar

A dining-room should be planned to accommodate the number of customers that can be catered for by the kitchen and vice versa, based on one or two sittings according to the type of clientele expected and the menu. The more the area can be filled with customers, the more profitable the operation will be, provided that comfort and enjoyment are not sacrificed. Within a given area the manager must be able to draw plans showing various ways of furnishing it to seat different numbers, leaving sufficient circulatory space. Flexibility is sometimes an asset in that it allows the room to be used for different functions according to need. Capacity is determined by usage and it is sometimes desirable to be able to shut off part of the room if demand is slack.

Different styles or forms of service dictate optimum space allocation in dining-rooms, as shown in Figure 14. With the exception of cafeteria service, the allowances include space required for sideboards. All these figures cover circulatory space, though gangways should be kept to the safe minimum to gain full use of space. The decision regarding what mixture of tables to use will depend on customers' requirements, but a balance of tables for two, four and six is recommended; tables for six will increase the capacity but may mean strangers sharing.

In the allocation of space for the dining-room, allowance must be made for storage and holding areas for furniture and equipment in intermittent use. Obviously this has to be in keeping with the seating capacity of the dining-room.

Also related to the dining-room are the dispense bar and cellar which supply alcoholic and non-alcoholic drinks. The dispense bar is the place where waiting staff order drinks for serving to customers in the lounge if there is no bar, and in the dining-room. As such it need only be a functional area, whether sited actually in the dining-room or, as is more usual, behind the scenes but close to the dining-room. It will carry all the stock, as dictated by the tariff or wine list, and the equipment necessary to keep the stock in good condition for service. The counter and circulatory space need only be sufficient for the number of persons working there and for a reasonable number of serving staff on the other side of the counter.

The space allocated to the dispense bar could be part of that apportioned to the dining-room and this would be determined by the type and volume of business done. As such it is difficult to give an exact figure as a guideline for the amount of space required.

It is also not possible to provide exact figures for the allocation of space for the

Figure 14   Allocation of space for various styles of service

Style of service	Allocation per customer (m²)
Guéridon service from a trolley or side table	1.8
Silver service on to plates in front of customers	1.5
Plate service	1.2
Banquet service on communal seating plan	1.0
Banquet service at separate tables	1.5
Cafeteria service (excluding servery)	0.8

cellar. Whatever form the cellar takes, the space allocation is governed by the extent of the wine list or bar tariff, the size of the establishment, and the volume of business. Space is also governed by the policy on purchasing – for example, whether drink is held in bulk storage, whether wine is bottled on the premises, or whether kegs or casks of beer are kept in stock. On the other hand, there could be frequent deliveries of easily obtainable supplies. The percentage of space allocated can therefore vary considerably and is more usually taken from the overall area devoted to the food and beverage operation, although quite often it can be part of the storage area.

By using the par system of stocking a bar from the cellar, it is possible to ascertain fairly exactly what amount of stock will be carried and from it the amount of space required to store it in. The amount of stock never varies because at the end of each day all the empty bottles, kegs, etc. are returned to the cellar and a requisition is made for each replacement item issued to restock the bar, thus standardising the allocation of space.

Customer amenities

A good restaurant should offer facilities other than the room where meals are taken: an entrance hall and reception area, cloakrooms for men and women, and a lounge bar or other kind of bar, will all help to give customers a good impression of an establishment as soon as they arrive.

The reception area and/or lounge should be designed to accommodate customers who wish to have a drink before the meal, or who have not booked a table and will have to wait for one to become vacant. The furnishings and furniture need to be relaxing and comfortable and in keeping with the general decor of the dining-room. A lounge bar may also act as a meeting place for members of the public – whether or not they are taking a meal – who like this kind of atmosphere as compared with that of a public house. A lounge bar will provide comfortable seating arrangements around the room rather than concentrating it around the bar counter, and as it is not the sort of place where customers come to spend an evening the allocation could be as low as 2.5m^2 per person, which would include the bar itself.

There are other kinds of bars, such as cocktail bars, where there would probably be more contact with the bartender as he or she prepares the drinks. A long counter with stools and less comfortable seating around it would therefore be appropriate. A public bar would obviously have a wider range of drinks than a cocktail bar, but its more functional nature means that an allowance of 1.5 m^2 per person is adequate.

Under Section 89 of the Public Health Act 1936, local authorities are empowered to require the provision of sanitary conveniences in such numbers as are considered necessary for persons using the premises. Licensing magistrates want to know if these needs are satisfied before they will grant a licence for the sale of liquor. The British Standards Institution (BSI) issued a Code of Practice for the guidance of restaurateurs in satisfying these requirements.

Closets

Male	1 per 100 up to 400 persons.	400 and over – 1 per 250.
Female	2 per 100 up to 200 persons.	200 and over – 1 per 100 or part.

Wash basins

1 for 1 to 15 persons, 2 for 16–35, 3 for 36–65, and 4 for 66–100.
Persons – this applies to male and female toilets.

An allocation of 3 m^2 per water closet is necessary; a wash basin requires 1.5 m^2 and a urinal 1.3 m^2.

Cloakroom facilities for the use of customers require up to 0.08 m^2 per person where there is an attendant, and 0.10 m^2 where customers hang up their own apparel.

Kitchen areas

The overall space available for installing a kitchen will vary greatly from one establishment to another, and each must be planned individually. It is important to bear in mind that the revenue-producing departments of the establishment have first priority as regards available space. These are the dining-room and, in a licensed restaurant, the bar; in the industrial sector they are the canteen with the vending machines or tea trolleys. The kitchen is not a revenue-producing area, although obviously the dining-room could not function without it. But it means that the allocation of space for this department must only be that necessary for it to carry out its function efficiently and safely.

There are no hard-and-fast rules about how large a kitchen should be to cater for a given number of meals. It is now accepted, however, that a kitchen requires only about half the space assigned to the dining-room. This rule-of-thumb measurement gives rise to the often quoted figure of approximately 0.5 m^2 of kitchen floor area for each chair in the dining-room, which gives a ratio of 1:2, although this normally only applies to industrial situations where the figure of 1 m^2 of eating space per person is acceptable. In a conventional restaurant with waiter service the allowances are different, and Figure 14 (page 55) shows how typical measurements of area per customer decrease as the scale of numbers increases. This cannot, of course, apply to the dining-room where a customer will still require the same amount of space whether the capacity is 100 or 600 and whether it is full up or not. The only variation to this is in an establishment that fills the seats more than once during a service period or during the hours of opening. Here the means of establishing the size of the dining-room is by knowing or estimating the volume of business at the peak periods of the day and allocating space to cope with this. The rate of turnover, or length of time a customer is estimated to take to consume a meal, has a bearing as it is accepted that at busy times of the day a queue may form to get into the dining-room, or customers are expected to go to the lounge bar until their table is ready.

Figures for large-scale kitchen installations are given by various bodies such as the BSI who recommend an allowance of 0.7 m^2 for a kitchen producing meals for 100 people; 0.5 m^2 for 250, and 0.46 m^2 for 500 people; these allowances are per person, so a kitchen producing 100 meals should have a total area of

70 m². Figures for kitchens producing school meals vary according to individual education authorities who suggest areas varying from 42 m² to 51 m² for 150 meals, and from 144 m² to 160 m² for 600 meals per day.

In arriving at any allocation of space, it is necessary to know what the area actually includes. For example, one kitchen may have all its ancillary sections in close proximity to it, another will have its servery counter on a different level and away from the production area, while yet another may have large preparation areas sited as part of the stores.

STORES

In allocating space for the stores, it is necessary to know the probable range of goods to be used, their rate of turnover, and the frequency of ordering fresh supplies. These factors apply mainly to non-perishables, as the perishable commodities are usually ordered on a daily basis and require only overnight storage space. By measuring the packages of items in general use, it is possible to arrive at the total amount of space required to house basic stocks and to plan storage space accordingly.

STILLROOM

The stillroom is part of the kitchen premises where hot and cold beverages, toast, rolls, croissants and brioches are dispensed. A knowledge of the function of the stillroom and the volume of business being done will provide information regarding the amount of space required for this department. The limited range of services offered by the stillroom dictates the items of equipment that have to be housed, and work study will show where these should be sited so as to avoid any wasted space. The kind of equipment installed determines whether the stillroom is operated by a stillroom hand or is self-service. In self-service stillrooms machines dispense hot water, tea, coffee and milk or chilled fruit juices at the touch of a button, stopping automatically after delivery of the correct quantity. A commercial-size toaster turns sliced bread into hot toast to the waiter's requirements, and a hot cupboard keeps rolls and similar items warm. A waiter can operate a juicer to make fresh citrus fruit juices from a container of halved oranges or grapefruit. The necessary serving equipment of warmed cups, mugs and jugs can be kept in the stillroom or in a nearby hot cupboard.

PLATEWASH AND POTWASH

These two ancillary departments should not be very demanding of space since the range of activities taking place in them is fairly restricted. The anticipated volume of work, the equipment, and the total number of staff likely to be working in these ancillary areas at any one time will dictate the size of each department.

Staff facilities and offices

By law, certain facilities have to be provided for staff. The figures for male and female staff toilets are the same: 1 closet for 15 employees, 2 for up to 30, and

5 closets for 76–100. Separate facilities for males and females must be provided. Depending on the size of lockers supplied for staff to hang their outdoor clothes or uniform in, the amount of space required will vary from 0.08 m² to 0.12 m² per member of staff. Changing rooms need to be large enough to hold all those arriving at the start of one of the shifts. The number of wash basins required for staff is the same as for closets, but only 1 shower per 10 staff need be installed.

A rest room should be provided where staff may relax when off duty for a short time or between shifts, with a separate one for the kitchen staff. This may be supervised by the personnel department or a social committee of members of staff, who will decide on the amenities needed. Apart from the furniture and fittings, pastimes in the form of a television set, video game, and books, newspapers and journals may be offered to help good staff relations. The amount of space provided could be based on a minimum of 0.5 m² per person on the staff payroll. The staff dining-room is an important part of this general area because in many cases meals are a perk of the job. It is now more usual to provide a central dining-room for all grades and kinds of staff where meals are served on cafeteria lines to coincide with meal breaks. The amount of room to allocate for this is approximately 0.75 m² per person, calculating the total area from the number of staff expected to attend at the peak period, or staggering mealtimes if space is at a premium. In addition there must be room for the service counter and storage space for food and equipment.

Staff meals

It is important that staff are made to feel a valued part of an establishment, and the quality of the meals they are given contributes to this. The food must be adequate, of good standard, and decently served in pleasant surroundings. Meals should not be repetitive or low-cost ones made of unused food cooked the previous day. Customer food can be served to staff after being correctly stored and reheated, but this would only be feasible in smaller establishments. Where many staff are employed it will be necessary to employ a staff cook to prepare meals from scratch with separately ordered foods. Some hotels and restaurants give the operation of the staff canteen to a catering contractor which will work to a given level at a fixed cost.

In large establishments the person in charge of the catering operation, and also those persons in charge of the main departments, require offices in which to carry out their managerial duties. Sometimes a clerk or secretary is necessary to do the clerical and administrative work of the department. Apart from these departmental offices, which are an integral part of the practical areas of the food and beverage operation, there are central offices where the work related to accounts, personnel and other business activities is carried out. The allocation of space for the departmental offices is usually included in the total area assigned to these departments, whereas the business offices employing staff to carry out administrative activities must conform to government legislation. In general these requirements are for a minimum of 3.7 m² per person engaged in the office; if the ceiling is lower than 3 m there must be 11 m³ of room space per employee. The space allocation must also take account of furniture, fittings and machinery.

Planning the areas

Once the total area of the catering operation has been decided and space has been allocated to the main departments and their supportive and ancillary areas, the next stage is to plan the way in which they will be furnished, fitted and equipped to meet the practicalities of production and service, and at the same time the customers' needs and expectations as identified.

Dining-room

The eating area or dining-room is where customers usually first come into contact with the establishment, so it is important that the initial impact is positive. Each establishment has its own requirements depending on the kind of menu and form of service, the necessary seating arrangements of open plan or division into booths, the prices charged, and the number of staff on duty at peak times. The entrances and exits, (including fire exits), toilets, cloakroom and bar, facilities for the disabled, and adequate circulation space all need to be planned to give maximum efficiency.

Basically, the layout and atmosphere resulting from it are dictated by the type of service offered in relation to the customers' needs. Consider two very different examples, a self-service cafeteria and a very conventional restaurant – in both cases it is important that the atmosphere is correct for each type of customer, since it will have an effect on their behaviour and colour their pleasure, despite the fact that in the first they will be in and out quickly whereas in the other they will have longer to absorb the surroundings.

The atmosphere created in a dining-room is an important part of its planning, as customers often choose where to eat because of a congenial atmosphere that suits them. Yet atmosphere is a very difficult thing to define: it can mean a relaxed, intimate feeling or a lively, noisy setting full of hustle and bustle. Both will appeal to different types of customers. In fact, the effect that the environment has on the senses is not consciously noted. Thus not only smell, hearing, looks, touch and taste but also temperature, pressure, balance and kinaesthetics play a part, and these senses convey meanings to the brain where they are processed in the psychological activity of perception. The feeling of atmosphere in a room is further moderated for the customers by the ongoing activities within the area to which they are exposed on entering, and by any previous association with the restaurant.

It is clearly important to provide an atmosphere which will attract the type of customers identified at the outset. To do this, the following environmental aspects must be considered:

- **visual** – colour, form, texture, illumination and the interaction of all these with the external environment
- **thermal** – temperature, relative humidity and air movement
- **auditory** – acoustics, music and other types of sound.

VISUAL ENVIRONMENT

Colour plays a big part in the creation of atmosphere and contributes to the 'feel good' factor which helps put customers at ease in a restaurant. There must be a perfect blend of colours including the surrounding walls and windows, the carpet and curtains, lampshades, pot plants and floral arrangements, the table and

Plate 3   The Bath Spa Hotel, Bath

chairs, and all the accoutrements that go to make a meal an experience. Cool blue and green colours give a feeling of relaxation, while warm yellow and red colours give a more stimulating, even an exhilarating feeling. In subtle ways the choice of colour combinations can create different feelings in the minds of customers, which is why fast-food emporiums are decorated in warm, light colours which help speed up the rate of turnover. In the case of an upmarket restaurant, deep colours with some gilding give a sense of warmth and security. Lighting is also important in creating atmosphere and includes natural light from windows and doorways. There are recommended lighting levels for the various sections of a dining-room and kitchen, depending on their size and use. Many different kinds of lamp bulbs are available, each giving a particular effect which can help create the desired atmosphere of a room. Candles are used to create a cosy environment, especially for evening meals and special occasions. The overall requirement is to make the room look inviting, to help customers look their best, and to enable them to read the menu easily. Emergency lighting is obligatory in case an incident occurs that demands a hasty exit or in the event of a power failure.

THERMAL ENVIRONMENT

Customers will enjoy their meal more if the temperature of the restaurant is just right. All public areas should be kept at a constant temperature of 15–18°C using unobtrusive air-conditioning, with relative humidity at 50–55 per cent. This will provide comfortable conditions.

AUDITORY ENVIRONMENT

Sound is an essential element in the creation of atmosphere in a dining-room, because it can give customers a feeling of belonging and of participation in the activities. Silence makes the room feel eerie, and loud noises such as a dish or piece of cutlery accidentally dropped by waiting staff will cause consternation. The pleasant hum of conversation, however, can add to the mood of the dining-room. Staff should be taught to work quietly and not to engage in idle chatter between one another or to start up a conversation with the guests. Background music such as piano or tape might be suitable for the venue.

Bars and cellar

A hotel may have several bars on the premises, each with a special theme – one like an upmarket public house, one like an American bar that serves cocktails and other mixed drinks and no beer, and usually one attached to the restaurant for resident guests and non-resident customers who wish to drink an aperitif before eating. Each one needs its own planning and space requirements according to the way it is run, how many bar staff are needed to run it, and what items are included on the bar tariff. There should be close access to the cellar where the bulk stock of drink is held.

The decor, furnishings and fittings of a bar should either be similar to that of the adjacent restaurant or reflect a specific theme, possibly to reinforce the name given to the bar.

The cellar holds bulk stocks of all the drinks on sale from the wine list and bar tariff, and there should be sufficient space for every bin number. Some of these may hold fine wines as they mature for several years for future sale; others are for table wines, fortified wines, aperitifs, spirits, liqueurs, mixers, beers and ciders, each with its bin number that matches the entry on the wine list. The cellar should ideally maintain an even temperature of 10–12°C all the time, the lighting should be dim, and there should not be any vibration from passing traffic, lorries being unloaded or heavy trolleyloads of supplies which might disturb the wines stored there.

Cloakrooms

Cloakroom and toilet facilities must be kept clean and secure at all times; many customers judge an establishment by the quality of these facilities.

Staff facilities

Staff accommodation, including changing and recreation rooms, toilets, shower room, dining-room or staff canteen and staff entrance, must be carefully planned and furnished. It is important to provide reasonable conditions that give staff the feeling of concern on the part of management for their well-being during breaks and when off duty. Access to trade journals and books, television, savings schemes, participation in team sports and bonus incentive payments are all features of personnel facilities.

Kitchen

The first step in planning a new kitchen, or the complete alteration of an existing one, is to ascertain its purpose – the kind of work that is to be carried out in it according to the menu it will use.

There are many kinds of kitchen plans, e.g. for a factory canteen, college refectory, hospital, home for the elderly, snack bar or high-class restaurant, each of which requires a different layout that is determined by the kind of customer to be catered for and the sort of food they expect.

The planning team will be involved from the outset to ensure that the kitchen complies with current building and other regulations. The following factors require careful consideration:

- The flooring must be very hard-wearing, slip-resistant, easy to clean, and strong enough to support heavy-duty kitchen equipment. It should slope gently towards the drainage gulleys.
- The walls need to be heat-resistant, crack-resistant and easy to clean.
- The ceilings must also be heat-resistant and easy to clean. They are usually suspended to hide pipes and ventilation shafts. It is possible to install overhead jets to spray foam over the stove in case there is a flash fire.

- The doors should have the bottom part protected against kicks and bumps from trolleys; there should be no handles and any glass must be safety glass. Fire exits must be clearly marked. Swing doors to the dining-room should be soundproofed.
- The windows must be made of safety glass. They do not necessarily have to open, but should give natural light that prevents staff from feeling cooped up.
- The gas supply should be controlled by a central switch so that the supply can be cut off if necessary. The electricity must also be governed by a main supply switch. Mains water must be piped directly to each item of equipment that requires a supply, as well as to the wash basins.
- The storage facilities must be adequate to accommodate every type of item in use, to keep them in ideal condition, and to keep them secure.
- Fire-fighting equipment, hand-washing basins, internal and external telephones, and notice boards must be placed in sensible locations.

Large groups which use the same menu in all their branches will have a master plan that is based upon the principles of their operation, including the seating capacity and expected volume of business. They will probably use the same equipment in each outlet and the same contractor for each new branch. Budgetary costs are known in advance.

A guideline for the allocation of space to the various sections of the kitchen gives approximately 5 per cent to the goods receiving area, 5 per cent to the storerooms, 5 per cent to the stillroom, 10 per cent each for the dish and pot washeries, and 10 per cent to the chef's office, kitchen secretary and staff room. This leaves 55 per cent for the three main departments of the kitchen, allowing 12–13 per cent each for larder and pastry and 30 per cent for the main kitchen parties of sauce, fish, roast and vegetables. These amounts take into account the necessary equipment and machinery needed in each section, and gangway space for ease of circulation between workbench and stove and to a refrigerator. Some pieces of equipment are used by several parties and should therefore be sited where all are able to reach them.

Lighting in the kitchen should be similar in colour to that of the dining-room so that prepared dishes look the same when presented to the customers. Lights fitted under the canopy over the stove must be capable of withstanding the intense heat and steam that rises, and should be designed to prevent glare and shadows. They should be low-energy lights. All kitchen lighting should be measured to provide the recommended level of 500 lux which is the Système Internationale (SI) unit of illumination and is equal to light energy.

Ventilation in the kitchen is essential to provide a comfortable working environment for chefs working over a hot stove, grill or fryer for several hours non-stop. Ventilation systems work by extracting hot fumes and stale air and bringing in fresh air from outside. They take strong cooking smells out of the kitchen and reduce condensation from boiling, baking and steaming ovens. Extractor fans are usually housed in a canopy sited over a bank of equipment which also incorporates the lights and possibly a fire-existinguishing system.

In a cook-freeze or cook-chill operation where the food preparation and packaging areas are separated from the cooking area, good ventilation should provide an air temperature of approximately 10°C to ensure hygienic conditions.

Every kind of refrigeration equipment, including the deep-freezer, cook-chill food holders, walk-in cold rooms, refrigerators, chilled cold buffet display units and trolleys, blast chiller ice wells and ice-making machines, are sited in appropriate places around the kitchen and its ancillary departments to keep all the different kinds of food and drink in ideal conditions. Raw food must be stored in a separate refrigerator from cooked food, especially meats. Optimum storage temperatures are: deep-frozen foods –18°C to –21°C; raw fish 1°C; meat, poultry, sausages and bacon 2°C; cooked meats and dairy products 3–5°C; cook-chill meals 3°C; sous-vide dishes 3°C; uncooked pastry 5°C; cakes, flans made with custard or cream 5°C; salads, pâtés and pies 7°C. Digital display thermometers fixed on the outside of the refrigerators show the temperatures inside by numbers and have a greater impact than a pointer or dial.

The function of the kitchen and its ancillary areas

The main kitchen is the central cooking area where all the main courses are cooked and served by a number of groups of cooks called parties, each carrying out a particular part of the menu. The main ones are the sauce partie which produces all the meat dishes cooked by boiling, stewing, shallow frying, poêling and braising; the fish partie which produces all the fish dishes except those cooked by deep frying and grilling; the roast partie which produces all roasted, deep fried and grilled fish, meat and vegetable dishes; and the vegetable partie which cooks all the vegetables on the menu, other than those which are deep fried and grilled, as well as the soups, farinaceous and egg dishes. Each of these parties is allocated a section of an island site adjacent to the service hotplate and surrounded by work benches. The site is composed of stoves, bain-marie, salamander, deep frying unit, stockpot, steamer, roasting oven and grill. Some of these items are for use by all the parties, while others are for the use of one particular partie.

The larder

The larder is the section of the kitchen which acts as a storehouse and preparation unit for many of the items on the menu. Going through the sequence of courses, it makes all cold hors-d'oeuvres and issues items needed for hot hors-d'oeuvres; it issues bones and chicken carcasses for making stocks; it produces garnishes such as quenelles for soups; it issues ham, tongue, bacon, etc. for egg dishes; it prepares fish and shellfish for cooking, e.g. egg and breadcrumbed, and mousselines; it carries out the butchering of joints and small cuts, and the tying and trussing of meat, poultry and game; it issues cold sauces and dressings; and it makes all cold buffet dishes, cold soups, fish and meat items, raised pies, terrines, all the salads, dips and dressings, centre pieces and ice carvings. It may also look after the cheese board or trolley, prepare the baskets of fruit and nuts for dessert, and make up several of the savouries for cooking by the roast cook. Every single item on an à la Carte menu is cooked to order and each item has to be issued from the larder to the partie that will cook it.

The pastry department

The pastry department is run as an independent unit by the chef pâtissier who, according to the volume of work, would be assisted by several demi-chefs, each responsible for a particular branch of pastry work. For example, one would make all the different kinds of pastry and doughs, bouchées, vols-au-vent, tartlets and flan cases and also the covering of pies. Another would make all the hot sweets listed on the day's menu. Another would produce the cold sweets, all the different kinds of ice-cream and sorbets, bavarois, mousses, fools and syllabubs. Another would specialise in sugar work and would also make the gateaux, petits fours and possibly the many items made from chocolate, pastillage and marzipan. Some establishments may employ a baker to make loaves of bread, rolls, croissants and brioches.

Vegetable preparation area

Nowadays vegetables are available in ready-to-cook form; they have been washed, peeled, cut as required and need only storage. A vegetable preparation area is necessary only in those establishments which purchase fresh vegetables as harvested from the field. A number of vegetable hands and several items of equipment and machinery are required together with sufficient space to accommodate them and a number of mobile sinks and storage bins.

Potwash and dishwashing departments

The potwash and dishwashing departments are of vital importance in the maintenance of high standards of hygiene of kitchen utensils and restaurant equipment.

The potwash needs skilled staff to ensure that all saucepans and cooking utensils are thoroughly cleansed and dried after each use so as to avoid the risk of cross-contamination. A large establishment will find that a potwashing machine produces the desired results and lessens the number of staff required. In a smaller set-up, a wall-mounted electrical pot scrubber will ease the burden of staff employed in this department.

The dishwashing department is where all used crockery, glassware, cutlery and other silverware are washed, sterilised and dried ready to be used again. A head plateperson supervises the efficient operation to ensure that the staff keep each service point supplied with the necessary equipment. The main item of fixed equipment is the dishwashing machine which must be big enough to deal with peak loads of all the different items and deliver them spotlessly clean, dry, smear-free, sterile and sparkling. There must be space to accommodate trolleys, spring-loaded crockery dispensing units, burnishing machines, waste disposal units and sinks. A glass-washing machine can be installed to deal with glasses instead of putting them through the dishwasher. These machines must have an integral break tank and an air gap to conform to the requirements of the water regulation council to prevent soiled water returning with the source of supply.

Waste disposal area

All the waste products from the catering department are taken to the waste disposal area. As much as possible should be placed into containers for recycling, including bottles, cardboard and tins. Plastic bags filled with waste can be compacted in a machine to a smaller size before being thrown into a paladin or skip.

Kitchen hygiene

A wall-mounted pressure hosepipe on a rewind hose reel will help keep the entire kitchen area clean. A scrubber-dryer mobile machine will remove grease and grime with brushes that can clean out any grout lines on tiled floors, leaving the whole department's floors thoroughly clean and hygienic. The catering manager or head chef must carry out a hygiene inspection of his or her entire department to a formalised programme, taking notes of any breaches of the regulations, faults that need to be corrected and higher standards attained. Under the Food Safety Act all food premises are subject to inspection by environmental health officers.

Further reading

Birchfield, J. (1988) *Design and Layout of Foodservice Facilities*. John Wiley & Sons
Jones, P. and Merricks, P. (1994) *Management of Food Service Operations*. Cassell
Knight, J. (1998) *Quantity Food Production, Planning and Management*. John Wiley & Sons
Lawson, F. (1995) *Hotels and Resorts: Planning, Design and Refurbishment*. Butterworth-Heinemann

7 Convergence of facilities II
Equipment

Overall needs analysis; Cost and budget influences; Equipment construction and manufacture; Ordering equipment; Kitchen equipment; Dining-room equipment; Equipment for bars and customer amenity areas; Equipping the ancillary areas.

When setting up a new catering operation, a large part of the initial outlay will be spent on equipment which includes both fixed and mobile items, kitchen machines, small items including crockery, glassware, cutlery and cooking utensils, as well as linen, furniture and furnishings. In addition to the capital outlay there needs to be an annual allowance for the purchase of replacement or additional items and a further sum for maintenance contracts to keep the production equipment and machinery in running order.

Before buying any heavy-duty equipment for the kitchen it is necessary to decide which fuel is going to be used, and for the dining-room it is important to decide the policy on service, atmosphere and the amount of space to be made available for the number of customers.

The total budget available has first to be divided amongst the main departments and, although it is obvious that the kitchen with all its necessary equipment will cost more to equip than the dining-room, this must not be at the expense of the latter. In fact the dining-room and public areas should have priority in the matter of funds.

The time will come when it is necessary to replace outdated or worn-out equipment or to resite existing equipment during structural alterations to the premises. These alterations may become necessary if the original purpose is changed in the light of customer demands. The financial implications have to be costed to ensure that the new system will be viable.

This chapter deals with the subject of equipment in the following sequence:

1 kitchen equipment
2 dining-room equipment
3 equipment for the bars and customer amenity areas
4 equipment for stores and other ancillary areas

It aims to introduce the reader to most of the items and facilities available. But first it is necessary to look at the factors connected with selection and purchase.

Overall needs analysis

An analysis of each item of equipment should be carried out in order to ascertain whether its purchase can be justified. This has to be done in relation to the menu and the service by following the movement of items of food through the various stages from their delivery to final distribution in the form of a meal for consumption in the dining-room. The production volume of the business has to be known so that the maximum number of portions envisaged equates with the capacities of the items of equipment. This in turn hinges on the policy of portion size and the form of purchasing, bearing in mind the difference between food in its raw volume and that of the prepared volume. Such an exercise will help to ensure that only essential items are considered for purchase and those which will be used less frequently are given lower priority. If possible these items of lower priority should be eliminated from the list by minor adjustments to the menu, and different but more useful and versatile items can then be considered.

Daily usage

An exercise in calculating the normal daily usage of each item of equipment and machinery as a percentage of the working day can also help in deciding what to purchase. It is well known that many processes take place at the same time. This exercise might reveal that these processes could equally well be done at different times, thus permitting better use of equipment and manpower and removing the need to duplicate items. As certain activities must always precede others, placing them in chronological order will assist in equipment choice and also show up possible bottlenecks.

Control of fuel

The optimum use of kitchen equipment and machinery has a bearing on fuel bills, and staff must make every effort to conserve energy. Even such a common practice as adjusting the flame to the size of the pan should not be overlooked, while the old idea of turning on equipment first thing in the morning and not switching it off until the end of the dinner service is no longer valid.

Equipment needs

Equipment needs will vary depending on the type of operation. Large-scale cost sector catering operations work to a fairly restricted menu. They need equipment suitable for bulk cooking for large numbers. Commercial firms must offer a fairly wide choice of dishes and therefore work with small-scale equipment. They run on an à la Carte system of good advanced preparation and quick cooking methods, so restricting the size and range of equipment required.

Menu influence

The type and amount of equipment required in the kitchen and dining-room will be influenced by the nature of the menu and service and the volume of business. High-class establishments may have additional requirements, e.g. for trolleys and lamps to be used for a buffet display at lunch or a daily roast joint carved in the room.

Furnishing other areas

Other areas must be considered as well as the kitchen and dining-room and all purchases justified. Suitable equipment and furniture must be chosen for the bar and lounge in keeping with the type of establishment. Storage areas for food and beverages require the right kind of cupboards, shelving and refrigeration. Staff amenity rooms need solid furniture for reading, writing and relaxing, as well as some leisure pursuits such as darts or snooker.

Needs analysis

To sum up, every item of equipment should be evaluated for its ability to meet operational needs, provide efficient output, and save labour or conserve fuel. It must be judged on quality and not on price; poor-quality furniture, furnishings and linen will soon need replacing.

Over-provision of equipment will lead to high operational costs, whilst under-provision usually leads to bottlenecks, causing inefficient production.

Cost and budget influences

There are two approaches to this topic, depending on the type of operation. In the first, the budget allowance is broken down to the actual cost of each item of equipment required then, if the sum exceeds that made available, it will be necessary to look for suitable alternatives at lower prices, hopefully of the same quality. In the second, the total cost of all items is requested to be put in the budget. It is also possible to put the whole project out to tender – the firm that bids successfully will draw up the plans, put it all together and hand it over as a going concern. Then again it is possible to lease the equipment without any capital outlay at all.

The purchase decision will be made by the management with the advice of the planning team. They will try to choose standard production items, knowing that specially constructed ones to suit their particular needs are going to cost much more. Consideration must be given to the cost and its relation to size, durability, usefulness or performance, design and finish – more expensive items are not necessarily the best or most desirable. Desirability is often a deciding factor in purchasing and the buyer looks at the gauge of the metal and the possibility of obtaining spare parts, but it should be recognised that advances in technology enable manufacturers to improve performance and put new improved models on the market. It is therefore necessary to obtain the most up-to-date machinery which gives good performance in relation to its cost.

Installation

The cost of delivery and installation of heavy-duty equipment must be included in the budget, bearing in mind that in some instances the floor may have to be strengthened or insulated.

Operating costs

It is important to calculate the operating costs of each item of equipment, basing this on its likely use and loading. The high cost of fuel demands economical use, and thermostats and sensory devices must be kept in good working order.

Maintenance costs

Upkeep costs may include a maintenance contract with a firm of kitchen engineers to service all equipment in all departments; it may include emergency call-out to do a vital repair job to keep the department in operation. The design of equipment has a bearing on ease of maintenance – the more straightforward it is, the cheaper it is to keep working, since manpower is the most expensive part of this contract. A planned programme of maintenance will help to keep all items of equipment and machinery in good working order.

The cost of replacing expendable equipment such as linen, furnishings and utensils that are worn out has to be included in the budget.

Equipment construction and manufacture

This relates to the materials used and the design and finish of items of equipment. They should be sufficiently solid to stand up to hard use, and should also look and handle well. The materials should be strong, non-absorbent and non-corrosive; thermal conductivity applies to some items, whilst lightness in weight and smoothness of finish apply to others. All equipment should be easy to clean so that standards of hygiene can be maintained. Restaurant furniture should combine elegance and practicality so that it suits the particular requirements of the establishment, yet be robust to give long service. The decisions whether to have chairs with arms, if they should be stackable, what material to use for the seats, how high the seats should be and how wide, all need careful consideration. Choose curtain material that does not need cleaning too frequently and stays attractive without fading.

Ergonomic requirements

The ergonomics of equipment should be studied so that their design suits the people who will use them and helps to make the working environment efficient. This includes a working height of approximately 100 cm for most jobs, or 90 cm for heavy work. A dining table should be 70 cm high and the seat of the chair 43 cm in height. The application of ergonomic principles helps to reduce unnecessary stress and increases the effectiveness of the staff employed. Work study is a part of the planning process and sets out to obtain the best use of manpower and resources by cutting out unnecessary movements and motion in carrying out any task. Making the best use of the equipment installed is a part of the work study.

As a result of the drive towards the free movement of goods between the countries of the European Union, manufacturers of large-scale catering equipment are now harmonising standards of gas and electric items to ensure that they pass agreed tests and satisfy the regulations which will give them the CE Certification Mark. They can then be sold and used in every country of the European Union.

Performance and usefulness

Equipment, whether a stove, an ice-making machine or a mixer, is evaluated by its performance which includes ease of operation. Performance refers to output or what amount can be produced in a given time. Manufacturers are able to give figures for output of certain foods in their items of equipment, basing them on production under ideal conditions which are not always easy to reproduce in ordinary practice. In large-scale or fast-food catering, performance is of great importance as it effects the length of time a customer may have to wait for food. Durability and reliability are part of this.

The furniture for the dining-room and customer amenity areas must be chosen with the following criteria in mind: its suitability, ease of movement, comfort, strength, design and materials used. The crockery, cutlery and glassware must be chosen to suit the standard of the dining-room and also for its durability, ease of replacement, functionality, weight and material used.

Ordering equipment

The techniques of ordering are described in Chapter 11, and the details given there hold good for the purchase of equipment. Great detail is required to obtain exactly the right goods at the right price, by giving precise specifications so that the goods purchased fulfil all requirements. When the decision to purchase equipment is taken lightly and without a full assessment, problems may arise which were not envisaged, such as difficulty in accommodating it, extra installation costs, lack of ventilation, unsuitability for its purpose, or poor operating performance.

Materials used

An understanding of the materials used to manufacture items of equipment, especially the new man-made materials, is necessary. In the past heavy-duty equipment meant not only that it had to perform heavy duties, but that it was solidly made of heavy-gauge cast iron or steel. Much modern equipment utilises lighter weight and thinner gauge materials such as aluminium, duraluminium and stainless steel.

Kitchen equipment

When purchasing kitchen equipment and machinery, whether new or second-hand, for a completely new kitchen or as a replacement item, it is important to consider the following questions:

- Is the item suitable for the style of cooking being used?
- Will it cope with the maximum number of meals to be served?
- Can it deal with the menu and form of service in use?
- Will it match and fit in with the other equipment?
- Is it economical in fuel consumption?
- Is it easy to keep in clean condition?
- Are safety factors installed within it?
- How durable is it? What is its lifespan? Will it withstand hard use?
- Will maintenance be easily available? What will it cost?
- Will the floor bear the item's weight?
- Can it be brought in through exiting doorways?
- Do staff need training before using it?
- Does it carry a warranty period?
- Is its price within budget allowance?
- Are there delivery and installation costs?

There will be a range of models of each item of equipment and machinery from different manufacturers, which may make it difficult to choose the ideal piece for a given situation. It can be helpful to inspect one in a working situation or at an exhibition where manufacturers and suppliers will have a stand.

The following details give an outline description of important items of equipment installed in the kitchen and its servery. It is not meant to be exhaustive, and the items listed are not necessary in every kitchen.

Fixed or heavy-duty kitchen equipment

THE KITCHEN RANGE

In the majority of kitchens this is the most used piece of equipment, mainly because of its versatility. It is a composite unit that is designed to cope with a number of tasks by using the top and oven at the same time. The traditional solid top has the advantage that if it is fully loaded with pans some can be boiling, others simmering and others just keeping warm. It can be uneconomical, however, because whether operated by gas or electricity it has to be kept on full all the time, whereas separate rings can be adjusted to suit the actual needs of the service, so cutting down on fuel costs. It is possible to have a half solid top with some individual rings. The oven can be thermostatically controlled with a heat source at the base and the heated air passing through the lining, thus giving convected heat. There is a tendency to have different heat zones in various parts of the oven, but the cook gets used to this. A disadvantage of the range is that it is ergonomically bad to have to bend down to manipulate the progress of food cooking in the oven; if the drop-door type is used when tending the food, it means stooping to the task. The range certainly makes full use of floor space and is enhanced by the overhead rack which is used to hold cooked foods and serving dishes. The practice of siting a grill or salamander above the stove has advantages, but also some disadvantages – it eliminates a potential bottleneck at the point of distribution, but can deplete the section of a supply of service dishes to hand.

An electrically operated range will take approximately 30 minutes to reach an operating temperature of 180°C, but because of good insulation will maintain good heat for up to half an hour after being switched off.

GENERAL-PURPOSE OVEN

This is a free-standing oven which can be loaded without bending or stretching and is therefore ergonomically better for staff. It may be operated by radiant heat, where the visible flame in the base gives a gradient of heat from bottom to top, and is very good for roasting. Convected heat, which is generated by semi-external burners housed below the bottom of the oven and enters the chamber through vents, is good for baking as the heat is even.

PASTRY OVEN

This kind of oven is more usually electrically heated because of its good heat retention and evenness of operation. It is made in separate decks, each operating independently and having a heavy bottom and a narrow opening of 12.5–22.5 cm; the number of decks would be built according to the establishment's requirements. This oven is more suited to pastry and bread baking than to general use.

REEL OR ROTARY OVEN

This is usually required for bakery work, but may be used for general baking and roasting. It has a wheeled mechanism carrying a number of racks on which the trays of food to be cooked are placed. The trays stay the right way up on a flexible axle and the wheels are driven by a powerful motor. This type of oven may be gas, electric or oil fired. It is very economical in a large-scale operation and gives a good even result. A version of this type of oven enables a loaded trolley to be wheeled inside and attached to a clasp at the top; this suspends the trolley just clear of the bottom so that it rotates when the oven doors are closed.

CONVECTION OVEN

Convected heat is efficient and when generated in an oven and circulated as heated air it gives an evenness of result that no other oven can match. This type is sometimes called the forced-air oven because the electrically driven fan can blow the air at 80 km per hour, reaching every part of the oven. As food cooks by the penetration of heat, vapour and moisture are released from the surface of the food and tend to slow down the penetration. With air being circulated at high speed, the heat penetration is faster and therefore speeds up the cooking process. This oven can be operated at a slightly lower temperature than an ordinary one and still give quicker results; shrinkage is lessened by its use. The oven operates better with a full load, but there should be room at the side of the shelves for the forced air to circulate.

A convection oven does everything a normal oven does except perhaps the baking of bread, but roasting, braising and ordinary baking and the reheating of bulk packs of frozen food are accomplished efficiently. Ergonomically they are good since they are usually free-standing or bench-mounted, and some models are loaded by pushing a trolley of food inside and closing the doors on it. The doors are side opening and have heat-reflective glass panels. When opened the doors should operate a fan cut-out switch to prevent hot air blowing on to the face of the cook. A timer that rings and shuts off the heat at the end of the cooking period is installed and an interior lamp shows how the cooking is progressing. Aerodynamic perforated oven linings give even temperature and high capacity, and low-pressure fans assist this. A humidifier is incorporated to prevent shrinkage and improve texture; it allows different dishes to be cooked in the same oven without transfer of flavours.

Table-top convection ovens in which the air velocity can be controlled are also available. They have an advantage over microwave ovens of similar capacity in that they take steel gastronorm containers and foil dishes.

COMBINATION OVEN

This kind of general-purpose oven combines hygienic fresh steam at 100°C and hot circulated air at 30–300°C in one appliance. It is available in electric or gas versions. The controls will operate:

1 the pressureless steam at 100°C, or for firm foods up to 110°C
2 the hot air for roasting, baking, gratinating and glazing
3 the combined effects of 1 and 2
4 vario-steaming for gentle cooking of bain-marie items
5 reheating of plated cooked meals.

A whole carcass of meat can be hung on a mobile spit for roasting. A temperature probe will switch the oven off when the desired internal temperature is reached. A sensor measures the humidity in the oven, from 0 to 100 per cent.

This type of oven is energy- and labour-saving. Normal oven loss in roasting meat is as high as 30 per cent, whereas in a combination oven it is only 18 per cent. The oven can be filled with gastronorm trays of different foods for cooking

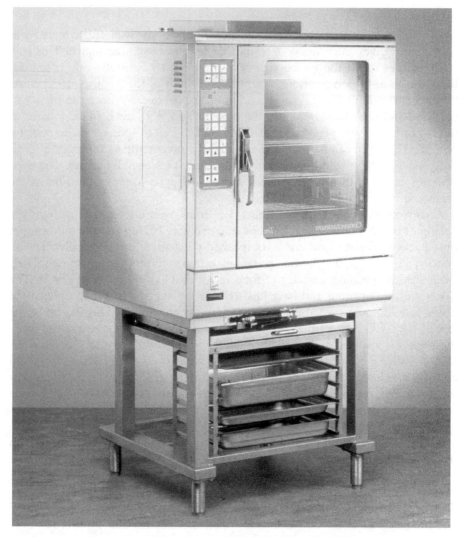

Plate 4   Convectasteam Combination Oven, by Falcon Catering Equipment

together without cross-flavour, and each dish can be removed as soon as ready without great loss of heat.

Meals for a banquet can be cooked in advance and regenerated at the precise moment of serving without any drying out. This kind of oven works well for yeast and pastry goods. Digital controls light up to show timing, temperature and humidity, and some are controlled by a computer system.

CONVOTHERM TEMPLOCK OVEN

This is a static or mobile oven for holding freshly prepared hot meals in covered bulk containers, plates or banqueting services at the ideal temperature from time of cooking to time of service without further cooking or drying out. It works from a 13-amp plug and looks good inside the restaurant or banquet hall. At other times it can be in use for prime cooking.

PIZZA OVEN

A Pizza oven is brick-built. It has a narrow opening door leading to a shallow baking chamber with a brick hearth. Individual pizzas are placed on this by means of a peel and cooked at a high temperature under intense radiant heat for a short length of time. For large-scale service, oblong baking trays are used and the resultant pizza is cut into portions.

TANDOORI CLAY OVEN

A tandoori oven is used exclusively for cooking tandoori items, including lamb kebabs, seafoods, tandoori chicken and nan bread. It was first used by the Mogul dynasty which governed Hindustan from the sixteenth century, and until its recent popularity was in use almost exclusively in Pakistan. It was originally cylindrical in shape, made of clay, and buried outside underground with only the top opening showing. It was fired by burning charcoal at the bottom for several hours until the oven got red hot. Then the previously marinated food, threaded half-way along a sharp skewer, was placed inside to rest on the bottom and cooked and basted until done. Nan bread was baked by sticking it to the side of the oven near the top. Stainless steel, free-standing tandoori ovens fuelled by high-pressure gas are now made for use by ethnic restaurants in this country.

MICROWAVE OVEN

Microwaves are electromagnetic radiation waves contained in the narrow band of radio wavelengths and were originally developed for use in radar communications. Microwave cookery differs considerably from other forms of cookery, but is not a principle of cooking in the same way that baking and boiling are. Few cooks obtain fully efficient use from it, mainly because they do not understand its role in the kitchen.

A microwave oven works by bombarding the food with electromagnetic waves given off by a magnetron. The energy is absorbed and causes the molecules in the food to oscillate at a very high rate. These vibrations cause intermolecular friction and create kinetic energy which is apparent from the vapour released from the food. The high-frequency radio waves cook the food from within, and the effective penetration appears to be 2.5 cm from every direction. This means that the thicker the food, the slower the rate of penetration. Moisture content and state of solidity also cause different rates of cooking.

The oven will not seal or colour foods, and the sinew or collagen in meat is not converted into tender, juicy, gelatinous matter as happens when roasted or grilled. A special browning plate is available that gives a pleasant appearance to meats cooked in this way, particularly to steaks, and some ovens are fitted with a turntable so that foods are cooked more evenly and quickly.

Cooking in a microwave oven is approximately seven times faster than in an ordinary oven; poaching and shallow frying can be done satisfactorily and regeneration and defrosting of cooked dishes is very good. As such it is frequently used at the point of service to ensure the food is very hot when distributed to waiting staff.

It is not possible to use metal dishes in a microwave oven as it causes a luminous discharge between the electrodes – even a gold band on a dinner plate causes this and the microwaves will gradually destroy the metal together with the glaze. Ceramic and glass dishes are used instead and these stay fairly cool during the cooking operation.

The size of microwave oven needed for a catering establishment depends on its use and the amount of food cooked in it. There is a range of models rated from 800 watts to 1,300 watts. Some are capable of operating on half or full power – half power is useful for quick defrosting of frozen foods. BS 5175 specifies the safety requirements of microwave cookers. If the oven is not cleaned regularly, food splashes on the door seal can cause leakage of the microwaves which are very dangerous to the operator; a small calibrated radiation reader can be used to check this.

When deciding what microwave oven to buy, the following points should be considered:

- Would a combined microwave and forced-air convection oven be more suitable for your needs?
- Is it a commercial size and not one designed for domestic use?
- Is the power output at least 1.2 kW?
- Can it carry out a certain amount of prime cooking?
- Does it regenerate frozen and chilled foods quickly?
- Is there a light inside it?
- Is it digitally programmed?
- Does it read barcodes?
- Does it have pre-set programming?
- Is food moved around on a turntable?
- Is there the space to site it close to the serving point?
- Does the purchase include an insurance policy on the magnetron?

COMBINED MICROWAVE OVENS

The **Mealstream** oven, sometimes referred to as a jet oven, is a heavy-duty oven which combines the advantages of microwave and forced-air circulation and will do all the common cooking processes with the exception of deep frying. Both sources of power should be used together, though it is possible to use them separately. The microwaves cook the food quickly, while the convected heat gives colour, flavour and texture that the microwaves alone cannot provide. As well as reduced cooking time, there is also less weight loss. The oven is suitable for regenerating frozen food and there is pulse power for defrosting frozen poultry prior to cooking. It is designed to take gastronorm trays and foil containers.

A **Maestrowave** oven is a commercial microwave with a grill and forced-air convection.

Ovens which combine microwaves, steam and hot-air convection are available with up to six shelves in which food can be placed while it is still cold. They are programmed by means of electronic touch pads and the internal temperature is controlled by computer technology. When the desired internal temperature of the food is reached the oven will turn itself off, thus saving energy whilst reducing heat loss by as much as 20 per cent. Staff using this kind of oven require initial training in order to gain maximum advantage from it.

CHINESE COOKING STOVE

This item has become popular outside China in kitchens which feature several Chinese dishes amongst others on the menu. It is made for the à la Carte service of stir-fry dishes which ideally have to be cooked at a very high temperature as quickly as possible.

It is manufactured as a solid-top range on legs with up to six or seven large round openings that will each accommodate a normal-size wok, sinking it half-way inside so that it is directly surrounded by the flames from a supply of gas. To stir-fry successfully very intense heat is essential, so as many as 48 high-rated burners are installed. The stove part is made to accommodate pans of stock or water with food in a bamboo or wooden steaming basket for cooking in the Chinese fashion. It is also useful for the quick method of sautéing for large numbers, though there is no cover for the openings.

It is usual to have a water tap sited on the stove so that the woks can be quickly swilled after use and the surrounding edge of the stove may be water-cooled through a gully.

A smaller lightweight wok cooker works by induction heating off a 3-amp plug for stir-frying oriental dishes in front of customers.

GRILLING EQUIPMENT

The true grill enables food to be put on an adjustable grill bar above the fire – it uses either charcoal or coke to give an intense heat without smoke or flame, forming a glowing bed that lasts without refuelling for a long period.

Gas-operated grills with mineral lava heaped on top give the glowing effect but not the same taste as charcoal, yet they are clean and efficient and may be installed in a dining-room where grills are a speciality.

A **salamander** is sometimes referred to as an over-fired grill as its source of heat comes from the top so that it will gratinate and glaze as well as grill. The heat is quite intense and when meat is grilled on the bars of a salamander, its juices tend to be extruded on to the tray beneath. By placing the meat on a tray to grill, the juices will not be lost and it will thus prevent much of the dryness found when grilling directly on the bars.

Grilling is also carried out on a **griddle plate**, which is a solid slab of cast iron or steel heated by gas from beneath or by electric elements. Some are ridged to brand marks on grilled meats, but a flat surface allows all kinds of foods to be dry fried, including eggs. The heat is conducted and it is necessary to have a film of fat to prevent food sticking. A lot of fumes and vapour are given off so ventilation is important and the air filters need regular cleaning. The capacity of a griddle, as for a grill, can be calculated by its dimensions and by how long a particular item takes to cook.

In a **contact grill** food is placed between two heated metal plates, the top plate being hinged. Both plates are electrically heated to give a quick result because of the dual heat source.

A **barbecue** is a type of grill which uses charcoal as the source of heat, or it can be fired by butane gas burning on to a bed of mineral lava or pumice shaped into brickettes.

A **toasted-sandwich machine** is useful for making the many different kinds of two- and three-decker sandwiches. The untoasted bread with the fillings inside is placed in the machine, the top is clamped down and the timer set. Whilst it is cooking the edges are sealed, and some machines divide the sandwich into halves or quarters ready for eating. This kind of sandwich is the Club Sandwich which is popular in most countries as a quick and satisfying snack.

FRYER

Deep-fat frying is the fastest method of cookery because it operates at 150–196°C. At these high temperatures, however, it is not easy to control, so unless a purpose-built item of equipment is used the result can be both unsatisfactory and costly. Two main types of fryers are used: the first where the fat is contained in a V-shaped pan and the heat is directed to each side, leaving a cool zone at the bottom; and the second where the electric element is in the pan of fat, heating the oil above but leaving a cool zone below. The purpose of the cool zone is to receive particles of food that would otherwise get burnt and spoil the oil. The smaller the top opening, the less exposure there is and consequently less chance of oxidisation of the oil.

Oil is an expensive commodity and should be made to last as long as possible; this means minimal absorption by the food and avoidance of breakdown caused by excessively high temperatures. The amount of oil necessary to fill the fryer is important – if it is possible to reduce the amount by putting in less food at a time, then it is possible to cook at a slightly lower temperature thus decreasing the amount of fat used but not allowing absorption. It is calculated that two and a half litres of oil are required per 500 g of food.

To obtain maximum use of oil or fat in a fryer it should be filtered after each service period while still warm, using a separate power filter machine that sucks out the fat through a fine strainer then pumps it back in after the oil reservoir has been cleaned. New designs of fryers have a filtration system built in to serve a bank of frying units. To extent the life of the frying oil, it is also recommended that the lid of the fryer is kept closed when not in use.

Control is essential for this item as there are obvious hazards in its use. A gas-operated fryer may have a snap-action thermostat adjustable up to 190°C, with a second overheat cut-off fitted to operate at 215°C in case of thermostat failure. A cooking timer also acts as an automatic cut-off. An electric fryer has the second

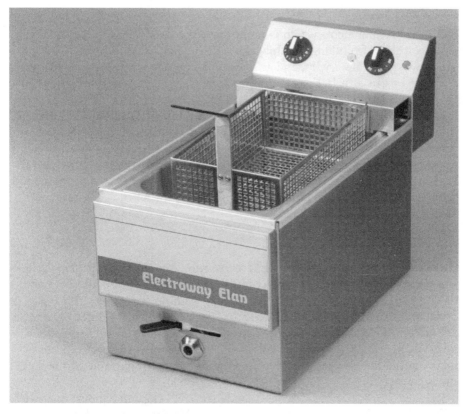

Plate 5   Electroway Elan Fryer, by Viscount Catering Ltd

thermostat bonded to the heating element which becomes operational if the main thermostat fails.

The capacity of a fryer is expressed in output of food, usually kilograms of chip potatoes per hour, taking them from the raw state.

PRESSURE FRYER

Deep frying carried out in a pressure-sealed frying kettle, which is usually computer controlled with digital control panels, keeps the natural juices and flavour inside foods. This item of equipment is therefore very suitable for frying raw chicken portions. The oil is heated to 190–250°C, and the food is then immersed and immediately sealed and coloured. The lid is sealed down and cooking takes place under pressure at 120°C. No further coloration takes place. The cycle is timed to switch off and exhaust before the lid can be opened; a pressure gauge indicates the pressure in the fryer and shows when it is exhausted. Foods must be coated before being submerged and, although it is possible to blanch chipped potatoes, this item of equipment will not fry them.

BRATT PAN

This item of equipment, which is often referred to as a multi-purpose cooking pan, is capable of fulfilling a number of tasks: it can be used for boiling, braising, stewing, shallow frying, and as a bain-marie. Claims are made for its use as a deep fryer, but as it lacks a thermostat control and a cool zone it is not really suitable.

The bottom of the pan is made of cast iron or stainless steel. It has a tilting mechanism which is labour-saving as the contents of the pan can be poured out rather than ladled. The pan size is normally 76 cm × 61 cm × 180 cm with a capacity of 32 litres or approximately 200 portions of food, and it can cope with 24–30 kg of shallow-fried meat per hour. The stainless-steel base may cause food to burn in certain spots, and it is best to thicken a stew when nearly ready rather than at the half-way stage.

BOILING PAN

There are three main types of boiling pans: the direct heated type; the double pan; and the steam type. The direct heated pan is good for boiling vegetables, making stock and thin soup. A steam boiling pan, or kettle as the small size is called, has steam under pressure circulating through the two walls of the pan. It differs from the double pan which is actually the direct type with some water in the cavity, and does not work as fast as the pressure type. All have stainless-steel linings and the smaller sizes can be tilted rather than having to run off the liquid through a tap.

The steam kettle cooks viscous liquids such as soup and gravy very well. Baskets that fit perfectly are used for batch cooking green vegetables, and it is possible to have a quick-chill type in which cold water circulates through the jacket to cool a sauce or a stew prior to chilling or freezing. A power mixer attachment will purée the contents of the kettle, and a mixing or agitating attachment will keep the contents well stirred during cooking time.

The sealed jacket contains water, rust inhibitor, anti-freeze and electric elements to produce the steam. The 22 litre and 45 litre models can be used over and over again during a busy service period and, as these do not need a lid because they work so quickly, it is easy to keep glancing at how the contents are cooking. Models with a capacity of 545 litres are also made, but with such a capacity it is obviously an advantage to bring the water supplies close by. Some boiling pans have a rectangular casing to give an orderly look to the battery of kitchen equipment.

STEAMERS

There are several types of steamer to choose from: the atmospheric steaming oven; the pressure steamer; the dynamic pressureless steamer; and the flash steamer. In a steamer there is no water to weigh down the food and cause distortion. Since the food must be cooked in perforated trays to allow the steam to cook it from all sides, there is also no cooking liquid.

The **atmospheric steamer** produces its own steam from the container of water at the bottom which is heated by gas or electricity; the water is fed in as required and controlled by a ball valve. When the water reaches 100°C it gives off steam which is trapped in the chamber to cook the food. The door is sealed to prevent escape. Five or six trays of food may be placed in to cook at the same time. To install this type of steamer, only fuel, an indirect water supply and drainage are required.

A **pressure steamer** allows cooking at a higher temperature than 100°C, shortening the cooking time and retaining more nutritional value, natural colour and flavour. Some models need water poured on to the base of the oven to produce steam; others generate steam by means of water jets onto the bottom of the steamer compartment. For steamed puddings the atmospheric steaming oven is best, but for batch cooking of potatoes and green vegetables, both fresh and frozen, the pressure steamer gives better results. It does, however, require great care as the slightest extra cooking time can spoil the colour of the food. The timing device will control the cooking, and there is often an audio as well as a visual signal to mark the end of the cycle, but the door will not open until all pressure has been vented. There is a danger of scalding water gushing out if an attempt is made to force the door open. Solid trays are available for steaming meat and chickens without losing all the juices. Only minutes are needed to cook vegetables, but larger items need nearly as long as in the atmospheric steamer.

Ovens that operate with steam in them but without pressure are used for cooking meats and are successful in keeping cooking losses very low. There is no build-up of pressure so the oven does not have to be sealed, though some models are dual-purpose and may be operated as a pressure cooker.

The newer type of **pressureless convection steam cooker** is smaller than the atmospheric type and it allows the door to be opened at any time without stopping the cooking process. It operates off a 5 kW electric supply. The steam generator is self-contained and operates at zero pressure, yet will cook trays of frozen peas in two minutes and beef at ten minutes per 450 g. Some foods such as rice need water in the pan and, where needed, juices can be retained when cooking meat by using a solid tray. This kind of steamer is usually enhanced with a computerised control system.

Combined steam and hot-air ovens that work on either or both of the heat sources are dealt with on page 75.

In a large-scale food production unit, the use of travelling or endless-belt ovens, fryers, grills and steamers are essential. They are timed to cook the foods to the correct temperature at a set speed.

General kitchen machinery

The following items of equipment are operated by electricity, though there are still some, such as slicing machines, that are operated by hand. These machines are referred to as labour-saving because they make light work of such chores as chopping, cutting, grating, mixing and peeling.

MIXING MACHINE

This is a frequently used machine in the kitchen because it can do a wide range of jobs very efficiently with just a bowl and three mixing attachments – whisk, paddle and dough hook. There are different sizes of mixers for different uses, small and medium table models and several sizes of floor-mounted ones. The size used to be stated in US quarts of 32 fluid ounces, but is now given in litres. With some models, different bowl sizes may be used by attaching a collar to take the smaller bowl, but this also means having two sets of mixing tools. Mixers have three-speed gears to obtain speedy aeration and smooth liquid mixes, and also for dense or elastic mixes such as fruit cake, hamburger mix and bread dough. Large models have a power lift to bring the bowl up to operating level, and a timer that allows staff to get on with something else whilst the mixer is working.

So many operations are carried out more efficiently with the mixer than by hand that it is difficult to visualise a kitchen without a mixer. Indeed so many people use it daily that the pastry department, larder and kitchen usually each need their own model. The versatility of a mixer in operating such attachments as a mincer, vegetable cutter and hamburger moulder can lead to a bottleneck where only one mixer is available and all sections need to use it.

HIGH-SPEED MIXER

A high-speed mixer takes up a small amount of room and produces much better bread dough than the normal mixing machine. It is useful if the policy is to serve bread and rolls made on the premises. It uses a system called the Chorleywood process, also known as the no-time dough, in which all the ingredients, including cold water and an improver, are mixed and developed at very high speed in a few minutes. The dough is then ready for moulding.

AIR WHIP

Another form of mixer is the air whip, which is useful where a large quantity of whipped cream is used in pastry work. This machines doubles the cream in volume and does not over-mix.

MOBILE TURBO-MIXER

A mobile turbo-mixer can be placed into a boiling pan to mash the contents. It saves having to remove food from the pan to the mixer and lessens the chance of it getting cold. A revolving knife unit is surrounded by an interchangeable sieve for fine or coarse mixes, and is lowered from its stand into the pan to produce, for example, mashed potato, vegetable purée or soup.

FOOD PROCESSOR

The kitchen machine that gets more use than even the mixing machine is undoubtedly the food processor, because it is capable of doing all the jobs that a mixer can do plus chopping, chipping, creaming, crumbling, dicing, grating, grinding, liquidising, mincing, puréeing, shredding and slicing of foods such as raw and cooked meats, vegetables, cheese, chocolate, coffee beans, egg whites and for making mousses, pâtés, quenelles and so on.

A plastic or stainless-steel bowl is locked into the motor and set in motion at the desired speed whilst the food is fed in through a chute and lid using the plunger. There are many different makes and several sizes of this machine, which quickly pays for itself by the amount of use it gets and by simplifying many tedious processes.

HEAVY-DUTY BLENDER

This is a widely used piece of machinery which saves the need to pass soups and purées through a sieve, although it may still be necessary to use a fine strainer after-wards to obtain the best results. It can process raw and cooked foods and is also useful for making emulsified sauces such as mayonnaise and salad cream. There is also a heated version that is capable of making a decent Sauce Hollandaise.

PACOJET MACHINE

This machine will mince or purée frozen foods at $-18°C$ to $-22°C$ straight from the freezer. It will also cut frozen items into rough discs by first freezing them in the container of the machine. When fish or chicken is left longer in the machine and the necessary ingredients are added, it will produce a perfect quenelle mixture. It can make a savoury or sweet mousse from frozen, cooked or raw materials; produce a pure fruit ice-cream; or even mix a fruit-based cocktail.

This machine has encouraged the formation of a chef's association known as the Pacojet International Circle. The association has the aim of dreaming up new ideas and dishes which are exchanged among the worldwide members who own a Pacojet machine.

LIQUIDISER

Hand-held liquidisers will purée and mix large amounts of soft foods, sauces, soups and mixtures of up to 100 litres from a 13-amp electric supply.

SOUP KETTLE

Rustic-style soup kettles keep the contents piping hot. The holder is surrounded by hot water, hot air or steam and can hold up to 75 normal portions without any loss or deterioration of taste and consistency. Soup kettles can also be used for holding and serving stews.

CAN-OPENING MACHINE

A can-opening machine is electrically operated, and a suitable free-standing table model that can deal with tins up to A10 size is essential in all kitchens. The machine inserts a blade into the can when switched on and stops when the lid has been detached. The lid is held by a retaining magnet.

VACUUM PACKAGING MACHINE

A vacuum packaging machine excludes oxygen from filled pouches in the sous-vide system of food production, thus preventing spoilage inside the vacuum packs. For production runs a probe is inserted into one of the batch to monitor temperature during storage (see also Chapter 14). Vacuum-packed products must be prepared under strict hygienic conditions, and chilled and stored immediately once prepared.

Larder machinery

BOWL CHOPPER

The bowl chopper has a set of knife blades that rotate as a steel bowl containing the food to be chopped goes round and round until the required degree of fineness is reached. This machine will continue chopping until a fine purée is formed, such as for a mousseline or pâté mixture. A food processor does exactly the same tasks and has the advantage of being mobile and less costly.

MINCER

A mincer can be operated by hand or by electricity and will produce a coarse or fine result according to which plate is used – there are several to choose from. It is also available for use in the hub of a mixing machine. Prepared sausage-meat can be fed through a mincer with a length of skin pulled over the extruder; it will fill the skin as the meat is pushed through by the mincer worm.

MEAT TENDERISER

A meat tenderiser pierces slices of steak fed through it with hundreds of fine needles which cut into the connective tissue and sinew. It is used to make cuts of tough meat more tender.

SLICING MACHINE

A slicing machine cuts sides of bacon or cooked and raw meat into slices of the desired thickness by means of a rotating round cutting blade. Hand-operated, gravity-feed and automatic machines are available; thickness of cut and speed of operation are adjustable. Raw meat can be chilled before being sliced. The machine must be taken apart after every use for thorough washing and sterilising.

BAND SAW

A band saw is used to dissect frozen or chilled carcasses and to cut meat into the required joints. It works very quickly and neatly through bones and rind. Safety precautions must be followed when using it.

SMOKING OVEN

A smoking oven has a compartment filled with hardwood chips or sawdust. These smoulder gently and generate smoke that cures the meat or fish, including salmon, eels, mackerel, haddock, trout, cod roe, which is hung from the top of the oven. The fish is turned or moved as necessary so that smoke reaches all parts of the surface. A supplementary source of heat such as a hotplate turned on to low to give a temperature of about 125°C helps to keep the food moist.

WRAPPING MACHINE

A wrapping machine holds a roll of polythene or clingfilm of food-use quality and has a heated wire that cuts it to suitable lengths. It is used to wrap items hygienically and to prevent foods from drying out in storage.

INSECT KILLER

An insect killer provides effective pest control by attracting, killing and collecting flying insects. It does this by means of a blue light system that can be wall hung or ceiling mounted and has replaceable tubes. These have superseded window screens, fly papers and sprays.

Vegetable preparation machines

POTATO-PEELING MACHINE

A potato-peeling machine rubs the skins off potatoes as they are whirled around inside the machine against the carborundum bottom and side-plates. Some machines have a timing device; if not, it will be necessary to lift the lid to see if they are ready to be let out into the sink, having turned off the water. Carrots can also be peeled in this machine.

CHIPPING MACHINE

An automatic chipping machine pushes peeled potatoes through a cutting disc, using different discs for the various kinds of chips from Pommes Allumettes to Pommes Pont-Neuf. It can chip as much as 18 kg of potatoes in one minute.

SHREDDER

A shredder can be attached to the hub of a mixing machine or, using the correct blade, to a food processor to produce finely or coarsely shredded, diced, grated and sliced vegetables. Some cheeses can also be prepared in this machine.

VEGETABLE WASHING MACHINE

A large-scale catering establishment can benefit from the installation of a vegetable washing machine which will thoroughly wash and drain most green vegetables and salad stuffs without causing damage to delicate leaves. They are made in several sizes.

Machines for the pastry department

ROLL-MOULDING MACHINE

A roll-moulding machine divides a rolled-out slab of bread dough into pieces of the desired size. It then starts to rotate and mould them into neat balls ready for proving.

BREAD MOULDER

A bread moulder takes pieces of dough and kneads and moulds them to the required shape before depositing them in the baking tins.

PROVER

A prover will hold bulk dough in a mixing bowl and provide the right level and amount of humidity to prove the dough. Then when it is moulded and trayed, it can be placed on the shelves for the second proving. It can be warmed by gas or electricity and requires a supply of fresh water.

ROLLING-OUT MACHINE

A rolling-out machine rolls out pastry to the desired thickness and dimensions. It is operated either by hand, turning the handle, or by electricity.

DIE-STAMPING MACHINE

A die-stamping machine has a number of dies of different sizes. A piece of pastry in a pan or mould is placed in the selected die and the top press is pulled down, flattening the pastry to line the mould in readiness for filling. The dies are for making various sizes of tartlet cases, flans, round, square and oblong pies, and tarts; it can also produce lids for these. The machine is electrically heated.

CREAM-WHIPPING MACHINE

A cream-whipping machine can be used to whip cream in the pastry department, increasing it up to two and a half times its original volume by incorporating air. It keeps its shape when piped out, unlike aerosol whipped cream which loses shape rapidly. These machines are made to whip amounts from $1\frac{1}{2}$ to 12 litres of cream.

ICE-CREAM OR SORBET MAKER

An ice-cream or sorbet maker churns a prepared mixture made traditionally with eggs, milk, sugar and cream or fruit, or using a commercial ice-cream mix, until it thickens and aerates under the intense refrigeration given off by the machine. It then has to be stored at −20°C in a cabinet used only for ices. When required for service, it can be removed to another cabinet held at −18°C. It is illegal to sell ice-cream that is warmer than −2°C. A sorbet must be kept at −18°, but should ideally be served as soon as it has been made.

Legislation demands that ice-cream mixtures be heated to at least 69°C for 30 minutes or 150°C for 2 seconds, then cooled to 7°C within one and a half hours until frozen. The Ice-Cream Regulations 1967 lay down minimum food requirements for ice-creams.

Stillroom machinery

EGG BOILER

An automatic egg boiler lowers an egg into boiling water, cooks it according to the time set, and then withdraws the cooked egg from the water immediately.

This means that the stillroom person no longer needs to watch over the eggs with an old-fashioned egg timer.

HOT WATER BOILER

A hot water boiler provides water at the correct temperature for brewing tea; it is drawn off into teapots or urns. As part of a café set, water can be sprayed over ground coffee in a side urn ready for bulk service. A steam nozzle may be attached for heating the milk. The boiler operates by electricity or gas, giving boiling water from an undercounter pressure boiler plumbed into a mains water supply. A drainage gulley is needed under the tap in which to empty waste water from warming and rinsing teapots and jugs.

ESPRESSO MACHINE

Espresso coffee is made with this machine. Finely ground, dark-roasted coffee is placed into a small container which is fixed into the water font. Steam is forced through the ground coffee, producing a very black, aromatic cup of coffee.

Cappuccino is also produced from an espresso machine by adding two parts of milk to one part espresso coffee and mixing them under the steam jet of the machine to give it a frothy head.

CONA COFFEE MACHINE

A Cona coffee machine is a patented coffee maker. A jug of cold water is brought to the boiling point. The hot water rises up a glass tube into a weighed amount of coffee housed in a glass funnel on top. After this the infused liquid is drawn down by vacuum into the lower glass or stainless steel jug ready for serving. If not needed immediately, the coffee can be kept hot on the built-in hotplate.

FILTER COFFEE MACHINE

A weighed amount of ground coffee is placed in a paper filter bag inside a funnel which leads into a jug standing on the built-in hotplate. Cold water is poured into the reservoir. When switched on, the water is heated by an electric element and sprayed over the ground coffee; it emerges as liquid coffee in the serving jug.

MILK-SHAKE MACHINE

A milk-shake machine is used where there is a demand for cold or hot flavoured drinks. It is in the form of a console with bottles of flavoured syrup for dispensing into the mixer compartment either by hand pump or push-button. The milk is shaken, together with any additional ingredients such as ice-cream or fruit, until frothy and velvety.

CHILLED BEVERAGE MACHINE

A chilled beverage machine holds fruit juices ready to serve. The juice is stirred by a paddle while being cooled by electric convections.

ICE-MAKING MACHINE

An ice-making machine is attached to an approved supply of water from the mains and sprayed on to refrigerated trays made with various indented shapes. When frozen, cubes are released into the storage bin by flash heating. Different shapes and sizes can be produced, as well as crushed ice. The cubes do not stick together in the storage bin.

For use in a bar, an ice dispenser can be fixed to the back bar which will feed the required amount of ice cubes straight into a glass held under the outlet and pushed up to release it. This is more hygienic than the traditional ice bucket kept on the bar counter where it may be open to contamination.

Ice comes under the Food Hygiene Regulations and must not be contaminated. The ice-maker bin must be cleaned and sanitised weekly and the cubes may not be touched by hand. The water must be tested regularly and a Water Research Council approved connection used on the water supply to the machine.

Refrigeration

To comply with legislation dealing with the storage of food, it is necessary to install several different kinds of refrigeration for different uses.

Frozen foods must be kept in a deep-freeze unit at –18°C. Chilled foods, other than cook-chill ones, should be held in a refrigerator that keeps them at 0–5°C. Cook-chill meals must be kept at 0–3°C. Sous-vide packs should be held at 0–3°C. Fresh meat and fish should be kept at 2°C. A general-purpose refrigerator should show 4°C on each reading. A cold room should maintain a temperature of 8°C.

It is essential that refrigerators are monitored regularly by using a temperature gauge affixed to each one, a hand-held probe or a digital temperature display, noting down the temperature on every occasion. The probe can also be used to monitor the temperature of products in the refrigerator, though it must be sanitised after each test. It should be used to check the temperature of perishable foods on delivery to ensure it has not risen unduly during the journey from the supplier's premises. Monitoring systems are now fitted to new refrigerators. They are placed in the warmest part of the interior and register air temperature on a chart recorder or display thermometer.

Chilled display cabinets are used to display dishes or portioned buffet items, salads, smorgasbörd selections and sweets in the restaurant. Items should not be put on display until the unit is already operating at a cool temperature, because constant opening of the door allows warm air from the room to enter.

A chilled display of raw food such as steaks, oysters, etc. should be arranged on trays on a bed of crushed ice. These open-counter displays have forced cooled air blown across the food and out.

Good practice regarding refrigeration includes:

- regular cleansing of the inside and outside; most have automatic defrosting and there is no need to turn off the current for several hours to melt build-up of ice

- regular servicing and maintenance by a professional person
- correct location away from areas where there is a high ambient temperature or high humidity
- ventilation at the rear where the cooling unit is sited
- not putting hot food in the refrigerator as it will raise the air temperature to an unacceptable level; it must be chilled quickly in a blast chiller to 4°C before storage
- storing raw and cooked food entirely separately, using separate refrigerators if possible
- having an internal light and alarm in cold rooms in case a member of staff is accidentally shut in
- when purchasing a new refrigerator, ensuring that the refrigerant does not contain chlorofluorocarbons (CFCs). CFCs are man-made chemicals that damage the ozoner layer.

Before purchasing any kind of refrigeration unit, it is advisable to gain an answer to each of the following questions:

- Is it the right size for its envisaged use?
- Will it fit the available space?
- Is the space well ventilated?
- Will it be sited close to cooking equipment?
- Does it work efficiently in a hot atmosphere?
- Is it economical to run?
- Is it hard wearing, made of stainless steel or plastic?
- Is it mobile?
- Is maintenance and service quickly available?
- Has it a good lock?
- Can it be opened from inside?

Caterers should be aware of the ban on the use of CFC-operated refrigerators and other equipment. In order to comply with EU Regulations which aim to prevent leaks of the refrigerant in the system, users must review their present maintenance procedures.

The Food Safety (General Food Hygiene) Regulations 1995 which cover England and Wales state that refrigerators must be set to work at a maximum temperature of 8°C. This is the maximum for keeping foodstuffs that are likely to support the growth of pathogenic microorganisms or the formation of toxins.

Insulated boxes are available for the transportation of hot, chilled and frozen cooked food, for example from a central production kitchen to satellites. These boxes are made from foam-injected polyethylene and are available in several sizes. They are lightweight and easily stacked. Chilled food packed in these boxes at 2°C for distribution in unrefrigerated vehicles will rise by only one and a half degrees to 3.5°C over a 3-hour period.

It is advisable to regenerate chilled meals as close as possible to the eating place, which means having a refrigerated trolley to transport them and a regenerating oven at the location. A regeneration trolley into which chilled meals are packaged and transported whilst working as a refrigerator can be switched on to regenerate when it gets to the serving point.

Food-service equipment

The ideal way of serving food so as to give maximum customer satisfaction is by the à la Carte system where food is cooked to order and served immediately. Under the Table d'Hôte system it is usually necessary to cook much of the food in advance of serving and to retain it in a heated zone until the customers arrive. It is during this holding period that rapid deterioration can occur unless food is held in the best possible condition so that it is safe and hot enough for customers to enjoy.

HOT CUPBOARD OR HOTPLATE

This item is used to keep cooked foods in good condition and also to keep plates and dishes warm. The optimum temperature setting for keeping food hot is 76–88°C, giving an internal temperature of 65°C; the recommendation is to keep the internal temperature above 62.8°C. The temperature for keeping plates warm is 65°C – at this heat they are just right for handling and the glaze is not damaged. Ideally crockery and silverware should be heated in a separate hotplate away from the food. An electrically heated plate-warming unit known as a Lowerator is the best way of maintaining the supply of hot plates and other items of crockery.

A hot cupboard can be sited in the kitchen area at the end of the production line and the cooked foods kept in it; a cabinet hot cupboard which has an upper and lower compartment is useful for this purpose. The hotplate or counter service hot cupboard is the point to which prepared dishes are brought for distribution. It has a plain top and sliding or rollaway doors on both sides of the cupboard part. It is heated by gas or electricity and sometimes from a live steam supply.

SERVICE COUNTER

A service counter for cafeteria and self-service operations would have a bain-marie top into which the containers of various components of the meal fit, with dry heat or hot water at the bottom to keep it hot during the service period. Reserves of food may be kept inside the hot cupboard. The operating temperature must ensure that the food both on top and inside is maintained at approximately 82°C so that it does not dry out or get cold. Service counters are usually made of stainless steel on the outside, possibly with enamel doors and mild steel interiors. It is helpful to have a water supply and drainage for the bain-maries.

The kitchen sections or parties need a bain-marie for keeping prepared foods in – either a large one for general use, or one for each section of the kitchen. Sauces and soups are placed in the bain-marie in special tall pots that take up little space, and are served from here. A stew, or prepared vegetables, will also keep hot in a bain-marie for Table d'Hôte service.

Cold foods for service must be kept cool in a refrigerated service counter which is manufactured as a closed-top, fixed or mobile unit with several insets and refrigerated cupboards underneath the counter top. It is used for the storage and service of cold foods, including cold sweets.

Modular equipment

Modular equipment is a great asset in the kitchen as it ensures that full use can be made of all available space for every major item of equipment. It makes sense to have baking dishes and all other containers made of a size that fits ovens, steamers, refrigerators, service counters, etc., particularly when the containers hold a given amount of food and therefore a definite number of portions.

The Gastronorm system of modular equipment is widely used because it is very adaptable and saves space. The full-size module is 527 mm × 324 mm and there are half, quarter, third, sixths and even ninth sizes, all with lids and to several depths for various uses.

This standardised system also applies to fixed and mobile equipment, including ovens, hotplates, refrigerators and trolleys. They are made to hold a given number of standard modular containers, or fractions of that size. This ensures that it is possible to utilise fully every centimetre of space, whether cooking joints in an oven or storing cooked foods in a deep freezer.

The containers are made of stainless steel, aluminium, polycarbonate and other plastic materials, some completely transparent. Food as hot as 100°C can be displayed in some plastic containers, which have a notch to hold serving spoons in readiness.

Small kitchen equipment

The following list gives an idea of the wide range of small kitchen equipment and utensils in everyday use.

- **Pans and moulds**: stewpans, braising pans, sauté pans, sauteuses, sugar boiling pans, bain-maries, pots, frying pans of all sizes and omelette pans, dariole, charlotte, savarin, jelly and all types of pastry moulds, as well as sponge tins, cake hoops and flan rings.
- **Cutting instruments**: slicers, graters, peelers, knives, corers, column and aspic cutters, spoon cutters, secateurs, cleavers, choppers and saws.
- **Thermometers**: sugar boiling, brixhydrometer, dough, brine, relative humidity and oven.
- **Strainers**: colanders, conical strainers, chinois, skimmers, salad basket, sieves, muslin and tammy cloths.
- **Kitchen utensils made of wood**: mushroom, triangle, chopping boards, sieves, salt box, spoons, spatulas and peppermills.
- **Other utensils**: whisks, fish grills, frying baskets, scoops, brushes, ladles, serving tongs, basins and pie dishes.

One of the most difficult decisions to make when purchasing small equipment is what kind of pans to buy, so a knowledge of what is available and the advantages and disadvantages of each should be helpful. Cooking pans are made of copper, aluminium, stainless steel or enamel, and some combinations are available. The properties of these and other small kitchen equipment are discussed below.

COPPER PANS

Copper pans have found favour with chefs for many hundreds of years because they give good, quick results from their high thermal conductivity. They are, however, expensive to purchase, difficult to keep clean, and the tin lining needs regular retinning. For these reasons they are no longer popular and in many kitchens serve only as ornaments that can give a golden glow to the kitchen.

STAINLESS-STEEL PANS

Stainless-steel pans are the choice of chefs because they are heavy, look good, and are made in all the traditional shapes and sizes of copper pans. Some are made with a base of copper to give an even spread of heat. They look clean and clinical and do not stain or wear out.

ALUMINIUM PANS

Aluminium pans are usually made from aluminium alloy because the base metal is soft and may get dented. Spun or cast aluminium pans with a ground base are good for heavy-duty use and can be used on electric and gas stoves. These pans are usually cheaper to purchase than any of the others, but may not have the same length of useful life. The metal tends to discolour both inside and out, and this is difficult to remove.

ENAMELLED PANS

Enamelled pans are made by spraying powdered glass mixed with clay and water and colouring matter on to iron or steel moulds and baking at a very high temperature. They are expensive to purchase and heavy to use. Their ideal place in the professional kitchen is as colourful service containers that customers can see as their food is served from them or on a guéridon.

NON-STICK PANS

Non-stick pans were developed for frying food using only a small amount of fat or, with care, no fat at all. A good-quality frying pan or sauteuse will have been treated with silicone coating several times. This will make it long lasting, provided that the pan is cleaned carefully without using a wire scourer.

IRON EQUIPMENT

Cast iron is a good material for making baking sheets, frying pans and roasting trays, as it does not warp or rust. Wrought iron is used for making frying pans in various sizes. They are somewhat lighter than those made from cast iron.

TINNED-STEEL EQUIPMENT

Tinned steel is tinplate with a very thin coating of tin on both sides. Many kitchen utensils are made of this material, including baking tins, patty pans, flan rings, serving spoons, and most wire items such as conical strainers, frying baskets, spiders and cake racks. The covering of tin gives good resistance to air and water corrosion, but after long use may wear off and the steel underneath will then rust if not dried after use. It is not usual to have these items retinned as it is cheaper to purchase new ones. Moulds are sometimes made of tinned steel but are now mainly of aluminium.

GLASSWARE

Fireproof glass cooking and serving dishes are attractive and often well decorated, but the drawback of using glass in the professional kitchen is the danger of breaking it, with the possibility of splinters of glass falling into food unnoticed. Its use should be confined to the dining-room, although it is often necessary to use glass dishes for cold sweets from the pastry department and salads from the larder.

EARTHENWARE

Earthenware serving dishes enhance the standing of an establishment where they are placed on to silver flats for presentation, with a silver cover to keep the food hot. The food may have been cooked in the dish or merely served in it. Some of these dishes are fireproof and withstand high oven temperatures, whilst others are only for serving cold items such as an hors-d'oeuvre selection.

PORCELAIN WARE

Porcelain ware is a very white china that is excellent for cooking as it withstands very high temperatures. Apart from the shallow round, oval and oblong dishes, other items include casseroles, egg cocottes, marmites, soufflé moulds and oeufs sur le plat dishes.

PLASTIC WARE

Man-made materials are so versatile that they are continually being developed as replacements for traditional materials. Nylon is used, for example, for pot scourers, brushes and string, and many machines have nylon gears. Vinyl is used as a flexible film for covering and packing foods to give hygienic display. Polythene is a rigid plastic used for making storage containers, mixing bowls, buckets, measures and dustbins; it is also produced as a film for food packaging and as refuse sacks. Polystyrene is a thermoplastic, made into transparent and translucent trays and dishes suitable for larder work. Phenolics are dark-coloured plastics used for heat-resistant saucepan handles. Urea plastics are used to make switches and handles for stoves and refrigerators. Melamine is a very hard plastic that is used for items of crockery and as basins. Polypropylene is of the same family as polythene and is formed into crates as used in dishwashing machines, and also to make pudding basins. Very lightweight trays and crockery as used for in-flight catering are made of methylpentine polymer.

KNIVES

Knives are part of the chef's personal equipment which no one else is allowed to use. They are usually made of stainless steel which has been hardened, tempered and precision ground. Each knife is either forged by heating and hammering or stamped out from a sheet of steel. It includes the blade, holster and tang which is covered by the handle. The handle can be made of wood or profilon, a plastic material that can be coloured.

Chefs are required to show 'due diligence' by carrying out their work in a hygienic manner, which means using different knives for different tasks. Manufacturers therefore give the knife handles different colours to avoid cross-contamination: red for cutting up raw meat; yellow for cooked meat; blue for cutting and filleting raw fish; green for fruits and salads; brown for cutting up raw vegetables; and white for dealing with dairy produce such as butter and cheese.

A chef's set of knives usually includes a cook's knife, paring knife, turning knife, filleting knife, boning knife, heavy chopping knife, palette knife, roasting fork, sharpening steel, peeler, canelle groover, trussing needle and larding needle.

CHOPPING BOARDS

Chopping boards are available in several sizes and in various thicknesses. They are made non-slip by the use of feet which are rotatable so that both sides of the board can be used. Substitutes for wooden chopping boards are based on rubber or plastic and do not cause splinters or harbour germs. The material is non-toxic and non-absorbent. They are made in the following colours: red for cutting raw meat; blue for raw fish; green for fruit and salads; brown for raw vegetables; and yellow for slicing cooked meats.

Some boards are made of white high-density polyethylene and have the use stamped indelibly along one side. This is of assistance to a colour-blind cook. With the coloured boards, it is useful to display a chart on the wall listing the code.

Care and maintenance of kitchen equipment

When equipment is cared for in a proper manner, it will give good service and last for a longer time than if routine care and maintenance is not carried out. This applies to fixed and mobile equipment and to small utensils. It is necessary to instruct staff in the correct way of cleaning and looking after equipment, and to draw up a planned programme which will ensure that every item is taken care of over a period of time and that nothing is neglected.

There are three levels of maintenance of equipment. The first is when the item is cleaned after being used – to ensure it is kept in a satisfactory state of hygiene. The second level is when the item is given a routine examination to see that there is nothing wrong with it – checking that no screws are missing, for example, or making sure that it has been oiled. The third level of maintenance is usually done under contact by a firm of kitchen engineers who will attend at regular contracted intervals to overhaul and clean each item thoroughly, test it, and confirm that it is in perfect working order.

Some of the metals used in the manufacture of equipment require special cleaning methods as follows:

- **Cast iron and mild steel** – this is cleaned with an abrasive such as wire wool or emery cloth.
- **Stainless steel** – this should be cleaned with detergent diluted in hot water and a cloth or nylon pad. If not properly rinsed stainless-steel items look smeary, but it is possible to finish them with a special finishing polish that gives a bright shine.
- **Aluminium** – this should be washed with hot water and detergent, but no washing soda because this will pit and tarnish it. The alloys of aluminium are harder than the natural metal, but can be scratched by using any harsh abrasive.
- **Stove enamel** – equipment made or finished with stove-enamelled fittings should be washed with detergent well diluted in hot water, then rinsed and dried. Only nylon scouring pads should be used to rub off stains.

Washing-up machines

DISHWASHING MACHINES

Dishwashers are made in several sizes, from front-loading batch models which can be bench mounted, to a conveyor-belt model which needs a large room to house it and several staff to operate it.

A batch dishwashing machine is operated by pushing a basket of dirties inside, closing the sliding door, and switching on the correct programme. It could be used for slightly soiled items, such as glasses or serving trays, or heavily soiled items, each having a set time from 1 to 10 minutes. The basket remains static or rotates during the cleansing process. An output of 1,000 items per hour means that this kind of machine is suitable for small establishments.

The belt of the conveyor-type machine has notches on which to load plates and silverware as well as baskets for cutlery and glasses. The items pass through pre-wash, wash, rinse and drying sections and then appear at the end ready to use again. The speed can be controlled to clean up to 9,000 items per hour.

POTWASHING MACHINE

A potwashing machine cleans saucepans and many other cooking utensils by injecting powerful jets of hot water all over them during a timed operation. It is impossible to open the door of the machine during this process. The pots are made ready for immediate use and any burnt-on food is discharged through the drain.

POT SCOURER

A pot scourer is mounted on the wall over the pot wash. When it is switched on, a wire brush at the end of a flexible sheathed shaft rotates and is pressed against the insides of the pots being washed. It is used to remove any food left sticking to the inside and outside of the saucepan and to burnish the outside.

HAND-WASHING FACILITIES

Hand-washing and drying facilities are required under food hygiene legislation. Hand basins with a supply of hot water, nail brush and bactericidal gel soap are essential, together with an electrically operated warm air hand-drying machine.

Waste disposal

An enclosed area must be allocated for the storage of waste material until it can be disposed of, and looked after by a kitchen or stores porter whose duty it is to keep it in a hygienic condition. The local council's cleansing contractor hires paladins for bulk rubbish to be collected regularly, or a private waste-disposal company will remove rubbish on contract. Recycling of wine bottles, cardboard and paper is environmentally necessary.

WASTE-DISPOSAL MACHINES

A waste-disposal machine can be installed to grind all waste (including plastic) with water to a sludge which is drained, compressed and bagged ready for disposal.

A smaller waste-disposal machine can be sited under a sink. When switched on, high-speed, rotating blades chop waste food and trimmings with water into the drains. For large-scale work waste material is deposited in the shute of a free-standing machine which is turned on at intervals as it fills up.

A waste-disposal machine for plate waste is sited where the dirties are brought from the dining-room to the dishwasher and scraped into the machine by waiting or wash-up staff.

INCINERATOR

An incinerator, preferably smokeless, reduces combustible waste to ashes. This would only be viable for a very large-scale operation using a lot of non-recyclable material.

WASTE COMPACTOR

A waste compactor reduces the volume of waste materials with upwards of 2,000 kg of force, quietly and economically, to one seventh of its size in half a minute.

BOTTLE CRUSHER

A bottle crusher crushes glass into minute particles ready for recycling. Different colour bottles should be dealt with separately.

Dining-room equipment

When customers eat in a restaurant, they are taking part in a ritual that is termed 'the meal experience' – an expression which encompasses all the sensations and emotions that have an effect upon customers and includes not only the food and service but also the atmosphere. The first of these, the food, is tangible, because the customer consumes the results of the acquired skills of the chef. The second, the service, is slightly intangible in that it is part practical ability and part social skills, which include the grace, presence and composure of the server and the charisma of the person in charge of the dining-room. The third part of the meal experience, the atmosphere, is intangible as no two customers gain a similar impression on entering the dining-room. They need to be made welcome by the waiting staff and when seated be able to take in the ambience of their surroundings which includes the decor, lighting, fittings, furnishings and temperature.

Furniture

Dining-room furniture is available in so many variations of finish and colour that only the most relevant factors can be dealt with here.

TABLES

Tables are purchased in standard sizes, with a supply of extensions and various table tops; square tables can be made long or round as required. Obviously the chairs and sideboards should be in keeping with the general decor, but this is not so important for the tables as they are nearly always covered by tablecloths and thus remain unseen.

CHAIRS

The chairs must be comfortable no matter what kind of room they are to be used in, and they should combine elegance and formality. They should be solidly made and without protuberances that customers might bump against, and very smoothly finished so as not to ladder women's tights. A space to put away chairs not actually in use is vital, as spare chairs stacked in the corner look bad.

SIDEBOARDS

Sideboards made especially for a restaurant will cost more than ready-made ones, but unless they are to be a feature of the room are best kept in the background. They are utilitarian items of furniture that hold the equipment needed to facilitate the service.

FINISHES

Finishes to furniture are intended to keep them looking good throughout their life. Plastic is used in many ways in the dining-room without necessarily making things look cheap. Designers use plastics to give shapes that wood cannot achieve, and in so doing offer greater variety, toughness and easier maintenance.

Chromium-plated steel tube, epoxy resin and stove-enamel finishes to steel, plastic-coated steel mesh and anodised aluminium finishes are all used in furniture manufacture. Wood is laminated with clear plastic melamine to give a tough finish and over-printed teak or rosewood patterns from photographs are sealed in, making it difficult to tell from the genuine article. Furniture is available in pine, beech, teak, oak, mahogany, rosewood and walnut, but mostly veneered. Modern veneers are usually coated with synthetic lacquer and can look authentic.

Crockery

BONE CHINA

This is the highest quality and most expensive type of crockery. The advantages of equipping the restaurant with bone china are that it looks much better than any other kind of pottery and is strong, very white and translucent; it is also vitreous and non-porous. Its strength makes bone china a good long-term investment.

EARTHENWARE

Earthenware crockery is usually much thicker than bone china; it is also not as white and is completely opaque. It weighs more than bone china but is much cheaper to purchase. It is porous under the glaze and is made in many colours.

PORCELAIN

Porcelain is made from 50 per cent china clay, 25 per cent quartz and 25 per cent feldspar. It is vitreous and translucent, though compared to bone china it has a blue or grey tinge. Much of what is used is made in France as oven-to-table ware.

STONEWARE

Stoneware is hard, tough and vitreous. It is available in deep colours and is very suitable for a thematic restaurant where coloured crockery is more appropriate than white.

OVEN-TO-TABLE WARE

Oven-to-table ware can be quite attractive because there is a wide variety of elegant shapes and sizes which are excellent heat conductors and retainers. No ovenproof dish can be put on the stove or in the oven without something in it, and it is unwise to subject it to rapid changes of temperature as the glaze may craze or the dish may crack. If a dish is marked flameproof, it means it is possible to cook in it on top of the stove. The various kinds of oven-to-table ware are:

- **Glass** – either opaque or transparent; very hygienic and with good thermal shock resistance.
- **Cast iron** – rough finish and very heavy, with a tendency to rust if not kept oiled.

- **Enamelled cast iron** – very strong and heavy, and very expensive; available in many colours and with decorations. The enamel can splinter if not used carefully.
- **Earthenware** – good heat retention but porous and may craze if subjected to a high temperature; not all are ovenproof.
- **Enamelled steel** – much lighter and cheaper than enamelled cast iron, but the lightweight ones develop hot spots; plain colours and stencilled decorations are available.
- **Porcelain** – withstands high temperatures; very strong and high thermal shock resistance, which means it can go straight into the deep freezer from the oven without cracking; available in all-white, brown exterior, and also in gold and silver for use particularly with cold dishes.
- **Terracotta** – very rough and cheap, but ideal for presentation of peasant-type foods; porous and unglazed and cracks easily.

DECORATION OF CROCKERY

Underglaze decoration is where the pattern is applied to crockery before it is glazed so that it is protected and does not come off with repeated washing. On-glaze decoration is put on after the crockery has been glazed and the items are then fired for a third time, but this kind is more likely to wear off. Banding is where a simple band of colour is applied to the rim. Gold banding is often used. This could be Best Gold, which is real gold with other precious metals fired on to the glaze. Liquid or Bright Gold has a metallic appearance and is not so durable as Best Gold. Acid Gold is not so widely used because it is the most expensive form of gold banding.

THE PURCHASE OF CROCKERY

When purchasing crockery, try to limit the number of different pieces by selecting those that will serve several purposes. Choose crockery that has an elegant yet functional shape; that will withstand being washed up several times each day; and that stacks firmly, taking up little storage space. Consider the suitability of each item:

- Are the handles of the cups easy to hold? Will they withstand frequent use?
- Should the plates be rimless?
- Do the saucers keep the cup in the centre?
- Will the coffee-pot spout be easy to clean?
- Will the teapot sit level when inverted for machine washing?

If crockery is to be printed with the name or motif of the establishment, it will mean placing a large initial order and having to pay extra each time more is ordered. If the order is for several thousand pieces it can be placed directly with a pottery, but if a stock pattern is chosen (and some stay in production for many years), it will be better to buy from a wholesaler or even a retailer who will be able to supply a small number of replacement items from stock. It takes a long time for a potter to put a particular order into production, and the order may have to be placed at least six months in advance.

Glassware

Soda-lime or soda glass is the ordinary type of glass used for making everyday drinking glasses. It can be made into tough glasses suitable for general use in a restaurant, thicker glasses for public houses, or beautifully shaped designs for high-class establishments. For a more elegant and more expensive range of glassware, an establishment could decide to buy lead crystal glass. Adding lead when making glass results in a softer glass that refracts light strongly and is easier to cut, giving a brilliant effect. The pattern on cut glass is made with abrasive stone wheels which cut in fairly deep. Moulded cut glass cannot be mistaken for real cut glass because it does not have its brilliance, and it is usually possible to see a line running down the side showing that it was machine-pressed in a mould.

It is possible to have the establishment's name or motif sandblasted on to glasses. Jets of abrasive sand and compressed air are directed through a stencil which eats away at the glass, leaving the pattern on it. The only coloured glasses used in catering are for serving German wines; they have the traditional colours of green for Moselle and brown for Hock incorporated into the stems.

Each kind of drink seems to require a different shape of glass. Although it is not possible to have just two or three general-purpose shapes, there is no need to have too many different ones, especially if cut lead crystal is chosen as being representative of the standard of the restaurant. For example, the old-style champagne glass has been virtually dropped in favour of a tall flute which allows the bubbles to keep rising and which could also double as a glass for white wine. It is necessary to have brandy glasses, one kind of glass for port and another for sherry, one for liqueurs, and goblets – often referred to as Paris goblets – which come in several capacities and are good enough for most wines and short drinks such as gin and tonic water.

Toughened glass withstands a lot of hard wear, but shatters into thousands of pieces rather than into splinters when dropped heavily. It is virtually shockproof and usually available as tumblers.

Disposable plastic glasses are available in half-pint and one-pint sizes for beer, and in many other sizes for all kinds of drinks.

Cutlery

Buying the cutlery for a dining-room is not just a matter of deciding whether to select stainless steel or plated silverware; it involves choosing from the very many designs available in both metals, and ensuring that they are comfortable to use and easy to keep clean.

Silver-plated cutlery is usually made in the traditional designs. It stains easily, but can be kept clean for a considerable time by using a long-term silver polish. It is advisable to buy only top quality silver-plated cutlery. This relates to the thickness of the deposit of silver plating on each item. If the cutlery is of poor quality, thin or badly used, the plating will wear off.

Stainless-steel cutlery of average quality is cheap but tough, and is labour-saving as compared with silver. The two best qualities are those marked 18/8, which indicates the use of 18 per cent chromium and 8 per cent nickel, and 12/12, which is 12 per cent each of chromium and nickel. The better qualities have a good finish, are comfortable to use and look elegant. The cheaper imported types are very lightweight and not very well designed, even though they may look attractive when first purchased. Unless it is washed quickly and well rinsed, stainless steel soon becomes dull in use because it tends to get stained by acids such as lemon or vinegar; it will not rust but it is difficult to keep it look-ing like new. It is available in matt or shiny finish and is often made with handles of bronze, wood, horn, ivory and celluloid. Some are made with tangs and others have rivets to keep the handles in place. Each can look good in its own particu-lar setting, but not all of them will stand up to the harshness of the dishwashing machine and the high temperatures of the water used.

Chrome or nickel-plated cutlery is still made and has the advantage of cheap-ness and toughness, but is being replaced by cheap stainless-steel items.

There is a wide range of items from asparagus tongs to ice-cream spades, and the menu of an establishment will determine what needs to be purchased. An establishment that specialises in grilled steaks, for example, may decide to purchase all knives with serrated blades for ease of cutting.

Serving dishes

Serving dishes are made of electroplated nickel silver (EPNS) or stainless steel in a wide range of shapes and sizes for particular purposes, from soup tureens to timbales. The shapes are traditionally oval and round, but can be oblong for modern-style dishes. The price will depend on the gauge of steel used, and whether it is finished with trimmed or wrapped edges and has a satin or shiny finish.

Some serving dishes are made in copper, usually with a polished 18/10 stain-less steel or nickel interior and brass handles. This kind of finish will not require retinning as it is resistant to heat and acids. Some are made so that the copper does not tarnish and are excellent for kitchen-to-table use. Aluminium service dishes are also made, but these soon become dull and are more suitable as under-dishes when used with earthenware. The lids for serving dishes can be aluminium as they are usually removed before presenting the dish to the customer.

Flat aluminium foil dishes are made in many sizes for cold buffet use where foods are arranged neatly for display. They are not suitable for serving hot foods at table.

Restaurant silverware should be kept in good condition. When dents, scratches, etc., have to be repaired, it is sensible to resilver the items at the same time. This should be cheaper than buying new and also saves the cost of sending them to the replating firm. A 20-year guarantee should mean that stained silver-ware which is properly polished in a burnishing machine will last longer than inferior quality EPNS goods.

Linen

Linen is the general term given to all the different kinds of tablecloths and table napkins, and the choice is governed by the standard of the establishment and by the frequency of laundering.

Linen is undoubtedly the best material, as its snowy white double-damask appearance is unequalled even by blends of linen and other fibres. Stains are easy to remove. Cotton is also good. It is available in a much wider range of colours than linen; and is also much easier to launder. Linen and cotton in a 50/50 blend can be further improved by the application of non-iron and stain-resistant processes. Man-made fibres are not very good as table napkins because they are not very absorbent, but they are suitable for use as tablecloths.

Tablecloths and table napkins are made in standard sizes to suit different requirements – tablecloths for long, square and round tables, and napkins in sizes up to 60 cm square. It is possible to have a full-size cloth on a table with a runner over it to take the stains, as this helps to cut laundry costs. It is usual to have a felt or baize cover under the tablecloth tied to the legs which helps to prevent the cloth from slipping. Some fabrics are plastic-coated which allows the tablecloth to be wiped clean. Waiting staff need a waiter's cloth of plain material for carrying hot dishes and cleaning the table.

A teacloth is an important item of linen because of its wide range of uses by many different members of staff. Its main use is for drying equipment after washing where this is not done by the action of the dishwasher. A teacloth must be absorbent so that a large number of items may be dried before it gets too wet to be effective. This means that the materials used to make them must be linen, cotton or rayon, or a combination which has been fully bleached and is lint free so that it leaves no fluff on glasses after being polished. Teacloths are used in the bar and dining-room for the specific use of polishing cutlery, crockery and glassware; they are issued to kitchen staff for the purpose of drying their knives after washing or for wiping pans and dishes before use. In practice they serve many other purposes, such as for removing pans from the oven.

Table mats have their uses mainly on formica tables where they can add colour, and on wooden tables which would be marked by a hot dish. Rush or cork table mats are essential on tables that do not have a heat-resistant finish, as linen will not protect them; plastic mats on a slippery surface tend to slide off.

When purchasing table coverings and napkins, waiter's cloths, teacloths and tray cloths, the probable cost of laundering all these items has to be considered. Some need to be starched and folded in a special way. A good laundry which can do this work at a reasonable cost and give a good return service will not always be easy to find. Many caterers prefer to use a linen hire service where the only costs are those of laundering and a hire charge.

Other items of dining-room equipment

These include flower vases, table numbers, bread baskets, cruets, finger bowls, ash trays, and many specialised types of serving tools such as asparagus tongs, snail tongs, lobster picks and so on. The choice of materials in which these items are made must be in accordance with the main type of equipment used.

TROLLEYS

Trolleys play a large part in food service, and it is therefore necessary to ensure that gangways in the dining-room are wide enough for them to move without difficulty. The wheels are very important as they often cause trouble in use and some types do not run smoothly on carpet – swivel castors are essential. If the dining-room is on two levels, it may be necessary to provide different trolleys for each level to save lifting them up and down. Where the restaurant provides a joint each day and likes to show it to customers at their table, it will be necessary to have a heated carving trolley made of carved wood and/or silver plate.

There is also the service trolley for guéridon work, incorporating a spirit or gas cylinder lamp to cook food. Even if the restaurant does not feature flambé work, there might be a special request for Crêpes Suzette.

A sweet trolley, hors-d'oeuvre trolley, cheese trolley, iced-salad trolley, cold buffet trolley, liqueur and cigar trolley may all have a part to play in some classes of restaurant. A general-purpose trolley for bringing in equipment or stock for laying up needs to be more practical than elegant since it will not be seen by customers. A truck to move stacks of chairs and table tops is also useful. Clearing trolleys operated by staff in a refectory should be narrow enough to get through the gangways and look good even when loaded with dirty items. For a self-clearing operation, high trolleys that will accept trays of dirty dishes are necessary.

Plate 6   The Woodside Trolley, from TSE Brownson

HEATERS

Heaters for keeping food and crockery hot are considered as part of the waiter's sideboard and may be built-in or free-standing. They are usually electrically operated and made of stainless steel or plate glass. Some are preheated on a stove and brought in, and some are slotted into a heated cabinet for removal as required. Others have candles or methylated spirit burners, and for some dishes a table hotplate heated by a candle is enough to keep dishes warm.

TABLE LAMPS

Table lamps give an intimate atmosphere to a room. The decision whether to have table lamps will depend on the size of the tables, but as some types also act as emergency lighting there is something to be said in their favour. It is not advisable to have a pendant light over each table, as the room arrangement may sometimes have to be changed around. Candles used in candelabra should be non-drip.

TRAYS

If skilled staff are employed there should be no need for waiter's trays in the restaurant, except for when clearing away at the end of the service. If trays are to be issued other than silver salvers used for serving drinks at a reception, they should be of a size that can go easily through swing doors and of a material in keeping with the class of establishment. They should not sag when fully loaded or have a moulded edge where food debris can lodge unseen.

Floor coverings

The choice and selection of floor coverings will depend on the kind of dining-room and the amount of money available. The covering selected will play a large part in creating the desired atmosphere. A traditional dining-room run on formal lines will need to offer a relaxed atmosphere, so a dark-coloured covering of good quality is desirable. In contrast, a popular restaurant will want to create a more lively atmosphere that is always fresh looking, lively and bright. Ease of cleaning, wearing properties, the possibility of replacing worn areas, resistance to stains from spillage and marks from furniture, and resistance to dirt, are factors to be taken into account.

The following types of floor covering are suitable for use in dining-rooms:

- **Tiles** – ceramic or quarry tiles are available in a wide range of patterns and colours and help to create a cool environment. They are inclined to be noisy in use but need not be slippery.
- **Vinyl** – usually foam backed to give a soft tread. It is available in rolls and as tiles in many patterns and colours, often representing tiles and other materials by being embossed or textured. It is inexpensive when compared with other floor coverings.
- **Carpeting** – this can be comparatively very expensive. It is available by the roll or as squares, and there are many different qualities and different mixtures of fibres that give a wide range of choice. The wearing quality varies, and even

all-wool carpets can wear differently. The thickness, backing, colour fastness, need for underlay, plain or patterned, colour, and relationship with the rest of the decor, must all be considered before deciding on its use.

- **Wood floors** – there are many kinds to choose from, including hardwood strips and blocks for laying in various patterns; parquet flooring available as short strips or glued in panels; and wood mosaic squares made of fingers of wood arranged in basket pattern. This form of covering is attractive, warm and hard-wearing, but it is expensive and excessive heat may cause shrinkage.

Other kinds of floor coverings used to give a particular effect include mosaic made of glass silica, bricks of various sizes and colours, terrazzo which uses marble chippings, natural marble, stone of various kinds and colours, cork tiles, linoleum and rubber.

Equipment for bars and customer amenity areas

There are many different kinds of bar, each having its own particular characteristics. Some serve every possible type of drink, whilst others may sell only wine. Some have a long counter to encourage customers to sit or stand and drink at the bar, whereas others have comfortable seating and waiters to take the order and serve. There is another type known as the dispense bar which is usually hidden behind the scenes and supplies drinks to serving staff for customers; there are also mobile bars which can be set up anywhere for a special function. The customer amenity areas of a high-class catering establishment include a foyer or reception and lounge area where people can wait for their friends or for their table to be ready; a cloakroom for leaving hats and coats; and the toilets.

Bars

When equipping a bar, it is important to ensure that the stock is kept in perfect condition and that whatever a customer requests is immediately available. This means that if draught beer is served, the cellar must be adjacent or there must be sufficient space under the counter for the range of casks and kegs. From the cellar there may be a need for hydraulic air compressors, suction engines and impeller pumps in order to facilitate the service and deliver the beer in good condition. It is necessary to keep wines in readiness for immediate service so there must be a refrigerator to hold white and rosé wines and a place of normal room temperature for red wine. A refrigerator shelf for bottles of beer, mineral waters and cider saves having to open the door of the refrigerator each time one is ordered.

In some establishments all washing is done centrally, so waiting staff would take all used glasses there. In others glasses are washed up in the bar either by an electric machine that will wash, rinse and dry a tray load in under two minutes, or by a water pressure machine that washes them whilst they are held over it. An ice-making machine should be sited in or near the bar, and if drinks are paid for at the point of sale, there should be a cash register or restaurant management terminal.

The following list shows the general range of utensils needed to operate a bar efficiently. An experienced bartender will seek to satisfy every customer requirement by providing every drink on the bar list, as well as any others that may be requested. This will mean carrying a full range of equipment where possible.

- **For cocktails and mixed drinks**: shakers, Hawthorn strainer, mixing glass and spoon, bar glass, squeezer, drinking straws, swizzle sticks, cocktail sticks, spirit measures, cutting board and knife, ice crusher, small ice bucket or bowl and tongs, soda siphon, jugs, ice pick, crown cork opener, corkscrew, bitters bottles, sugar sifter, nutmeg grater, blender.
- **For wine sales**: ice buckets and stands, corkscrew, champagne cork remover, carafes, strainer and funnel, salvers, wine knife.
- **For cigars and cigarettes**: humidor, cigar cutter, cigar matches.

Foyer and/or reception

Where there is a foyer or reception area, generally only chairs and small tables, either fixed or free-standing, are required. The reception head waiter's desk may be sited here or just inside the dining-room; telephones for external and internal calls can be here or at the cashier's desk.

Cloakroom and toilet

The provision of toilet facilities is decided by local government regulations which state the number and type of facilities to be provided according to the possible number of persons on the premises at any one time. This naturally decides the total area to be allocated for these services. Toilets and wash basins can be selected in accordance with the standards of the establishment, and this applies to the ladies room with its furnishings of chairs, mirrors and dispensers for special needs. Hand-drying equipment can be roller towels, individual towels, paper-towel dispensers or warm air hand-dryers. Instead of providing soap, soap dispensers are useful accessories to the general washing and tidying facilities for customers.

Provision for the storage of hats, coats, umbrellas and other carried items is dependent on the class of establishment. At one end of the market the provision of hat and coat stands in the dining-room is sufficient, whereas for a high-class establishment an area, usually adjacent to the toilets, is called for. This requires some sort of staffing, shelving and counters for the efficient holding of personal effects, and a well-organised security system.

Equipping the ancillary areas

Goods receiving area

There should be adequate space to receive the expected size and amount of any delivery, with the possibility of having two suppliers arriving at the same time. A table or bench is needed to inspect goods properly; a platform scale or a set of scales to check the weights; and a trolley or truck to transport goods from the area into the stores.

Stores

There can be several kinds of stores for different sorts of commodities, but in general all that is required is shelving fitments that make the best use of available space. Ideally they should be adjustable, with the possibility of adaptation for all types of goods and resiting if necessary. Ready-made systems have this advantage over fixed built-in shelving. Bins for storage of dry goods make better use of space if they are square rather than round. If root vegetables are stored, the decision whether to keep them in the original sacks or to turn them out will determine what kind of bins are installed.

Refrigeration is needed for perishable commodities such as dairy produce, vegetables and salads, meat, poultry and fish.

Scales and measures for issuing commodities to the various departments are necessary, and office equipment may be required such as a computer, typewriter, telephone, fax machine, calculator, desk, chairs, filing cabinet and shelving for books and boxed or filed items.

Cellar

The requirements for the wine and spirit store include racks for laying wines horizontally in order to keep them in good condition, lockable cages for spirits and liqueurs, mobile baskets for empty bottles, and trucks and special trolleys for the transfer of goods from cellar to bars. If bottling is carried out in the cellar, specialised equipment such as bottling and labelling machines, trestles and funnels will be needed.

Further reading

Fuller, J. and Kirk, D. (1994) *Kitchen Planning and Management*. Butterworth-Heinemann

Kirk, D. and Milson, A. (1991) *Principles of Design and Operation of Catering Equipment*. Butterworth-Heinemann

8 Convergence of facilities III
Fuels, services, safety and hygiene

Environmental issues; Energy conservation policy; Fuels; Fuel
applications; Water supplies; Ventilation; Waste disposal; Safety;
Food hygiene; Personal hygiene; Cleaning materials; Fire
prevention.

This chapter concludes the sequence of bringing together everything necessary to
ensure the efficient and profitable running of a catering business. It covers many
topics directly connected with the kitchen department, including fuel and water
services, working conditions, safe catering and hygiene. Much of the legislation
mentioned in this chapter emanates from the European Union Commissioners,
which means that it applies to each member country of the EU.

Environmental issues

Caterers in all branches of the industry must consider how the running of their business affects the natural world and its resources. Every business should have its own
policy of good environmental practice that will prevent global warming, pollution,
depletion of the ozone layer, destruction of tropical rain forests, and bad food
production and processing methods. The combustion of fuel has an effect upon the
atmosphere both within and without the premises. A policy is needed that reduces
consumption and protects the environment, thus saving fossil fuels and other non-
renewable natural resources. Other issues in catering include the safe disposal of
waste materials such as used frying oil, bones, fat and swill; support for the recycling
of used bottles, paper, cardboard and cans; and control of potentially harmful detergents, disinfectants and toiletry sundries. The use of CFCs is banned in all products
and should no longer effect the world's ozone layer. A 'Green' campaign for every
kind of organic product has been launched, and environmentally friendly food-
processing methods such as Modified Atmosphere Packaging are now in use.

Energy conservation policy

Every business needs to draw up an energy conservation policy to govern the use
of fuel, which should then be implemented by members of staff at all levels.

The policy document must cover all fuel supplies and installations for heating, cooking, lighting, insulation, ventilation and air-conditioning in accordance with a preventative maintenance contract. All this should prevent fuel wastage or misuse, and each departmental head should be made responsible for constant monitoring of fuel usage. Old and worn-out equipment and machinery inevitably consumes more energy than modern items which are designed to function economically.

An example of how new technology cuts fuel consumption is the heat recovery unit in a potwashing or dishwashing machine. This cuts the amount of humidity in the atmosphere by means of a pump which draws the vapour in the hot air back inside the machine, condensing and recycling it back into the washwater tank and boosting the heat of the rinse water.

Fuels

The two main fuels used in the catering industry are electricity and gas. Both are versatile and have several uses, often together as in a fan-assisted gas oven or a gas-fired stove top with an electric oven underneath. It is not normally necessary to make a choice of fuels when planning a kitchen unless the establishment is beyond the reach of an electricity powerline or gas pipeline. Other sources of fuel are coal, charcoal, liquid petroleum gas and butane gas.

Fuel consumption is governed by staff working in the departments of a catering establishment who should be constantly encouraged to turn off or turn down the heat and light whenever possible.

Every item of cooking equipment and machinery has its fuel rating measured in kilowatts. The greater the number of dishes on the menu and the more diverse their methods of cooking, the larger the number of items of cooking equipment required to produce the menu and thus the higher the fuel bill.

Codes of practice govern the way in which the fuel supplies are connected to the premises and to each piece of equipment.

Electricity

This fuel is measured by the megajoule (MJ) and its consumption is by the kilowatt (kW), one unit of which is equal to 3.6 MJ. It is a secondary energy source in that it is produced by steam-driven turbines, the steam being generated from coal, natural gas, oil or nuclear energy. It is a highly efficient fuel, clean in use and free from fumes; therefore no sophisticated ventilation is needed. It can be used to power every kitchen appliance as well as giving illumination and providing an air-conditioned work environment. A drawback is that a heavy-duty electric cooking range takes some time to reach cooking temperature and retains the heat long after being turned off. By using flexible cables and sockets, it is possible to make this equipment mobile so that it can be moved around.

Gas

Many chefs prefer gas to electricity, and it is estimated that about 80 per cent of professional kitchens are equipped with gas-fired items. This is because the flame can be seen and visually adjusted, giving instant control. It is a very safe fuel as most gas appliances are fitted with flame failure devices and a central isolating stop valve cuts off the supply from the meter in an emergency. The addition of an electricity supply will light up the inside of the oven; give automatic ignition; drive an oven fan; provide exterior warning lights, digital temperature and timing controls; and allow for the insertion of interior heat probes and, for baker's ovens, electrically operated revolving shelves and steam injection.

Gas stoves date from the late nineteenth century and took time to attain their present popularity. In places where no supply of piped gas is available for the operation of a kitchen on either a permanent or temporary basis, e.g. an outdoor catering event, liquified petroleum gas (propane gas) is available in cylinders which can be connected to ordinary gas-burning equipment to give a good service.

Solid fuel

Kitchen ranges fired by solid fuel go back to the year 1708 when Thomas Robinson designed a stove consisting of an open coal fire and boiling top with an oven underneath. Count Rumford who lived from 1753 to 1814 used his scientific knowledge to design many different kinds of cooking and heating stoves. Gradually these methods of cooking were replaced by new inventions such as the Aga stove designed by the Nobel prize winner Dr Gustav Dalen. This was first introduced into this country in 1929. It was designed to run economically on solid fuel, although it now also operates on oil or gas. Although Aga stoves are mainly installed for domestic use, they can often be found in restaurants and private hotels where users praise them for their efficiency.

Large solid-fuel ranges are still manufactured to meet the demand of chefs who appreciate the challenge of producing distinctive results which they say cannot be obtained from the other more convenient fuels. Modern ranges are often finished with coloured bandings and are highly burnished to give an old-fashioned look to a professional kitchen.

Fuel applications

Pressure cooking

Pressure cooking is a variation of steaming where the cooker is placed over any form of heat. The fixed lid traps all the steam emitted from the contents and builds up high pressure which cooks the food quickly. The pressure must be allowed to subside before the lid is unlocked.

Induction cooking

The induction cooking system is a remarkable technological advance in the design of cooking equipment. Using this system the consumption of electrical energy begins only when a saucepan is placed on the stove top. Induction heat is generated by sending electric current through a spiral coil which creates an intense magnetic field when a pan is placed on it. A vitroceramic plate covers the coil and supports the pan, and gives an immediate reaction. The pan must be made of a special steel; ordinary pans made of copper and stainless steel must be fitted with thermic detachable bottoms. Fuel consumption is in proportion to the size of the pan, but is controllable and consumes much less energy than a normal electric stove.

Halogen hob stoves

A halogen hob uses a halogen tube lamp beneath the vitroceramic plate on a cooker top marked with the circumference of saucepan bases. This shows where the pan must be placed to obtain the heat which comes from infra-red radiation. The action is fast, very efficient and without heat loss.

Water supplies

Water services include not just the supply of water to a location but also drainage and sewerage. Mains water that goes straight to the taps is for drinking and cooking purposes, whereas cold water from a tank in the building is for toilets, dishwashers, potwashers, waste disposal units and showers and is not drinkable.

Hot water is produced and stored by a central boiling plant to supply bathrooms, radiators, wash basins and sinks. Drainage from kitchen sinks and gulleys usually has to pass through a grease trap sited outside the building and needs regular cleaning.

A hosepipe for cleaning areas must have an approved double-check valve fitted to prevent any contaminated water being sucked back into the mains. Washing-up machines must comply with the Water Authority's by-laws. These specify that the water must be drawn from a dedicated supply which has a type-4 air gap to prevent a backflow of contaminated water.

Ventilation

Food preparation rooms must have adequate natural or mechanical ventilation, and environmental health officers will inspect them to see if the correct conditions are met. The ambient air temperature of a preparation room should be kept at approximately 15°C. Any mechanical ventilation system must be kept clean and in good working order, including the motor, fan, ducting and filters. Natural ventilation is not ideal and open windows must be covered with insect screens. The environmental health officer uses a hygrometer to test the relative humidity; an anemometer to test air movement; and a thermometer to determine the temperature of the room. Contaminants such as carbon monoxide gas, bacteria and mould spores, and any build-up of dust and grease on pipes and ducts, must be eradicated.

Waste disposal

Catering establishments have to get rid of a lot of liquid and solid food waste as well as cardboard, plastic and metal packaging materials. Waste has to be removed from preparation areas as quickly as possible so that it does not start to smell or attract pests. Swill and rubbish bins must be emptied into bulk waste containers kept well away from the kitchen area. Bins must be kept clean, preferably by using bin liners and covering them with lids. Liquids and semi-liquid food waste can be disposed of in a waste disposal unit or through a drainage system which can cope with it.

The chef or departmental manager has a duty to carry out inspections of the waste disposal system to ensure that legislation is not being contravened.

Safety

Under the Health and Safety at Work Act 1987, employers and employees have a duty to ensure there are no risks to the health and safety of all persons who work at or visit the premises. Regulations drawn up under this Act are enforced by the Health and Safety Executive (HSE) and by the local authority's environmental health department. There are five major points to be remembered:

1 Any hazardous incident should be traced back to the root cause of why it happened.
2 Potential hazards must be identified and remedied quickly.
3 Top management must determine health and safety policies and be involved in monitoring every aspect of health and safety.
4 Managers and supervisors must be fully accountable for health and safety performance in the areas for which they are responsible.
5 All employees must be thoroughly trained in safe working practices and receive continuous education and guidance on the elimination of hazards.

The Royal Society for the Prevention of Accidents (ROSPA) runs health and safety courses for all levels of staff by sending out visiting advisors. The Industrial Society provides health and safety courses for its core members.

The highest risks in the catering industry are slipping, falling, tripping, coming into contact with hot surfaces, lifting heavy items and handling them in the wrong way, being struck by an object, catching dermatitis, and developing upper limb disorders. Employers must make risk assessments of these and any other hazards, and competent persons must be appointed to help the company comply with the regulations and legislation. Both full- and part-time staff and all new entrants must be made aware of their responsibilities in this matter.

The Workplace (Health, Safety and Welfare) Regulations 1992 state that floors must be non-slip where appropriate and kept free from anything that might cause a person to slip. They also state that measures must be taken to prevent people from falling any distance that would injure them and to prevent objects such as pans falling on them. Handling and lifting of heavy items that might cause injury are covered by the Manual Handling Regulations. These state that staff must be given training in how to lift heavy objects correctly.

Every establishment must, by law, have a first-aid box. Under the Health and Safety (First Aid) Regulations 1981, the basic contents of the box should include 1 pair of disposable gloves, 2 large and 4 medium sterile dressings, 6 safety pins, 20 individual sticking plasters in a pronounced colour, 2 sterile eye pads, 4 triangular bandages, and an HSE guidance leaflet.

Safety rules

All kitchen staff should take the following everyday precautions:

- Always wear the correct uniform or protective clothing and proper footwear.
- Ensure that pilot lights are on before turning on the main gas jets.
- If there is no pilot light or automatic ignition, have a lighted taper ready before turning on the gas.
- Do not place any full containers, especially those holding hot liquid, above eye level.
- Avoid carrying heavy pots of boiling water across the kitchen single handed.
- Allow a pan containing hot fat to cool before moving or carrying it across the kitchen.
- Do not plunge or empty a frying basket of damp food into a pan of hot fat without having a spider to hand to take some out if it starts to boil over.
- Do not draw pots too near the edge of the stove or table where they could get knocked off.
- Keep the handles of pots on the stove away from direct heat.
- Sprinkle lids and handles just brought out of the oven with a dusting of flour to act as a warning sign.
- Use a dry oven cloth or folded kitchen cloth when handling hot saucepans.
- Always carry knives with the points downwards, and do not leave them in a sinkful of water before washing them.
- Mop up any spillage of water or fat on the floor immediately and if necessary sprinkle the area with some coarse salt to prevent people slipping.
- Do not run in the kitchen and do not attempt to barge past fellow workers.
- Be aware of where the first-aid kit is kept and know who to call in an emergency.

- Know where the fire-fighting equipment is housed. Know which extinguisher to use and how to use it, according to what is burning.
- Beware of cuts caused by meat bones, fish bones and fish shells which can quickly become septic.
- Do not start chopping or cutting on a butcher's block when other implements are nearby.
- Always work methodically and cleanly. Try to stay calm during the busy service period.

Safe operation of kitchen machinery

There is a tendency for kitchen staff to become over-familiar in the use of machinery and to disregard instructions and safety standards, accepting that the machines are there to make the job easier by doing all those tasks that demand concentrated effort. Staff must be trained in the use of the machines they will be using; the likely dangers from electric shock; the dangers of using mixing, slicing, chopping and mincing machines; and the need to see they are hygienically washed and reassembled after each use.

The Provision and Use of Work Equipment Regulations were introduced in 1992 with the objective of ensuring that employers keep each item of equipment in perfect working order and that staff are trained to use them correctly. Failure to comply with these regulations can lead to prosecution. The environmental health officer is entitled to ask to see records which show that equipment was properly installed and staff received proper training in its use.

Warning notes regarding the use of equipment must be displayed on or by the machines. Each new item of kitchen equipment has to pass a rigorous safety test, but could still be hazardous in the hands of untrained staff. Each electric appliance must be tested regularly; a hand-held tester can be used to check that the earth bond and insulation are in order.

Food hygiene

In the UK, the Department of Health has prime responsibility for food hygiene. It works jointly with the Ministry of Agriculture, Fisheries and Food (MAFF), the Department of the Environment, and the local health authorities and environmental health departments to ensure that adequate controls are applied and that action is taken and properly coordinated in the event of an outbreak of food poisoning.

The Department of Health aims to protect the health of the public by combating microbiological contamination of food, removing hazardous food from the food chain, containing outbreaks of food poisoning, encouraging good hygiene practices, and providing advisory and consultancy services related to catering, dietetics, hotel services and pest control to all catering establishments.

To show due diligence, a chef must be constantly on guard throughout the chain of processing food from delivery to cooking and serving. A chef can require staff to take a basic food hygiene course run by the local environmental health department or other agency. The course deals with food poisoning prevention, personal hygiene and cleaning procedures. Common examples of bad food handling practice include:

- using the same chopping board for cooked and raw food which can cause cross-contamination
- poor storage facilities which mean that cooked and raw foods are kept together in a refrigerator; a separate unit for each is desirable, but if not possible raw items must be at the bottom.
- incorrect temperature control of refrigerators and serving points; cooked food must be held at 63°C, and food being prepared must be handled quickly and returned to the refrigerator with undue delay
- misuse of wash basins and sinks for cleaning foods and equipment
- staff not washing their hands after using the toilet, handling raw food, or touching the face or mouth.

Food hygiene legislation

The main legislation on food hygiene is the Food Safety Act 1990. This gives authority to environmental health officers to issue notices of improvement to businesses that do not meet satisfactory hygiene requirements and empowers them to close down any business that might pose a risk to the public health. It includes offences of selling or supplying food which fails to meet food safety requirements. The Food Premises (Registration) Regulations 1991 require that owners of food businesses register their premises with the local authority to ensure they are inspected.

The European Union aims to harmonise food laws between all member states. The EU Directive on Food Hygiene sets out general hygiene principles and conditions for foodstuffs applicable to all food businesses. It covers design and structure of premises, facilities, equipment, operation and personal hygiene of staff. It requires that all food handlers are trained in food hygiene. It also places a responsibility on owners to analyse food hazards and identify where they may occur, known as Hazard Analysis Critical Control Points (HACCP). Critical control points are the stages of the production line where hazards could arise, such as possible bacterial contamination, foreign bodies such as insects, broken glass, metal objects, chemical and bad handling practices. A Department of Health publication called *Assured Safe Handling* gives guidance on this.

Food poisoning

The reputation of a restaurant or other catering business could be damaged overnight if just one customer makes a complaint to the local environmental health officer that he or she became ill soon after eating a meal at that particular establishment. A capable chef is constantly vigilant to prevent a customer making a complaint that the food served is 'off' by seeing that it is perfectly fresh on delivery and properly stored until the time it is cooked and served. If there is any doubt about its freshness, the food should not be served.

The possibility of food poisoning is avoidable, but staff should know how to deal with an incident should the need ever arise. They should be made aware of the procedure to follow: keeping samples of the foods being served so they can be analysed; collecting data on a special form stating when and how it happened, and what emergency action or treatment was taken; and assuming full control of the incident rather than involving a third party.

Outbreaks of food poisoning are always caused by bacteria which do not die simply because they are in a clean kitchen. Most outbreaks originate in meat or poultry which is already infected with salmonella or *Clostridium welchii* when delivered. The salmonella will be destroyed by cooking to the correct internal temperature of 70°C and so should the clostridia, but there is always the chance that some spores will remain and multiply given the right incubating temperature. If foods are left simmering at a low temperature or cooled down slowly in a warm atmosphere, dormant spores may come to life or the food may become recontaminated.

Any protein foods, including dishes containing milk and eggs, which are left standing about at a temperature within the zone of 10–60;°C are at risk. The most dangerous zone is between 36.1°C and 37.7°C, which is about blood temperature.

Salmonella is found in raw meat, poultry and eggs. It has an incubation period of 12–36 hours. Infection leads to fever, diarrhoea, vomiting and headache which can last for a week. *Clostridium welchii* may be present in raw meat and causes diarrhoea. The incubation period is 8–22 hours. An outbreak of a particularly harmful strain of *E. coli* bacterium which contaminates meat and dairy foods – *Escherichia coli* 0157:H7 – was responsible for many deaths recently, mainly the elderly and weak. *E. coli* releases a toxin in the gut that destroys body cells. Poor hygiene practices in abattoirs are a cause of it.

Foods that need special care are reheated dishes, brawn, bought meat pies, gravy, stock, cream cakes, cooked and raw shellfish, and cold meats.

The local environmental health department must be notified of an outbreak of food poisoning. It will try to find the extent and cause of the incident and will decide if there is a case for prosecution. Statements will be taken from customers and staff and the caterer must try to field a defence of 'due diligence' as a means of proving that all reasonable precautions were taken and that staff had acted diligently to avoid the possibility of an outbreak of food poisoning. The caterer has to prove that every possible care in the preparation of the meal had been taken; that the food had been properly stored and cooked; and that monitoring and safety checks had been carried out.

It is necessary to use a control system to monitor temperature and time throughout the cycle from transportation to delivery, storage and cooking. A

Figure 15   Guide to food safety temperatures

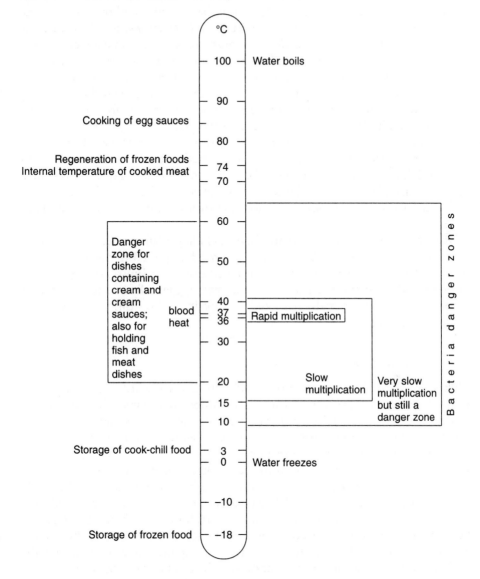

hand-held probe records temperatures from 50°C to 150°C, with the time and dated stored in the instrument's memory or transmitted to the storage system of the kitchen computer. A guide to food safety temperatures is given in Figure 15.

Use of leftover foods

It is usually feasible for a chef to estimate the number of meals likely to be served on any day of the week during the whole year by taking note of the number of table bookings, the number of residents if part of a hotel, the number served on the same day last year, the weather and the social calendar, and the events of the day. Unforeseen circumstances may upset these calculations, in which case the number of meals served will be less than those prepared. In some establishments the surplus food is served as staff meals; in others it may be collected by a charitable body for disposal to poor and hungry citizens. The chef can take the decision to recycle good-quality leftover food by including it in the next day's Table d'Hôte menu in the form of classic dishes, but this is frowned upon by environmental health officers and should be avoided.

Any usable leftover food must be arranged tidily on trays or other suitable receptacles, marked with the time and date, covered, and refrigerated at a temperature of 5°C or less. If suitable, it can be served cold the next day or transformed into a hot dish, but it must be heated to a temperature of at least 70°C and maintained at 63°C during the service period. Leftover food must be used within 48 hours.

Swill is the name given to waste food, including plate waste, which is kept separate from other refuse for selling as pig food. A pig farmer who buys swill from a catering establishment must be licensed from the Ministry of Agriculture, Fisheries and Food and must transport the swill hygienically and heat-sterilise it before feeding it to animals. It should be kept in cool conditions at its source before being collected.

Irradiation of foods

This is a method of preserving food by subjecting it whilst still very fresh to rays from the electromagnetic spectrum or by using accelerated electron beams. Certain foods can be subjected to treatment by gamma rays and X-rays which cause ionisation of foods. (Ions are electrically charged groups of atoms formed by the loss or gain of one or more atoms.)

Food for irradiation is prepared in the normal manner, packaged and passed by conveyor belt through a continuous active radiation field of gamma rays produced by radioactive cobalt. These penetrate food more thoroughly and their intensity can be better controlled than ordinary X-rays which are generated by beaming accelerated electrons on to a metal target. The intensity of the gamma rays is affected by the density of the food being irradiated and also by the distance between the source of radiation and the food being processed.

The amount of radiation absorbed is measured by a meter which shows it in KGy or KiloGrays. The maximum should not exceed 10 KGy.

Only top-quality food is worth preserving by irradiation. The method destroys some of the microorganisms present in the food which would eventually cause it to spoil if left. It does not affect the food in any way and no chemical changes are detectable; indeed, it is indistinguishable from the fresh product. Foods that benefit most from irradiation are strawberries, prawns, papayas, pork and poultry products; no additives or preservatives are needed.

Irradiated foods have to be labelled under the Food (Control of Irradiation)

Regulations 1990 and Food Labelling (Amendment Irradiated Foods) Regulations 1990. Customers should be told if any dish on the menu contains any irradiated foodstuffs. It has been proven that consumers can eat these products without risk to their health.

Personal hygiene

The following rules are applicable to staff engaged in the production and service of food and drink to the general public:

- Wash your hands before starting work and before handling food or dishes, and always after using the toilet.
- Keep any cuts or sores covered with a distinctive coloured waterproof dressing that can be easily traced should it fall off when mixing foods.
- Do not start work if you have an open sore on the hands or any skin infection.
- Do not continue to work using an ingredient such as flour to which you are allergic.
- Do not go to work if you are suffering from a throat infection or have bowel trouble.
- Dress in a clean uniform and try to keep it clean. Wear it only while on duty. Wear good footwear.
- Take pride in your professional appearance.
- Keep your hair neat and wear a chef's hat on duty.
- Do not smoke anywhere in food premises.
- Do not cough or sneeze over food.
- Keep your fingernails short.
- Wear disposable gloves when mixing foodstuffs.
- Do not wear a wristwatch, bracelet, earrings or necklace as they can harbour bacteria and could get caught in machinery.
- Do not taste foods by dipping a finger in it or by using a pencil; use a clean spoon and wash it between tastings.

Cleaning materials

In many businesses all the cleaning is carried out by a contractor, but this does not lessen the responsibility for absolute cleanliness on the part of the owner who is answerable to inspectors of the local environmental health department. The hygienic cleanliness of catering enterprises is governed by legislation, and each departmental head must know the necessary standards that the contractor must achieve and maintain. This entails a knowledge of cleaning procedures and the nature of cleaning materials used, which can then form a programme of action and checklist of important points. Contractors may have to carry out their work during night hours, but routine cleaning needs to be carried out during working hours, with daily, weekly and monthly activities which must include pest control of insects, mice, rats, and possibly birds. Cleaning materials must be chosen carefully and in the knowledge of where and how they are to be used. The person responsible for ordering them must know the needs of the various departments and the types and brands of cleansers and disinfectants available and their packaging.

A wide range of cleaning materials are used, including:

- detergents, soap, scouring powder, soda and oven cleaner
- disinfectant
- water softeners, including salt
- special solvent for use in grease traps
- cleaner for air filters
- floor and furniture polish
- cleaner for removing stains from silverware
- upholstery cleaner
- toilet cleaner, air freshener and toilet rolls
- disposable dishcloths, scourers, dusters and rubbish sacks
- small items of equipment, including nail brushes, scrubbing brushes and mop heads.

Other items kept in the cleaning store are tapers, matches, light bulbs, disposable gloves, and candles for the dining-room where featured and for use in the event of electricity failure.

These materials are costly and must be controlled by making sure the correct quantity of the right cleansing material is used for each particular job. They must be stored away from foodstuffs under lock and key. Cleaning equipment, both hand and mechanically operated, must be kept in an efficient and safe condition and staff instructed in its correct usage.

Modern synthetic detergents are made of a mixture of chemicals with a wetting agent, water softener, emulsifier, germicide, and a rinsing aid to ensure a streak-free finish. Bleach is a bactericide, but is dangerous to the user if not properly diluted and can taint surfaces if not well rinsed off. Quaternary Ammonia Compounds (Quarts) are effective cleaners, though not against all pathogenic substances, and are used mainly for washing kitchen utensils and worktops.

The cleansers in general use are:

- alkaline detergent for removing grease from deep fryers, ovens, walls and floors
- detergent degreaser for use on thick grease and charred residues on baking trays and machines
- detergent sanitiser for work surfaces after they have been cleansed of soilage
- neutral general-purpose detergent for all kinds of dishes, saucepans, glassware, walls and floors
- decarboniser – a heavy-duty cleanser for baked-on deposits in ovens on stove tops and from baking trays

- abrasives in powder form for heavily used equipment that requires thorough scouring
- acid descalers for dissolving hard water stains and hardened scum in bain-maries.

The Control of Substances Hazardous to Health (COSHH) Regulations 1988 impose a duty on managers to review working practices which could expose employees to potentially hazardous substances. It covers substances such as bleach, oven cleaners, anti-fungicidal solutions and various cleaning agents that are irritants or toxic, causing burns to the skin. They must be used only in a well-ventilated area.

Fire prevention

A fire certificate is a legal requirement for all premises where more than 20 people work, and a fire officer has to inspect the building in order to draw up a comprehensive list of the requirements. The owner or occupier has to make a fire risk assessment and is responsible for installing adequate fire precautions in association with the current health and safety framework.

Further reading

Hendrik *et al.* (1991) *Food Policy Trends in Europe*. Ellis Horwood
Jukes, D. (1997) *Food Legislation of the UK*. Butterworth-Heinemann
Kirk, D. (1998) *Environmental Management for Hotels*. Butterworth-Heinemann
Stretch, A. and Southgate, H. (1991) *Food Hygiene, Health and Safety*. Longman

9 Provisioning I
Commodities

Purchasing specifications; Meat; Beef; Veal; Lamb; Mutton; Pork; Bacon; Offals; Poultry; Game birds; Game animals; Fish; Shellfish; Vegetables; Fruit; Nuts; Dairy produce; Fats and oils; Meat substitutes; Condiments and seasoning agents; Essences, flavourings and colourings; Confectionery goods; Sweetening agents; Beverages; Cereals; Delicatessen and speciality goods; Charcuterie; Value-added foods; Auxiliary items.

This chapter deals with most of the commodities in general use in the kitchens and dining-rooms of all kinds of catering establishments. It gives descriptions, quality points, sources of supply, purchasing units, seasonal availability, storage guidelines, and the technical terms used to describe many of the items in the language used by caterers.

The importance of provisioning can be judged by the amount of money spent on commodities, which ranks with that spent on the salaries of the entire staff of an operation. Thus it is important to ensure that the money is spent wisely and that the people who are authorised to do the buying obtain the best value by ordering the right goods at the right price and of the right quality for the particular establishment.

Purchasing specifications

The person responsible for buying any kind of commodity should be capable of striking a bargain with a supplier on the basis of his or her recognition of the quality of the goods offered. A specification for each item on the provisions list will ensure that the people who will actually be using the commodities accept them as being exactly right for the needs of the operation. A specification is a detailed written description of each commodity which helps to ensure that each time it is ordered it totally matches the prescribed requirements, or with only minor discrepancies, thus giving constant quality for the particular kind of business it is being bought for. The specification must be agreed by both the user and the supplier and be used every time that item is ordered and delivered; thus there will be no dispute between the two sides.

Purchasing specifications are discussed further in Chapter 11.

Quality standards manual

A large catering company may decide to draw up a manual that gives buyers and suppliers information of the quality standards required for all its branches. In the form of a code of practice, it will stipulate that supplies must be produced in accordance with current food legislation and that the purchaser has the right to inspect suppliers' premises without prior warning to ensure that the building is suitable for its use, that it is run under correct control, and that the staff observe food hygiene regulations. The code of practice will require that goods are properly packed and labelled and correctly stored before delivery, and that the delivery vans are clean and, if necessary, temperature controlled. Suppliers, in turn, must keep quality control over the firms that supply them with basic ingredients and equipment. The purchaser can further demand to see records of analysis of products, use of a metal detector, and any other safeguards concerning quality control.

Meat

Meat is the word used to describe the flesh of animals which is prepared for human consumption and includes the offals or interior organs. There are four main types of meat in general use: beef, veal, pork and lamb, and sometimes mutton. Meat is not a seasonal commodity and it is possible to include it in all its forms on menus throughout the year. The one exception is new season's lamb, either home-killed or from New Zealand, which may be featured on a menu when it first appears each spring. At one time pork was considered to be a seasonal commodity, but this is no longer the case.

Meat is composed of muscle, connective tissue, fat and bone in various amounts according to the type, age, sex and breed of animal. The muscle part is the actual lean flesh and is composed of bundles of muscle cells which are held in place by the connective tissue. The connective tissue is mainly collagen, which softens during cooking; this should not be confused with the tough sinew which does not become tender and should be removed from the joint. The fat of meat varies in colour from the hard white fat of lamb to the deep yellow of old cow beef. The size of bones and their hardness is an indication of the age of the animal.

In most catering establishments the amount of money spent on the purchase of meat outweighs that of all other commodities put together. It is estimated that more than 30p of each £1.00 of expenditure in the kitchen goes on meat in its various forms. This is because meat is the main item on most menus and, except for vegetarians, plays a part in everyone's diet each day. Its importance also derives from its nutritional value as the most valuable source of protein – the substance in the diet which promotes growth and repair of body tissues.

Religious and cultural beliefs may affect the kind of meat a particular person and even a nation will consume. To some people beef is obnoxious, whilst to others pork is absolutely forbidden because of religious laws. A caterer needs to know the rules governing the eating habits of such groups so as to avoid serving unsuitable meat.

Meat purchasing

Meat can be purchased as a whole carcass or as wholesale trade cuts; it can also be bought in ready-to-use cuts such as chined best ends and loins, chops, cutlets, escalopes, noisettes and steaks. If bought whole or in large cuts, proper storage and preparation facilities must be made available to a qualified butcher or larder chef, and it will probably be necessary to purchase a fixed or mobile bandsaw.

Meat is available in fresh, chilled, frozen and vacuum-packed forms. Apart from British meat there are imports from the EU, Uruguay, Zimbabwe, Argentina, Holland, New Zealand and several other countries.

A specification for the purchase of fresh meat should include the following details:

- country of origin
- classification or grade
- name of the joint or cut of meat
- weight of the cut within a limited tolerance
- the thickness of the joint and how it was prepared
- the thickness of any fat covering
- packaging and labelling.

Maturation and storage

Some kinds of meat improve by being hung to mature for a certain length of time which helps to make it more tender and improves its flavour. Average times for maturation are:

- beef – seven to ten days
- lamb – two to three days
- pork – one to two days.

Veal can be used straight after slaughter.

Meat which is vacuum packed will mature slowly over six to eight weeks. It should be kept in the wrapping and stored at −3°C. Wholesale butchers have ideal facilities for maturing meat at the correct storage temperature and at the right degree of humidity over the optimum period.

Fresh meat should be kept in a refrigerator at 2°C and a relative humidity of 80–90 per cent. Cuts of meat should be laid on trays, covered to exclude the air and stored in a refrigerator at 5°C. This will prevent it from drying out and losing weight.

Conservation or premium grade meat comes from animals that have been reared at a high standard of animal husbandry without having been subjected to hormone injection, fed on additives, or reared under intensive farming methods. This grade will be entirely authentic, wholesome and tender, and as the name implies will command a premium price in the market.

Visual lean

When ordering diced or minced meat ready to use, the butcher should give details of the visual lean component. Good quality stewing or minced meat should not contain more than 10 per cent fat, thus ensuring 90 per cent lean meat. Poorer quality meat might have up to 30 per cent fat quantity. The amount of visual lean required can be incorporated into the specification.

Beef

Beef is the name given to meat obtained from domestic cattle and is the most widely used kind of meat. The best breed for beef is believed to be the Aberdeen Angus, which is a small, stocky animal; other breeds are the Herefords and short-horns and crosses of these. Charolais cattle have been brought over from France to cross-breed with some British stock to improve the quality.

A whole side of beef is divided into two quarters between the tenth and eleventh ribs which gives a hindquarter with three rib bones and a forequarter with ten rib bones in it. Each quarter will weigh from 60 kg to 80 kg from a heifer or up to 90 kg from an older animal.

Chilled beef should be stored at –2°C so that it keeps hard on the outside and soft within. Frozen beef should be hung at a temperature of –18°C.

Hindquarter

A hindquarter of beef has most of the best-quality cooking joints and is mostly used in high-class establishments. Figure 16 shows the position of joints on a hindquarter of beef.

Figure 17 lists the joints that can be cut from a hindquarter of approximately 70 kg, together with approximate weights and optimum uses of each.

Small cuts of beef are prepared from some of these joints, which may be prepared on the premises or purchased in the form of portion-controlled meats. They are listed in Figure 18.

Forequarter

A forequarter of beef provides only one good-quality roasting joint – the fore rib. The remainder of the carcass is more suitable for braising or stewing. This

Figure 16   Hindquarter of beef

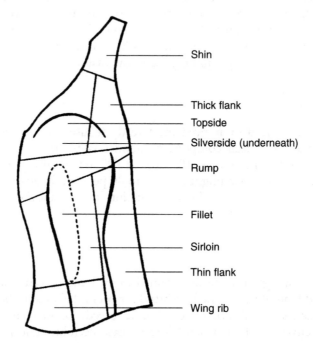

- Shin
- Thick flank
- Topside
- Silverside (underneath)
- Rump
- Fillet
- Sirloin
- Thin flank
- Wing rib

Figure 17   Joints from a hindquarter of beef

Name of joint	Approx. weight	Optimum uses
Shin or leg	7	Consommé, stewing
Topside	8	Roasting, braising, stewing
Silverside	10	Pickling for boiling, stewing
Thick flank	10	Roasting, braising, stewing steaks
Rump	9	Steaks for grilling
Sirloin	10	Roasting, poêling, steaks for grilling and shallow frying
Fillet	3	Roasting, poêling, steaks for grilling and shallow frying
Wing rib	4	Roasting
Thin flank	8	Boiling, stewing

In addition there is a kidney and a quantity of suet.

suggests that the forequarter is generally tougher than the hindquarter and has a slightly higher bone and fat content.

When cutting beef for stewing, it is preferable to use meat from one cut rather than to have it mixed from more than one joint. The meat from, for example, the clod is tougher than other joints.

Figure 19 shows the position of joints on a forequarter of beef.

Figure 20 lists the joints that can be cut from a forequarter of beef of approximately 70 kg, together with approximate weights and optimum uses of each.

Figure 18 Small cuts from a hindquarter of beef

Name of cuts	Description	Average portion weight (g)
Sirloin steak	Steak cut from a boned sirloin	180
Double sirloin	Double thickness steak cut from a sirloin	350
Minute steak	Thin sirloin steak flattened	150
Porterhouse steak	Steak cut through a whole sirloin with the bone and fillet	550
Chateaubriand	Thick steak for a minimum of 2 people, cut from the head of the fillet	250
Fillet steak	Steak approx. 3 cm thick, cut from the upper part of the fillet	180
Tournedos	Round steak cut 3 cm thick from the centre of the fillet	120
Filet mignons	Small steaks cut from the tail end of the fillet	2 × 75
Rump steak	A thick slice of the rump	150
Point steak	Steak cut from the triangular corner of the rump	150

Figure 19 Forequarter of beef

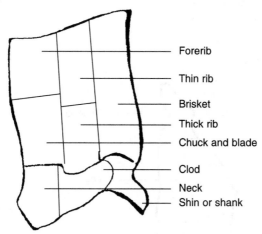

- Forerib
- Thin rib
- Brisket
- Thick rib
- Chuck and blade
- Clod
- Neck
- Shin or shank

Figure 20 Joints from a forequarter of beef

Name of joint	Approx. weight (kg)	Optimum uses
Fore rib	6	Roasting
Thin rib	8	Braising
Brisket	16	Boiling, braising (pickled for boiling)
Thick rib	8	Braising
Chuck and blade	10	Braising, stewing
Clod	8	Stewing, mince
Neck	8	Stewing, mince
Shin or shank	6	Stewing, mince

No small cuts are prepared from this part of the carcass, except for perhaps a large steak cut from the fore rib.

Veal

Veal is the name given to meat from calves that have been reared on a special diet that includes milk. This produces tender, pinkish-white coloured flesh with a delicate flavour and only a thin covering of creamy white fat. It has no marbling of fat and can be dry if not cooked with care. The bones are heavy in proportion to the amount of flesh and they also are pinkish-white in colour.

Supplies are mainly from Holland and France with a lesser quantity of home-produced veal, available only as fresh and ready to use. It should be kept refrigerated at 4°C.

Veal is available in the following joints: hindquarter; leg with rump; loin and rump; saddle; shoulder; and best end. It is also possible to purchase by the carcass and the price will be less than for the best cuts, but there will be some stewing meat to be utilised.

Figure 21 shows a carcass of veal viewed from the side and the usual joints into which it is dissected.

Figure 22 lists the joints that can be cut from a carcass of veal of approximately 140 kg, together with approximate weights and optimum uses for each. It also shows the small cuts obtainable.

Figure 21   Carcass of veal

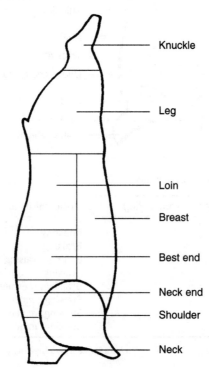

Knuckle

Leg

Loin

Breast

Best end

Neck end

Shoulder

Neck

Figure 22   Joints from a carcass of veal

		Name of joint	Approx. weight (kg)	Optimum uses and small cuts
Hindquarter	Cut from the leg	Leg	33	Roasting, poêling, braising
		Knuckles	7	Stewing; cut into thick sections on the bone (osso bucco)
		Cushion	7	Roasting, poêling, braising; cut into escalopes, grenadins
		Under-cushion	7	Roasting, poêling, braising; cut into escalopes, grenadins
		Thick flank	8	Roasting, poêling, braising; cut into escalopes, grenadins
		Rump	7	Roasting, poêling, braising
		Saddle	22	Roasting, poêling,
		(Loin	11)	Roasting, poêling; cut into chops for grilling and shallow frying
Forequarter		Best end	8	Roasting, poêling; cut into cutlets for grilling and shallow frying
		Neck end	6	Stewing
		Neck	8	Stewing
		Breast	7	Roasting, stewing, braising
		Shoulder	17	Roasting, poêling, braising, stewing

In addition there is a kidney attached to the loin.
The bones from the leg weigh approximately 2 kg.

Lamb

A lamb is a young sheep of up to one year old; after this it is called mutton. British lamb is available as fresh meat all the year round and is larger than the imported frozen and chilled forms from New Zealand. Welsh and Scottish lamb are sometimes available under their respective names; and occasionally it is possible to feature présalé lamb reared on salt marshes near the coast, and Pauillac lamb or house lamb which is well known in France for its fine flavour and tenderness.

Lamb is available in the whole carcass, as half lambs cut between the saddle and best end, and as joints. Fresh lamb should be stored at 3°C and frozen lamb at –18°C.

Figure 23 shows two views of a carcass of lamb and the usual joints into which it is dissected for catering.

Figure 24 lists the joints with their approximate weights as cut from a PM grade New Zealand lamb; it also shows the optimum uses and small cuts obtainable.

Figure 23   Carcass of lamb

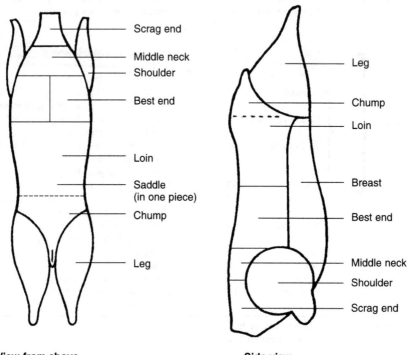

View from above   **Side view**

Figure 24   Joints from a carcass of New Zealand lamb

Name of joint	Approx. weight (kg)	Optimum uses and small cuts
Shoulder	2 × 1½	Roasting, stewing
Leg	2 × 2	Roasting, boiling; cut into leg steaks
Breast	2 × ¾	Roasting, stewing
Middle neck	1	Stewing
Scrag end	¾	Stewing
Best end	2 × 1¼	Roasting; cut into cutlets for grilling
Saddle or	4	Roasting, poêling
2 Loins		Roasting, poêling; cut into chops for grilling or into noisettes or rosettes for shallow frying

Mutton

Good-quality mutton is mainly imported in frozen form from Australia and New Zealand, although British mutton can also be purchased. It is usually available only from wholesalers. The meat is darker and more strongly flavoured than lamb, and equivalent joints are at least 25 per cent heavier.

Pork

Pork is the meat of a pig which has been specially reared for its particular uses in the butchery and catering trades. Good-quality pork comes from animals of up to 12 months of age. The flesh is light pink in colour and firm in texture, with a minimum covering of milky white fat and thin clear skin. The bones are small in proportion to the flesh. For special occasions some farmers can supply small, plump sucking pigs. British pork is best and is available all the time, usually cut into sides or as wholesale cuts. Pork does not improve by hanging to mature it and should be used fairly quickly. Store at 3°C for a minimum length of time.

Figure 25 shows a carcass of pork viewed from the side and the usual joints into which it is dissected for catering.

Figure 26 lists the joints that can be cut from a side of pork of approximately 23 kg, together with approximate weights and optimum uses for each. It also shows the small cuts obtainable.

Bacon

Bacon is the cured flesh of a pig that has been bred especially for this purpose. The meat is preserved by being salt cured or immersed in a brine and then

Figure 25   Side of pork

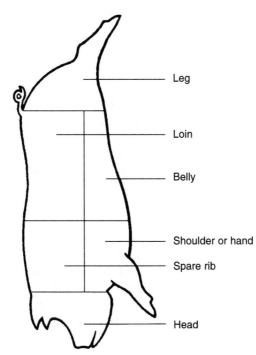

Figure 26   Joints from a side of pork

Name of joint	Approx. weight (kg)	Optimum uses and small cuts
Leg	5½	Roasting, boiling
Loin	6	Roasting; cut into chops for grilling and shallow frying, escalopes
Spare rib	3½	Roasting; cut into chops for grilling; shallow frying and braising
Shoulder or hand	3½	Roasting, stewing, pies, forcemeats
Belly	3	Boiling, pies, pâtés, stuffings, forcemeat
Head (½)	2	Boiling for brawn

smoked. Recipes for brine vary between firms of bacon curers. Some include sugar, in which case the bacon can be labelled as sweet cured. Dry curing consists of rubbing or injecting salt into the flesh. Smoking varies with the type of sawdust used and the length of time allowed; the smoke usually has antiseptic properties.

British bacon is excellent, as is that imported from Denmark and Holland. If purchased by the side, it should be dry and have a nice smell with flesh that is lean, firm and pale pink in colour with a minimum of fat. Store bacon at 10°C.

Figure 27 shows a side of bacon and the usual joints into which it is dissected for catering.

Figure 28 lists the joints that can be cut from a side of bacon of approximately 23 kg, together with their approximate weights and optimum uses. It also lists the small cuts obtainable.

Offals

Offals are the edible internal organs and other parts of livestock, including the heart, liver, kidneys, feet, caul, tripe, tail, tongue, lung, brains, sweetbreads and head. They are available fresh or frozen and are always in season, although some such as a calf's head, chitterlings and caul may be difficult to obtain. They should be firm to the touch, heavy in weight, and look and smell fresh. They need the same careful storage as other meats.

Poultry

Poultry embraces all the domesticated birds that are reared for the table, including chickens, ducks, geese, guinea fowl, turkeys and pigeons. All these birds should be plump, neatly plucked and have a fresh smell. Chickens and turkeys have white flesh; ducks, geese and guinea fowl are slightly darker; and pigeons have quite dark flesh.

Figure 27   Side of bacon

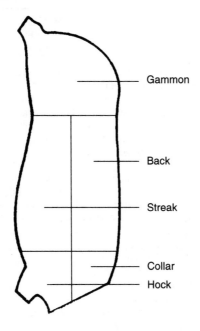

Gammon

Back

Streak

Collar

Hock

Figure 28   Joints from a side of bacon

Name of joint	Approx. weight (kg)	Optimum uses and small cuts
Hock	3½	Boiling; pies
Collar	3	Boiling; pies
Back	7½	Cutting into bacon chops; slicing into rashers for shallow frying and grilling
Streak	3½	Cutting into rashers for shallow frying and grilling
Gammon	5½	Boiling; braising; cutting into gammon steaks for shallow frying and grilling

All poultry is available throughout the year in fresh, chilled or frozen form and is usually bought in standard weights to yield two, four, six or eight portions according to type and size. Except for poussins and pigeons which are priced per bird, poultry is charged by the number of birds at so much per kilogram. Chicken, turkey and duck are also available as small cuts, including supremes, magrets, escalopes, boned legs, drumsticks, and diced for stewing.

Fresh poultry should be stored at 5°C for a short period only; frozen poultry should be kept at –18°C.

Figure 29 lists the general range of poultry available, together with descriptions, weights and suitable cooking methods.

Figure 29   Poultry

Name	Description	Best average weight	Suitable cooking methods
Chicken	A well-fleshed medium size bird; good colour and excellent flavour	1¼–1¾ kg	Roasting, grilling, shallow frying, poêling
Fowl, fattened	A larger well-fleshed chicken of excellent colour, flavour and texture	2–2½ kg	Poaching, poêling
Fowl, boiling	An old hen; needs prolonged cooking	2–3 kg	Boiling
Poussin	A very small milk-fed chicken	Single: 350g Double: 600 g	Roasting, grilling
Turkey	Large bird with excellent flesh to bone ratio; flavour stronger than chicken but still very good; can be dry if overcooked	5–12 kg	Roasting, boiling
Duck and Duckling	Loses a lot of weight in cooking because of high fat content; dark tender flesh of excellent flavour; can be dry if overcooked	2–3 kg	Braising, roasting, poêling
Goose	Similar to duck but much larger and flavour more pronounced; high fat content; the older bird can be tough and need braising; Very good flavour	5–7 kg	Roasting, braising
Guinea fowl	Slightly smaller and thinner than a chicken with yellow skin and darkish flesh; very good slightly gamey flavour; can be dry and stringy if overcooked	1½ kg	Roasting, poêling
Pigeon	Dark flesh which can be decidedly tough and stringy in an older bird; strong almost gamey flavour	500 g	Braising, roasting, poêling, grilling

Recently ostrich meat has become widely available. It is used more as a substitute for beef than as poultry, its flavour and colour being between beef and venison with a marked taste. It is very lean and is suitable for use as steaks rather than joints. Also available are peacocks and emu meat.

Game birds

These are wild birds which are usually shot for sport then sent to market where a firm of game dealers pluck and dress them ready for the table. Sometimes they are sent straight to the kitchen where a larder chef will have to prepare them for cooking. It is necessary to see that no shot is left in the flesh. As shown in Figure 30,

Figure 30 Feathered game

Name	Description	Season	Average number of portions per bird	Suitable cooking methods
Capercaillie	Like a very large grouse; slightly dark flesh; tender and a very good flavour	Aug–Dec	10–12	Roasting, pies, terrines, escalopes
Grouse	Grey plumage with grey furry legs; very tender when young, up to 18 months; perhaps the best of all game birds; excellent and distinctive flavour	12 Aug–15 Dec	1–2	Roasting Old birds – pies, puddings, terrines
Partridge	Smaller than the grouse; when young and plump, very tender; the grey-legged partridge is better quality than the red-legged; excellent delicate flavour	Oct–Feb	1	Roasting Old birds – braising
Pheasant	A largish bird; the cock bird is very beautiful but the hen is usually much plumper and more tender; the flesh is whitish but inclined to be dry and needs to be larded and well basted when roasted; needs to be hung for some time to develop its gamey yet excellent and delicate flavour	Oct–Feb	2–4	Roasting, poêling Old birds – braising
Plover	Small plump bird, the best for eating being the golden, grey and green plovers; they are now mostly protected species in the UK and thus rarely available; excellent, delicate and distinctive flavour	Oct–Feb	1	Roasting
Quail	Small, plump and very fatty bird mostly reared commercially on quail farms; should be eaten very soon after being killed; good texture, tender and very good delicate flavour	All year	2 per portion	Roasting
Snipe	A small marsh-feeding bird with long legs and bill, dark flesh, good texture and excellent flavour	Aug–Mar	2 per portion	Roasting
Teal	Small species of wild duck; pronounced flavour which is sometimes fishy; needs to be young and if roasted not overcooked	Aug–Mar	1	Roasting, braising
Wild duck	In the UK this refers to the Mallard; very dark flesh which can be lean and tough if not young and carefully selected; strong pronounced flavour which can sometimes be fishy	Aug–Mar	2	Roasting
Woodcock	Similar in appearance to the snipe but larger; enjoys a high reputation for gastronomic excellence	Oct–Feb	1	Roasting

there are closed seasons when it is illegal to shoot game, so unless frozen birds are used, feathered game is a seasonal commodity. The quality of a game bird is shown by its plump breast, the spurs on its legs, and the end of the breastbone which should be soft and pliable.

L'Extravagance Culinaire d'Aldermen

This title was given by Alexis Soyer (1809–59) to a dish he prepared for a feast held in the Guildhall at York on the 25th of October 1850. It was a magnificent function for 260 mayors and aldermen, hosted by the Lord Mayor of London with the Prince Consort as guest of honour. Soyer was at that time a cult chef who kept himself in the public eye whilst running the kitchens at the Reform Club in St James. He invented the dish and served it to the top table only, the other 240 guests eating the by-products.

He ordered 180 items of different kinds of poultry and game birds, including chickens, ducks, turkeys, pheasants and grouse, from which he removed the two smallish pieces of flesh attached to the carcass when the birds' legs were removed. The French term for these is 'sots l'y laisses'. Each of the privileged guests received 20 pieces sautéed and garnished à la Toulousaine, with the addition of a boned and stuffed bunting, a trussed crayfish, asparagus tips and turtle meat. The other guests had the more common remains of the birds.

The Extravagance became known as the 100 guinea dish because the cost of the ingredients came to 105 guineas or £110.50. It isn't known if Soyer served this innovatory and sumptuous dish at any other functions over which he presided, certainly not in Ireland where he set up soup kitchens during the famines of the 1840s to feed and nourish the starving population.

Game animals

The various kinds of deer, both wild and farmed, and hares and rabbits come under the heading of furred game. It is now also possible to feature wild boar on the menu as these are being raised on farms in this country, though they are still hunted in the forests of Europe.

Venison is the flesh of deer, including the fallow, roe and red deer, and is distinguished by its deep reddish-brown colour. It should be obtained from an animal of up to four years of age to ensure tenderness. Gamekeepers send their animals to game dealers who skin and prepare them into sides for hanging to allow the meat to mature. The Game Act covers seasonal availability.

A hare also improves if it is hung downwards for a few days after it has been

Figure 31   Furred game

Name	Description	Season	Average number of portions per bird	Suitable cooking methods
Venison	Dark flesh with little fat; excellent if slightly strong flavour; often needs larding and marinating for many preparations; the flesh of older animals can be very tough and stringy	July–March	Depends on size and weight	Roasting, stewing, braising, grilling
Hare	Dark flesh with a pronounced gamey flavour; can be tough with a coarse texture in older animals; needs marinating for many preparations; be careful of splintered bones and shot	Aug–March	6–8	Stewing, roasting
Rabbit	Whitish flesh with a delicate almost chicken-like flavour, tender and of good texture; do not hang for long as the flesh quickly develops taint; beware of splintered bones and pellets in those that have been shot	All year	4–6	Stewing, roasting

skinned and drawn. The diaphragm should be left untouched so the blood can be used in the preparation of jugged hare. A young animal is preferable as its flesh is less stringy.

As with hare, a young rabbit is preferable because it will be more tender and tasty, plump, fresh-smelling and with white flesh. Fresh and frozen rabbit is always available.

Figure 31 gives brief details of the main kinds of furred game. Other wild or exotic meats include bison, kangaroo, alligator and crocodile, all available from specialist suppliers. Some are reared on farms. The alligator meat comes from the Yangtse river in China, the crocodile from Zimbabwe.

Fish

In most catering establishments fish is the second most important commodity after meat. It is a very versatile commodity – there are many different kinds on the market which can be used in a variety of different ways on several courses of the menu. Fish is also nutritionally good whether fresh or frozen, salted, smoked, pickled or canned.

Fish is a perishable commodity that deteriorates quickly if not stored in a fish refrigerator or under crushed ice to keep it moist.

Quality points of fresh whole fish include prominent bright eyes; deep red-coloured gills; moist, glazed skin with any natural scales intact; a fresh smell; and firmness to the touch. Fillets of fish must be cleanly cut and of an even size and weight according to specification.

Salt-water fish

This refers to fish caught in the oceans which are available in commercial quantities either in fresh or frozen form. Most salt-water fish are in season all year round, although bad weather can affect availability and price. Some are farmed, so the seasons do not apply to them. Figure 32 gives details of the salt-water fish which are generally available, divided into white fish and oily fish.

Freshwater fish

Fish from the rivers and lakes are not generally available commercially except for salmon and trout; apart from these, freshwater fish do not often appear on menus. Figure 33 on page 144 gives details of freshwater fish in common use, divided into white fish and oily fish.

Exotic fish

Many exotic species of fish are available fresh from all over the world, either whole or as fillets in a vacuum pack which will keep fresh for several days until the package is opened. The fish listed in Figure 34 on page 145 are imported from several tropical regions, mainly from the west coast of Africa, the Seychelles, the Pacific Ocean, and the Indian Ocean and Tasman Sea around Australia. 'Aus' indicates those from Australia.

Preserved fish

Many kinds of fish are suitable for being pickled, salt cured or smoked, which preserves them for future use and adds to their taste. Various kinds of vinegar and wine together with seasoning and flavouring agents are used for pickling fish. Roll mops are a well-known example of fish treated in this way. Smoked fish is first salted then cold or hot smoked to dry it out and give added flavour and aroma. Finnan haddock, Arbroath smokies and kippers are examples of smoked fish that need further cooking before being served. Smoked salmon and smoked trout are eaten without further cooking. Some of these items are sold in vacuum packs.

No special storage is needed for pickled fish in hermetically sealed jars; if home-made it should be kept refrigerated at 8°C. Smoked fish should be kept in cold storage.

The following list gives a brief description of the pickled, cured and smoked fish in general use:

Arbroath smokie – a small size, whole smoked haddock named after the Scottish town where it is produced.

Bismark herring – a whole herring opened out flat, the bone removed; pickled in vinegar.

Figure 32   Salt-water fish

Name	Description	Best season	Suitable cooking methods
White fish			
Bass	Large round fish of up to 100 cm; silver with dark back and firm flesh; with very good flavour	Aug–Mar	Poaching, baking, grilling, steaming
Brill	Large flat fish with red-brown skin on one side and very small scales; close fairly firm texture; good flavour similar to but not quite as good as turbot, and the flesh is not as white	June–Feb	Braising, poaching, shallow frying
Cod	Fairly large round fish; grey-green skin with dark spots and silvery belly; good firm texture with clearly defined flakes, very good flavour. Small fish are known as codling	June–Feb	Boiling, poaching, grilling, shallow frying, deep frying
Coley	Medium size round fish similar to cod, having greyish-pink flesh; fairly firm texture; fair to good taste. Cheaper than many other fish. Also known as coalfish or saithe	Aug–Feb	Poaching, shallow frying, deep frying
Conger eel	Large size marine eel of up to 200 cm in length and thick in proportion; upper jaw overlaps the lower one	Mar–Oct	Stewing, bouillabaisse
Dab	Small flat fish with light brown skin and rough scales; fairly firm opaque texture; fair to good flavour. Usually served whole with the head removed	Sept–May	Grilling, shallow frying, deep frying
Flounder	Similar to lemon Sole	Mar–Nov	Baking, braising, poaching, shallow frying
Haddock	Medium size round fish similar to cod but with a dark patch on the shoulder and pronounced scales; good flaky texture; very good delicate flavour	Mar–Feb	Baking, poaching, shallow frying; deep frying
Hake	Medium-large round fish of the cod family but longer and narrower in proportion; slate-coloured skin; fairly firm flaky texture; very good flavour that compares favourably with haddock. Also called gem fish	June–Mar	Baking, grilling, poaching, shallow frying, deep frying
Halibut	Very large flat fish with smooth dark olive-coloured skin and marbled white underside; good firm texture that is flaky but inclined to be dry; very good flavour	June–Mar	Braising, grilling, poaching, shallow frying, deep frying
John dory	Oval body which is flat-sided with large spiny head and fins; olive-brown skin with metallic sheen; firm texture; excellent flavour that rivals that of Dover sole or turbot. Also called mirror dory	All year	Braising, poaching, shallow frying, deep frying
Monkfish	Ugly, large head, brown skin and white flesh with a sweetish flavour. Also called angler fish	All year	Braising, grilling, poaching, stewing

Figure 32   (cont.)

Name	Description	Best season	Suitable cooking methods
White fish (*cont.*)			
Plaice	Flat diamond-shaped fish with brown skin with red spots; soft texture that breaks easily; good to very good flavour that sometimes has a slightly 'muddy' taste	May–Feb	Grilling, poaching, shallow frying, deep frying
Sea bream	Round fish with large head and broad back fin; orange-red to brown skin; fairly firm, flaky texture; fair to good flavour; slightly off-white colour when cooked. Also called tarwhine	June–Feb	Baking, braising, grilling, poaching, shallow frying, deep frying
Sole, Dover	Flat fish; elongated oval shape; brown to dark grey upper skin, white underneath; close, firm texture that detaches easily from the bone when cooked; excellent flavour	May–Feb	Grilling, poaching, shallow frying, deep frying
Sole, lemon	Broad flat fish with brownish-yellow upper skin, white underneath; softer texture and much less flavour than Dover sole	May–Mar	Grilling, poaching, shallow frying, deep frying
Skate	Flat fish of the ray family; only the two triangular side pieces known as wings are used; fairly soft ribbed texture; excellent flavour. Skate is always skinned but never filleted	May–Feb	Poaching, shallow frying, deep frying
Turbot	Large flat fish; brown to dark slate-grey skin with tubercules on upper side, no scales; firm texture with pronounced flakes; excellent flavour. Small ones are called chicken turbot	Apr–Feb	Braising, grilling, poaching, shallow frying
Whiting	Medium size round fish; long compact body; grey to olive-brown on back and silver below; fairly firm and flaky texture; very good delicate flavour	June–Feb	Baking; poaching, shallow frying, deep frying
Oily fish			
Bonito	Round fish of up to 70 cm in length; member of the tuna family with stripes along the body	All year	As escabeche, grilling, shallow frying, also salted, canned
Herring	Medium size round fish with bluish-silver skin and large easily removed scales; fairly compact soft texture; excellent identifiable flavour. Herring lends itself to processing by salting and curing	May–Dec	Baking, grilling, poaching, shallow frying, pickling
Mackerel	Medium size round fish of the tuna family; dark green silvery skin marked with black wavy bands; fairly flaky, softish texture; excellent distinctive flavour. Mackerel must be used as fresh as possible	All year	Baking, grilling; poaching, shallow frying

Name	Description	Best season	Suitable cooking methods
Oily fish (cont.)			
Mullet, red	Smallish round fish with red back and silvery pink belly and big broad scales; firm, flaky texture; excellent distinctive flavour. Red mullet must be used very fresh as it quickly deteriorates. Grey mullet are also available	May–Nov	Baking, grilling, shallow frying
Pilchard	Silvery-bluish colour. Small, young ones are called sardines	Jan, Feb, April, Nov Dec	Grilling; shallow frying
Sardine	Very small round fish of pilchard family with silvery skin; compact lightly flaky texture; excellent pronounced flavour. Sardines are most usually sold in canned form	Jan, Feb, April, Nov, Dec	Grilling; shallow frying; deep frying
Sprat	Small fish of herring family, similar to sardine but with flat sides; firm texture with light opaque flakes; excellent flavour	Oct–Mar	Grilling, shallow frying
Tuna or Tunny fish	Bluefin tuna are fished around Britain's coasts and in the Mediterranean. A large round fish with compact flesh; weighs up to 200 kg	All year	Shallow frying, braising, stewing
Whitebait	Tiny round silvery fish thought to be the fry of herring, pilchard and sprat; eaten whole after deep frying giving crisp, crunchy texture; excellent distinctive flavour	Apr–Sept	Deep frying

Bloater – a whole herring first cured by salting then very lightly smoked; usually served grilled as a breakfast dish.

Buckling herring – a whole herring that has been fully smoked; can be eaten as it is purchased or further cooked.

Smoked eel – the whole eel, fully smoked; served cut into sections free from skin and bone.

Finnan haddock – a medium size haddock, boned out and opened flat with the head removed; slightly salted and lightly smoked to give a yellow colour. Served poached as a breakfast, high tea or supper dish.

Gravlax – middle cut of raw salmon, boned and skinned, flavoured with salt, sugar, pepper, chopped dill and acquavit, and marinated for 2–3 days. Eaten raw as an hors-d'oeuvre.

Kipper – a herring opened out and the centre bone and head removed; lightly salted and fully smoked to give a deep brown colour. Grilled and served as a breakfast dish.

Figure 33   Freshwater fish

Name	Description	Best season	Suitable cooking methods
White fish			
Carp	Plump round fish with olive golden-brown skin and yellowish belly; firm flaky texture; good flavour which is sometimes muddy if not correctly farmed	Oct–Apr	Baking, braising, poaching, deep frying
Pike	Elongated round fish with dusky olive-brown skin; yellow sides and silvery belly; coarse dry texture; very good flavour	Winter	Baking, poaching; stewing
Sparling or smelt	Long small round fish with silvery skin; delicate smell of cucumber; opaque, yet friable texture; excellent pronounced flavour	Sept–Mar	Baking, grilling, shallow frying, deep frying
Oily fish			
Eel	Elongated snake-like fish with brown, grey or green coloured skin; close oily texture; good distinctive flavour	All year excepting May	Braising, poaching, stewing, deep frying
Salmon	Large round fish with steely blue skin and silvery belly; firm, well-flaked texture; excellent flavour; pink to red coloured flesh	Feb–Aug	Braising, grilling, poaching, shallow frying
Salmon-trout	Round fish similar in appearance to salmon but smaller and darker skinned; firm, well-flaked texture; excellent flavour; pink to red coloured flesh that is more delicate than that of salmon. Also known as sea trout	Mar–Aug	Braising, grilling, poaching, shallow frying
Trout	Small round fish of several different species; brownish black to silvery in colour or with rainbow effect; firm finely flaked texture; excellent flavour; light creamy-brown to light pink coloured flesh	Feb–Sept All year from trout farms	Braising, grilling, poaching, shallow frying

Maatjes herring – the Dutch version of the Bismarck herring is spiced during curing.

Mackerel – available as the whole fish or fillet smoked to a golden brown, sometimes flavoured with crushed peppercorns; served as an hors-d'oeuvre.

Roll mop – the whole boned herring or a fillet of herring, rolled up with a few slices of onion and pickled in vinegar with aromats. Served as an hors-d'oeuvre.

Smoked salmon – the whole side salted, then smoked until the outside is dry but the interior still moist; served cut into very thin slices.

Salt cod – the opened and boned cod, dry salted until it becomes very hard; it will keep indefinitely; needs long soaking before being cooked.

Smoked sprats – these are cured and smoked whole for serving as an hors-d'oeuvre.

Figure 34   Exotic fish

Name	Best season	Cooking methods
Barramundi – also called freshwater perch (Aus)	Oct–Mar	All methods as for cod
Blackfish – also called drummer (Aus)	All year	Baking, deep and shallow frying; grilling
Blue grenadier (Aus)	Mar–Oct	Baking, deep and shallow frying, grilling
Boar fish (Aus)	All year	Baking, braising; poaching
Croaker – also called black drum and red drum (Aus)	All year	Baking, braising, deep and shallow frying, grilling
Dart fish – also called swallowtail (Aus)	Oct–May	Baking, shallow frying
Emperor – also called capitaine rouge, lascar and sweetlip	All year	All methods as for bream
Flathead – there are several varieties, e.g. dusky, tiger	Apr–June	Baking, deep and shallow frying, grilling
Garfish – also called needlefish	All year	Baking, frying, grilling
Grouper or groper – also called coral trout and vielle platte (Aus)	All year	Baking, braising, frying, grilling, poaching
Hapuka	All year	As for sea bass, particularly roasting
Jewfish – also called jewey and mulloway (Aus)	All year	All methods
Jack – also called horse mackerel, trevally, pompano and kingfish (Aus)	All year	Baking, braising, frying, grilling, poaching
Leather jacket – also called file fish (Aus)	All year	Braising, poaching
Murray cod (Aus)	June–Aug	All methods
Orange roughy (Aus)	All year	Shallow frying, grilling
Parrotfish (Aus)	All year, but best in June	All methods
Pomfret	All year	Baking, braising, frying, grilling, poaching
Redfish – also called ocean perch and norway haddock	All year	Baking, braising, deep and shallow frying, grilling
Ribbonfish	Apr–Aug	As darnes for baking, frying, grilling
Shark	All year	As supremes for sautéing and stewing, fins for soup
Snapper – also called bourgeoise therese and vara vara	All year	As supremes and darnes for baking, braising, grilling
Swordfish – includes marlin	All year	Baking, braising; poaching, stewing
Trumpeter (Aus)	All year	Baking, shallow frying, grilling, poaching

Smoked sturgeon – this is usually imported as whole smoked fillets, prepared in the same way as smoked salmon.

Smoked trout – whole cleaned trout of 200–300 g, smoked for use as an hors-d'oeuvre.

Fish offals

The roes and livers of certain fish are available in various forms and can be used in certain dishes including hors-d'oeuvre and savouries. The main ones in general use are:

Cod roe – available in fresh form, usually ready-boiled for further use. It is also available as smoked cod roe which is served as an hors-d'oeuvre.

Herring roe – the soft herring roe from the male fish is esteemed as a gourmet dish, being used as a garnish with fish dishes or poached and served on toast as a savoury. The hard roe from the female of the species may also be used but is not so acceptable. Soft herring roe is also obtainable in frozen and canned form.

Liver – fish liver is rich in Vitamins A and D. Cod and halibut livers are usually converted into oils for medicinal purpose.

Shellfish

There are two main groups of shellfish: crustaceans and molluscs. Crustaceans have an external articulated shell and jointed limbs; the different types are listed in Figure 35. Molluscs are soft-bodied animals contained in single or double shells; the different types are listed in Figure 36 on page 148. This group also includes the cuttlefish, octopus and squid, although they do not have shells.

All shellfish deteriorate quickly whether bought alive or cooked, and must be used soon after being caught. They should feel heavy in relation to their size, and the shells of molluscs must be tightly closed. Frozen shellfish such as prawns, crabs and lobsters are invariably cooked before freezing. The larger fresh crustaceans are bought by number and approximate weight from a wholesale fishmonger who should be able to supply every kind of shellfish.

Vegetables

Vegetables play an important part in most people's diet because they are traditionally served as an integral part of a main meal. Certain ones are served as a course on their own and others make excellent garnishes. Vegetables are also an important source of vitamins and mineral salts. Given the right care in cooking, their nutritional value can be maintained. They should not be overcooked but kept slightly crisp.

Figure 35   Crustaceans

Name	Description	Best season	Suitable cooking methods
Crab	Oval shell with two claws and eight legs; reddish-brown colour which deepens after boiling; long thickish fibrous flesh from the claws that is firm and slightly chewy; dark meat from the body is soft and moist; very good distinctive flavour	Apr–Dec	Boiling, and for further processing
Crawfish	A large lobster-like shellfish with no claws; light reddish-brown colour that stays after boiling; fairly coarse texture; good flavour not so pronounced as lobster. Also known as rock lobster or spiny lobster	Apr–Oct	Stewing, boiling, and for further processing
Crayfish	A miniature lobster-like shellfish from streams and rivers; dark blue that changes colour to bright red when cooked; smooth, firm fibrous texture; excellent flavour	Winter	Boiling, stewing
Lobster	Smooth blue shell with claws of uneven size; changes from blue to red when cooked; firm, white flesh with an excellent flavour	Apr–Nov	Boiling, grilling, stewing
Prawns	Bright grey when fresh, turning pink after cooking; firm, slightly chewy texture; excellent flavour. King prawns from warm seas are much larger than British prawns	Feb–Oct	Boiling, and for further processing
Scampi (Dublin Bay prawn)	Shellfish similar to the lobster but smaller and with more elongated claws; orange pink colour and whitish legs that do not change after cooking; softish texture that is slightly chewy; excellent distinctive flavour	Apr–Nov	Boiling, poaching, stewing, shallow frying, deep frying
Shrimps	Similar to the prawn but smaller; grey-brown to pink in colour; firm slightly chewy texture; excellent flavour	Feb–Oct	Boiling, and for further processing

Vegetables are graded by EU regulations, Class 1 being the highest quality. Good-quality vegetables are crisp, fresh, well coloured, heavy in relation to size, firm without wrinkling, and show no signs of decay. Most vegetables are available all the year round, though shortages can occur to home-produced and imported vegetables due to weather conditions and transport hold-ups.

Vegetables are usually packed well to prevent damage during transit. They are supplied in diverse units according to kind such as bunch, bundle, count, tray or sack. It is best to order leaf, flower head and legume vegetables daily for immediate use. Sacks of root vegetables can be stored for a certain length of time if there is a dry, dark storeroom available. Frozen vegetables must be kept in the deep-freeze cabinet at –18°C.

Organically farmed vegetables which have been grown without the use of

Figure 36   Molluscs

Name	Description	Best season	Suitable cooking methods
Cockle	Small bivalve with ribbed shells; chewy, rubbery texture; fair to good flavour	May–Dec	Boiling, steaming
Mussel	Long narrow bivalve with greeny-blue to black shells; partly soft and partly chewy texture; good flavour. Care must be taken that mussels are from uncontaminated waters	Sept–Mar	Boiling, and for further processing
Oyster, native	Round, flat bivalve having ridged shells; soft texture; excellent flavour. Native to Britain	Sept–Mar	Usually eaten raw; also poaching; deep frying
Oyster; cupped	Imported oysters; deep rugged shells	All year	
Scallop	Bivalve with radial ribs on shells – one flat the other convex; white flesh and orange colour roe; fibrous, chewy texture; excellent flavour		Poaching, stewing, shallow frying; deep frying
Cuttlefish	Oval shape up to 25 cm with eight short tentacles; it has an internal bag of ink and a soft bone through the middle	All year	Stewing, shallow frying
Octopus	Soft sac-like body with strong jaws, a central bag and eight tentacles; usually needs beating to tenderise it	May–Dec	Braising, stewing, shallow frying
Squid	Torpedo-shaped body with tentacles, with an ink sac and cuttle bone; similar to a cuttle fish. Small ones are called calamari	May–Oct	Stewing, poaching, shallow frying, deep frying

chemical fertilisers are viewed by many customers as being more like nature intended – tastier and healthier than vegetables produced by 'conventional' methods which rely heavily on inputs of chemicals to produce a high yield and therefore greater profit. See page 351 for information on genetically modified foods.

Figure 37 gives details of the root and green vegetables in common use – divided into roots, tubers, bulbs, leaves, flowers, fruits and seeds, legumes, and stems and stalks. Figure 38 on page 153 lists exotic vegetables which may not always be readily available.

Potatoes

Potatoes make a valuable contribution to the British diet. They are popular and versatile in use and have a good vitamin C and protein content. There are hundreds of different varieties, each with best uses; some are available nation-wide and others only locally.

The two main groups are new potatoes, which are harvested when their foliage

Figure 37   Root and green vegetables

Name	Description and quality points	Best season
Roots		
Beetroot	Round or elongated in shape with reddish-purple flesh; best when firm and round, not sprouting, and not too large; available raw or ready cooked	All year
Carrot, new	New season carrots should be used immediately; should be of a reasonable size for preparation and of good colour	May–June
Carrot, old	Should be firm, of good shape and stubby rather than over-elongated, unblemished especially during winter months, of a good colour, and not split or broken	All year
Celeriac	Variety of celery; the thick turnip-like root only is used; should be firm and heavy in relation to size, not damaged or rotting; discolours quickly whilst being prepared	Autumn–Winter
Parsnip	Long white to yellow tapering root; best when medium size; should be fresh looking, without blemish or soft brown patches; the flavour is improved after having been touched by frost before being pulled	Autumn–Winter
Radish	Pungent small root of many varieties, some round, oval or long and tapering. Select when young, not too large and firm; should have a good colour with fresh green leaves and should not be split	Spring–Autumn
Salsify	Long white root which should be firm and not too thin or too thick; also known as the oyster plant; scorzonera is a larger variety with black skin	Autumn and Winter
Swede	Large turnip-shaped root with yellow flesh; should be firm and without blemish, not too dirty and heavy in relation to size. The smaller ones have the better flavour	All year except Jul–Sept
Turnip	Swollen root with white flesh, either round or elongated; should be firm and unblemished; should not be spongy or wormholed. The small early season ones are crisper and better flavoured	May–Feb
Tubers		
Artichoke, Jerusalem	A very knobbly tuber with white watery flesh; best when not too small or too misshapen; should not be wrinkled or flabby but firm and crisp	Dec–Feb
Potatoes	Should be firm, well shaped, free from blemishes, not tinged with green, and without too much soil attached. See Figure 39 for list of varieties	All year
Potatoes; sweet	Similar in shape to the potato with very soft sweetish flavour somewhat perfumed; usually served as a vegetable rather than as a potato; should be firm, heavy and evenly coloured	All Year
Bulbs		
Chives	Small thin member of the onion family with very delicate flavour; should be bright green and freshly cut with no discoloured stems or flowers	Spring–Summer

Figure 37   (cont.)

Name	Description and quality points	Best season
Bulbs (*cont.*)		
Garlic	Round white bulb divided into many segments called cloves; strong pronounced smell and flavour; should be dry and firm to pressure with unbroken outer skin and no signs of sprouting	All year
Leek	A member of the onion family; best with long white stems shading to pale then to dark green at the top; should be plump, clean and unblemished with no signs of wilting or yellowness	All year except May
Onion	Perhaps the most widely used flavouring for cooking. Should be firm, dry, compact in shape, even in size and have no signs of sprouting; moistness and softness to pressure is a sign of decay. There are many varieties, the large Spanish onion being the mildest in flavour. If stored properly it will keep well for some months	All year
Onion, button	These are the first onions to be cropped just after they have formed a nice round bulb; should be of even graded size, small and with no signs of sponginess or sprouting	Summer
Onion, spring	These are the thinnings of the onion bed; should not be too bulbous at the root and should have a good colour ranging from white to dark green with no signs of wilting or discoloration	Spring– Summer
Shallot	Member of the onion family with many varieties; usually small, compact shape but a tendency to grow into separate cloves; colour of the flesh ranges from light green to pale violet; should be firm without any sprouting; any softness or sponginess is usually a sign of decay	All year
Leaves		
Brussels sprouts	Variety of cabbage which produces small round growths called sprouts in the axils of its leaves all along the central stem; should be small, tight and compact and of a good bright green colour	Sept–Nov
Cabbage, green	Member of the Brassica family of which there are many varieties, some smooth-leaved and others curly-leaved such as the Savoy cabbage; select those which have a good colour with unblemished leaves	All year except April and May
Cabbage, spring	Early season cabbage which has not yet developed much in the way of heart; very tender and of a very good colour when not overcooked; should be fresh and crisp without blemished leaves	Jan– Mar
Cabbage, red	Should be firm and compact with a good reddish purple colour; reject if there is too much opening of the leaves and any sign of limpness or dehydration	Aug–Feb
Cabbage, white	Very heavy in relation to size, very firm and close texture, and pale green to white in colour. Also called Dutch cabbage	All year

Name	Description and quality points	Best season
Leaves (cont.)		
Cabbage, Chinese	Also known as Chinese leaves; looks like a cross between a large cos lettuce and a celery but larger and heavier; long white leaves that are very crisp; reject if limp and wilted. Also known as pak-choi	All year
Chard	This is the name given to the leaves of a beet grown mainly as a leafy vegetable; dark green in colour with whitish mid-ribs. Best when young and fresh; when old can be very stringy. The mid-ribs can be stripped and cooked separately like sea-kale	Autumn–Winter
Chicory	Has longish thin stalks, white at the base to a green frizzy top; should look fresh and be crisp without any blemishes. The long thin root is roasted and blended with coffee	Summer
Corn salad	Small deep green leaves on a small stem; should be fresh without wilted or blemished leaves	Spring
Endive, Belgian	Variety of cultivated chicory; has closely packed, long blanched leaves which are just yellowy green at the top; should be selected when very firm and unopened and with no signs of brown on the outside leaves	All year
Kale, curly	Dark green, curly leaves without any heart; select when crisp, unblemished and not too many stalks	Jan–Mar
Lettuce, cabbage	Similar in shape to a small cabbage; should be crisp with a good firm heart; check for rotting leaves or browning in the centre of the heart	Apr–Sept
Lettuce, cos	Elongated shape, deep green in colour with close-packed leaves; should be crisp and unblemished with no signs of brown rust disease	Summer
Lettuce, iceberg	Large, light green, crisp, densely packed leaves; should feel heavy in relation to size and very firm	All year
Lettuce, little gem	Small size, compact, resembles a miniature cabbage	
Sorrel	Broad green leaves that look similar to dock leaves; should be fresh looking and crisp with no discoloration; used as a garnish rather than as a vegetable	Spring
Spinach	Fresh-looking green leaves; best without too much hard stalk; should not be sandy or dirty	Aug–Nov
Watercress	Best when packed in named grower's bunch; should be bright green with short stalks and no discoloured leaves	All year
Flowers		
Artichoke, globe	A member of the thistle family; only the unopened flower head is used; should be tight and close packed. Large ones provide the artichoke bottom which is the flat part out of which the flower grows. Small varieties can be eaten whole when young	June–Sept
Broccoli	There are many varieties of this vegetable which is similar to cauliflower though having a smaller head and of different colours – white, dark green and purple. Select well-shaped and close-packed flower heads with no wilting green leaves on the outside. There are early sprouting varieties	Feb–Sept

Figure 37   (cont.)

Name	Description and quality points	Best season
Flowers (cont.)		
Cauliflower	A variety of cabbage used for its unopened flower head which is referred to as the 'curd'. This should be well formed, tightly packed, of a good white to light yellow colour and with no signs of spotting. Reject any where the flower is opening and loose	All year except April
Fruits and seeds		
Aubergine	Elongated pear-shape, dark purple in colour with yellowy flesh; should be plump, firm and glossy with no signs of wrinkling or other blemishes	June–Oct
Courgette	Small baby marrow; best when not too large; should be crisp and firm with no signs of blemish on the skin	May–Aug
Cucumber	Many varieties, of which the most commonly used are hothouse cultivated. The small variety is known as the gherkin. The best quality salad cucumbers should be selected fresh and crisp with no signs of flabbiness, preferably as straight as possible, approx. 25 cm in length and not too thick	All year
Marrow	Should be young and firm though the skin must not be hard but a good dark green colour; best size is approx. 30 cm long	June–Sept
Pimento	Hollow pod with a few seeds; crisp shiny outside with short stem; available as green, red and yellow varieties; also called peppers or capsicums. Should feel firm and crisp and have no signs of wrinkling or flabbiness	
Sweetcorn	The seed of the Indian corn or maize plant, frequently served on the head (cob); these should be young, well filled, and covered with fresh green leaves; the grains should be milky looking in colour and soft; they should not be hard and yellow	Jul–Sept
Tomato	Many varieties of a branching plant, which bears a bright red fruit; should be firm, of even shape and a good colour. Also available as cherry and beef varieties and in sun-dried form	All year
Legumes		
Bean, Broad	A large, broad pod which should not be flabby or going dark; best when young and well filled with small beans which do not require skinning when cooked	Jun–Aug
Beans, French	A green pod which is eaten whole or cut when the beans inside are barely formed; should be stringless, crisp, straight, flat and not showing the shape of the beans through the pod	June–Dec
Beans, runner	Another green pod eaten usually sliced; best when young and small; should snap crisply; reject if too large, flabby, dry, yellowish in colour, or the shape of the beans is showing through the pod	Jul–Sept
Mangetout	A flat green pea pod cooked and eaten whole; should be crisp, very green in colour and not too large or broad	Summer

Name	Description and quality points	Best season
Legumes (cont.)		
Peas	A green pod of which the peas only are eaten; should be plump and crisp without being over full or too tight and of a good green colour. Usually purchased ready-shelled	May–Sept
Stems and stalks		
Asparagus	A plant of the lily family of which the young shoots are used as a vegetable; select when straight with tight unopened heads; wrinkling and browning at the stalk ends is a sign of staleness. Good varieties include Lauris, Evesham, Argenteuil, Malines and Genoa. The thinnings are sold in bundles under the name of sprue	May–July
Celery	A plant cultivated for its long leaf stalks; best when white and crisp with a good firm heart; check for discoloration insect damage to the interior	All year
Fennel	A plant of which the swollen base of the leaf stalks form a very tight bulbous shape; should be white with little green showing; check for splitting or brown discoloration	June–Oct
Kohlrabi	The swollen base-stem of a member of the Brassica family; looks very similar in some respects to the turnip; should be not too large but firm and heavy in relation to size; if too large and old kohlrabi are inclined to be woody	Apr–Jul
Seakale	A plant cultivated for its leaf stalks which are usually blanched and forced; should be a good whitish colour without blemishes and be crisp and firm	Dec–June

Figure 38   Exotic vegetables

Name	Description and quality points
Bean Sprouts	Quick growing, elongated with sprouting tops; very low in calories; used mainly in Chinese dishes and raw in salads
Breadfruit	Round, oval or pear-shaped fruit, the size of a small melon; some are seedless; taste is similar to a sweet potato
Christophine	Tastes like marrow and cucumber; looks like a ridged green or white pear or may have a smooth skin
Dasheen	Large tuber up to 20 cm long with brown, hairy skin; use as for potatoes. Eddoe is a small version
Mooli	Resembles a long radish or parsnip; smooth white skin and bitter taste
Paksoi	Similar in looks to Chinese leaves but with dark green shoots and thick stem

Figure 39   Main crop potato varieties

Name	Description and quality points	Suitable uses
Alcamaria	Pale yellow skin and flesh; waxy; long oval shape	Boiling, salad
Cara	White skin with pink eyes; creamy flesh; round to oval	Boiling, baking, roasting, chips
Desirée	Red skin and yellowish flesh; firm texture; mild flavour	Mashed, chips
Dunbar Standard	White skin; mealy texture; mild flavour	Mashed, chips
Estima	Light yellow skin and flesh; oval shape	Boiling, baking, chips
Golden Wonder	Russet brown skin; floury texture; distinctive flavour	Roasting, baking, crisps
Kerry's Pink	Pinkish white skin; floury consistency	Roasting, baking, chips
King Edward	White skin with patches of pink; floury	Roasting, baking, mashed
Linzer Delicatess	Yellow skin; firm texture; small elongated shape	Salads
Maris Piper	White skin; creamy flesh; floury; oval shape	Baking, boiling, roasting, chips
Pentland Dell	White skin; creamy flesh; floury; oval shape	Baking, chips
Pentland Squire	White skin and flesh; floury; round to oval shape	Baking, roasting
Pink Fir Apple	Pinkish skin; yellow waxy flesh; irregular shape	Salads
Romano	Pink skin and creamy flesh; waxy texture, creamy flesh; round to oval shape	Baking, boiling, Roasting, chips
Wilja	Rough yellow skin; pale yellow flesh; elongated oval shape	Boiling, baking, chips
Nadine	Fairly large round shape; firm texture	Boiling, baking, chips

is still green, and main crop potatoes, which are not harvested until their foliage has died back. The best known new potatoes are Jersey Royals, Maris Bard and Carlingford, but other kinds are imported. Figure 39 lists the names of the best known main crop potatoes and their optimum uses.

Potatoes

There are more than 120 different kinds of potato, but only about 30 kinds available commercially. Each variety has its own quality of texture, taste, cooking uses, size, shape and skin colour. Britons eat at least 2 kg a week on average, mainly in the form of chips, mashed, roast or boiled, as an accompaniment to a main item of fish or meat.

Recipe books give dozens of ways of using potatoes, as a vegetable, a garnish, and in a supper dish as the main ingredient. They can be featured in each course from hors-d'oeuvre to relévé. They can also be used in making pastry and rolls.

Potatoes contribute a quarter of the daily adult requirement of vitamin C and contain 2 per cent protein, 1 per cent mineral salts, 2 per cent dietary fibre, 15 per cent starch, 79 per cent water, and a little fat; a standard 100 g portion yields 80 kilocalories.

Potatoes have played an important part in the British diet since the end of the eighth century and will continue to do so. New potatoes are harvested from March to July whilst the foliage is still green. Main crop potatoes are called old potatoes and are not harvested until the foliage has died back.

Despite the premium price obtained for the earliest Jersey Royals, potatoes are still the cheapest kind of vegetable though the price is increasing gradually each year. A few years ago potatoes fetched £169 per tonne, but by 1996 they had increased in value to £356 per tonne and are likely to follow this upward trend.

Two varieties of sweet potato are also available. One has yellow flesh and a dry, mealy texture. The other has darker orange flesh and is sweeter and more moist; it is also known as a yam. Both varieties have brown skins.

Edible fungi

Edible fungi should look fresh and clean with tight gills; they dry out and wilt quickly and should not be washed until they are wanted for cooking. The best-known varieties are listed in Figure 40 on page 156.

Pulse vegetables

Pulses are the edible seeds of leguminous plants which are removed from their pods and dried. Pulses in general use include lentils, split peas, marrowfat peas, chick peas, butter beans, haricot beans and kidney beans. They should be dry but not dried out, have a good natural colour, and be fairly fresh so that prolonged soaking is not necessary before cooking.

Cooked pulses can be made into hors-d'oeuvres, soups, salads, pâtés and are useful for vegetarian and ethnic dishes. The soya bean is a very useful pulse, being the base for soy sauce, a meat analogue and tofu as used in Japanese cookery.

Fruit

Fruits are used throughout the menu because their distinctive flavours marry well with many fish and meat dishes. Fruits and fruit juices make good first courses; fruit soups are popular, especially cold ones; savoury and sweet fruit salads are old favourites; and every category of the sweet course uses fruit. The fruit basket

Figure 40   Edible fungi

Name	Description and quality points	Best season
Cep	Also known as the flap mushroom; very fleshy, wide and flat and brown in colour. Select when young and fresh with minimal damage	Autumn
Chanterelle	Irregular funnel shape; bright egg yellow in colour; toughish texture; aroma of apricots and slight taste of pepper. Inclined to be fragile when raw, so select as undamaged as possible	Summer and Autumn
Field	White or brown, silky smooth cap which is flat or convex; light pink gills; excellent for frying and grilling whole	Autumn
Morel	Has an irregularly pitted cap which is somewhat conical in shape; yellowish-brown in colour with a white short stalk. Select when young and fresh	Autumn
Mushroom	The cultivated mushroom rather than the field mushroom is now more generally used in catering and is available in three grades: buttons which should be small, firm and white with no signs of opening; caps which are larger, partially opened but still white and firm; and flats which are the fully opened mushroom, darker in colour and much larger. All mushrooms should be selected when fresh, unbroken and unblemished	Cultivated all year; (field July–Oct)
Oyster mushroom	Brown-grey in colour; shaped like an ear; their delicate flavour needs careful cooking	Cultivated all year
Shiitake	Grows on wood of dead trees; usually sold dried for soaking before use mainly in oriental dishes	All year
St George	Looks like a field mushroom with a white to yellow cap and thick stalk; the gills are closely packed. A fragile fungus with a strong flavour	Summer and Autumn
Truffle	Black with hard, rough skin; should be even in size with very strong flavour and aroma; the best come from the Perigord region in France. White truffles have a more pronounced flavour and are mostly found in the Piedmont region of Italy	

for dessert and fruit petit fours completes the list, not forgetting crystallised, dried, glacéd and candied fruits.

Figure 41 gives details of fruits in common use – divided into hard, citrus, stone, soft and other fruits. Figure 42 on page 159 lists exotic fruits which may not always be readily available.

Figure 41   Fruits in common use

Name	Description and quality points	Best season
Hard fruits		
Apple, cooking	Many varieties, the best known being the Bramley; should be even, firm and unblemished. Best flavour when picked late and stored for some time	Autumn–Spring
Apple, dessert	Many varieties including imports from several countries; should be of medium size, a pleasing colour, firm and have a good aroma. Good eating varieties include Cox's Orange Pippin, Golden Delicious, Laxton and Granny Smith	All year
Pear	Best known varieties are Williams, Comice, Beurre Hardy, Conference; should be medium size, even shape, firm and juicy, and not over-ripe	All year
Citrus fruits		
Grapefruit	Imported from many countries, all mainly of good quality. Choose large size fruit with smooth firm skin and even colour; should be heavy and juicy; some pink-fleshed ones are available	All year
Lemon	Used for flavouring and garnishing only; select even, oval shape, with good yellow skin which should be thin; must be juicy and with not too many pips	All year
Mandarin	Mandarin, tangerine, clementine and satsuma are all small varieties of the orange. They have slight differences of size and flavour; some have loose skins but most should feel firm	Winter
Orange	Two main varieties, the Valencia and the Navel, the latter being seedless; they should be firm, ripe, of a good colour and juicy. Many hybrid varieties are available, including Ortanique, Shamouti, Tambor and Temple	All year
Stone fruits		
Apricot	Pale to deep orange colour; nice aroma and flavour. Check for bruising	Summer and Autumn
Cherry	Available as yellow, red, dark red and black varieties; also the Morello cherry for garnishing. Check for ripeness and freedom from blemish	Spring and Summer
Damson	Looks like a small plum; deep blue colour; used for cookery	Sept
Greengage	A variety of plum, yellow to green in colour; used when of a good size and ripe as a dessert fruit, but mainly used for cooking	Aug–Oct
Nectarine	Very similar to a peach, but with a smooth skin and not usually so large; care should be taken that they are ripe, with the flesh firm but juicy. Check for bruising	Summer
Peach	A round stone fruit with velvety skin; golden-yellow and red in colour with white or yellow-orange flesh and a distinctive flavour; should be firm but juicy. Good-quality fruit imported from Italy and France. English hothouse peaches are available during the winter but are expensive	Summer

Figure 41   (cont.)

Name	Description and quality points	Best season
Stone fruits (cont.)		
Plum	Oval stone fruit with smooth skin. There are many varieties with different colour skins ranging from yellow to dark purple. Some large varieties such as the Victoria plum make excellent dessert fruits when ripe and juicy. Check for bruising and insect damage	Aug–Sept
Soft fruits		
Blackberry	These grow wild, but cultivated varieties have a better flavour and are larger. Check carefully for insect damage and maggots	Aug–Oct
Cranberry	A small dark red berry with a very tart taste used mainly for a sauce. Select those of a good even red colour. Check for rotting berries and unwanted stalks	All year
Currant, black, red and white	These should be bold in size, fresh, juicy and with not too much stalk; used mostly for cooking	July–Aug
Gooseberry	The small green ones are used for cooking; the larger varieties, when ripe may be served as a dessert fruit	June–Aug
Loganberry	This resembles a raspberry but has a soft seedless flesh; used mainly for cooking	July–Aug
Raspberry	These should be whole, large, fragrant and sweet; it is advisable to examine underneath the contents of punnets as mouldiness starts very quickly here; do not store for any length of time	June and July
Strawberry	Many varieties are grown; choose medium size fruit which have a good red colour and are sweet, well flavoured, and clean and fresh	June–Aug
Wild strawberry	Cultivated ones are available; should be small and multi-coloured with a wonderful aroma and flavour	Summer
Other fruits		
Avocado pear	Dark, shiny green to purple skin which can be smooth or rough; used mainly as a savoury fruit; imported from Israel, USA, southern Africa. Select when ripe with soft flesh but firm to the touch. Mottled brown skin can be a sign of being over-ripe	All year
Banana	These are picked whilst green and ripened for sale; should be yellow, firm and unbruised, and in bunches rather than loose	All year
Fig	Fresh figs are green to deep purple in colour with a smooth skin and reddish pulp. Select when unblemished and fairly firm to the touch; should not be split or over-soft	Autumn
Grape	These are available as black or white; they should be plump and in neat bunches with their bloom unblemished and with no bad ones discernable. Belgian hothouse and Cape grapes are best for dessert	All year

Name	Description and quality points	Best season

Other fruits (cont.)

Name	Description and quality points	Best season
Melon	These should be firm, heavy and without blemishes; fragrant varieties include Cantaloup, Charentais, Honeydew, Musk and Ogen. A ripe melon will have a pronounced perfume and be soft to touch at the flower end	All year
Pineapple	These should be fairly firm, heavy, fragrant, have fresh-looking leaves, browny-yellow skin, and a good shape and size; they should be stored in a humid atmosphere	All year
Rhubarb	Although strictly a vegetable stalk, rhubarb is classified as a fruit as far as catering is concerned. The stalks should be a good colour, firm and straight, with not too much leaf; forced rhubarb is pale pink and has thin stalks, outdoor is red and has thick stalks. Reject if limp and discolored	Apr–June

Figure 42   Exotic fruits

Name	Description and quality points
Carambola	Usually referred to as star fruit because the wings resemble a five-pointed star; thin yellowy waxy skin and sweet-and-sour taste
Custard apple	Oval pear shape; yellow skin with reddish markings; served cut in half for eating with a spoon. Also known as anona fruit
Guava	Plum or pear-shaped fruit with thin green to yellow skin and a ring of seeds inside; its sweet smell is better than its musky taste
Kumquat	A tiny orange with a thin rind and aromatic smell; eaten whole and raw or cut into slices
Kiwi fruit	Egg shape with furry brown skin; deep green flesh with black seeds and tangy flavour
Lichee	Small oval fruit with a hard mottled skin; pearly, jelly-like flesh and scented flavour and aroma
Loquat	Yellow-orange coloured skin; looks like a small plum. Also known as Japanese medlar
Mango	Fairly large yellow-orange coloured round or oval fruit with a large clingstone and sweet-smelling flesh
Mangosteen	Round fruit with thickish browny-purple skin; plump white segments with a very fragrant taste and smell
Passion fruit	Egg shape with a hard wrinkled browny-purple skin and acidy-sweet flesh with black, edible seeds. Also known as granadilla
Pawpaw	Shiny yellow skin and pinky-apricot flesh with dark grey, edible seeds in the centre; usually served sprinkled with lime juice
Persimmon	Resembles a large orange-coloured tomato with a prominent calyx; the sweet-tasting flesh is eaten when the fruit is very ripe, using a spoon. Also known as the sharon fruit or kaki
Rambutan	Small, dark reddish-brown fruit with a furry skin and long seed; can be peeled, deseeded and cut into slices or served like a soft-boiled egg

Figure 43   Nuts

Name	Description and quality points
Almond	Oval in shape; very distinctive flavour; used for dessert and as shelled, split, nibbed, flaked, ground or shredded for pastry and kitchen use
Brazil	Slightly curved and elongated three-sided nut, used mainly for dessert
Cashew	Small kidney-shaped nut usually served roasted and salted
Chestnut	Shiny brown, round nuts similar to a horse chestnut; used mainly in pastry work but also in the kitchen; sold candied as Marrons Glacés
Hazelnut	Small round nuts; used in pastry work and for dessert; also referred to as a filbert
Macadamia	Good-quality nut similar to a cashew nut; also known as Queensland nuts because they are grown there
Peanut	Oval-shape, light brown and available in the shell, skinned and with skin on; used salted in the bar and at receptions
Pine kernel	Very small nut obtained from various species of pine cones, mainly in Italy; used mainly for pastry work
Pecan	Similar in shape and taste to the walnut, but smoother and sweeter; used mainly for serving at cocktail parties
Pistachio	Small soft, green-fleshed nut covered with a purple-green skin; used mainly for cooking purposes
Walnut	Has a light brown crenellated double shell; used for dessert, pastry work and in the kitchen
Water chestnut	This is actually a tuber grown in China and Southeast Asia. It is used as garnish or a vegetable in Chinese dishes; and available mainly in cans, cooked in water

Nuts

Nuts have many uses in cookery. They are mainly used in the pastry department, in ground and whole forms, for cakes, pastries and petits fours. However, they can also be used as garnishes and in pâtés and stuffings. With a selection of fruit they form part of the dessert. Shelled nuts are appreciated in the bar with drinks.

Nuts in shells should be bold and heavy; shelled nuts should look clean, fresh and even in size, and feel heavy in relation to their size. Most nuts are imported. The best selection of nuts in shells is timed to coincide with Christmas. Shelled and ground nuts should not be stored for too long as they quickly lose their flavour, aroma and crispness. Figure 43 lists the nuts in general use.

Dairy produce

Dairy produce refers to commodities which are based on milk, including cream, yoghurt, ice-cream, butter and cheese. Eggs are also discussed under this heading. Dairy products are an important source of protein and calcium.

Milk

Milk is used widely in catering in many different drinks and dishes. Most milk is pasteurised to destroy bacteria, which means it is heated to 72°C for 15 seconds and then cooled rapidly. It is available in many different forms:

- **Homogenised milk** – the fat content is distributed evenly throughout the milk.
- **Semi-skimmed milk** – approximately 1.5 per cent fat.
- **Skimmed milk** – less than 0.3 per cent fat.
- **Channel Island milk** – milk from Jersey and Guernsey breeds containing nearly 5 per cent fat.
- **Sterilised milk** – homogenised milk heated in the bottle to 100°C for 20–30 minutes. It will keep for several weeks without refrigeration.
- **UHT milk** – homogenised milk heated to 132°C for 1–2 seconds then poured into containers and sealed. It will keep for several months. Also known as long-life milk.
- **Evaporated milk** – the water content is distilled off to leave a concentrated form of milk. It is bought in cans.
- **Condensed milk** – skimmed milk is mixed with water and then boiled under pressure until it reduces to a sticky consistency. It is bought in cans.
- **Dried milk** – produced by evaporating the water from liquid fresh milk until it forms solids.

Fresh milk should be kept refrigerated at 5°C and used within one or two days. Dried milk powder should be kept in an airtight container.

Cream

Cream is used to add richness to dishes, and as a garnish or for decoration purposes. It is separated from milk by mechanical centrifuge and then made available in the following forms:

- **Single cream** – 18 per cent fat; does not whip.
- **Double cream** – 48 per cent fat; keeps its shape when whipped and piped for decoration.
- **Whipping cream** – 40 per cent fat; used for decorating cakes.
- **Soured cream** – soured by bacteria to give a savoury, piquant taste; suitable for use in many dishes, especially those of Russia, eastern Europe and Scandinavia.
- **Creme fraîche** – pasteurised cream with the addition of a culture that gives it a slight acid taste and thick richness.
- **Clotted cream** – 55 per cent fat; heated to 82°C to produce its characteristic flavour.
- **Aerosol cream** – long-life cream in aerosol cans for squirting directly on to foods. The effect collapses quickly.

All fresh creams must be refrigerated at 5°C.

Yoghurt

Yoghurt is made by treating pasteurised skimmed milk with a bacterial culture which is then incubated to give the desired taste and texture. *Lactobacillis bulgaricus* and *Streptoccus thermophilus* are the cultures used. Plain yoghurt can be set, which is like junket, or stirred, which is smooth and fairly thick. Many of the flavoured yoghurts have a stabiliser or thickener to suspend the fruit pieces or purée or other flavourings. Frozen yoghurt is also available, either in low-fat or creamy form. As well as being a dessert in its own right, yoghurt can be used to finish soups, sauces and stews, for dips and salad dressings, and in pastry work.

Ice-cream

Whether bought from a manufacturer or made on the premises, ice-cream must be stored at –20°C. When required for service, the estimated amount should be transferred to an ice-cream service cabinet set to operate at –18°C (0°F).

The Ice-cream Regulations 1967 specify the minimum percentage amounts of fat and sugar that ice-cream must contain. When the mixture is made it must be pasteurised by heating to 69°C and held there for 30 minutes, or at 80°C and held for 15 seconds. It must then be cooled to 7°C within one and a half hours and frozen quickly using a recording thermometer. A record must be kept of its production. Its serving temperature must not be higher than –2°C.

It is advisable to make sorbet for immediate use as it loses its taste and texture by long storage. Ready-made sorbet is kept at –18°C so that it does not go rock hard and lose its original consistency when served.

Butter

Britain, Denmark, France, Holland and New Zealand are the biggest exporters of butter. Each has its own characteristics and price.

All butter is made by churning fresh cream. English butter is sold as sweet cream butter which is mild and smooth, usually salted and possibly coloured; it may not contain more than 16 per cent water. Butter made from cream that has been allowed to ripen is made with a lactic acid culture which helps to accelerate the ripening process and gives a very slight sour taste to the finished result; often it is salt-free. Blended butter is made by mixing several kinds together which gives it a softer texture.

Many flavoured butters are available including garlic, herb, rum and brandy. Concentrated butter, which has a fat content of 96 per cent, is ideal for cooking purposes. Ghee is butter that has been clarified to eliminate the milky deposit.

Butter can be bought in 12.5 kg blocks and 250 g and 500 g packs, preferably in foil packaging as it can absorb other flavours. It is best kept refrigerated at 5°C and can be frozen for up to three months.

Cheese

Cheese is made from milk by souring it with a bacteria then adding rennet which causes it to clot and set. It is then cut and scalded by heating to remove all the whey, milled with the addition of dairy salt, and pressed into shape in moulds. It is then left to ripen and mature. Cheese can be classed as hard, firm, soft, cream and blue cheese, each having its own characteristics. It should be purchased according to demand and used as soon as possible to avoid drying out. Some cheeses may improve by being kept for a few days, but maturing should have been done by the supplier. It must be kept covered in a cool, clean place where it will not become hard and dry, at 5–7°C. It should be brought to room temperature in advance of service.

Figure 44 gives details of the most popular cheeses and their countries of origin. In addition to the hundreds of cheeses available, some of the traditional cheeses are now flavoured or mixed to give added interest to the cheese course under new names such as Cheviot (cheddar made with chopped chives); Charnwood (cheddar cheese smoked then coated with paprika); Huntsman (a layered cheese consisting of stilton and double gloucester); Red Windsor (cheddar cheese with a marbling of elderberry wine), and many others.

Eggs

Hen's eggs are an extremely useful and versatile commodity because they can be used in so many ways and can emulsify, enrichen, thicken, bind, coat and glaze foods. In a fresh egg, the yolk will have a good round curve and the white will cling closely around it. The colour of the shell and the yolk have no bearing on the nutritive value of the egg. Fresh eggs are graded as extra large, large, medium and small.

Other types of egg can be obtained. Frozen egg is available for use mainly in bakeries; powdered egg has been dehydrated; pasteurised egg is available as yolks alone and whole eggs, flavoured with either salt or sugar. Pasteurised egg can be kept at ambient temperatures, whereas fresh eggs are best kept in a refrigerator at 10°C. It is recommended for making cold sauces such as mayonnaise instead of fresh yolks which may carry salmonella germs. Gulls' eggs when in season are usually bought as hard-boiled, as are quails' eggs which are available all the year.

Fats and oils

Fats are non-dairy products based on animal or vegetable fat or oil, hydrogenated, flavoured and coloured according to name. Margarine is not a true substitute for butter and has its own role in catering. General-purpose margarines are suitable for table use for those who do not appreciate the quality of butter, and in all sorts of cookery. They are sold under many brand names. Cake margarine is easy to cream and has the ability to absorb the sugar and eggs. Pastry margarine gives good results for all kinds of pastry. Puff pastry margarine is made to be highly plastic so that the layers of fat and dough can be built up strongly.

Other fats include lard, which is made from the fatty tissues of pigs. It has a firm yet plastic texture and no taste or smell until it is melted for frying. It is used successfully in making pastry.

Figure 44   Cheese

Name	Country of origin	Description	Shape	Approx. weight
Hard cheese				
Parmesan	Italy	Made from cows' milk; delicate granular texture; straw colour; hard, brittle and crumbly; sharp fruity flavour; used mainly for cooking purposes	Cylinder	24–39 kg
Firm cheese				
Bel Paese	Italy	Made from cows' milk; smooth consistency; creamy colour; lactic smell and mild flavour	Thick disc	2 kg
Caerphilly	UK	Made from cows' milk; sold fresh and young; has a wettish texture; mild slightly sour flavour; white in colour	Round flat	3½ kg
Cheddar	UK	Made from cows' milk; firm texture; white to yellow colour; slightly nutty flavour; very good for cooking	Cylinder or box	18–27 kg
Cheshire	UK	Made from cows' milk; crumbly texture; available as orange or white coloured; very salty and fatty, excellent flavour	Cylinder or box	22 kg
Derby	UK	Made from cows' milk; resembles cheddar; good flavour and texture; can turn sour quickly	Rectangle	6 kg
Edam	Holland	Made from cows' milk; smooth red or yellow rind; nice round shape; rubbery texture; pale yellow colour; slightly nutty taste	Ball	1½–1¾ kg
Emmenthal	Switzerland, France	Made from cows' milk; smooth rind; yellow colour with large round holes; good aroma and flavour; firm texture	Cartwheel	80–98 kg
Gloucester, double	UK	Made from cows' milk; golden red or white colour; mild bland flavour; good texture	Cylinder	28 kg
Gouda	Holland	Made from cows' milk; stiff, yellow wax rind; little smell, bland taste; smooth texture	Round flat	3 kg
Gruyère	Switzerland, France	Made from cows' milk; smooth skin, light yellow to amber in colour; small holes spaced far apart; firm texture; good smell; fruity flavour; very good for cooking	Large	29–39 kg
Leicester	UK	Made from cows' milk; deep orange-red in colour; very mild flavour; melts quickly	Cylinder	13–18 kg
Mozzarella	Italy	Made from buffalos' milk; oval or round shape; very white with rubbery texture; strong lactic smell; mild flavour	Variable	½–1 kg

Name	Country of origin	Description	Shape	Approx. weight
Firm cheese (cont.)				
Stracchino	Italy	Made from cows' milk; pink rind, yellow colour; strong smell and fruity flavour; soft supple texture	Square	1–2 kg
Saint-Paulin	France	Made from cows' milk; smooth rind and velvet smooth texture; very mild flavour	Disc	2 kg
Wensleydale	UK	Made from cows' milk; white, slightly sour-tasting cheese that is sometimes aged to develop as a blue veined cheese	Cylinder	4½–5½ kg
Soft cheese				
Brie	France	Made from cows' milk; soft thin white rind; straw coloured; supple texture; nice smell and pronounced taste	Flat disc	1.8–3 kg
Camembert	France	Made from cows' milk; white rind; ripe flavour but not over-ripe or too runny in texture; should be slightly firm when ready to serve	Small flat disc in round box	250 g
Carré de l'Est	France	Made from cows' milk; soft white rind; smells slightly of mushrooms; bland flavour	Small square	120–260 g
Munster	France	Made from cows' milk; smooth shiny red rind; very strong smell and flavour	Disc	0.3–1.5 kg
Pont-l'Eveque	France	Made from cow's milk; smooth golden rind; nice smell and pronounced flavour; soft, supple texture	Square	350g
Cream cheese				
Boursin	France	Enriched cows' milk cream cheese; very soft texture; sold flavoured with garlic, herbs, or pepper	Square	100 g
Cottage	UK	Curd cheese made from skimmed milk with a grainy texture; low fat content	Round containers	250–500 g
Demi-sel	France	Salted cream cheese with mild flavour, wrapped in foil	Small square	75–100 g
Fromage-frais	France	Smooth soft cheese made from skimmed milk that is not left to mature; can also be used in soups, sauces and sweet dishes	Small containers	75–100 g or more
Petit-Suisse	France	Cylinders of very white unsalted cream cheese; must be eaten fresh	Small cylinder	30 g
Quark	Germany	Made with pasteurised milk in very low fat to full cream styles	Round containers	250–500 g

Figure 44   (cont.)

Name	Country of origin	Description	Shape	Approx. weight
Blue vein cheese				
Bleu d'Auvergne	France	Similar to Roquefort but made from cows' milk; strong smell and sharp flavour	Flat cylinder or smaller packs of varying size	2–2½ kg
Danish Blue	Denmark	A blue veined cheese of reasonable quality, but in a different class from Stilton and Gorgonzola; rather sharp taste	Thick disc	2½–3 kg
Gorgonzola	Italy	Grey-red skin; soft runny texture and strong smell; white to yellow colour with even veining	Cylinder	6–8 kg
Mycella	Denmark	Similar to Gorgonzola; a better quality of Danish Blue	Cylinder	5–9 kg
Roquefort	France	Made from sheeps' milk; should have uniform veining, salty flavour, firm but smooth texture	Tall cylinder	2½ kg
Stilton	UK	Crinkly grey rind; abundant blue veins; good strong aroma and flavour; firm smooth texture when properly matured	Tall cylinder	4–4½ kg

Shortenings make good cakes and pastry and are produced, under various brand names, from liquid and semi-liquid oils that are hydrogenated into white fats.

Suet is made from white beef fat from around the kidney by finely grating and dusting it with rice flour; vegetable suet is made of hardened hydrogenated vegetable oil.

Vegetable, fish and animal oils are used to manufacture spreads for making sandwiches, as well as cooking fats for deep and shallow frying. They are made solid by the process of hydrogenation. Some are low in cholesterol and others are recommended for vegetarians and dieters, each with its own brand name.

Liquid oils in general use include soya bean oil, corn oil, rapeseed oil, ground-nut oil and sunflower oil. Olive oil and sunflower oil are useful for making mayonnaise. Olive oil is available as extra virgin and virgin which are the first and second pressings. Hazelnut, walnut and other oils from nuts are expensive and used mainly in salad dressings. The normal frying temperature of oil is 175–190°C, according to the kind of food being deep fried.

Meat substitutes

These products have been developed to satisfy the ever-growing demand from people who want to avoid eating any kind of meat. Statistics show that 50 per cent of the UK's population now eat meat only two to three times a week and want something else to make up their diet. They are happy to eat meatless sausages, burgers and shepherd's pies made with vegetable protein obtained from soya beans, peas, wheat and fungus, all made to resemble meat.

- Soya beans are processed into textured vegetable protein in minced or cubed form which can be made into stews, casserole, pies and made-up dishes. The milk expressed from soya beans is fermented and made into a soft yellow slab known as tofu. It has a delicate flavour and is a staple of Japanese and Chinese cuisine.
- Arrum is made of pea and wheat protein and can be used in the same way as soya bean products.
- Quorn™ is produced from a tiny fungus which grows naturally. It is fermented and processed into a pale yellow dough and formed into flakes and mince, coagulated with white of egg to prevent it disintegrating when cooked.

These meat-free substances are high in protein, low in fat, and contain little cholesterol.

Condiments and seasoning agents

These ingredients are important for adding flavour and aroma to foods before, during and after cooking, generally in small amounts. Herbs and spices should be bought in small quantities, using them while still fresh and to maintain their partic- ular aroma and flavour. Most of these items are general grocery supplies, though fresh herbs are obtained from a greengrocer. The nature of the establishment and menu will determine what kind and quantity of these items should be kept in stock. So long as they are kept airtight, no special storage conditions are required.

Salt

Salt is essential to human life, but it needs to be used with discretion as it is contained naturally in many foods as well as being used to preserve foods such as bacon, ham, cheese and fish. Salts are available for different uses, including fine table salt for filling salt-cellars; slightly coarser kitchen salt; coarse freezing salt; sea salt made of crystallised concentrated saline; bay salt made by evaporat- ing sea water; and the several flavoured salts made by adding dehydrated garlic, herbs, celery seed, onion and so on. Oriental salt is ordinary salt mixed with ground dried chillies. Low sodium salt is preferred by people on a low-salt diet.

Monosodium glutamate tastes very salty but is in fact hydrolised wheat used to give extra flavour to dishes during or after cooking, especially Chinese food.

Pepper

Pepper is a spice which grows in the form of peppercorns in several South-East Asian countries. Black peppercorns are picked in the unripened stage and sun-dried.

White peppercorns are picked when ripe on the same plant. Green peppercorns are unripe berries usually packed in brine. Red peppercorns are not true peppercorns though they have a peppery flavour; they are also sold in jars or cans packed in vinegar. Mignonette pepper is made by grinding a variety of black and white peppercorns in a peppermill.

Ground pepper is a fine cream-coloured powder, the quality of which stems from the peppercorns used to make it; poor quality pepper is greyish in colour. Cayenne pepper is very pungent because it is made of ground dried chillies and is used only sparingly in cookery. Paprika is a sweet tasting, very red coloured mild form of pepper made from red pimentoes. Tabasco is a hot pepper sauce made from fermented red chillies.

Mustard

Mustard is available in a wide range of different styles and flavours, all based on the seeds of three varieties of the mustard plants of the Cruciferae family. The main kinds are English, which is hot and strong and is bought in powder form or ready to use; French, which is usually dark, mild and acidy and is always bought ready to use; German, which is mild and sweet; and American, which is also mild and of a light colour. Other mustards are made from coarsely ground or crushed seeds, with different kinds of vinegar, with wine or verjuice, or flavoured with honey, herbs or garlic.

Vinegar

Vinegar is the fourth item in a cruet and it has a lot of uses in cookery as well as on the dining table. Malt vinegar is the best and is brewed from malted barley or wheat which gives it a dark brown colour and strong flavour. Distilled vinegar is refined malt vinegar and is colourless and quite sharp to the taste. Poorer quality vinegars are made of diluted industrial acetic acid which has been coloured and flavoured.

Other vinegars are now widely available and can be useful in dressings. Wine vinegar is available as red, white and sherry; flavoured vinegars contain tarragon, chilli, garlic or raspberry; cider vinegar is made from apple juice and is pale yellow in colour; balsamic vinegar is a matured, dark, sweet-flavoured vinegar made from the juice of the trebbiano grape, matured in oak casks.

Stock

A major fear of any chef is that he or she may one day fall foul of the environmental health officers when they come to inspect the kitchen. In the past one of the likely causes of food poisoning was the way in which the communal stock-pot was looked after – it was common practice to let it boil all day, turn it off and leave it at night, then carry on cooking it day after day, throwing in any suitable scraps. Environmental health officers have clamped down on this and insist that homemade stock is cooked to at least 63°C for not longer than 24 hours. This has led to increased use of commercial stock bases that can be made up as required, as cheaply as homemade stock. Every possible flavour is now available in paste, cube or concentrated liquid form.

Pickles, chutneys and sauces

These accompaniments are used at the table for customers to add to a plate of cold meat or on hamburgers and sausages, though the several kinds of chutney are usually served with curried foods. They are usually packed in bottles or jars under well-known proprietary brand names. The range of pickled items includes red cabbage, olives, beetroot, gherkins, small onions, walnuts, and the mixed blends such as mustard pickle, Branston and piccalilli. Chutney is made from mango, apples, apricot, peach, ginger and tomato. Sauces include Worcestershire, soy, chilli, oyster, barbecue, brown and tomato, some of which are called ketchup. The jellies also come under this heading: rowan, cranberry and redcurrant.

Herbs

Herbs are the leaves and stems of plants which give their specific aroma and flavour to food; some are in everyday use while others are used only in a particular dish. They should be used sparingly. Most are available in dried form and need to be kept in airtight containers as they soon lose their properties. Many are available in fresh form.

The following list gives brief details of the better known herbs.

Balm – a lemon-scented leaf used mainly as a tisaine and in fruit punch.

Basil – has a very strong flavour that blends well in tomato and pasta dishes and in salads.

Bay leaves – can be used fresh or dried, but the dry leaves are best; must be used sparingly.

Bergamot – has the pungency of sage plus the scent of rosemary.

Borage – these hairy leaves have the aroma and flavour of cucumber and are used mainly in drinks; the five-pointed blue flowers are crystallised for use as cake decorations.

Cardamom – grows as green, black and white pods; the seeds are ground and used to make curry powder, to flavour black coffee, and in sweet and savoury Middle and Far Eastern dishes.

Chervil – a fern-like leaf spray with a fresh spicy taste of aniseed.

Chives – long grass-like shoots smelling sweetly of onion; nearly always used fresh.

Cumin – a hot, bitter-tasting spice used in curry and in Mexican dishes.

Galingale – hot, strong, red-coloured spice sold in root and powder forms; has the aroma of cardamom, ginger and camphor.

Garlic – has a very strong smell when raw, but the smell and flavour are not so pronounced when cooked.

Lemon grass – highly lemon-scented fresh leaves, much used in the cookery of South-East Asia; also available in dried powder form.

Marjoram – greyish soft leaves similar to basil but more subtle in flavour, though quite pungent in dried form.

Mint – mainly used as an accompaniment with lamb and mutton in the form of mint sauce; there are many varieties.

Oregano – very like marjoram but more pungent and hot.

Parsley – this herb is indispensible in all good kitchens; it is used mainly as a garnish, either fresh, chopped or deep fried.

Rosemary – spiky leaves with a very aromatic smell and flavour; used mainly in Italian cooking.

Sage – grey-green hairy leaves used mainly in stuffings for pork and duck.

Savory – similar in appearance to thyme but has long, narrow leaves and a pungent, peppery aroma; useful as a flavouring in stuffings.

Star anise – fruit of a tree of the magnolia family in the form of a star with a strong spicy taste and the aroma of aniseed; widely used in Chinese and Scandinavian cookery.

Tarragon – long, thin, green leaves growing on a long stem; has a distinct tart aromatic flavour; used in many sauces and stews, and blanched leaves may be used as a decoration.

Thyme – there are many varieties of this herb, the most commonly used being garden thyme; subtle flavour and excellent aroma.

Turtle herbs – a mixture of dried aromatic herbs which includes basil, marjoram, thyme, chervil, fennel and rosemary, usually purchased ready prepared in sachets for giving flavour and aroma to turtle soup.

Spices

Spices are flavouring agents made from seeds or roots that are dried to bring out their inherent aroma and flavour. They are available whole, in powder form, and some as liquid essences, each adding its own tinge of pungency to the foods they are added to, both savoury and sweet.

The word spice comes from the same sources as species, meaning class of an object, and refers to any dried aromatics. Most spices originate in the area from China south to Indonesia, South India and Sri Lanka. The following list gives details of those in current use.

Allspice – dark berries which combine the aroma and taste of cinnamon, cloves and nutmeg in themselves; used whole as pickling spice and ground as a part of mixed spice; sometimes called pimento or Jamaican pepper.

Cassia – the bark of an evergreen tree of the laurel family; rolled into quills it is like coarse cinnamon; in powder form it is a constituent of mixed spice.

Chilli powder – usually a mixture of dried ground chilli peppers, aromatic seeds, spices and herbs; can be mild or fiercely hot to the taste.

Cinnamon – the inner bark of a species of laurel; available in rolled sticks or powdered form.

Clove – the dried flower buds of a tree; available whole for flavouring and in ground form for spicing such items as buns, mincemeat and apple pie.

Curry powder – available commercially in many different formulas, with no one single recipe for its composition. Basically it is a blend of mild and hot spices including cinnamon, coriander, cloves, allspice, ginger, nutmeg, mustard, cayenne and black pepper, and turmeric. Depending on the type of curry dish required, some of these may be omitted and others added.

Curry paste – this is mixed curry spices in an oily base which eliminates the raw taste because the ingredients have been cooked together.

Ginger – grows as a root in Asia, Africa and the West Indies; it is dried then either preserved in syrup, crystallised, or ground to a powder.

Mace – scarlet-coloured lacy network found inside the shells of nutmeg and has a slightly more pungent flavour than the actual nutmeg; available as blade mace or ground.

Mixed spice – a powdered blend comprising cinnamon, coriander, cloves, nutmeg and ginger. Many are made as spice essences.

Nutmeg – has a pleasant crisp aroma that makes it blend with most items made with milk; available as the whole seed or in ground form.

Saffron – this is the dried orange-coloured stigmas of the mauve flowering crocus; it has a warm bitter aroma, an exquisite flavour and golden colour; a very small quantity will produce the desired result; available as the original stigmas and in ground powder form; very expensive.

Turmeric – a member of the ginger family; its brilliant yellow colour is useful in the manufacture of pickles, chutneys and mustard blends; the flavour is not very pronounced but adds to the total spiciness of curry powder.

Christopher Columbus

King Ferdinand and Queen Isabella of Spain sponsored Christopher Columbus to sail to the Far East to bring back spices and gold. They wanted to monopolise the merchandising of spices throughout Europe as a means of replenishing their diminishing exchequer. Columbus left Palos on the 3rd August 1492, but instead of ending up in India or China he found himself in the Caribbean which he called the West Indies.

Caterers owe a debt of gratitude to Columbus – he brought back chilli peppers, a much more powerful spice than ordinary pepper which then fetched the same price as silver. We also owe to Columbus such everyday ingredients as haricot beans, maize, sweet potatoes, avocados, aubergines, bananas, pineapples and cane sugar which he brought back from his fourth voyage in 1502 to be cultivated in Europe.

Seeds

Dried seeds of various herbs and spices may be used instead of the fresh or dry forms, where appropriate.

Aniseed – small oval seeds with the smell and taste of liquorice; used for their digestive properties.

Caraway – elongated seeds with the taste and smell of aniseed; useful as a digestive; used in rye bread, seed cake and in pickles.

Celery – small brown seeds with a strong flavour and smell of the vegetable.

Coriander – small, slightly oval, ripe seeds used in several sweet dishes and also in ground form for curry powder.

Cumin – have a similar flavour to caraway seeds and are used for pickling and in Near East foods; in ground form they are included in curry powder and chilli powder.

Dill – used to sprinkle on rolls, in cooking sauerkraut, in pickling cucumbers, and for making dill water for babies.

Fennel – have an aniseed aroma and flavour; used in pickles and for cooking certain fish and meat dishes.

Fenugreek – very small reddish-brown or yellow seeds with an exotic flavour and aroma; used in curry powder and chutney.

Juniper – small dark berries used in cooking sauerkraut; they also blend well in game dishes.

Poppy – tiny, slate-blue seeds; often used to sprinkle on rolls and loaves and are an ingredient of Russian cookery.

Sesame – small, ovoid two-celled seeds of an East Indian herb that also yields sesame oil; used to give a nutty flavour to oriental dishes and widely used to coat rolls and biscuits.

Essences, flavourings and colourings

These items are used mainly in the pastry department for giving flavour, aroma and colour to cakes, pastries, petits fours, icings, ice-cream and many other sweets. They must be used sparingly so as to contribute only a background of flavour to the dish.

The essences in general use are authentic distillations and syrups or artificial ones produced in laboratories. For example, genuine vanilla essence is distilled from vanilla pods grown mainly in Madagascar; a cheaper version is based on coal tar derivatives but has an authentic flavour and aroma. Some essences combine the correct colour and flavour, for example the yellow colour of lemons and their taste.

Many flavourings are used in the kitchen and the pastry department for providing a subtle yet essential finishing touch to dishes, such as deglacing a pan after sautéing an item or finishing a consommé, and more especially for flavouring a gateau, an ice-cream dish or fruit sweet. The main flavourings are spirits and liqueurs, including Grand Marnier, Kirsch, Maraschino, Tia Maria, Brandy and Rum, and also Sherry, Port and Vermouth.

Colourings are used mainly for icing on cakes, but can assist in restoring colour lost during the cooking process. Care must be taken in their use, and only natural food colours should be allowed such as genuine cochineal pods, pistachio green colour and flavour, and egg yellow.

Confectionery goods

The following commodities are used mainly for pastry work and are readily obtainable from normal suppliers:

Angelica – the candied stem of the plant of the same name; used mainly as a vivid green item of decoration.

Fondant – an icing that can be made on the premises by cooking a sugar syrup to 115°C then working it, but is usually purchased ready made.

Gelatine – made from the protein produced from boiling the bones and hides of animals; available in powder and leaf forms to make jellies and to set cold sauces and mousses.

Marzipan – can be made from a combination of ground almonds, sugar and egg yolks, or purchased ready made for making into petits fours, biscuits and as a layer on a birthday, wedding or Christmas cake.

Sweetening agents

Sugar

Sugar is the most widely used sweetener and is made into several forms from sugar cane or sugar beet, both of which produce identical sugars. White sugars include granulated, caster, cube, icing, nibs and preserving; brown sugars include demerara, Barbados, soft brown and pieces, each having its own shade of colour and taste. All are allied to fairly specific uses in cookery to give the desired results. Coffee crystals are coloured, transparent, rough pieces for serving only with coffee.

Syrups

Syrups are produced from molasses which is the liquid remaining from the refining of cane sugars. Glucose syrup is widely used in commercial pastrywork and for preserves. It is a viscous, colourless, clear sweet syrup, also known as corn syrup and confectioner's glucose, made by treating starch with acid. Maple syrup is made from the sap of the maple tree and is used mainly for pouring over waffles.

Honey

Honey is made by bees from the nectar of flowers. The colour and aroma of honeys differ according to the kind of nectar taken by the bees. Honey can be used as a general sweetener in the same way as sugar, but it has a distinctive flavour.

Artificial sweeteners

Saccharine is not widely used in cookery, but Sorbitol, which is manufactured by catalytic hydrogenisation of glucose, is used in making chocolates, sweets and preserves, particularly for use by diabetics.

Beverages

This section gives details of the main hot beverages on sale in most restaurants. It includes information on tea, coffee, cocoa, hot chocolate and several proprietory brands of drinks, many of which can also be made for drinking cold. All products used for making beverages are sold in airtight or vacuum-packed packets that keep the contents fresh until first opened. Once opened, they should be kept well sealed or placed in an airtight container.

Tea

Tea is imported in dried form from many countries including China, India, Kenya and Sri Lanka, and is blended by tea firms into a range of different qualities and flavours to suit customers' tastes. Apart from the well-known brand names of blends, there are a number of special teas: Earl Grey is delicately scented with bergamot; China tea has a delicate aroma, flavour and colour, and is best drunk as it is poured or with a slice of lemon; Japanese tea has a flavour of jasmine; Russian tea is made from teas grown in Caucasia and is served with lemon rather than with milk. Decaffeinated tea is available for customers who suffer from a heart complaint. The traditional names of the different kinds of tea grades, such as Pekoe, Orange Pekoe, Souchong, Darjeeling, etc., are used by tea merchants rather than as brand names.

The way to make good tea is to warm the teapot, add the right amount of tea, pour on the right amount of water that has just come to the boil from cold, then let it brew for at least three minutes, covered with a tea cosy.

Iced tea is popular in hot weather and is made by cooling freshly brewed tea and serving it plain with ice cubes.

Coffee

The coffee we drink is brewed from 'green' coffee beans imported from Brazil, Columbia, Java, Costa Rica, Jamaica, Kenya and several other countries. The beans are roasted to the required stage, ground to the desired grade and usually blended. Three kinds of coffee beans are grown. Arabica is the best quality; it has only half the caffeine content of Robusta which ranks as second quality and is used mainly for making instant coffee. Liberica is the third type and is also used for instant coffee.

Blended coffee may be made from a mixture of all three and carry a name such as Breakfast, After Dinner, French, Viennese, Catering brand, etc. Dried figs are used in what is known as Viennese coffee and chicory in French coffee. Coffee beans, ground coffee and instant coffee are available in decaffeinated forms. Decaffeination is done while the beans are still green, i.e. before they are roasted; it tends to be slightly sweeter than ordinary coffee and once made goes stale quickly.

Coffee can be brewed in bulk in a café set which has a source of hot water for brewing then holding the made coffee and the heated milk in the other container. It is usually made in one of the following ways:

1 in a filter machine, where the correct quantity of water is heated and sprayed through the funnel holding the measured amount of coffee, into a serving jug which is kept on a heated plate
2 by perculator, which boils the water in the jug, sending it up a tube and over the ground coffee in its container continuously until it is switched off
3 a cafetière, in which the ground coffee is placed in a glass, metal or plastic jug and filled with boiling water to brew, then the plunger is pressed down to trap the coffee grounds at the bottom.

Turkish coffee should be made with what is called Mocha coffee, a fine variety that is exported through the port of Mukalla on the Red Sea; it is brewed in a special copper coffee pot. Espresso coffee is usually made by the cupful by forcing steam on to finely ground coffee to produce fairly concentrated coffee.

Iced coffee is made by adding ice cubes to black coffee. If desired, it may be decorated with a rosette of whipped cream.

Cocoa

Cocoa is grown in several African and South American countries and exported as dried cocoa beans. These are then ground and some of the fat content removed in the form of cocoa butter. The powder is used to make a hot drink by mixing it to a smooth liquid with hot water or milk or a mixture of both. Drinking chocolate is made by adding sugar and sometimes powdered milk to fat-reduced cocoa powder.

Proprietary beverages

These are warm and soothing bedtime drinks, sometimes called nightcaps, which claim to give sound sleep. Examples are the well-known brands Horlicks and Ovaltine and other malted drinks.

Cereals

Cereals are grains produced from cultivated grasses. They are processed according to their end use and form a staple ingredient in most dishes. The following cereals are most widely used:

Barley – the source of pearl barley and barley flour which is used to thicken and enrich soups and can be used to make bread in its plain form; also available as malt flour in which the barley is allowed to germinate and hydrolyse the starch to maltose before being milled.

Buckwheat – this cereal is known as Saracen's corn and is of the dock family; the seeds resemble small beechnuts and are finely ground for making blinis and other Russian foods.

Maize – the source of corn meal, which in its coarsely ground state is used to make polenta; also cornflour and custard powder.

Oats – mainly used for making biscuits, porridge and muesli; it is available in coarse, pinhead and fine grades.

Rice – a staple food of at least one-third of the Earth's inhabitants. Bulk supplies come mainly from the USA, Australia, Italy, India and South America. Many different types are available including white (both long and short grain), brown, wild, Basmati and Arborio. It can also be ground for use in puddings.

Rye – grown and widely used in Eastern European countries, mainly for producing flour to make rye bread which is a solid, close-textured, dark-coloured loaf, sometimes flavoured with caraway seeds.

Wheat – processed to form semolina and flour; used extensively in bread and cake making. Durum wheat is grown in semi-arid climates such as North Africa and Spain for making into farinaceous products.

The following commodities, though not strictly cereals, are included here because of their association with these products.

Arrowroot – obtained from the underground stem or root of the manioc plant grown in the West Indies. It is pulped, dried and finely milled as a thickening for soups, sauces and gravies.

Sago – comes from the pith of the sago palm tree which grows in South-East Asia. It is roasted and milled into various grades and sizes and used in puddings.

Tapioca – made from the rhizomes of the cassava plant which are roasted and milled into flakes or seeds.

Breakfast cereals

Breakfast cereals are based on one or other of the cereals listed above which have been processed with flavourings and colourings, with or without the bran or germ, into the familiar shapes of the proprietary brands. Muesli is a mixture of several natural products including nuts, fruits, oats and sugar for eating as a breakfast cereal. All cereals must be stored in a cool and very dry store where they are safe from contamination by insects.

Delicatessen and speciality goods

These commodities are everyday items on the menus of deluxe hotels and restaurants where customers are more interested in the novelty and rarity of a dish than its price. These items do not often appear on the menus of medium-class restaurants because they are too expensive and cannot produce sufficient gross profit.

Caviar

Caviar is the salted roe of several species of sturgeon caught mainly in the Caspian Sea around the shores of Iran and Russia and in the rivers Volga and Ural which run into it. The quality of caviar varies between the different species of sturgeon: Beluga caviar is the best and most expensive; Ocietrova is the second best; and Sevruga, which has the smallest size eggs, is the cheapest because it is the most plentiful. Pressed caviar is also made and the roes of other kinds of fish including whitefish and lumpfish are dyed black as mock caviar. Red caviar comes from salmon.

The general term used to denote the finest quality caviar is Malossol, which indicates the amount of salt used rather than the actual species of sturgeon. Imperial and Royal Black are brand names given to high-quality caviars. The high price of caviar is because of its rarity and worldwide demand. Its handling and preparation are crucial to its quality and freshness. Caviar is packed in tins of 250 g and 500 g which must be stored at around 1°C, if possible under crushed ice when it will keep for several weeks. It is imported by specialist firms that can offer advice on its handling and service.

Foie gras

Fois gras is the name given to the livers of geese and ducks that have been force-fully fed, though not cruelly, to create a larger than normal size of liver. The livers are graded according to colour and size. Foie gras is sold in many different forms: in the raw state; steamed for pâtés; sterilised in an earthenware terrine; as a parfait mixed with diced or chopped truffle; 'en croûte' as either an oblong or tall cylindrical pie; in a can with madeira or port-flavoured jelly; or as a paste.

The centre of production was originally Strasbourg in France where most of the long-established firms such as Feyel, Rougie and Bruck are based. Foie gras is produced in other parts of France, especially in Toulouse, and also in Hungary and Israel, but Strasbourg holds pride of place as the city of origin and for producing foie gras of the finest quality. Fresh, raw and cooked foie gras must be kept under refrigeration and used as soon as possible because it is very perishable.

Truffles

Truffles are valued for their natural black colour and unique aroma, and are highly prized for their scarcity value as shown by their other name, 'the black diamond'. The truffle is a subterranean mushroom that lives in contact with the roots of a tree, usually an oak, around which a burnt patch can be seen. Young truffles need 7–10 months from the end of April to reach maturity and are harvested, some in summer and some in winter, by a specially trained dog who can locate them by their smell. The truffles are taken to one of the 10 truffle markets in France where the law of supply and demand rules the prices paid.

Fresh truffles are sold at these markets in brushed form. Dealers and chefs who are good judges of quality will bid for, say, a year's supply then peel, prepare and deep freeze them for use as required. Other than this they are sold in 50 g, 100 g and 250 g tins as either peeled or unpeeled, with truffle juice which is kept from when the truffles are first sterilised when they lose about 25 per cent of their weight. This juice is highly valued for cooking purposes. After opening a tin of truffles, any left can be kept moist by covering with madeira wine.

White truffles are used mainly in Italian dishes and are often grated raw over pastas. They are mainly found in the Piedmont region of northern Italy.

Snails

Snails are popular as a hot hors-d'oeuvre. This is quick and easy to prepare by putting canned, cooked snails in the accompanying packet of snail shells, filling with snail butter and reheating in a hot oven. It is also possible to catch large snails, preferably the 'gros Burgogne' species, and to put them in water to degorge before boiling over a period of several hours then using according to a recipe.

Turtle meat

Turtle meat is available in dried and canned forms for use in garnishing real turtle soup. It is imported from Australia and the Cayman Islands.

Ham

Ham is produced from hind leg of pork, cut with a rounded end, then cured and smoked by a particular process according to traditional methods associated with a particular region. A gammon is a cured leg cut from a side of bacon. Among the best known hams are:

- **York** – dry salted, lightly smoked and matured for three to four months which gives it a mild flavour, pink colour and firm texture
- **Bradenham** – cured with the addition of molasses to produce a dark outer coating and bright red meat
- **Virginia** – wet cured with the addition of molasses and smoked with hickory wood.

All these have to be cooked before they are ready for consumption. Other hams are cured over long periods for eating raw, then cut into tissue paper-thin slices as an hors-d'oeuvre. Some of the well-known names are Jambon de Bayonne from France, Parma from the city of that name in Italy, Westphalian from Germany, and Serrano from Spain.

Bird's nests

Bird's nests are made by the sea-swallow on the cliffs of the Annam coast of Java and the islands off the coast of Malaya, and are collected at great risk by the inhabitants of these regions. The bird builds the nest by producing a thick white liquid from its salivary glands. The nest is cleansed and packed in tins for export ready to be soaked before cooking in a consommé as Bird's Nest Soup.

Frog's legs

Frog's legs are the back legs only of the small green frog, preferably caught in a clean environment. They are well soaked before use then threaded on a skewer at about 12 pairs per portion, ready for cooking by any of the accredited recipes.

Vésiga

Vésiga is an unusual commodity that has a place in several dishes of Russian origin. It is the dried, whole spinal column and bladder of a sturgeon and requires long soaking and cooking to render it tender, but even then does not have much taste.

Charcuterie

This term is used to describe the range of goods produced by a pork butcher and includes cooked and raw items made mainly from pork and its offals and a few other kinds of meat. This interesting range of goods includes prepared, cooked or dried and smoked products made in large or small sausage shapes which may need a certain amount of further cooking. The lightly cooked ones include black pudding, frankfurters, saveloys, boudins, teewurst and cervelat; the cooked and lightly smoked kinds are mortadella, mettwurst, bierwurst; and the smoked ones are pepperoni, salami, chorizo and kabanos. In addition there are the terrines, pâtés, galantines, brawns, liverwurst, pork pies, and finally the many kinds of sausages that are suitable for boiling as well as those which are usually fried or grilled.

The cured and smoked products can be safely hung in a dry store where there is good air circulation, but all the others need to be kept under normal refrigeration. It may be advisable to take a daily delivery, according to the requirements of the menu.

Value-added foods

These are commodities which have been partially or completely prepared by the manufacturer, who has prepared the product with the addition of certain other ingredients that make the item ready to cook or already cooked. Thus all the basic preparation is done in the factory and the items are then packaged and sold in a chilled, frozen, sous-vide or ambient state that consequently makes life easier for the staff of a kitchen where the foods are being used. At the basic level it could be the preparation of a supreme or magret; then the same item crumbed or stuffed and crumbed; then the item in a cooked form, possibly with a suitable garnish and sauce; and finally the item as a complete main meal – each stage having added a certain value to the basic ingredient.

Auxiliary items

Under this heading is included a wide range of articles that have an important though subsidiary part to play in the efficient operation of a catering establishment. It includes official stationery items used in the chef's or caterer's office, as well as items used in the kitchen and dining-room to assist results and enhance presentation. The official documents for use by the catering manager, buying officer, head chef, head waiter and head cellarman are authorised by the employer and cover all internal and external correspondence, all ordering of supplies, all issues within the departments, and all control documents in use. Writing implements, waiter's check pads, menu blanks, till rolls, requisition pads and ordering forms are examples of these items. They will be kept in the care of the secretary or other responsible person who will order and issue as required.

Many chefs and catering managers do most of their clerical work on a computer, and a kitchen clerk or secretary will carry out much of their work on a similar machine. A printer, word processor and desktop publisher are also likely to be necessary for the efficient running of the office; this means that disks and databases, stationery and electrical points are necessary. A computer can act as a machine for correspondence; a personnel control list with details of every member of staff; a record of business done and kitchen percentage figures; a record of orders placed on nominated supplies; a database of ingredients and calorific values; a recipe file; and also a menu compiler, dish coster, stock controller, purchasing specifie and production planner.

The other kinds of paper in daily use are dish papers and doileys, pie collars, ham and cutlet frills, greaseproof paper and baking parchment. Other small items that may be needed include clingfilm, aluminium foil, plastic and foil dishes and containers of various shapes and sizes and lids for them, cocktail sticks, kebab sticks, sandwich and cheese flags, paper table coverings and table napkins where used, place cards, menu blanks, wine lists, bar tariffs, sample banquet menu booklets and themed celebration advertising notelets. All these have to be kept in stock to meet the likely demand.

Genetically modified foods
As this book goes to press, genetically modified foods are increasingly making the headlines. See page 351 for more on this topic.

Further reading

Kent, N. and Evans, A. (1993) *Technology of Cereals*. Butterworth-Heinemann
Kirk, R. and Sawyer, R. (1991) *Pearson's Composition and Analysis of Food*. Longman
Lawrie, R. A. (1991) *Meat Science*. Butterworth-Heinemann

10 Provisioning II
Wines, spirits and beverages

Wine; The wines of France; The wines of Germany; The wines
of Italy; The wines of Spain; The wines of Portugal; The wines
of Australia; The wines of New Zealand; The wines of South
Africa; The wines of the United States of America; The wines of
South America; The wines of Eastern Europe; The wines of
England; The wines of other countries; Organic wine; Spirits;
Liqueurs; Aperitifs; Beer; Cider and perry; Non-alcoholic drinks;
Bitters; Cigars; Planning the wine list; Cellar and bar stock
control; Laying down stocks; Promoting beverage sales.

Drink is a commodity about which the buyer needs to be knowledgeable in
exactly the same way as he or she does for food. A comprehensive knowledge of
the subject of wines and spirits requires a depth of study beyond the compass of
this book which can only offer a guide to the varieties, purchase, storage,
handling and sale of drink.

A wine list should be drawn up to complement the food on the menu. Its
extent and scope will be governed by the consumers' spending power, the
amount of capital the business is prepared to tie up in laying down stocks, and
the amount of cellar space required to store these items. The expected turnover
of stock is also a contributory factor.

The sale of wines and spirits is a profitable part of the food and beverage operation as it bears fewer overheads, but although it is much easier to control than
food, this control should be as foolproof as possible.

Wine

Wine is the naturally fermented juice of grapes, the sugar in the grapes being
converted into alcohol. The alcohol content of table wines such as claret,
burgundy, and hock ranges from about 7 to 13 per cent, which is low when
compared with most spirits which are on average 40 per cent alcohol. The various kinds of wine fall into three categories – still, sparkling and fortified – and
they are made as white, pink and red. The juice of all grapes is white or very pale
yellow, which means that white wine can be made equally from black grapes or

white. The colouring of pink and red wines develops as the skins and pips of black grapes are left in contact with the must or grape juice, so colouring it.

The variety of grapes used in making a wine gives it its characteristics. There are many different varieties of wine grapes, the finest of them being the Cabernet Sauvignon, the Pinot Noir, the Chardonnay and the Riesling. Great wine is usually produced from a single variety; other wines are frequently produced from several varieties of grapes.

The soil on which the grapes are grown, the way the vines are cultivated, the climate in which they grow, the climatic conditions whilst growing, all have an effect upon the wine produced. For example, grapes grown in the northern zone of production have less sugar, are lighter and have less alcohol than those grown in the more southerly parts, but they are higher in acid and so keep longer.

Purchasing wines

Wine making and selling is a huge international business employing many people. In some countries it acts as a major source of revenue. The caterer needs a professional knowledge of drink and must constantly seek to improve this knowledge. In the practical sense the buyer should be able to judge not only the great wines of Bordeaux and Burgundy, but also respectable wines for everyday drinking that can be put on the wine list without detracting from its distinction. It is the search for and appraisal of these lesser known wines that demonstrate the ability of the buyer.

White, rosé and red house wines can be kept for sale by the bottle, carafe or glass and should be sold at a reasonable price that makes them attractive to drink with the Table d'Hôte menu. But house wine does not have to be a cheap wine of no distinction; the brand selected should satisfy the wishes of the clientele as regards quality and price and it should be possible to continue to obtain a supply over a reasonably long period.

Some wine merchants and other suppliers of wine offer a service of person-alised wine labels for use on bottles of house wine. Labels are printed with the name of the restaurant which adds a certain cachet to the product, as though it has been specially selected and imported by the restaurant owner. The labels are usually put on by the supplier; details about the origin, quality, grape, etc. would be included on the back label which has to conform to European legislation.

Storage

The standard bottle of wine contains 75 cl, sometimes written as 750 ml; a half bottle of wine holds 37.5 cl; a magnum holds the equivalent of two bottles, which is one and a half litres. A one-litre bottle holds 25 per cent more wine than a normal bottle. Many bottles carry the European Union e sign which authenti-cates the amount of the contents.

The shape of the bottle and its colour varies according to the country or region of production. The two main shapes are the high shoulder kind used for bottling clarets from Bordeaux, and the sloping neck kind used for Burgundies. The wines of Alsace come in long thin bottles that are a good 5 cm taller than ordinary bottles, but the wine label always indicates where the wine was bottled.

Red wines are invariably bottled in green or brown glass and white wines in green glass. Young wines for early drinking and dessert wines are bottled in white or pale amber glass.

Champagne and sparkling wines have to be bottled in thick glass to resist the internal pressure and, when full, can weigh as much as 600 g more than a bottle of ordinary wine; the cork has to be covered with a wine muzzle. Corks vary in size from 3.5 to 5.5 cm in length according to the quality of the wine and country or region of origin; the cork is usually branded with brief details of the wine's origin.

Corked wine

A 'corked' wine can be a frightening problem for a sommelier and is not an uncommon occurrence in a busy restaurant where hundreds of bottles of wine are served daily. It is caused by a faulty cork which taints the contents causing a growth of mould and a musty smell. It could also be caused by storing wine in an upright position which causes the cork to dry out and allow air to get in and spoil the wine. Wine does not 'breathe' through the cork as is sometimes stated.

The problem of a tainted natural cork can be overcome by bottling wines in screwcap bottles, but this downgrades the wine somewhat. Vintners are now using new plastic corks with the trademark 'Supreme Corqs' – squashy elastic stoppers which seal the bottle firmly. They are made in several colours and have to be drawn with a corkscrew. They allow bottles to be stored upright and are ideal for fine wines which need maturing over time. A second kind of artificial cork is the French-made *tage*, composed of a hard plastic material which looks exactly like a real cork. It seals in the wine but once drawn is difficult to push back in if the whole contents are not drunk immediately.

To keep wines in good condition it is advisable to store them in a cellar or wine store at a constant temperature of approximately 10°C and humidity of 70–80 per cent, free from draughts and vibration and kept in semi-darkness. Some wines are so popular and sell so quickly that they can be kept upright in their cases or bins. Quality wines should be kept in bins in the horizontal position so that the cork is in contact with the wine which will prevent it from oxidising. Fortified wines and spirits should be stored vertically, usually under lock and key.

Wines brought from the cellar to the dispense bar must be prepared for sale. White, rosé and blush wines should be cooled to approximately 7°C; reds should be brought to a room temperature of approximately 15°C.

Some establishments may buy wine by the cask and have the cellarperson care for it and eventually bottle it. This wine in the wood is described as being 'on ullage' before it is ready for bottling. Ullage is also the name given to the space between the level of the wine in a bottle and the cork.

Wine by the glass

For customers who want to drink wine with their meal or in a public bar but don't want a full or half bottle, opened bottles or wine boxes can dispense a selection of wines by the glass. There are several kinds of apparatus which look good on display in the bar or behind the scenes in the dispense bar that keep the wines in good condition and at the correct serving temperature for immediate sale. The amount of wine per glass should be in accordance with statutory regulations.

BYO

An unlicensed restaurant can use the BYO abbreviation in its advertising to encourage customers to bring their own wine to drink with the meal. A small charge will be made to cover the cost of handling, serving and provision of glasses.

The wines of France

There are six major wine-growing regions in France, each of which produces some remarkably good wines; they are Bordeaux, Burgundy, Champagne, Alsace, Loire and Côtes du Rhône. There are other regions which produce a large quantity of good-quality but lesser known wine; among these are Savoy, Provence, Languedoc Roussillon, the Jura and the Dordogne, and they are usually featured as French regional wines.

The wine growers of France are governed by the Ministry of Agriculture's classifying system of guaranteed authenticity, which protects the buyer from being sold wines of dubious origin and doubtful character. There are two terms used on French wine labels to denote the authenticity of the contents: AOC (Appellation d'Origin Contrôlée) indicates that it is a fine wine that has been made in accordance with the local practice of the place named on the label; VDQS (Vins Délimités de Qualité Supérieure) indicates a more simple wine that comes from an area other than the main designated AOC areas. The conditions for entitlement are laid down by a body called the Institute National des Appellations d'Origins des Vins et Eaux-de-Vie, which is abbreviated to INAO. Many wines have the name of the district on the label as further proof of authenticity, for example Appellation Beaune Contrôlée means that the wine will have come from any vineyard in the Côte de Beaune. Even a first growth wine such as Château Rieussec will have Appellation Sauternes Contrôlée included on its label.

The main shippers of French wines are all firms of great standing and may be relied upon to supply wines of the required quality in wholesale lots. The names of some of the most well-known ones are Bouchard Aîné, Bouchard Père et Fils, Calvet, Deinhard, Dopff, Geisweiler, Harvey, Hugel, Jaboulet-Vercherre, Latour, Lebegue, Patriarch, Jules Regnier, and Thorins.

Bordeaux

When a connoisseur of wine thinks about the subject dearest to his or her heart, thoughts automatically turn to France and more specifically to the region known as Bordeaux from whence come more fine red and white wines than anywhere else in the world. The red wine that comes from this region is known in the UK as claret.

The best wines of this region were classified into an order of quality as long ago as 1855, being graded into 1st, 2nd, 3rd and 4th or 5th growths together with Bourgeois, Artisan and Peasant growths. The list was revised in 1966 under different headings and, as well as being given numbered growths, they were graded into Outstanding, Exceptional, Superior and Good growths; but in general the 1855 grading is still used. All the different districts and communes of Bordeaux are listed, there being nearly 150 well-known wines that give great distinction to any wine list. They are, of course, wines that are in great demand and therefore command high prices, but besides the classified wines there is a vast production of mainly good to excellent table wines whose quality is guaranteed by the name of the broker or shipper appearing on the label.

There are 12 districts of Bordeaux producing both red and white wines and each district is divided into communes or parishes (see Figure 45). The following paragraphs give a general description of the wines of the main districts and the names of their most notable communes.

MÉDOC

Médoc is the largest district of Bordeaux and the one where most of the great red wines are produced. They are all different in character, but in general are astringent when young, developing into elegant wines of subtle yet fragrant bouquet with a robust body. There are five notable communes, each embracing many famous vineyards; these are Saint-Estèphe, Pauillac, Saint-Julien, Margaux and Cantenac. The whole district is sometimes divided into Haut-Médoc and Bas-Médoc, but the term Bas is not often used thus making the division of little value.

GRAVES

Graves is the next large district and is noted for its gravelly soil; it is the only place in Bordeaux that produces both red and white wines of considerable note, there being three times as much white as red.

The white wines of Graves are dry, fruity and very individualistic with good acidity so they keep well. The red wines are full bodied and very robust. Although Château Haut-Brion was the only red wine from Graves to be included

Figure 45 Bordeaux wines

Notable commune	General description	Examples of notable names	Classification

Main district – Médoc

Notable commune	General description	Examples of notable names	Classification
Saint-Estèphe	Produces mainly red wines, full bodied and rich but not so notable as those from other Médoc communes. A few classified growths; many good to excellent Bourgeois growths	Ch. Montrose (R) Ch. Calon-Ségur (R) Ch. Rochet (R)	2nd growth 3rd growth 4th growth
Pauillac	Produces the largest quantity of wine of the Médoc, full bodied, great bouquet, generally distinguished. The list of fine wines is lengthy and there are many very good Bourgeois growths	Ch. Latour (R) Ch. Mouton-Rothschild (R) Ch. Pontet-Canet (R)	1st growth 2nd growth 5th growth
Saint-Julien	Produces outstanding red wines that are even finer than those of Pauillac and fuller than the ones of Margaux	Ch. Léoville-Poyferre (R) Ch. Gruaud-Larose (R) Ch. Beycheville (R) Ch. Talbot (R)	2nd growth 2nd growth 4th growth 4th growth
Margaux	Produces many remarkable clarets of great breeding and keeping qualities. Some dry white wine also produced	Ch. Margaux (R) Ch. Rausan-Ségla (R) Ch. Palmer (R)	1st growth 2nd growth 3rd growth
Cantenac	Outstanding quality red wines with very distinctive characteristics	Ch. Brane Cantenac (R) Ch. Palmer Ch. Pouget	2nd growth 3rd growth 4th growth

Other communes

Ludon – Produces many good Bourgeois clarets as well as a 3rd growth
Cussac – Produces good red wines that resemble those of Saint-Julien
Listrac – Produces many sturdy and inexpensive clarets, some good Bourgeois growths
Moulis – Produces large quantities of very dependable and well-balanced red wines

Main district – Graves

Notable commune	General description	Examples of notable names	Classification
Pessac	Produces the finest of the red Graves; they keep well and remain sturdy	Ch. Haut-Brion (R) Ch. Pape Clément (R) Ch. La Mission-Haut Brion (R)	1st growth Classified growth Classified growth

Figure 45 (cont.)

Notable commune	General description	Examples of notable names	Classification
Main district – Graves (cont.)			
Léognan	Produces very distinguished red and white wines	Ch. Carbonnieux (W) Ch. Haut-Bailly (R) Ch. Olivier (R & W)	Classified growth Classified growth Classified growth
Martillac	Produces red and white wines; the red are better on the whole and are sturdy and mature slowly	Ch. Smith-Haut-Lafite (R) Ch. La Tour-Martillac (R) Ch. La Garde (R)	Classified growth Classified growth Bourgeois
Talence	Produces a few good red wines and one of the finest white Graves	Ch. La Ville-Haut-Brion (W) Ch. La Tour-Haut-Brion (R)	Classified growth Classified growth

growth

Other communes

Beautiron, Cadaujac, Castres, Gradignan and Portets produce some principal red Bourgeois, Artisan and Peasant growths as well as some excellent unclassified red and white wines

Notable commune	General description	Examples of notable names	Classification
Main district – Saint-Emilion			
Saint-Emilion	Robust full-bodied wines, of excellent colour and keeping qualities	Ch. Ausone (R) Ch. Beauséjour (R)	1st great growth 1st great growth
Graves-Saint-Emilion	Produces wines that are very similar to those of Saint Emilion	Ch. Cheval-Blanc (R) Ch. Figéac (R)	1st great growth 1st great growth

Other communes

Lussac-Saint-Emilion – Produces some very full inexpensive red wines and a large amount of white under the appellation of Bordeaux Blanc

Montagne-Saint Emilion – Produces full-bodied red wines of good quality, less expensive than St Emilion

Puisseguin-Saint-Emilion – Produces strong full-bodied red wines of good value

Parsac-Saint Emilion – Produces poorer quality wines than from Saint Emilion, but full bodied

Saint-Georges-Saint-Emilion – Produces some good-quality red wine

Sables-Saint-Emilion – Produces some acceptable fruity young red wines that are best drunk young

Notable commune	General description	Examples of notable names	Classification
Main district – Pomerol			
Pomerol	Produces some fine as well as a large quantity of good average red wines. Most are short-lived	Ch. Pétrus (R) Ch. Certan (R)	Exceptional growth Unclassified
Lalande de Pomerol	Produces red wines that are very similar to Pomerols but somewhat less fine	Ch. Bel-Air (R) Ch. de la Commanderie (R)	Unclassified Unclassified
Néac	Produces some very good red wines; generally soft and smooth and usually inexpensive	Ch. Garraud (R) Clos du Castel (R)	Unclassified Unclassified
Main district – Sauternes and Barsac			
Sauternes	Produces the most famous sweet white wines in the world; they are very smooth, have a remarkable bouquet and a high alcohol content. Those of good vintages are very long lived	Ch. d'Yquem (W) Ch. La Tour-Blanche (W) Ch. Filhot (W)	1st great growth 1st growth 2nd growth
Bommes	Produces white wines which are similar in every way to those of Sauternes	Ch. Lafaurie-Peyraguey (W) Ch. Sigalas-Rabaud (W)	1st growth 1st growth
Barsac	Produces excellent white wines similar to Sauternes though somewhat less sweet but of greater delicacy	Ch. Climens (W) Ch. Coutet (W) Ch. Romer (W)	1st growth 1st growth 2nd growth
Preignac	Produces white wines similar in most respects to those of the communes of Sauternes	Ch. Suduirait (W) Ch. de Malle (W)	1st growth 2nd growth
Fargues	Produces some very good sweet white wines of the usual Sauternes quality, including one 1st rowth	Ch. Rieussec (W) Ch. de Fargues (W)	1st growth Classified growth
Other districts			
Bourg and Blaye	Produces both red and white wines of medium quality though full bodied. Sold as Côtes de Bourg and Bourgeais and as Côtes de Blaye or Bordeaux Rouge		
Premieres côtes de Bordeaux	Produces mostly white wine that is mellow and soft to sweet and some sound inexpensive red wines		
Fronsac and côtes-de-Fronsac	Produces some good, robust red wines similar to the Pomerols, usually of good value		

Figure 45 (cont.)

Notable commune	General description	Examples of notable names	Classification
Other districts (cont.)			
Entre-deux-Mers	Produces vast quantities of ordinary and inexpensive white wines, much of it sweet, but increasing quantities of dry white wine are being produced. The red wines from this district are not very distinguished and are sold as Bordeaux rouge or Bordeaux Superieur		
Sainte-Croix-du-Mont	Produces very sweet and fruity white wines that are heavier than the Sauternes and of less elegance. Well-known names include Ch. de Tastes and Ch. Grand Peyrot		
Loupiac	Produces very sweet and heavy white wines, similar to Sauternes but nowhere near as elegant		
Cerons	This district adjoins Sauternes and Barsac but is officially part of Graves. It produces very good sweet wines, golden coloured with a high alcohol content and similar in many respects to those of Sauternes		

in the 1855 classification list, there are now many more well-known names and the lesser-known ones are also very good. The communes of Graves are Pessac, Léognan and Martillac.

SAINT-EMILION

Saint-Emilion is a district of Bordeaux that produces many remarkable wines which are almost up to the standard of Médoc, being very rich and high in alcohol. The list of great growths contains many well-known names. There are a number of communes within the district, including Lussac-Saint-Emilion, Parsac-Saint-Emilion and Saint-George-Saint-Emilion.

POMEROL

Pomerol is the district next to Saint-Emilion and the smallest of them all. The wines produced here are all red and are rich and full bodied with a deep colour and perhaps a little more breeding than the wines of Saint-Emilion. The communes of Pomerol are Lalande de Pomerol and Néac.

SAUTERNES AND BARSAC

Sauternes and Barsac are two main parts of the same small district of Sauternes and give their names to two of the greatest sweet white wines of the world: Château d'Yquem and Château Climens. Barsac is in fact a wine from Sauternes, but has its own appellation and prefers to keep its slight distinction. The sweetness of these wines comes from allowing the grapes to shrivel and dry and then to develop the so-called Noble Rot, which increases the concentration of sugar and thus its high alcoholic content. These wines are highly perfumed, very rich to the taste and keep for a long time.

OTHER DISTRICTS

The other districts of Bordeaux are Bourg, Blaye, Entre-Deux-Mers, Fronsac, Premières Côtes de Bordeaux, Sainte-Croix-du-Mont, Loupiac and Cérons. All produce both red and white wines in large quantities. The red ones are soft but rich and fruity. Many of the white wines from these districts are blended and include some that resemble Sauternes, being quite sweet.

Burgundy

This region produces wine second only to that of Bordeaux. Its wines are more full bodied and heavy in contrast to the delicacy of claret. Both red and white wine is produced and many are great wines which can command very high prices. Most of the wine produced in Burgundy is red, but the few whites produced are all very well known and include Chablis, Meursault and Pouilly-Fuissé.

The main districts of Burgundy are the Côte de Nuits, Côte de Beaune, Côte Challonaise, Mâconnais, Beaujolais and Chablis. Between them, Beaujolais and Mâconnais produce more wine than all the other districts of Burgundy put together.

CÔTE DE NUITS

The Côte de Nuits district produces deep, fruity, full-bodied red wines that keep well and become smoother and more round with time. The notable communes are Gevry-Chambertin, Chambolle-Musigny, Vosne-Romanée, Nuits Saint-Georges, and Vougeot (see Figure 46).

CÔTE DE BEAUNE

The Côte de Beaune district produces wine that is fruity and soft and matures more rapidly than that of the Côte de Nuits. The town of Beaune is the centre of the Burgundy wine trade and more than 60 shippers have their head offices and caves there. The Hospice de Beaune is a charity that receives its support from the proceeds of the wine it grows in its own vineyards that have been left as legacies. The wine is sold at public auction every November, and bottles bear details on the label stating that they have been purchased at this great charity sale and giving the names of the donors. The seven notable communes of Côte de Beaune are Aloxe-Corton, Pommard, Beaune, Volnay, Meursault, Puligny-Montrachet, Chassagne-Montrachet, and Santenay (see Figure 46).

CÔTE CHALLONAISE

The Côte Challonaise district lies just south of the Côte de Beaune. Two communes, Mercury and Givry, produce mainly red wine; and another two, Rully and Montagny, produce mainly white. Rully also produces a large quantity of sparkling wine, made by the méthode champenoise. These sparkling Burgundies may be white, pink or red, and as a general rule are sweeter and more full bodied than Champagne.

MÂCONNAIS

The Mâconnais district produces large quantities of fairly good red and white wine and is most famous for its Pouilly-Fuissé, a quality white wine. Many of the lesser white wines are sold as Mâcon Blanc. The red wine from this district is named simply Mâcon.

BEAUJOLAIS

The Beaujolais district produces a vast quantity of red wine sold under the labels of Beaujolais-Villages, Beaujolais-Supérieur, and just plain Beaujolais. All are made from wines from various parts of this large district, the best ones bearing the name of the commune where they are grown. These are Brouilly Chénas, Chiroubles, Côte de Brouilly, Fleurie, Julienas, Morgon, Moulin-à-Vent and Saint-Amour. Beaujolais is generally a lighter wine than other Burgundies and is usually drunk whilst young. Some from the better-named vineyards, however, can be kept for three to four years.

CHABLIS

The Chablis district lies at the northern end of Burgundy and produces only light, dry, white wines that are well known as being the ideal accompaniment

Figure 46   Burgundy wines

Notable commune	General description	Examples of notable names	Classification

Main district – Côte de Beaune

Notable commune	General description	Examples of notable names	Classification
Aloxe-Corton	Produces red wines similar to those of the Côte de Nuits (including good keeping qualities) and also some outstanding white wines. These are similar to the Chablis but are more full bodied	Corton-Charlemagne (W) Corton Clos de Roi (R) Le Corton	Great growth 1st growth Great growth
Pommard	Produces light, fruity, well-rounded red wine. These wines are very popular and named vineyards on the label are sometimes the only guarantee of authenticity	Clos de la Commaraine (R) Pézerolles (R) Les Poutures (R)	1st growth 1st growth 1st growth
Beaune	Produces very good-quality red wines that mature quickly, as well as some white. The commune wines are often blended wines; wines with a village name followed by Côte de Beaune can be quite good	Les Cent Vignes (R) Champs-Pimont (R) Clos-des-Mouches (W)	1st growth 1st growth 1st growth
Volnay	Produces some fine red wines of good colour and bouquet. Can be drunk fairly young, but the best of the named vineyards keep well	Clos-des-Ducs (R) Clos-des-Chênes (R) Caillerets (R)	1st growth 1st growth 1st growth
Meursault	Produces some excellent white wines, very dry but with a certain softness. A certain amount of red wine is also produced, most of it sold under the Volnay label	Clos des Perrières (W) Genevrières (W) Charmes (W)	1st growth 1st growth 1st growth
Puligny-Montrachet	Produces perhaps the finest dry white wines; generally full bodied with a remarkable bouquet. Le Montrachet is undoubtedly the greatest	Le Montrachet (W) Chevalier-Montrachet (W) Batard-Montrachet (W)	Great growth Great growth Great growth
Chassagne-Montrachet	Produces some excellent white wines and almost an equal quantity of red wines; these are generally not quite such good quality, although there are a number of excellent 1st growths	Ruchottes (W) Clos St-Jean (R) Morgeot (W)	1st growth 1st growth 1st growth
Santenay	Produces some good dry white wines and some soft and full-bodied reds of which only three are classified as 1st growths	Les Gravières (W)	1st growth

Other communes

Savigny-les-Beaune, Monthélie and Auxey-Duresses all produce mainly fair to good red wines with a few respectable classified 1st growths

Figure 46 (cont.)

Notable commune	General description	Examples of notable names	Classification
Main district – Côte de Nuits			
Gevrey-Chambertin	Produces big heady red wines of good colour, full bouquet and finesse. They keep well and develop smoothness	Latricières-Chambertin (R)	Great growth
		Charmes-Chambertin (R)	Great growth
		Chapelle-Chambertin (R)	Great growth
		Chambertin–Clos-de Bèze (R)	Great growth
Chambolle-Musigny	Produces fruity red wines of very good colour, good vinous flavour and smooth body that have great breeding unequalled by any others. A little excellent dry white wine is also produced	Musigny (R)	Great growth
		Les Amoureuses (R)	1st growth
		Les Combottes (R)	1st growth
Vosne-Romanée	Produces outstanding red wines of great breeding, elegance and keeping qualities. Production of the classified growths is small, resulting in high prices	Romanée-Conti (R)	Great growth
		Richebourg (R)	Great growth
		La Tache (R)	Great growth
		Les Petits-Monts (R)	1st growth
Nuits Saint-Georges	Produces very soft full red wines with good bouquet. They are inclined to be a little less dry than a great deal of wines from the more northerly vineyards of Burgundy. A great deal of sparkling Burgundy is also produced	Les Pruliers (R)	1st growth
		Les Richemones (R)	1st growth
		Clos-des-Grandes-Vignes (R)	1st growth
		Clos de la Maréchale (R)	1st growth
Vougeot	Clos de Vougeot is the largest of the vineyards in the commune; it produces red wine of great quality and excellent bouquet, but perhaps not so full bodied as Chambertin. The remaining production of the commune except for a few small vineyards, is sold under the Vougeot label. A very small amount of white wine is also produced	Clos de Vougeot (R)	Great growth
		Clos Blanc de Vougeot (W)	1st growth
Fixin	Produces some excellent classified red wines. The commune wines are generally very good in quality and value	Clos-de-la-Perrière (R)	1st growth
		Clos-du-Chapître (R)	1st growth
		Clos Napoléon (R)	1st growth
Morey-Saint-Denis	Produces some very good, full-bodied red wines which are slow maturing and keep well. The best growths compare favourably with those of Gevrey-Chambertin	Clos de Tart (R)	Great growth
		Bonnes Mares (R)	Great growth
		Clos des Lambray (R)	1st growth

for fish dishes. As with Beaujolais, the demand far outstrips production. The wine is pale straw-yellow in colour, very clean on the palate, with a very delicate flavour that is almost flinty. The best Chablis is classified as Grand Cru and comes from several small vineyards next to each other; the bottle may bear the name of the particular vineyard. Chablis Premier Cru often has the name of its vineyard on the label and there are also some 1st growth wines from single vineyards. The name Chablis by itself on the label without a Cru number or named vineyard is of lesser quality. Petit Chablis is a very light blended wine suitable for carafe sales.

Champagne

This is undoubtedly the most famous wine in the world and has become associated with celebrating great occasions. Champagne is the name of the area east of Paris around the city of Reims, which is strictly defined as the only place where grapes may be grown to produce this wine. No other sparkling wine may be sold as Champagne, even though it is made by the same method and grapes.

The grapes are sold by the growers to the Champagne firms, which do the pressing, blending and bottling in their own cellars deep underground. The temperature is kept at 4°C all year round. Apart from a little pink Champagne, only white wine is produced and only certain years are declared as being a vintage, which makes them very expensive. Non-vintage Champagnes are blends of wines of several years. Vintage Champagne has to be tested and approved by a panel of experts and cannot be sold until at least three-years-old.

The quality of a Champagne is denoted by the name of its shipper, who may or may not own a vineyard. The finest Champagnes are made by the firms of Krug, Bollinger and Roederer. Other well-known shippers are Ayala, Heidsieck, Lanson, Mercier, Mumm, Perrier-Jouët, Piper Heidsieck, Pol Roger, Pommery et Greno, Moët et Chandon, Taittinger, and Veuve Clicquot.

The degree of sweetness of Champagne is printed on the label: Brut – very dry; Extra-Sec – quite dry; Sec – slightly dry; Semi-Sec – fairly sweet; and Doux – sweet. Champagne is available in bottles (75 cl); magnums (1½ litres), Jeroboams (3 litres); Rehoboams (4 litres); and Methuselas (6 litres).

Côtes du Rhône

The wines from this valley of the Rhône, lying between Avignon and Lyons, are known as Rhône wines. They are fairly big and heavy, dark red in colour and ideal for drinking with game dishes. Many of the names are well known such as Châteauneuf-du-Pape, Hermitage and Crozes-Hermitage; the lesser ones are bottled under the Côtes du Rhône label. Tavel is the most famous rosé wine of France and it comes from this area. It has abundant flavour and bouquet and, like all rosé wines, should be drunk young.

Alsace

This important wine-growing area is in northern France around the city of Strasbourg. It produces elegant white wines which are dry and fruity and have a very fragrant bouquet. The tall slender green bottles are labelled with the name of the type of grape, the name of the village or a brand name, and the name of the grower. Riesling, Traminer and Gewürtztraminer are some of the names of these wines. The words Grand Vine, Grand Cru and Grande Reserve are used to describe superior wines with good alcohol content.

Loire

The Loire Valley covers a large wine-growing area producing many well-known wines. The wines are named after the districts where they are grown. They are mainly white and range from dry to slightly sweet. A few reasonable red and sparkling wines are also produced, as well as the popular Anjou Rosé.

The districts of the Loire are Pouilly-sur-Loire, Pouilly-Fumé, Sancerre, Reuilly, Vouvray, Saumur, Chinon, Anjou, Côteaux du Layon, and Muscadet. The sparkling wines come from the Vouvray and Saumur districts and are labelled Crémant de Loire. They are made by the méthode champenoise. The red wines are light. They should be drunk whilst young and are excellent when slightly chilled. Pouilly-Fumé is a delicate dry white wine with a slightly smokey perfume which comes from the particular grape used. These include Chenin Blanc and Sauvignon Blanc. The reds are made from Cabernet Franc and Gamay.

Regional Wines

The wines from the less notable districts of France may not enjoy the prestige of those from the great wine-growing areas but are very presentable and merit their place on any good wine list. The following are the well-known districts with a few examples of the better known wines:

South West (Dordogne): red – Bergerac, Côtes de Bergerac, Cahors, Gaillac; white – Montravel, Bergerac, Monbazillac; rosé – rosé de Bearn; sparkling – Gaillac.

Provence, including Var: red – Bandol, Domaine des Moulières, Ch. de Selle, Domaine des Mauvannes; white – Cassis, Blanc de Blancs.

Jura: red – Château-Chalon, Château d'Arlay; white – Poligny; rosé – Rosé d'Arbois; sparkling – Etoile.

Savoy: red – Frangy, Marestal, Monthoux, Ayse Arbin; white – Crépy, Seyssel Apremont, Marignan.

Languedoc: red – Corbières, Minervois, Costières, Fitou; white – Clairettes, Banyuls, Bellegarde, Musacat de Frontignan; sparkling – Blanquette de Limoux.

Corsica: red – Sartene, Calenzana, Paviglia.

The wines of Germany

The wine-growing areas of Germany lie in the southern and western parts of the country along the banks of a number of streams that flow into the Rhine. Two main types of white wine are produced: Hock and Moselle. Hock is a term used in the UK to denote wine grown on or near the Rhine, while Moselle denotes wine from the river Moselle and its tributaries, the Saar and the Ruwer. Some red wine is produced but little exported. The following details relate to white wine.

The vineyards are the most northerly in Europe and under such conditions and climate it is not easy to produce good-quality wine, yet some of the German wines are counted amongst the really great wines of the world because they are refreshingly delicate, fragrant and long lasting.

Germany's wine laws define and control the types of wine made and divide them into six main classes:

1 **Tafelwein** – table wine made of German wine blended with wines of other countries in the EC.
2 **Deutscher Tafelwein** – table wine made entirely of German wine.
3 **Landwein** – wine from one of the many regions; dry to medium with good body.
4 **Qualitätswein bestimmter Anbaugebiete (QbA)** – quality wine from a specific area.
5 **Qualitätswein mit Prädikat (QmP)** – quality wine of a higher standard.
6 **Qualitätswein garantierten Ursprungs (QgU)** – quality wine from a guaranteed source; this is the equivalent of the French Appellation Contrôlée.

There are nine major wine-growing districts in Germany: Baden, Franconia, Mittelrhein, Mosel-Saar-Ruwer, Nahe, Rheingau, Rheinhessen, Rheinpfalz and Württemburg. The Rheinpfalz is sometimes referred to as the Palatinate. These districts are divided into areas, and within these are the named vineyards. Wines from a collection of vineyards in one of these small areas can be blended provided they are all of equivalent quality. Figure 47 gives a brief description of the wine-growing districts and some of the well-known wines from each.

A German wine label will give the following information:

- the area of production
- the quality classification
- the vintage year
- the village or composite area
- the name and address of the shipper
- the brand name, if any
- the name of the grape from which the wine is made
- if a Prädikat wine, its name, e.g. Spätlese
- the official control number
- the contents followed by the symbol e which shows it is a measure approved by the EU.

Figure 47   German wines

District	Description	Well-known wine names
Baden	Fresh wines with a flowery bouquet and delicate flavour	Nonnenberg, Sonnenberg, Kirchberg, Altenberg
Franconia	Dry wines of good quality and character; full bodied	Juliusspital, Wachenheimer, Ruppertsberger, Deidesheimer
Mittelrhein	Delicate wines with good bouquet but very little body; much of it is made into sparkling wine	Klosterberg, Fürstenberg, St Martinsberg
Mosel-Saar-Ruwer	Very light, delicate wines tending towards sweetness; good elegant bouquet; low alcohol content; some are slightly effervescent	Bernkastel, Piesporter, Bockstein Würzgarten, Sonnenuhr, Brauneberg, Zeltingen, Scharzhofberg
Nahe	These wines combine the features of Hock and Moselle and are very attractive, being steely and of fine aroma	Bockelheim, Neiderhausen, Kreuznach
Rheingau	Delicate wines with excellent aroma; may take some time to mature and become very elegant	Erbach, Mittelheim, Winkel, Rudesheim, Hallgarten
Rheinhessen	Mellow, mild and soft wines; the fine ones are fruity and of great elegance	Nierstein, Oppenheim, Nackenhiem
Rheinpfalz	Mild, mellow wines that are rich and without acidity; some are very sweet	Neustadt, Durkheim, Forst, Deidesheim
Wurttemberg	Produces mostly red wines, some good rosés	Spätburgunder, Schillerwein

The producer may put the year on the label if over 85 per cent of the contents are of that year and the wine has the characteristics of the year. Where two varieties of grapes are named they are given in descending order; if only one is named it will form at least 85 per cent of the content.

The following terms are used in conjunction with Prädikat wines:

- **Kabinett** – a quality wine just above that of QbA wine.
- **Spätlese** – wine made from late-gathered and very ripe grapes, producing a rich sweet wine.
- **Auslese** – wine made from only the best quality grapes, any bad ones having been excluded.
- **Beerenauslesen** – wine made from selected individual grapes when over-ripe and full of sugar.
- **Trockenbeerenauslesen** – wine made from individual grapes left to rot and become semi-dried in the sun until like raisins; it is therefore very sweet and more concentrated.
- **Eiswein** – wine made from grapes left on the vines until the cold weather freezes them; this gives a fine wine of concentrated flavour.
- **Originalabfüllung and Originalabzug** – this means that the wine was bottled by the producer.

Liebfraumilch as a name was originally given to many mildly agreeable Rhine wines, but is now a quality designation for wines from Rheinhessen, Rheinpfalz,

Rheingau and Nahe. Hock is the name given to German table wine from the Rhine area and made from Riesling or Sylvaner grapes or their crossings.

Germany also produces a great quantity of sparkling wine made by the Champenoise and Cuve Close methods. Schaumwein is the name given to any basic sparkling wine; Sekt is sparkling wine of better quality which is at least nine months old.

The wines of Italy

Italy is the world's largest wine producer. The ancient Greeks called it Oenotria Tellus, 'the land of vines'. The vine grows profusely all over Italy, and the characteristics of the wines vary considerably in relation to their location and altitude. Nevertheless the quality of Italian wines competes favourably with all the other wine-producing countries. There is a tremendous variety of different kinds of wine and no less than 13 main districts of production, some of them covering vast areas. Most of Italy's best red wines are produced in the Piedmont region.

Italy's wine laws delimit the zones of production and control production. A wine with the letters DOCG (Denominazione d'Origine Controllata et Garantita) on the label means that the wine is not only controlled but also has a guaranteed denomination of origin. It will have the names of the grower and wine merchant on the label in addition to the information required for a DOC wine. The letters VQPRD are also used on labels to show the wine is of good quality and produced in a determined area of the European Community.

There are a number of words used on labels to describe the contents: Riserva – aged in cask or bottle; Superiore – a slightly higher alcohol content; Vendemmia – vintage year; Secco – dry; Abboccata – a sweet wine; Frizzante and Spumante – sparkling.

The following list gives the main wine-producing regions, with examples of some of their better known wines:

Calabria: red – Ciro, Savuto, Donnico.

Campania: red – Falerno, Ischia Rosso, Gragnano; white – Lacrima Christi, Falerno, Greco di Tufo.

Emilia-Romagna: red – Lambrusco, Gragnana, Sangiovese; white – Albana, Trebbiano.

Friuli: white – Verduzzo, Riesling Renano, Picolit.

Latium: white – Frascati, Est! Est!! Est!!!, Montefiascone.

Lombardy: red – Valtellina, Sassella, Grumella, Valgella Sforzato, Frecciarossa, Botticina; white – Frecciarossa, Lugano, Riviera del Garda Rosato.

Marches: red – Rosso Piceno, Rosso Cinero, Sangiovese; white – Verdicchio, Orvieto.

Piedmont: red – Barbaresco, Barbera, Barolo, Carema, Nebbiola, Grignolino, Dolcetto, Malvasia; white – Erbaluce, Caluso; others – Asti Spumante, Moscato d'Asti, Vermouth.

Puglia: red – San Severo, Santo Stefano; white – Moscato di Salento, San Severo.

Sardinia: red – Vermentino, Vernaccia, Cannonau, Ciro di Cagliari; white – Nuragus, Moscato di Bosa.

Sicily: red – Corvo, Segesta; white – Corvo, Segesta, Zucco; others – Marsala.

Trentino: red – Santa Maddalena, Caldaro; white – Trentino Riesling, Lagrein.

Tuscany: red – Chianti, Elba Rosse, Brunello di Montalcino; white – Montecarlo Bianco, Vernaccia di San Gimignano, Vino Santo.

Umbria: red – Torgiano, Sagrantino, Rubesco; white – Orvieto, Grechetto.

Veneto: red – Bardolino, Valpolicella, Recioto, Valpantena; white – Lugana, Soave, Conegliano-Valdobiadene, Tokai.

Vermouth

Both sweet and dry vermouths are produced in Italy, mainly in or near Turin in Piedmont where most of the large firms have their headquarters. Vermouth is a fortified wine, mostly made of white wine. Brandy is added to give it extra strength, and the addition of many different spices and herbs gives it a distinctive smell and flavour. Dry vermouth has an astringent taste and light colour and is usually referred to as being French-type vermouth; sweet vermouth is popularly known as Italian vermouth. There are red, rosé, white and vintage varieties.

Marsala

Marsala is a fortified wine from Palerno in Sicily. It has a very attractive bouquet, high alcoholic strength and amber colour. It is much used in cooking. Some bottles may be marked with the letters OP (Old Particular), LP (London Particular), or SOM (Superior Old Marsala).

The wines of Spain

Spain is the third biggest wine-producing country in the world. It has 27 controlled districts regulated by the Instituto Nacional de Dominaciones de Origen (INDO), which exerts control over a large quantity of good-quality wine.

The best-known districts are Rioja, Valdepeñas and Catalonia, and of these three the wines of Rioja are the finest, the best of them coming from Rioja Alta and Rioja Alavesa. Rioja red wines improve with keeping, both in cask and bottle, and become mellow and of great character; the word Reserva or Reserva Especial indicates mature wines. Valdepeñas is on the other side of Spain, south of Madrid, and produces big, full-bodied red wines that are light in colour but high in alcohol, and also white wines that are dry and full-bodied. Both should be drunk young and fresh. Catalonia is the district around Valencia and produces some very good white and rosé wines. Away to the south-west is Ribera del Duero, the home of Spain's most expensive wine Vega Sicilia, a deep, intense red wine which is expensive and rare.

Spain also exports some very good sparkling wines made by the Champenoise and Cuve Close methods.

Sherry

Spain is probably more famous for its sherry than for its table wines. This wine takes its name from the town of Jerez de la Frontera in Andalusia, where all the bodegas (wine storage sheds or cellars) are to be found. The vineyards producing the wine lie to the north-west and south-west of Jerez. The main variety of grape grown is the Palomino, although others such as Pedro Ximenez, Mollar and Mantuo are also widely grown.

Sherry is made by what is known as the Solera system, where wines which have been fortified with brandy are put into oak casks stacked on top of each other. The bottom row contains sherry that is ready to draw off for sale, and as this is done the casks are refilled from the row above which is younger sherry. That is filled in turn from the row above and so on. Wines of different kinds and qualities are kept in different Soleras. This means that sherry is a blend of wines of many different years, but it also means that each firm can keep the particular quality of its brand names the same year after year. There cannot, of course, be a vintage sherry.

Sherry is thus a blend of wines fortified with brandy to give it a strength according to type of between 15 and 18 per cent alcohol by volume. Its use is mainly as an aperitif and it is made in many varieties:

- **Manzanilla** – very dry, pale in colour, medium body
- **Fino** – very dry, pale in colour, medium body
- **Amontillado** – dry, pale golden colour, fairly full body
- **Oloroso** – sweet, full bodied, golden colour, nutty flavour
- **Cream** – sweet, smooth, deep golden colour
- **Brown** – very sweet, dark brown colour, nutty flavour.

The manufacturers recommend that all these types be served cool, either by chilling the bottle or pouring the sherry over ice cubes, but this is a matter of taste and many prefer it served at room temperature.

Some other fortified wines are produced in Spain, including Malaga and Tarragona. Both are very sweet and suitable as an accompaniment with dessert. They have the same alcoholic strength as sherry. Montilla is a wine that is quite similar to sherry and made by the Solera system, but because it is produced outside the delimited zone it cannot be classed as sherry.

The wines of Portugal

Portugal has several demarcated regions, each producing its own kind of wines which together add up to a good many varieties. All are made of indigenous grapevines, unknown outside Portugal. The region called Barraida produces good reds and sparkling whites. The reds are full and fruity with a tannic edge and keep well for five years or more. It also produces the sweet fortified wine called Moscatel de Setubal. Dão, a remote mountainous region in central Portugal, produces rich, garnet-red, earthy wines which do not reach their best until after at least ten years. The Douro region offers some deep-coloured but soft velvety red wines and dry, nutty whites which are good everyday drinkers. Vinho Verde lies in the north-west corner of Portugal and produces most of the exportable crisp and young white wines and some well-known reds, including Quinta da Aveleda, Casa Garcia and Dom Basilio.

Port

The most famous wine of Portugal is port, the fortified wine produced in the town of Oporto on the River Douro. Port can be served as an aperitif, particularly the white variety, but it is mainly served at the end of the meal. It is the ideal accompaniment to Stilton and the nuts of the dessert course.

The varieties of port are as follows:

Vintage port – this is deemed fit to be bottled whilst still young in the sure knowledge that it will keep for many years. It is bottled after about two years in cask and marked with the year, then left to mature and improve with the passage of time. A heavy sediment is thrown and vintage port has to be carefully decanted before being served; the white 'splash' on the bottle shows how the bottle was binned and indicates that the crust will be on the opposite side.

Vintage character – this is good ruby port to which is added some older port to give body and flavour, rather than being left to mature as for authentic vintage port. It does improve in bottle.

Crusted port – this is the port produced in a non-vintage year and is given the same care as for vintage port; it can be made from a blend of wines of several different years. As the name implies it throws a sediment.

Ruby port – this is a fairly young port that takes its name from the lovely rich ruby colour of new port before it is stored; it is fruity but rough.

Tawny port – this is a port that has been allowed to mature so that it loses its ruby colour and becomes a deep amber, increasing in flavour to a mature nutty taste.

White port – this is made from white grapes only, but otherwise is the same as red port except that it is usually chilled and served as an aperitif.

Madeira

Madeira is an island in the South Atlantic which belongs to Portugal and which gives its own name to the very fine wine produced there. The island is actually a defunct volcano. The vines are grown on the slopes which are so steep that no mechanical means of cultivation can be used, and the must from the crushed grapes is carried down in goatskins. Fermentation of the wine is halted by the addition of brandy made from ordinary Madeiran wine and is then heated up to 60°C. Madeira is a blended and fortified wine with an alcoholic strength of about 20 per cent. It is made in several varieties:

- **Sercial** – very dry, delicate, pale to golden in colour
- **Verdelho** – medium sweet, golden colour
- **Bual** – medium sweet, golden colour, rich enough for a dessert wine
- **Malmsey** – very rich, very sweet, fragrant, dark colour, served as a dessert wine.

Madeira keeps very well and continues to improve for many years. It is frequently used in cooking.

The wines of Australia

Australia exports its wines worldwide to more than 70 countries, and in addition sends many of its vintners to other wine-growing countries across the world to give expert advice. The climate of Australia is ideal for wine growing and makes every year a 'vintage' year. The grape harvest can continue from mid-January right through to June, picking the bunches as they come to peak perfection.

The best-known vineyards are in the Barossa Valley in South Australia. They include Seppelt, Hardy, Orlando and Penfold, all well-known proprietors, and Coonawarra which was first established by Wynn's. New South Wales is the second largest wine-producing state. It embraces Hunter Valley, Mudgee and Murrumbidgee, with McWilliams as the biggest producer making more than 20 million litres every year. The south-eastern state, Victoria, includes the Great Western area which is famous for some outstanding sparkling wines. The Yarra Valley and Bendigo, Western Australia's vineyards, are centred around the Margaret River and Swan Valley and house several new winegrowers. Tasmania is rapidly making a name for its Chardonnay and Pinot Noir, and some French champagne makers are taking an interest in the island.

The wines of Australia have attained such a high reputation that there has been a need to increase the extent of its vineyards to meet its ever growing demand. Its present total of 48,000 hectares is being increased to 81,000 hectares and total production is set to reach 1.3 billion bottles per year by 2010. This increasing demand from more and more countries across the world has led to the mergers of many of Australia's vineyards into four major wine-producing companies, but there will still be a lot of small vineyards producing small quantities of exciting wine which finds its way into export markets.

The wines of New Zealand

Wine growing in New Zealand has a history going back to the early part of the nineteenth century. It has attained a high reputation for its young white wines made from classic European grapes, and light red wines which are now made by modern production methods. Among the well-known producers are Cooks, Corbans, Montana and McWilliams. The climate is similar to that of Europe on both the North and South Islands, with vineyards at Gisborne, Hawke's Bay, Canterbury and Marlborough.

Most of New Zealand's vineyards are planted on North Island, and Hawke's Bay and Henderson are the main centres of production of fine wines and many different estates. On South Island the majority of growers are centred on the Marlborough region.

New Zealand is better known for its fine white wines than for its reds, though these are gaining in reputation all the time. The climate of New Zealand is ideal for producing white wine, but rather cool for robust red.

- The Chardonnay vines benefit from a cool ripening period. This gives the grapes an intense flavour which is softened and improved by maturing in new oak barrels. Good brand names are Babich, Collards, Delegat and Hunters.
- The Chenin Blanc vines yield a range of flavours from very dry to rich, even with some sweetness. Good brand names are Collards, Cooks and Montawhero.
- New Zealand's Gewürztraminer rates second only to that of Alsace, with a pungent taste and scent that is very refreshing. Gisborne and Matawhero are good brands.
- The Müller-Thurgau vine is the most widely grown of all, yielding nearly a third of total production. Among the brand names are Cooks, Matawhero and Montana.
- Rhine Riesling has a good reputation for good white wines as a varietal or in a blend as made by Collards, Corbans and St Helena.
- The Semillon grape produces very refreshing whites such as Delegats, Montana and Villa Maria. It is also blended with Chardonnay or Sauvignon Blanc with very good results.
- The red wines of New Zealand are produced from the world's best-known vines, including Cabernet, Merlot, Pinot Noir and Pinotage.

The wines of South Africa

The wines of South Africa have always had a good reputation which rivalled those of Australia, New Zealand and California. More recently there has been a marked improvement in their quality and popularity which enhances the prospect of their inclusion in all wine lists. The KWV, which is a major wine-growers cooperative, has been influential in the country's wine industry for 75 years and has encouraged the planting of new vineyards and the use of new methods of vinification to improve the quality and quantity of wine produced. Ten years ago some 50 per cent of production was distilled into brandy and industrial alcohol.

Most South African wines are ready for drinking soon after bottling; some are made from a single grape variety and many are varietals. The only native vine is the Pinotage, but all the world's great vines are now grown here and, because South Africa enjoys such a wonderful climate and the soil suits them, these vines have a different taste than those from the same stock grown in other wine regions. Vines grown include Cabernet Sauvignon, Merlot, Pinot Noir, Chardonnay, Sauvignon Blanc, Chenin Blanc and Cape Riesling.

South Africa also produces excellent sherry- and port-type fortified wines similar to those made in their original countries of Spain and Portugal. Brandy is made using the same quality gradings as in France, and several other spirits and liqueurs are produced, the best known of these being the orange-flavoured Van der Hum.

The wines of the United States of America

The United States of America is the world's sixth largest wine-producing country, with wine being made in no less than 43 of the 50 States. However, 90 per cent of North America's wine comes from California, with New York State producing most of the rest.

The main wine-growing areas of California, which encompass 800 vineyards, are Napa Valley, Monterey, Santa Clara and Alameda County. Vines are planted on the mountain sides and in the valleys where they enjoy ideal growing conditions brought about by the chemical composition of the soil which also possesses good drainage. The ideal climate and use of modern methods guarantee quality wine.

In viticulture it is of vital importance to ensure that the vines are properly trained and fed and that the grapes mature at the required time. A rainfall at the wrong time will have an adverse effect on a particular vintage. If it rains during the harvest period in California, helicopters are sent up to blow-dry the vines. The harvest can therefore be gathered at the exact time when the grapes contain the desired concentration of organic salts, minerals and sugar that will produce a wine of first-class quality. The University of California at Davies has assisted wine producers in the selection of grape varieties, methods of training and pruning the vines, vinification and maturation processes. It initiated temperature-controlled, cool fermentation which is one of the reasons why Californian wines have achieved so many awards in wine-tasting competitions against many long-established European vineyards.

American wine makers came to realise that their products were good enough to compete not only at wine fairs but in the international market. Aided by good promotion and advertising, they decided to export their wines and soon gained a high reputation, particularly for those from California.

Among the 160 or so Californian wineries are Christian Brothers in Napa Valley, the largest one there, run by a religious order; Firestone in the Central

Coast area; E. and J. Gallo at San Joaquin who make a wide range of high-quality wines in the world's largest winery; Inglenook in Napa and San Joaquin, which is one of the oldest of the great wineries; Paul Masson who markets very reliable wines in the middle range; Robert Mondovi in Napa who produces wines of great character as well as general table wines; Sebastiani in Sonoma, an old-established firm which produces table and dessert wines; and Sonoma Vineyards, which has a high reputation for its Crown Cabernet and also produces fine sparkling wines in conjunction with Piper-Heidsieck, the well-known French Champagne house. All produce great wines.

Most of America's wine comes from established European vines and a few from hybrids of French and American growth. The country's own vines are the Catawba, Concord, Flora, Moore's Diamond, Niagra and Zinfandel. Catawba gives a pale red wine; Concord is grown in New York State on a large scale but its wines are not of a high quality; Flora produces a sweet white wine; Moore's Diamond is a white grape of ancient American origin, as is Niagra; Zinfandel is the most outstanding wine and produces red wines of many qualities from high to intense.

The wines of South America

This includes the wines produced in Argentina and Chile. It is possible that wine will soon be exported from Brazil where production is newly under way.

Argentina

Argentina is believed to be the fifth largest producer of wine and therefore exports its good-quality wines for others to enjoy. The best Argentinian wines come from the Mendoza region on the slopes of the Andes. Some are made from local grapes such as the Malbec which produces some of the very best reds, and increasingly from Cabernet Sauvignon and Andean Chardonnay vines.

Wines are produced in bodegas which bear the name of the property and/or the producer. Examples are Bodegas Norton, where Pedriel, a very fine Chardonnay, is produced; and Bodegas Bianchi, which is noted for its Don Valentin and Particular wines. Large wine cooperatives make enormous quantities of bulk wine and sherry-type wine. Brandy, known as pisco, is produced in Argentina as well as in Chile, Peru and Bolivia. A Pisco Sour is made from this brandy in the form of a shaken cocktail with lemon juice, egg white, gomme syrup and ice cubes.

Chile

Chile produces many wines of some repute under ideal growing conditions, most being varietals. All the best wines are produced in the Central Valley section.

Concho y Toro is the most important firm in Chile, having several bodegas where St Emiliana and Marques de Casa Concha are produced. Miguel Torres of Bodegas Torres has moved into Chile after making his name in the family firm in Penedés in Spain, and is producing some very good white wines by the cold fermentation method and reds from Cabernet Sauvignon vines. The four qualities of Chilean brandy are Selección, Especial, Riservado and Gran Pisco, all of which are aged briefly in oak vats.

The wines of Eastern Europe

This section includes Bulgaria, Hungary, Romania and the Republics of the former Yugoslavia.

Bulgaria

Bulgaria exports several very good varietals which are named after the grapes they are made from; some from the native vines such as Dimiate, Fetiaske, Gamza and Reatzitelli; and others from the classical Cabernet Sauvignon and Chardonnay vines. These and many blended wines are exported by the state vine monopoly, several under the Euzinograd and Mehana labels. Gamza and Mavrud grapes yield very drinkable reds, the latter being noted for its dark colour, good tannin content and plummy flavour. Pliska, Pomories and Preslav are Bulgarian brandies, listed in order of quality.

Hungary

Hungary produces one of the world's most exclusive wines, the unusual sweet-tasting, golden-coloured Tokay Aszu Eszencia. This is made by adding puttonyos, a sugary syrup or paste expressed from shrivelled Noble Rot grapes of the Furmint vine, to ordinary wine. The word Aszu means syrupy or the sweetest of the range of Tokays. Tokay Eszencia is low in alcohol, extremely rare and very highly priced and prized; these wines are only available in 50 ml bottles.

Not all Hungarian wines are so exclusive. Egri Bikaver, usually known as Bull's Blood, is a fairly robust red wine. The word Balaton on the label of a Hungarian wine indicates a good quality wine from the shores around Lake Balaton; Pes indicates a sweetish wine made from Riesling grapes. In general, Hungarian table wines have a good reputation for their firmness and character.

Romania

Romania now makes several western European-style wines from the Cabernet and Chardonnay vines which have replaced many of the fairly sweet reds and whites which were produced for export to Russia. Romanian wines are very acceptable and give good value for money. Those from Dealul Mare are full of flavour and dark in colour with a slight sweetish aftertaste. Murfatler is known for its sweet wines and probably the best known of all Romania's wines, Cotnari, a hearty dessert wine which is made from the native grape Grasa.

Yugoslavia

Yugoslavia no longer exists as a single country and the pleasant Laski Riesling and Lutomer Riesling and other wines for which the country was renowned are now labelled with the name of one of the six republics into which it has been divided. The good red wines come from the central and southern regions, but wine is produced in every republic excepting the central mountain range. Procupac and Vranat are two of these.

As in neighbouring countries, the Cabernet and Merlot vines give good results. Native vines are also used: Blatina yields acceptable reds from the Mostar area; and Plavak, which is grown along the coastline of Dalmatia, yields a heavy, sweetish red.

The wines of England

There are 413 vineyards in England and Wales, but only 20 operate on a commercial scale. Most of the wine produced in England is white of German stock, mainly Müller-Thurgau vines, yet the resultant wine is quite different from its German counterpart. The best English wines are crisp, dry and have a Cox's apple flavour which is quite distinctive. There isn't enough warmth and sunshine for the vines to flourish, so early ripening ones are planted. Wine-producing techniques continually seek to increase the quality by getting the grapes to ripen under unreliable English weather conditions. Some reds, rosés, sweet and sparkling wines are also produced which are fragrant and flowery. Lamberhurst is England's largest vineyard with 14 hectares under cultivation – still very small compared with some of the vineyards of the Napa Valley of California which cover 2,500 hectares.

A good wine list should include a range of British wines, including those from the Isle of Wight and Jersey.

Wines of other countries

Austria

Austrian wines are fairly light and fragrant. Most are white wines which are similar to those of Germany. The same wine terms are used. They are usually drunk while still young and fresh and do not equal the elegance of the best German wines.

Greece

Greek white wines have traditionally been treated with retsina. This is the resin from pine trees which helps to preserve the wine while giving it the distinctive flavour popular with the Greeks. There are now many new styles of light and dry white wines, aromatic rosé wines and some good red ones.

A new appellation system governs the production of many new-style Greek wines. Domestica on the label indicates a popular brand name for both white and red wine. Other well-known names are Mavrodaphne, a rich dessert wine, and Samos, a golden, very fragrant sweet wine from the island of the same name. Ouzo is the aniseed-flavoured aperitif, usually drunk chilled and clouded by the addition of ice cold water.

Israel

Israel has traditionally produced heavy and very sweet whites and reds for use on festive and religious occasions, and these are still sold, usually under the Carmel brand name. They are made under strict Kosher rules. In the 1970s producers benefited from Californian wine-producing technology and started to expand their vineyards which now cover much of Upper Galilee and the Golan Heights. Cabernet Sauvignon, Sauvignon Blanc, Semillon and Grenache vines have been planted which add distinction to the range of wines on offer, including soft reds and dry to sweet and sparkling whites. The best-known Israeli liqueur is Sabra, which tastes of oranges and chocolate.

Lebanon

Lebanon is notable for its high-quality Château Musar, a mature red wine made from Cabernet Sauvignon, Syrah and Cinsault grapes by Serge Hocher. Other good wines are Domaine des Tourelles and Domaine de Kefraya.

Organic wine

Organic wine is made by traditional methods without using chemical fertilisers in the soil in which the vines are grown and pesticides and herbicides on the growing vines. Any kind of vine can be grown in this way to meet the requirements of people who are concerned about the damage caused to the environment by what they think are unnecessary additives used to increase growth and yield. Growers know that the word organic on the label gives the wine added cachet and fetches a premium price.

These wines taste the same as those made by modern methods and the grapes enable connoisseurs to distinguish easily which vines they come from. Most wine lists include a number of organic wines under the headings of red, rosé and white or under the country of origin.

Spirits

Spirits are made by distilling a fermented liquid to concentrate essential flavours and to increase the alcoholic strength. The process is usually carried out using a patent still known as the Coffey still, although some spirits including malt whisky are produced in a pot still.

Substances as diverse as rice, potatoes, maize, corn and fruits are used. The most popular spirits are brandy from grapes, whisky from barley, gin from grain, rum from sugar, and vodka from potatoes or wheat. The French name for a spirit is eau-de-vie.

Spirits are really made for drinking on their own, but are versatile in use and go well with carbonated waters and in cocktails. They should be stored upright in the bottles, not lying down as for wine.

Brandy

This spirit is made by distilling ordinary white wine, which means that every wine-producing country can produce brandy. Although France produces the best brandies, some good-quality ones are also produced in Germany and Spain.

Cognac is the name given to brandy produced in a strictly limited district in what is known as the Champagne country of Charente in France. There are seven areas of this district and Cognac is a blend of brandies distilled in these areas. The wine is kept for five years before being distilled. It emerges as a fiery, raw liquid which needs to be matured in oak casks to become smooth and develop its distinctive bouquet. Some Cognacs have the words Fine Champagne on the label, indicating that at least 50 per cent of the content is brandy produced in the two major areas which are the Grande and Petite Champagne areas.

The label on a bottle of brandy is marked with stars or letters to denote the quality:

- one star – not less than three years old
- two stars – not less than four years old
- three stars – not less than five years old
- VOP (Very Old Pale) – from five to ten years old
- VO (Very Old) – from seven to twelve years old
- VSO (Very Superior Old) and VSOP (Very Superior Old Pale) – over ten years old.

Once bottled there is no further improvement, and there is no such thing as vintage brandy. Liqueur brandy would be a blend of mature brandies, the age having made them mellow but not sweet.

Armagnac is a brandy distilled from wine produced in the Armagnac district in France. It is not so well known as Cognac, but the best quality is highly praised by connoisseurs who appreciate it for its pungency and body in contrast to the smoothness of Cognac. Three-star Armagnac is five years old; VSOP is 20 years old; and XO is 40 years old.

Whisky

There are several types of whisky, the most popular being Scotch. This is made from barley which is malted, dried over a peat fire, then crushed, mixed with water and fermented with yeast. This liquid is heated and, as the vapour condenses, is immediately redistilled. Wheat is used in the same way to make a grain whisky, and the popular Scotch whiskies are a blend of these two. The difference between the various brand names lies in the different whiskies blended together to produce a particular flavour. None is less than three years old.

Irish Whiskey is made in the same way as Scotch whisky except that the malt is kiln dried and the smoke from the peat fire does not come into contact with it. It has a different taste to Scotch, being more fiery.

Bourbon, Corn and Rye Whiskeys are American types made respectively from grain (must be no less than 51 per cent maize), maize and rye.

Gin

This spirit is distilled from grain, usually maize, in a patent still which delivers it as ethyl alcohol. This is redistilled to give a pure and mellow spirit which is then diluted and flavoured with juniper berries, dried citrus peel, coriander and various other flavourings. It is ready for drinking after three to four weeks.

Genever Gin is Dutch gin, which is distilled four times then allowed to mature in wooden casks. It has more aroma and flavour than English gin and can be drunk as an aperitif. It is sold in tall 72 cl earthenware bottles at 71° proof.

Vodka

This spirit is made from potatoes or grain and is virtually tasteless and odourless. It is meant to be drunk neat and ice cold, but can be used in cocktails. Zubrowka is a yellow vodka flavoured and coloured by a grass grown in Poland. Vodkas are also imported from Russia and the Baltic countries.

Rum

This spirit is distilled from the fermented juice of sugar cane or by-products of the sugar factory made into molasses. Brown rums are full bodied and have a distinctive smell, whilst white rums are light bodied with very little taste or smell.

Other spirits

Other spirits in common use include:

- **Calvados** – an apple brandy produced in Normandy; it is quite fierce.
- **Grappa** – distilled from the residue of grape crushings in Italy.

- **Kirsch** – a white, delicately flavoured spirit made from cherries and cherry stones; produced in France, Germany and Switzerland.
- **Marc** – distilled from the residue of grape crushings in France.
- **Tequila** – a fiery spirit distilled from cactus of the agave species in Mexico.

There is also a large range of colourless eaux-de-vie derived from fruits such as damsons, mirabelle plums, pears, raspberries, strawberries and pine-apples.

Spirit measures

The European Union has standardised many laws that cover the sale of food and drink. Of the previous Imperial measures only the pint will remain, so there will be no further need for conversion charts. The sale of spirits, including whisky, gin, brandy and vodka, is by either 25 ml or 35 ml measures and optics. The old 6-out measure became illegal at the end of 1994 and licensed premises must display a notice saying which measure is in use. The 25 ml measure is the equivalent of $^7/_8$ fl oz, and the 35 ml measure is approximately the old $1^1/_4$ fl oz, which used to be called a double.

Liqueurs

Liqueurs are sweetened and flavoured spirits normally served at the end of a meal or used as a flavouring in foods. They differ according to the type of alcohol used as a base, such as brandy or whisky, and the particular flavouring agent used. Some of them have digestive properties from the herbs and spices used in their manufacture. Most countries produce a liqueur that is based on the popular national spirit and there are many hundreds available, but only about 20 are in very popular demand.

The best known liqueurs are shown in Figure 48. They are usually sold in 24 ml measures and contain between 37 and 43 per cent alcohol by volume.

Aperitifs

As the name implies, these drinks are designed to stimulate the appetite before a meal. They are served in measures of 100 ml, slightly more than for a liqueur but less than for a glass of wine. It is usual to serve them chilled or with ice in the glass. The flavour is derived mainly from herbs and spices, and quinine is used in many of them. The liquid base is usually wine and most of them are sweet.

Figure 49 on page 214 shows the most widely used aperitif drinks. In general they contain between 16 and 25 per cent alcohol by volume.

Figure 48   Liqueurs

District	Country of origin	Flavour	Base
Advocaat	Holland	Egg yolks	Brandy
Apricot Brandy	UK, Hungary	Fresh or dried apricots	Brandy
Atholl Brose	UK	Oatmeal, honey, cream	Whisky
Bénédictine	France	Herbs and roots	Brandy
Chartreuse (green and yellow	France	Herbs. Green has a higher alcohol content	Brandy
Cherry Brandy	UK, France, Germany, Holland	Cherries and cherry stones	Brandy
Cointreau	France	Orange	Brandy
Crèmes	France	Very sweet. Available as Crème d'Ananas (pineapple), de Bananes (banana), de Cacao (cocoa), de Café (coffee), de Cassis (blackcurrant), de Fraises (strawberry), de Framboises (raspberry), de Menthe (mint)	Brandy
Curaçao	Holland	Orange	Brandy or gin
Drambuie	UK	Honey	Whisky
Fiori d'Alpi	Italy	Flowers and herbs	Brandy
Grand Marnier	France	Orange	Brandy
Kümmel	Holland	Caraway and cumin	Grain spirit
Lindisfarne	UK	Honey	Whisky
Malibu	Holland	Coconut	Rum
Maraschino	Yugoslavia	The best is distilled from Marasca cherries, in Dalmatia	
Parfait Amour	France	Violet colour from violets or pink colour from rose petals	Brandy
Southern Comfort	USA	Peach, orange	Bourbon whiskey
Tia Maria	Jamaica	Coffee, spices	Rum
Triple sec	France	Highly rectified Curaçao	
Van der Hum	S. Africa	Naartjes (species of tangerine), other fruits, herbs and spices	Brandy
La Vieille Cure	France	Roots, herbs	Armagnac and Cognac

Beer

Beer is an alcoholic drink made from yeast-fermented malt, flavoured with hops. It is available in a great many forms and from many different breweries which may sell their beers locally, nationally or internationally, according to popularity. The main types of beer available include:

- **Pale ale** – light in alcoholic strength rather than in colour.
- **Brown ale** – coloured brown but light in alcoholic strength.

Figure 49   Aperitifs

Name	Flavour	Base
Amer Picon	Orange, Gentian, quinine	Wine and Brandy. As an aperitif – mixed with Grenadine and Cassis and diluted with water
Byrrh	Quinine, Brandy	Wine
Campari	Herbs	Grape spirit
Dubonnet	Quinine and Bark. Available as Red and Blonde	Wine
Fernet Branca	Herbs and Barks	Wine
Pernod	Aniseed, herbs	Wine
Pineau des Charentes	Cognac	Fresh pressed grapejuice
Quinquina	Quinine	Fortified wine
St. Raphaël	Quinine. Available as Red and White	Wine
Vermouth	Herbs, spices, orange. Available under many brand names as White, Red, Rosé and Dry; also vintage	White wine

- **Mild** – mild tasting; can be mixed with a stronger beer as mild and bitter, mild and brown, or stout and mild.
- **Bitter** – strongly flavoured with hops, giving it a characteristic bitter flavour.
- **Stout** – brewed from well-roasted malt which makes it very dark in colour. There are several brand names. Guinness is the most famous of these and is noted for its head or foamy top. It must be looked after carefully and stored at 13–16°C to be in perfect condition.
- **Lager** – available under various brand names, many imported. A popular beer because it is pleasantly pale, cool and refreshing.

Beer is available in bottles, cans and as draught from keg or cask. Keg beer is sealed in metal containers which guarantees it will keep in perfect condition. A cylinder of carbon dioxide is connected to the keg through a reducing valve which forces the beer under pressure to the dispenser.

Real ale is delivered in casks and just before leaving the brewery has some finings of isinglass added. In the cellar it is rested on stillions and in a few hours will be ready for serving.

Cider and perry

Cider is made from apples, the juice being allowed to ferment naturally. It is a refreshing drink but can be of high alcoholic strength. It is thought by some people to be innocuous, but dry rough cider can be very strong. Cider is sold on draught by the measure, in bottles or cans, still or sparkling, sweet or dry, and as vintage cider.

Perry is not so well known as cider, but in the form of a mini-bottle of Babycham is very popular. Perry is made from pears in the same way as cider.

Non-alcoholic drinks

Mineral waters include all the natural spring waters bottled and sold commercially for drinking alone or mixing with other drinks. They come from many different countries and many of them are from spas where people go to drink or bathe for medical reasons. They are still or sparkling, alkaline, aperient or sulphur, and all contain certain mineral salts to a greater or lesser degree. They should be chilled before serving. The best-known mineral water in the UK is Malvern water; the best known from France are Evian, Perrier, Vichy and Vittel; and the best known from Italy is St Pellegrino.

Carbonated drinks are commonly referred to as mineral waters or mixers and are used to dilute other drinks or are drunk on their own. They include tonic water, soda water, bitter lemon, dry ginger ale, American ginger ale, cola, ginger beer, lemonade and orangeade, and are available in returnable or non-returnable bottles and cans of many sizes.

Other non-alcoholic drinks include squash, e.g. orange, lemon, lime and barley water, and natural juices, e.g. orange, grapefruit, cranberry, pineapple and tomato. In high-class establishments the juice served will be freshly pressed from the fruit. Syrups are used in long drinks and cocktails and include Cassis – blackcurrant; Cerise – cherry; Citronelle – lemon; Framboise – raspberry; Gomme – plain syrup; and Grenadine – pomegranate. Peppermint, lime, banana and mint are others.

Bitters

Bitters are concentrated flavourings which add a subtle taste and aroma to many drinks and dishes. Orange, lemon and lime bitters are used to give fragrant aromas, and Angostura Bitters add aroma and flavour and help to whet the appetite. Unterberg Bitters are made in Germany and are similar to Angostura Bitters. Amer Picon and Fernet Branca, although mostly drunk as aperitifs, are often used as mild bitters for mixed drinks. Bitters are used in minute quantities – about 4 drops per 100 ml of a mixed drink are sufficient.

Cigars

Many restaurants prohibit smoking, but some have a smoker's section or permit smoking in the lounge or foyer where the coffee is served.

At the end of a fine meal, customers who wish to smoke should ask their fellow guests if they mind and, if nobody objects, request the sommelier to bring the humidor.

A humidor is a cedar-lined container for keeping a selection of cigars in good condition so that they are firm yet spongy rather than dry and crackly. The airtight container has a humidifier, which is a pad moistened regularly with distilled water in a metal grille, and a hygrometer made of sensitive human hair which registers any changes in the humidity. Cigars can be polluted by strong-smelling items such as flowers, fruit, spirits and perfume and can be affected by excessive heat, dampness and draughts.

There are several sizes and shapes of cigars and many kinds of tobacco used to make them. The inside filter is usually different from the binder and outer wrapper. The art of making a good hand-rolled cigar lies in the plaiting of the filter, its maturing and fermenting from green to brown.

Boxes of cigars are colour coded: C is the darkest, CC medium brown, and CCC the lightest. Dark brown cigars have the greatest aroma.

The main sizes are Corona (14 cm), Petit Corona (13 cm) and Churchill (18 cm) – all with straight sides; Torpedo has a pointed end and a Perfecto has tapering sides.

A hand-rolled cigar such as those made by Santa Damiana in the Dominican Republic, the Hoy do Monterrey Excalibur from Honduras, and the Cohiba from Havana, are so exclusive that people are prepared to pay £25 for the privilege of smoking one.

Planning the wine list

The aim of each licensed catering operation should be to persuade every customer to have something to drink with a meal; not only does it tend to make the meal something more of an occasion, but it helps the firm financially since the profit margin on the sale of drink is better than on food. In order to promote the sale of drink some thought must be given to the planning of the wine list, which in turn will influence the bar tariff and, where applicable, the banqueting wine list (usually an abridged version of the full wine list). The wine list, like the menu, can therefore be seen as a marketing tool. Bear in mind that wine is a significant part of the customer's bill, especially when sold at three times its cost price. If too highly priced, customers may select the house wine or other cheaper one.

The wine list should ideally be planned alongside the menu, with the manager of the dining-room, head waiter or wine waiter taking leading roles in consultation. Normally the menu will determine the kind of wines to be offered, although for some restaurants a superb wine list will to some extent dictate the style of the menu. As with the planning of the menu, the wine list must conform with the policy of the establishment as regards sales of alcoholic drink. The demands of customers will decide if magnums, half or quarter bottles should be stocked, whether wine will be served by the glass or carafe, how many sections there will be on the list, and the number of wines in each of them. The customers' spending power will decide whether fine wines or only ordinary table wines are listed and what the tariff is. The location of the bar, staffing and service procedures will affect the inclusion of aperitifs on the wine list or whether these go on the bar tariff. The importance of aperitifs in promoting appetite and sales, especially if profitable cocktails are featured, should not be overlooked.

The person responsible for compiling the list must have sound knowledge of wine, and a reputable supplier who carries all the important wines and can maintain supplies should be chosen. Some large establishments and groups maintain their own central depots and cellars and much of the buying is done directly through shippers and vineyards. If possible, a tasting should be held of each wine to be included on the list.

The wine, the consumer and the occasion

It is of the utmost importance that the wine list matches the type of operation and that it meets with the customers' expectations. The opening hours of business will influence the range and extent of the list, even though the class of business may be the same. For example, compare a restaurant that is open only for lunch with another, such as a hotel, where lunch, dinner and special functions are catered for. In the first case the range of fine wines would not be so extensive and the emphasis would be on those excellent wines more suited to the time of day and the demands of more hurried meals. In the hotel a wider range of the finer wines would be expected to cater for gourmet dinners and special functions.

The selection and range of wines

The selection and range of wines offered by an establishment must be sufficiently varied and large enough to suit all the possible tastes of its clientele. The choice available should be appropriate for the particular type of business. For instance, an ethnic restaurant would be expected to offer wines from its own country. A small bistro would be expected to offer good wine at reasonable prices, either bottled or in carafe but with limited choice. A deluxe restaurant would be expected to offer a multi-choice list of good to fine wines and liqueurs. Within these ranges, though, basic tastes and likings should be taken care of, including personal preferences for wines which are still, sparkling or fortified; red, white or rosé; dry, semi-sweet or sweet; light, medium or robust; ordinary to better; and reasonable in price to more expensive. The quality of the house wines and their prices must match the status of the establishment.

The sequence of the wine list

The sequence of wines on the wine list is not as clearly defined as for the menu. The customer expects to find dishes in a certain sequence with one or two minor exceptions such as cheese before or after the sweet. With wine, however, the choice is usually left to customers as to what they will drink and in what order. Nevertheless, the host will still expect the quality wine list to follow a well-established sequence. There can be minor differences in order, accent and range, but the pattern is usually the same. The essential information required for each listed wine includes the number and name of the wine, the date or vintage, the measure, and the price.

THE NUMBER

A number is usually given to all still, fortified and sparkling wines by the compiler of the list, and this corresponds to its bin number in the cellar. Spirits, liqueurs and cider have different storage arrangements; as proprietary brands they are in continuous production and can always be held in stock. Numbering makes it easy for customers to order, sometimes sparing them the embarrassment of having to read a long title in an unfamiliar language, and for the waiter to take the order – the number reinforced by its name acts as a check. It is also easier and more reliable to use the number and name for requisitioning from the cellar.

THE NAME OF THE WINE

The name of the wine should be given in full and, in the case of fine wines, should include its particular growth and region or area of origin, e.g. Château Calfon-Ségur 3ème Cru, Pauillac. The name of the shipper can be given for other wines.

DATE OR VINTAGE

Either may be used as a heading for the actual year of the wine's vintage where given. Of the Champagnes, only vintage Champagne is dated.

BOTTLES AND MEASURES

The range of bottles offered is determined largely by demand. It is usual, however, to offer bottles, half bottles and magnums of the better red Bordeaux and Burgundies; bottles, half bottles, magnums and sometimes double magnums of Champagne; bottles and half bottles of most French and German white wines and also of some sparkling wines. Most other wines are offered in bottles only. The measure for spirits such as brandy and whisky must be stated by law. The standard measures are either 25 ml or 35 ml. Other drinks such as sherry are priced by the glass.

PRICE

This should be given next to the column relating to bottle size or measure. Each section should start with the cheapest wine and then list the other wines in ascending order to the most expensive.

Banqueting wine lists

Wines included on a banquet or special party menu are normally selected from the establishment's wine list, although sometimes customers will bring in their own wines. In this case they would be charged a nominal sum for service and use of facilities. Where selected from the wine list, the choice is usually made by consultation between the manager or head waiter and the customer, and is made with reference to the menu to ensure that the wine suits the quality and special characteristics of the food. An individual customer is obviously quite entitled to drink what he or she wants in any order and at any temperature desired, but when a number of people are sitting together and eating the same food, it is essential that all are satisfied with the type, quality and order of wines served.

Rules of wine service

The following list summarises the details of wine service.

- The progression of wines served in a menu should be in an ascending order from the more ordinary to the finest, from the lightest to the full bodied, and from the youngest to the oldest. In short, this means serving wines in ascending order of quality.
- White wines are best served before red wines, except sweet ones which can be served with the sweet dish. Dry white wines are best served with fish and shellfish and white meats such as poultry, pork and veal.
- Champagne may be served throughout a meal, though a dry wine is best with all courses up to the sweet course when a demi-sec or doux Champagne would be more suitable.
- Red wines are best served with dark meats; the more robust Burgundies are ideally suited to rich, highly flavoured beef and game dishes.
- Sweet white wines such as Sauternes, Barsac, Tokay, Beerenauslese and Piccolit are best served with the sweet course, though Sauternes goes well with foie gras as a first course.
- Port is an excellent wine for serving with cheese and dessert.
- If a savoury is served instead of a sweet, the red wine served with the preceding course will be suitable.
- Rosé wines, as a compromise, can be served with any course of the menu, but would be inappropriate for a fine, well-chosen menu of gastronomic excellence.
- It is not wise to serve wine with any hors-d'oeuvre or salad which has been dressed with vinegar and oil, as vinegar has a bad effect on wine and makes it acidic.
- Asparagus and eggs should not be eaten with wine; they create a taste which destroys the quality and flavour of both the food and the wine.
- It is quite acceptable for wines from more than one country to be served with a meal, provided, of course, that they are of suitable quality and compatible with the food served. Differences in the style of wines can always add interest to the proceedings.

Staff

The skill and expertise of staff responsible for the storage and service of alcoholic and non-alcoholic drinks must be consistent with the needs of the particular wine list being used. At all levels this requires a knowledge of the qualities and characteristics of all the items featured, together with the ability and skill to store them in optimum condition, to keep them ready for service, and to serve them in the correct manner and at the right temperature. In short, the quality of the staff must match the quality of the wine list.

All staff concerned with this area of catering should keep up to date with new developments in viticulture and vinification. This requires not only personal endeavour on the part of the individual, but also that management provides time and opportunity for staff to attend educational courses concerned with the subject.

Cellaring and storage

Storage must be considered together with the problem of continuity of supplies. If an establishment decides it will be cheaper to buy in cask and to bottle on the premises, then this requires the right staff and equipment together with sufficient working space in addition to storage space. In the case of fine wines in bottle, the establishment has to decide how large a stock should be carried and how much capital it can afford to have tied up in this. Smaller cellar space is required for medium quality wines bought in on a regular supply basis and where the major stock is held by the supplier, but very often this can result in fluctuating prices unless this has been agreed on a contract basis.

Continuity of supplies

This poses no problems as far as branded spirits, liqueurs, beer and mineral waters are concerned. They are always available and good ordering procedures will ensure that adequate stocks are carried. With wines, however, there can be problems because the same wine of different years or different vineyards in the same area can vary greatly, and more importantly there is only a limited amount of any one vintage available. This can mean alterations to prices, or deletions and additions to the list if precautions are not taken to ensure an adequate level of stocks. Buying procedures have to be delicately balanced with the fluctuations of supply and demand if the listed wines are to be on offer for a reasonable length of time. Customers like to find the wines they prefer still available for some time; frequent chopping and changing of the listed wines can be confusing and irritating.

Pricing

A policy of marking up wine by a very high percentage could make it possible to have the gross profit on food sales at a reasonable rate, provided, of course, that the sales of wines could be kept at a high enough level. A careful balance must exist between the turnover of sales and the percentage of mark-up, bearing in mind that the customer expects value for money. It might be sensible to consider using a sliding scale for marking up the cheaper wines as compared with the more expensive. A 300 per cent mark-up for a bottle of wine costing £2 wholesale would look reasonable, whereas the same mark-up on a bottle costing £10 may appear unreasonable.

Descriptions

For some establishments it can be helpful to include a description on the wine list of the area from where each wine comes, together with short descriptive notes on their taste. For others, recommending certain wines for certain foods, and perhaps offering a wine of the day, can be an acceptable way of helping the customer. In first-class establishments these points are always the responsibility of the wine waiter, and one of his or her prime functions is to be able to advise the customer truthfully, from knowledge and experience.

Cellar and bar stock control

This is carried out on similar lines to all other goods, and all the details given for those (see Chapter 11) apply to the control of liquor in the cellar which is in fact a basic holding store, and to the bars which are the selling points. The cellar holds stocks of all the items shown on the wine and bar lists according to the expected turnover. Figure 50 shows a sample bin card used in the cellar for issues of a particular wine.

Each bar will maintain a sufficient stock of every drink on the list to satisfy known demand and send a requisition to the cellar as necessary to keep stock at the appropriate level. In some establishments all empty bottles are returned to the cellar for replacement by full ones to bring the stock level back to normal.

A dispense bar is the place where drink is kept in readiness for serving in the dining-room or lounge. It therefore has to carry a stock of every drink that is offered for sale to the establishment's customers. In a residential establishment it supplies guests' requirements in their rooms where this service is offered. Nothing should be served by the dispense barperson without a signed check to support the withdrawal from stock. At the end of each service period a consumption sheet is completed and sent for control, together with the checks received from waiters to support all the issues.

The person responsible for the food and beverage operation needs a good knowledge of bar work, as only in this way will he or she know if every drink is served to the required standard and also that no breach of the licensing laws or unacceptable practices take place. Staff pilfering is a known area of concern. Problems include giving short measures or free drinks; ringing up incorrect figures on the cash register; taking money from the till; and bringing in bottles of spirit while pocketing the sales proceeds.

One of the ways of maintaining control is by linking the existing optic or other dispensing measures to a micro-processor which will monitor every dispense

Figure 50   Bin card for wines

Item: Mateus Rosé			Bin No. 36
Supplier: Century Wine Co.			
Date	Received	In hand	Issued
January 20_ _			
1		50	12
4	120	38	–
6		158	12
7		146	24
10		122	10
16		112	24
18		88	12
22		76	24
27		52	24
30		28	12
31		16	6
February		10	–
2	120	10	24
5		106	12
7		94	12
8		82	24
16		58	12

transaction. This kind of system acts as a control which identifies any shortages between consumption and takings, as well as any surpluses. A computer will handle delivery notes, requisitions, stocktaking, stock consumption, cellar receipts and issues, and the profitability of each sales outlet; reports can be produced whenever required and for any time period. Ordering can be assisted by identifying slow-moving stock and examining stock turnover.

Control of alcoholic beverages is discussed further in Chapter 15.

Laying down stocks

One of the most important functions of the cellarperson is laying down stocks of wine in order that they mature until the stage of perfection for drinking is reached. At one time most establishments bought wine from the grower or shipper when it was cheap and stored it carefully until it was ready for drinking. This meant that the cellar was the repository of very valuable assets and that the cellarperson had to know how to treat the stocks and to monitor their development. Few caterers today can boast about the size and value of their cellar stocks and many are quite happy to leave a wine merchant to hold stocks and supply requirements. The capital tied up in cellar stocks can be put to greater advantage in a high-interest bank or building society account.

Promoting beverage sales

Beverages make an important contribution to the profitability of an establishment, because the product is non-perishable and its provision requires a minimal amount of care and labour input.

The marketing of beverages in a restaurant requires the same attention as given to the planning of the food operation. Beverages are complementary to food, so the selection of all beverages, wines and spirits ought to enhance as well as support the food operation. In effect, a plan of action resulting in a clear policy statement relating to the marketing of drinks and beverages needs to be drawn up and all concerned in the unit must be involved in its execution.

The staff involved in the marketing of drinks and beverages must be carefully selected and trained to ensure that they can discharge their responsibilities effectively. Their training should involve:

- product knowledge of wines, beers, spirits, liqueurs and non-alcoholic beverages
- an appreciation of food and wine combinations
- understanding of customers' needs
- knowledge of merchandising techniques
- treatment of the product, handling, temperature and presentation
- stimulating or assisting impulse buying.

Tools and techniques

The main tools in wine and spirit promotion are the bar and wine lists which should be prominently displayed for customers' use. When customers arrive at the bar for a pre-meal drink, the aperitifs or cocktails list should stimulate them to make a choice which appears more appealing than the standard drink available at home.

Sparkling cocktail shakers, mixing bowls and frosted ice containers displayed on the front of the bar contribute greatly to the special environment and professional presentation of the bar activities.

At the entrance of the dining-room, a simple but elegant display of small wine casks surrounded by a few artificial vine leaves and grapes and eye-catching wine bottles will subconsciously remind customers that wine is a normal part of the meal occasion. A liqueur trolley placed in the vicinity will act as a further reminder and stimulus.

On arrival at the table the customers should be offered an aperitif, and as soon as the food has been ordered the wine list should be left for them to study its contents. The sommelier, whose uniform should be distinguishable from the rest of the staff, should make a quick judgement of the customers' requirements in relation to the purpose of their visit and then proceed to offer advice on suitable wines in relation to their food choice. The customers must retain the impression, however, that the choice has been made by them and that the sommelier is there only to offer guidance on the content of the wine list.

Figure 51　Possible food and wine combinations

Food	Wines
Hors-d'oeuvre	Dry white, possibly red if meat predominates
Smoked salmon	Pronounced dry white, e.g. muscadet, moselle
Oysters	Dry white, e.g. sancerre, brut champagne
Caviar	Champagne, vodka
Pâté de foie gras	Gewürztraminer, traminer
Soup	Dry sherry, dry madeira
Pasta	Dry red, chianti type
White fish	Medium white, e.g. chardonnay, moselle, meursault
Oily fish	Rich white, e.g. hock, chablis
Veal	Rosé, light red, e.g. beaujolais
Pork	Rosé, light red, e.g. beaujolais
Beef	Deep red, e.g. mature médoc, pomerol, burgundy
Lamb	Deep red, e.g. claret, burgundy, rhône, barolo
Poultry	Medium red, e.g. young Médoc, burgundy, rhône
Game	Rich red, e.g. pommard, mature côtes du rhône
Cheese	Port or other red fortified wine
Dessert	Sweet red, tokay, sauternes, demi-sec champagne
Coffee	Spirits, brandy, whisky, marc, grappa

Various wines may be served with different courses, but it is counter-productive to suggest choices in relation to traditional practices such as white wine with fish.

At the end of the meal a liqueur or spirit may be offered with the coffee if it is felt that the customers would appreciate it.

Because of the legal restrictions on drinking and driving, many customers prefer to drink lightly. Sales of mineral water have therefore increased dramatically over the last few years, contributing greatly to the profitability of this aspect of restaurant service.

Further reading

Brown, G. (1995) *Classic Spirits of the World*. Prion

Davidoff, Z. (1984) *The Connoisseur's Book of the Cigar*. McGraw Hill

Foulkes, C. (ed.) (1994) *Larousse Encyclopedia of Wines*. Larousse

Halliday, J. (1998) *The Australian and New Zealand Wine Companion*. Angus Robertson

Hayter, R. (1996) *Bar Service Levels 1 & 2*. Macmillan

Johnson, H. (1991) *The Story of Wines*. Manderin

Robinson, J. (ed.) (1999) *The Oxford Companion to Wine*. Oxford University Press

11 Provisioning III
Purchasing, storage and issuing

Purchasing; The buyer; The principles of purchasing; Methods of
buying; Standard purchasing specifications; Sources of supply;
Receipt of goods; Storage; Physical requirements of stores;
Refrigeration; Prevention of contamination; Stores equipment;
Rotation of stock; Stock levels; Stores control documents;
Stocktaking and valuation; Security of stock and stores premises;
Stores issuing; Payment of accounts; Electronic control.

Purchasing

Knowledge of the principles of purchasing and the requirements for storage of
the materials used is a key to the efficient operation and success of any catering
business. Purchasing must follow the management's policy as expressed in the
items offered for sale on the menu and wine list. The menu governs the quality
and range of foodstuffs to be purchased; the bar tariff and wine list decide the
contents of the cellar; and the person appointed to do the buying contributes
much to the success of the enterprise. In addition to the consumable products, a
large number of non-food items such as small kitchen utensils, cleaning equipment, crockery, glassware, linen, paperware and cleaning materials must be
purchased. All this equipment requires control of storage and issuing in the same
way as consumable items. Firms of catering suppliers now serve hotels and
restaurants with every possible type of fish, shellfish, meat, poultry and game in
fresh, chilled and frozen forms, and all kinds of groceries plus small kitchenware.

The buyer

The job of buying goods for a catering establishment is a difficult one that
demands a comprehensive knowledge of commodities and the ability to make the
best use of the business's funds to yield maximum profit. In talking of a buyer,
we recognise that only large establishments have such a qualified person and that
in small firms the buying will be done by the proprietor or manager. In some
establishments the catering officer or food and beverage manager is the responsible person; in some hotels the head chef buys all the perishable commodities

for daily use. The decision as to who buys depends on the policy of the particular type of business or operation. A group may have nominated suppliers who give a discount for the business received from the total number of branches, or head office may simply permit the manager of each unit to buy locally from the best sources of supply.

The purchase of wine requires a particular and specialised knowledge to ensure that the wines selected are suitable for the type of establishment and clientele and will form a satisfactory wine list. Similarly, policy will decide the contents of the bar list which, together with the wine list, acts as the blueprint for cellar stock in the same way that the menus do for the food store.

The principles of purchasing

The person responsible for buying needs to define the basic principles he or she should follow to ensure that the decisions taken are effective. Some of these principles are:

1 Buy on quality, not on price alone.
2 Buy goods at the right price, at the right time, and of the right quality.
3 Know the seasonal availability of goods.
4 Foresee market trends to avoid possible supply problems.
5 Know the menu and wine list and the pricing policy of the firm.
6 Have more than one supplier for the main commodities.
7 Do not open too many small accounts.
8 Use only reliable suppliers.
9 Know the stores capacity and avoid over-ordering.
10 See that all goods are inspected on delivery.
11 Obtain discounts where possible without this affecting the quality and delivery of goods.
12 Ensure that only one person is responsible for the buying.

The buyer must work closely with heads of department in order to understand their requirements for the commodities they use. There is a big difference between placing orders and buying goods professionally; merely asking a supplier to deliver certain items without asking the quality, price, source and pack is poor practice and will not gain the respect of the supplier.

Methods of buying

There are three broad levels at which buying can be carried out, each relating to a particular size and volume of business:

1 **The primary market**, where goods are bought at the source of supply (grower, producer or manufacturer) or at a central market such as Smithfield

or New Covent Garden in London. Buying from these sources demands very large orders at regular intervals.

2 **The secondary market**, where goods are bought wholesale from a distributor. This gives the buyer the advantage of wholesale prices and possible discounts.

3 **The tertiary market**, where goods are bought from a retailer or local cash-and-carry warehouse.

Contract buying

Under stable financial conditions, suppliers are able to agree to supply a large enterprise with its entire requirement of a particular range of commodities at an agreed price for a period of one year or longer. Inflation and problems with supplies deter firms from tendering for this sort of business unless clauses in the contract allow for price rises at frequent intervals, which rather takes away the essence of what contract buying is all about. In the case of a contract with a firm of butchers, the price could be set midway between those charged on a certain day at Smithfield meat market and as recorded in a meat trades journal for that particular quality. For vegetables it could be the market price at Covent Garden Market plus a percentage for handling and delivery. There is a lot of work involved in making out a contract; there may not then be many firms offering to tender, and there are often questions about quality, price and delivery problems during the life of the contract. The difficulty of foreseeing the possible trend of prices, the increase in wages, and the cost of fuel for delivery make this form of buying more hazardous than it used to be.

Some local authorities, or consortiums of several county councils, run central stores depots where every conceivable item of equipment and certain non-perishable commodities are either held in stock or can be supplied by nominated manufacturers or wholesalers and delivered at specified intervals. To house all the goods, a warehouse is necessary together with staff to run it and lorries to deliver the orders; there are thus several overheads to be added to the price of goods and this may make prices less competitive.

One of these consortiums is The Buying Agency (TBA), a body which has been set up to supply the needs of the public sector of the catering industry. It aims to satisfy the needs of its members who are engaged in local authority catering, such as organisations who have successfully bid for contracts to run services previously done by direct labour. It covers the field of social and welfare establishments such as rest homes and day centres, schools, hospitals, colleges, municipal catering outlets and meals-on-wheels production centres. The agency nominates manufacturers who will supply goods made to specification under discount agreements. Having evaluated the equipment and all other items and ensured that they operate efficiently and meet safety standards and the needs of the purchaser, the agency then places firms of suppliers under contract. Most items of heavy-duty equipment, mixing machines and vending machines, crockery and cutlery, paper and plastics are covered. The TBA complies with European Union legislation for competitive tendering and the requirements of the General Agreement on Trade and Tariffs (GATT).

Rental of equipment

In the case of equipment and machinery it is possible to rent, hire or lease the required items on terms of a number of years. The agreement can cover insurance, maintenance, replacement and servicing. Thus a new business can be started without any capital expenditure on equipment and the charges will be paid out of revenue. Hire charges are tax deductible, equipment is covered by warranty, and items can be upgraded as new and improved ones come on the market.

Cash and carry

This method of purchasing food, drink and minor items of equipment is useful for small firms. The owner can obtain a pass enabling him or her to buy in what is, in effect, a wholesale supermarket, collecting the requirements, paying by cash or cheque, and taking the goods to a car or small van for transport. To buy at a cash and carry it may be necessary to give a VAT number or to purchase a minimum amount over a period. In this method of buying it is necessary to bear in mind the unseen costs of the person's time spent going to the warehouse and back, the amount of petrol used, and the running costs of the vehicle. There may also be the need to have ready cash to pay for the goods. It is an impersonal way of buying as there are few staff to discuss quality and prices. Discounts are not normally given and it would probably be necessary to purchase 50 cases of a particular item before being allowed to see the manager to bargain for a better price – then the problem of where to find storage space may arise.

Market buying

A very large firm may find it pays to employ a buyer to go to the main markets each day they are open, to purchase goods actually on display. In Arnold Bennett's book, *Imperial Palace*, there is a description of Jack Craddock buying meat in Smithfield at 5 a.m. for delivery the same day to the hotels he worked for. It highlights the problems and satisfactions of the traditional method of buying. The buyer must be very knowledgeable about purchases and be able to obtain the exact quality required and to negotiate the keenest possible prices.

It is also possible for a small firm to purchase its requirements in the major London markets by using the services of an agent who will walk through and buy on the caterer's behalf and have it delivered that day by a carrier, charging a percentage for the service.

Standard purchasing specifications

An experienced buyer can sum up the quality of goods delivered by using inherent expertise, but it is an admission of a lack of liaison between buyer and supplier to have to reject an item because it is not of the required standard. It could happen that a substandard item of produce has to be used because there is not time to wait for it to be exchanged. An expert buyer will seek to avoid such an occurrence by drawing up a standard purchasing specification for every commodity needed. It requires much thought and the assistance of the chef or person who uses the goods to draw up watertight specifications which, once approved, will be referred to every time the item is delivered. A standard purchasing specification is a statement of particular criteria related to quality. It acts as a point of reference between purchaser and supplier. The use of a standard purchasing specification should ensure uniformity of standard and consistency of quality. A copy is sent to relevant suppliers so that each knows what is expected. It may be useful to involve a supplier in the initial stages since the buyer might be asking for the impossible.

The following is an example of a typical standard purchasing specification:

SUPPLIER'S QUALITY AND PREPARATION SPECIFICATION   No. M10
Product: Foreribs of Beef
1 No cow or bull meat or meat designated as commercial or manufacturing will be supplied.
2 Joints to be cut from a chilled, unfrozen carcass of English, Scottish or Irish origin. Intervention beef may be supplied if originating from animals that conform to home-killed beef of the same grade.
3 The unfrozen carcass or joints must be stored at approx 3°C for 8–10 days prior to delivery.
4 No joints from an excessively fat or lean carcass to be supplied.
5 Joints to be prepared by removal of the spinal sinew and gristle, the chine bone to be freed and replaced and the rib to be tied.
6 The weight range to be 4½–5½ kg.
7 Delivery to be by refrigerated transport during which the temperature of the meat must not reach more than 10°C.
8 Prepared joints must be wrapped and sealed with the weight noted on each one. They must be delivered in a receptacle of good hygienic standard.
9 No meat supplied shall have been cut from a frozen carcass that has been defrosted for preparation.
10 All products must comply with the provisions of the Food and Drugs Act 1955, the Weights and Measures Acts 1963 and 1976, and the Trade Description Acts 1968 and 1972.

This example of a purchasing specification for minced beef shows the requirements which must be met by the supplier:

Minced Beef Specification

Carcass type:	Fresh
	United Kingdom, Eire
	Steer, Heifer
Cuts to be used:	No head meat or offal to be included. Chuck and blade, sticking piece
Trim level:	Free from tendons, ligaments, discoloured tissue, blood vessels
Fat level:	90% visual lean
Preparation:	Minced through 5 mm blade, once only
Packaging:	In sealed bags of 2½ kg

A product specification drawn up by a manufacturer for the supply of goods to a caterer would include the following information:

- product name and code number
- packaging details
- date of manufacture
- best before end date
- storage information
- instructions for use
- description of the product
- hygienic handling
- ingredient declaration
- nutritional values
- additives used in manufacture
- product microbiological standards

Each completed standard purchasing specification should have an identifying number.

Sources of supply

Several hundred different commodities are needed to fulfil the menu requirements of an establishment run on traditional lines and where food is prepared from raw. A quick-food snack bar or other similar place that runs on a limited choice menu also needs to buy many different commodities such as rolls and cakes as well as the basic brand items. The major staples of meat, fish and vegetables are usually purchased as required on a daily basis and if the order is fairly substantial two suppliers of each could be used. It is sensible to ask for a quotation from several suppliers in order to obtain the keenest price for a consistent quality.

Some suppliers issue a weekly price list showing what the commodities cost and what is available, with any special offers listed. Other suppliers send a representative to see the buyer each week when the market can be discussed and the order taken. Large wholesalers print a price list for distribution to customers to last as long as possible until all-round price rises make it obsolete; individual price increases can be notified weekly. Provision lists are also issued on a weekly basis and current wholesale prices for categories of commodities are given in the weekly trade journals. Some catering weeklies include a list of food prices for the week and a monthly food cost index showing on a percentage basis how prices have fluctuated over a period of time.

Wine will be bought from a shipper if the quantity involved is considerable, or from a local wine merchant who may be an agent for some growers but can obtain steady supplies so that the wine list can remain constant over a period of time.

Stationery, paperware and cleaning materials are bought in quantities sufficient to cover the needs of the catering department over a certain period of time and according to the size of storage areas available for keeping them safe. A cook-freeze or cook-chill production unit using foil and plastic containers would buy them in bulk from a manufacturer or wholesaler, but storage space is then required for minimum delivery quantities which could run into tens of thousands of each size. There is an enormous variety of powders, liquids, creams, sprays and pastes for cleaning purposes and the buyer has to know which is the most effective for the price.

A reserve stock of small utensils is necessary to replace those that get broken or worn out and the buyer must know the catering equipment specialists who can supply good-quality professional items.

Receipt of goods

Official order forms bearing an order number and printed with the name and address of the establishment are used to cover all orders placed with suppliers, even though orders may have been telephoned to save time. A sample order form is shown in Figure 52 (page 240). The order forms sent to suppliers are their only authority to deliver goods and claim payment for these goods.

With up to 50 per cent of sales being spent on the purchase of food, it is vital that all goods ordered are actually received. At the unloading bay or delivery point there must be a foolproof system for inspecting and receiving goods. Except for mail, all goods must be delivered to one point. There must be a reliable check for quality, quantity and price, and no blind receiving without delivery notes. A record of what goes out through the back door is also of importance.

No payment for goods received can be made until the receiving office informs the accountant that it is in order to pay for them.

It is usual to despatch perishable foods directly to the kitchen where the chef can check their suitability. Failure to inspect them can lead to higher costs and lower quality and it is important to ensure that the chef can devote adequate time to this aspect of the job. If, after inspection, goods are found to match the copy order and meet every requirement, they can then be accepted and a signature given. This is usually done by signing a copy of a delivery note or invoice, and it is this signed invoice which acts as authority to pay for goods received.

If there are discrepancies between what is written on the invoice and what has actually been received, or what was agreed when the order was placed, then the invoice must not be signed. It can, however, be noted on the invoice that there is some problem which has to be resolved concerning the transaction. In these days of high delivery costs when the delivery worker may not be able to wait whilst a big load involving, say, a hundred cases of varied items is checked against the delivery note, it is permissable to sign that the total consignment has not been examined. This ensures that any queries can be taken up with the supplier afterwards. This also applies to deliveries that are left after the stores have closed for the day and the van driver leaves the goods in the area in the knowledge that they will be safe until the following morning.

Storage

Once goods are received into stock they should be regarded as capital, with each item worth a sum of money; in this light the value appears more real than when they are looked upon only as commodities. The storeroom must be regarded as a strongroom for the safe keeping of valuables. This is only one aspect of storage, but underlying the whole subject is the need to keep everything under strict control and in perfect condition.

Siting of stores and cellar

If possible the food store and the cellar should be on the same level as the kitchen and dining-room so that it is not necessary to install a goods lift or to have to haul heavy goods up and down stairs. The food store will be cool if it faces a northerly direction and neither it nor the cellar need have windows.

In a large establishment the office which is the receiving point should be sited where it overlooks the delivery point, and the distance from there to the actual store should be minimal. Space is required to site a weighing machine and for trucks and trolleys to be parked when not in use. The distance from store to kitchen and from cellar to dispense bar should not be too far.

Automated handling of deliveries by means of an endless belt or overhead rail is worth investigating to see if labour can be saved. Some wholesalers now put the complete consignment for an establishment on one of its own delivery trolleys so that the entire load can be wheeled into the stores and avoid double handling.

Area allocation

The area allocated for storage should not be excessive, just sufficient to tie in with the kind of business being run. A conventional operation where all food is prepared from raw and receives a daily delivery needs little or no storage area, only refrigerators. A fast-food operation requires a very small store in which to keep its limited range of goods; in fact they could be left in open storage since control is by count.

Non-perishable goods

With as many as 500 non-perishable commodities in canned, bottled or packaged form to be kept in stock, these items can take up valuable space. Using the menu as the determinant and knowing the average rate of usage, it is feasible to apportion just sufficient space for a minimum stock of each commodity. The frequency of issuing and the quantities given out at one time have an effect upon the storage area needed. For example, canned goods may be issued by the case or by single tins. Cases may be stored on slats on the floor, whereas individual tins are best arranged on shelves. Foodstuffs that are packed in sacks may be issued as they are or in smaller amounts, in which case they will be emptied into bins to make it easier to weigh them out.

Perishable foods

Perishable foods include fish, meat, poultry, vegetables and fruit, and it is usual for these to be taken into stock by the chef after they have been inspected for weight, price, quality and suitability. They are kept in the larder until issued to the relevant partie, where they can be stored in the partie's refrigerator.

Cellar stock

All drinks are delivered directly to the cellar where items are placed in their respective bins either in readiness for service or, if applicable, to age and mature. The total area can be subdivided as required to provide sections that are more suitable for particular kinds of drink. For example, quality wines bought 'en primeur' must remain undisturbed for several years until they reach their peak. All wines require a constant temperature and dim lighting, regardless of the weather or time of day.

Cleaning materials

Cleaning materials must not be kept with foodstuffs, because even though they may not be strong smelling, they can pass their odour to commodities kept nearby. The layout of the store and positioning of goods should be planned to avoid the possibility of cross-contamination.

Physical requirements of stores

As well as the goods in store, stores staff have to be given consideration. The store should be a cool place, but conditions for staff must not fall below levels set in the Shops, Factories and Offices Act. The Act states that working conditions must be endurable; staff cannot be expected to work efficiently if the air temperature goes below 6°C.

An ambient temperature of 10°C is ideal for storage of non-perishable goods, but extremes should be eliminated. Hot water pipes that run through the store may cause localised hot areas and lack of ventilation can give rise to condensation which may affect goods such as cereals and canned foods.

Temperatures should not be allowed to fluctuate widely as this will cause spoilage and deterioration. We are not suggesting that store and cellar be insulated from the surrounding environment or that they be air-conditioned in order to provide the ideal atmosphere. It is a matter of making the best use of the space provided, using knowledge of how different goods keep under certain circumstances.

Humidity must also be considered. The amount of water vapour in the air is strictly limited but can increase as the temperature rises. When air that is saturated with water vapour cools, it gives up the excess vapour in the form of droplets of water which can cover the floor and walls and make conditions unsuitable or even dangerous. Relative humidity can be described as the amount of water present in the air, as a percentage of the maximum amount possible at a given temperature.

Refrigeration

With few exceptions all perishable commodities need to be kept in cold storage, which means having built-in coldrooms or free-standing refrigerators. Not long ago it was the practice to have a general-purpose coldroom. This is now illegal and it is necessary, for example, to keep raw meat in a separate refrigerator from cooked meat and to ensure that there is no transfer of smell and taste from one commodity to another because of close storage. The ideal set-up is to have a series of reach-in refrigerators, one for each separate class of commodity in the raw state, and to provide each kitchen partie with its own refrigerator for storing basic preparations.

The following gives an outline of refrigeration requirements for the various classes of perishable foods.

Meat

Fresh meat in carcass form should ideally be hung in a temperature of 2–4°C for sufficient time to become tender; joints and cuts should be spread out on trays on shelves and any drip wiped away regularly. Storage of meat requires 80 per cent relative humidity. Chilled meat can be stored at –2°C for up to one month; boneless meat in vacuum packs will keep for several weeks until opened when it must be treated as fresh meat. Frozen meat should be kept deep frozen at –18°C until required for use, then kept at 6°C until defrosted.

When meat that has been stored in the refrigerator is brought out to be prepared for cooking, the air surrounding it will be cooled to the temperature of the meat and the moisture content of the air will be condensed on to the surface of the meat, making it appear to be sweating. This moist surface will encourage the growth of spoilage organisms, which is why meat should not be brought back and forth from the refrigerator for cutting up to order.

Fish

Fresh fish should be kept in the fish tray of a refrigerator designed for this purpose, which allows any water from the fish to drain off. Crushed ice helps to prevent desiccation of fillets of fish and keeps them smelling sweet. If live fish are kept, the fish tank must be fitted with an oxygen supply and be fed during

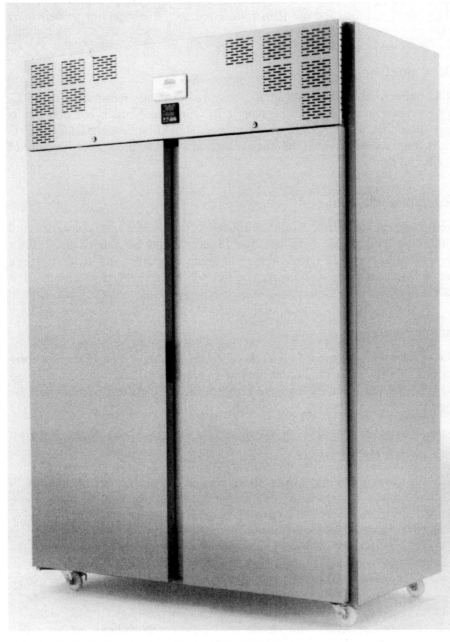

Plate 7   Sadia Refrigerator, from Viscount Catering Limited

their stay in the larder or restaurant if kept on display. For best results it is usual to purchase live shellfish, but they should be kept on ice and cooked as soon as possible. Fresh fish should be stored at 0–2°C; frozen fish should be stored at –18°C until required for use then transferred to the refrigerator to defrost at 6°C.

Dairy produce

Milk, butter, cheese and cream should be stored in a dairy refrigerator at 5–7°C. Whole cheese in the rind can be kept at 10°C in a cool larder. For best results eggs should be kept cool, but as with cheese should be brought back to 15°C when ready to use or serve. All must be kept covered to prevent any transfer of smells and flavour.

Vegetables and fruit

Fresh vegetables and fruit should be treated as perishables and kept under cool conditions until required for use, but ideally should be ordered daily. Root vegetables do not need refrigerating and green vegetables and salad stuffs are safe at 8°C. Soft fruits such as strawberries will ripen slowly at 5°C, melons at 10°C.

Frozen foods

The storage temperature for all kinds of frozen food is –18°C. If kept for long periods, it may need protection against freezer burn. Stocks of frozen food must be rotated correctly and the temperature of the deep freezer must be constant.

Clarence Birdseye

Clarence Birdseye (1886–1956) was an American inventor who once worked in Labrador as a fur trader. During the four years he was there he took note of the fish coming ashore from the fishing fleets, frozen hard because of the freezing temperature at sea.

Back home in America he experimented with frozen foods and developed a method of deep freezing to preserve foods for future use. The automatic freezing machine he invented was patented in 1924 and frozen goods gradually came into use; now a deep-freeze cabinet is an important piece of kitchen equipment in most homes and catering establishments. At first frozen foods used to come as solid blocks, but are now mostly individually frozen before packaging.

Clarence Birdseye's name lives on as the brand name of high-quality frozen food made by Unilever.

Prevention of contamination

The storeroom and cellar must be kept in a clean condition at all times and staff encouraged to be conscious of the need for good hygiene standards. Infestation must not be allowed to develop unchecked. Mice and rats must be prevented from entering under outer doors or by means of drainpipes, and all foods should be kept in rodent-proof containers. Flies can be killed by installing an electrically operated fly killer with an ultraviolet tube to attract and an electric grill to kill them. Birds, weevils, grain moths, cockroaches, beetles and silver fish are difficult to stop once they have gained a hold in a place. A contract with a firm of pest exterminators will keep pests in check and eventually rid the premises of them. The environmental health officer will advise on protection and decontamination.

Stores equipment

The fitments installed in the stores should aim to use the available space to maximum advantage, with shelves of an ideal depth and passage ways that will accommodate a trolley without being wasteful of space.

Shelving

The shelving must be stout enough to take anticipated loads and capable of being altered if the layout needs to be changed at any time. Regulations forbid the storage of open foods on the floor. Floor space should be used only for storage bins, preferably on castors, and for cases of canned foods, though they ought to be on slats to prevent them getting damp when the floor is washed. Goods in frequent use should be stored close to the issuing point at a height of one metre; goods in only occasional demand can be on higher shelves and at a distance from the serving counter. It is advantageous to know the range and kind of goods which will be used, their packing, and the estimated frequency of ordering and delivery, as this will determine the amount and type of shelving or cupboards required.

Shelving can be bought in modular form as free-standing with a load-bearing limit, as wall-mounted and adjustable, or in self-assembly packs. They can be made from wood, chrome wire, laminated plastic, aluminium alloy or other rust-free metal. It is worth considering the use of mobile racking that can double as trolleys on receipt, storage and delivery of goods to service departments.

Scales

The most important pieces of equipment in the store are the scales required for weighing receipts and issues. A platform scale is required for checking heavy goods on delivery and smaller sets of scales for weighing out goods as requisitioned. It is not advisable to move scales around and, to be completely level, they must be placed on a firm, even surface at the most useful point. A maintenance contract with the manufacturer will ensure correct issues and receipts.

Other items

Other items of equipment required are a desk and chair for use by the store-person, a ladder to reach goods from high shelves, refrigerators, tables, bins, containers, measuring equipment such as scoops and knives, and washing and drying facilities.

Rotation of stock

A principle of first in, first out (FIFO) must be followed so that old stock is not allowed to accumulate. This means putting the fresh delivery behind existing stock and always issuing goods at the front first. In the case of dry goods such as rice and milk powder stored loose in containers, it is advisable to deplete stock before tipping in the new delivery. Some commodities have a strong smell or ripen during storage, which means they must be used before they become over-ripe and obnoxious.

All goods, even canned goods, have an optimum shelf-life during which time they are at their best; thereafter they gradually lose quality. If condensation makes the store damp, canned goods may rust and in time the metal will deteriorate and affect the contents. The storeperson should have a good working knowledge of the shelf-life of commodities and thus be able to prevent anything exceeding it.

Stock levels

It is important to set a minimum and maximum stock level for each commodity. The minimum level must be set so that the store will never completely run out of stock, bearing in mind the time required to obtain fresh supplies. The maxi-mum level is set taking account of space available, amount of capital to be tied up in stocks of goods, regularity of deliveries and rates of issues. Bin cards show-ing issues and stock in hand are necessary to maintain stock levels.

The only time when agreed stock levels may be disregarded is when a supplier offers a greatly reduced price for a bulk order, but the buyer must first be sure that storage space is available and that the commodity is one that will be used constantly. In many stores there is a stock of items which, because of a change of chef or a new menu, no longer gets used and slowly gathers dust and starts to deteriorate. Notification to the compiler of menus can usually take care of this problem.

The buyer will be given a budget figure showing how much of the firm's capi-tal may be tied up in the form of goods in stock. Money can earn more on deposit with a bank than as goods on shelves. If, however, the class of business includes the selling of fine wines, then stock levels should be set as high as possible. Not only do fine wines appreciate in value, but once sold they are often impossible to replace.

Stores control documents

The activities of the stores and cellar need to be carefully controlled. A series of forms acts as records of each transaction for the receipt and issue of goods. A document is necessary to authorise every movement of goods in and out of stock. The following account of the receipt and requisitioning of goods gives examples of the forms in general use. There are several different versions of these, but in general they provide the basic details which govern all individual transactions.

Ordering

Orders for goods must be written on an official form in an order book, usually in triplicate, and must be signed by an authorised person. Some orders are placed by telephone, but must still be covered by an official order. All orders will have a number printed on the page. The top copy is sent to the supplier and is the means of obtaining payment for the goods supplied. The second copy is kept in the store for checking against the delivery note and invoice when the goods arrive, and for entering into the filing system. The third copy remains in the order book for any queries which may arise; any alterations such as short delivery or non-availability should be noted on it.

Figure 52 shows a sample order form of the kind used by a group or authority for ordering supplies. The order can be written or typed in and prices can be entered as agreed by telephone or from the price list issued by the supplier. The form may be designed for folding and sealing.

Figure 53 shows a sample order form used for supplies ordered under contract. The following supply conditions will be printed on the back of the form:

1 The specifications regarding quality as laid down by the purchasing officer must be adhered to.
2 A delivery note must be sent with the goods.
3 The amount as indicated must be supplied; no over-supply will be accepted.
4 The prices set out under contract agreement are not to be increased without notice.

Some wholesalers with a contract to supply all the establishments within a company or authority find it practical to print order forms which list every commodity in use, with a few lines for the buyer to write in items outside the normal range. A pad with a year's supply all correctly dated may be given to each unit. The week's order is written in triplicate and handed to the driver for the following week at the time of delivery of the current week's order. The duplicate comes back as the delivery note and the authorisation to pay the account. This

Figure 52   Sample order form

Universal
H O T E L   L T D

Pondtown Rd, Stornfold

To: Knightley & Co. Ltd
10–18 Charles Rd
Cross Trading Estate
Bilstown

Order No. 12882

Please supply: £   p

5 × 10 litres Bestco frying oil
1 × 2½ litres olive oil
10 kg long grain rice
1 × 1 kg tins ground ginger
2 kg cornflour
5 kg sultanas
5 kg currants
1 case sauerkraut
12 × 300 g jars Café Hag
10 × 500 g drums grated Parmesan

Please quote the above order number on your invoice.

Signed: _____

Date: _____

system avoids the need to write out official order forms. Figure 54 shows a sample form of this type.

Some suppliers employ sales staff who phone establishments to solicit orders, give current prices, make special offers, and discuss the market situation. Others employ representatives or salespeople who make regular visits to establishments. They assist the buyer in making out an order by quoting the supply availability and actual prices, as well as any special lines. Some firms send sales/delivery people with vans loaded with their range of goods for the buyer to decide what is required on the spot. In all these cases it is essential to write out an order form to cover all the items ordered or purchased.

Deliveries

There should always be someone on duty to receive incoming goods. It is always better to check deliveries when they arrive than for someone to sign the note

Figure 53   Sample order form for contract use

ORDER FORM			No. J 21863

ORDER FORM   No. J 21863
Date:

Universal
HOTEL LTD

Pondtown Rd, Stornfold

Please supply the undermentioned goods:

Amount	Item	Unit price	Specification no.	Cost £	p
180	Lemon sole fillets and bones		35		
2 kg	Peeled prawns, fresh		18		
12 kg	Smoked haddock fillets		3		
10 × 2 kg	Scampi, jumbo		16		
30 kg	Whole cod, headless		28		
6 kg	Kippers		4		

Please see conditions on reverse of form.

To: James Fish Suppliers & Co., Hull

Signed: _____
          (Purchasing Officer)

saying 'unexamined', with the bother of taking up any discrepancies on the phone later. When goods are delivered they should be checked against the order and delivery note for exactness, and weighed or counted and inspected for quality. If standard purchasing specifications are part of the established procedure, the goods need to be carefully checked against these specifications. Where prices appear on the delivery note, they must be compared with the agreed price and any variation taken up with the supplier. The goods must be taken into the store immediately and not left lying around outside. The various items must be entered into the goods received book if one is kept; if not, in the ledger or on the bin cards.

Figure 55 shows a sample delivery note.

The following points relate to delivery notes:

1 The form of delivery note can vary widely; some firms have every item they supply printed on the note, with only the number of units ordered needing to be entered. Very often prices are not included on the delivery note.

Figure 54   Combined order form, delivery note and authorisation to pay

INVOICE ORDER

To Messrs Gravender & Sharmer, Thalmar House, Charnton. CN1 7RT

Please supply the goods indicated during the week ending:

To: Foreman Green School

Signed: E. Gregory   Date: Order No. H 0372

Commodity	Unit	Unit No.	Units req.	Unit cost	£ p	Commodity	Unit	Unit No.	Units req.	Unit cost	£ p
Apple, solid pack	A10	6001	6			Currants	3 kg	7001	2		
Apricot pulp	5 kg	6002	3			Dates	5 kg	7002			
Gooseberries	A10	6003				Desiccated coconut	3 kg	7003			
Mandarin oranges	A10	6004	6			Glacé cherries	1 kg	7005	2		
Peach caps	K3	6005				Mixed peel	3 kg	7006			
Pineapple crush	A10	6006	6			Prunes 50/60	12½ kg	7007			
Pineapple rings	A10	6007				Raisins, seedless	12½ kg	7008			
Baked beans	A10	8010	18			Sultanas	12½ kg	7009			
Broad beans	A10	8011				Almonds, flaked	500 g	7010			
Celery hearts	A10	8012				Almonds, ground	3 kg	7011			
Carrots, whole	A10	8013	6			Almonds, nibbed	500 g	7012			
Sweetcorn niblets	75 oz	8014				Walnuts, shelled	3 kg	7013			
Tomato purée	1 kg	8015	24								
						Lemon essence	500 ml	4003	1		
Beans, butter	3 kg	9010	1			Raspberry essence	500 ml	4004			
Beans, haricot	3 kg	9011				Strawberry essence	500 ml	4005			
Lentils	3 kg	9012				Vanilla essence	1 litre	4006			
Peas, yellow split	3 kg	9013									
Pearl barley	7 lb	9014				Sugar, caster	50 kg	3101	1		
Rice, Japan	25 kg	9015	2			Sugar, Demerara	5 kg	3102			

Figure 55   Sample delivery note

DELIVERY NOTE

James Fish Suppliers
HULL

To: Universal Hotel
    Pondtown Road
    Stornfold

Your order No: J 21863   Dated: No.   07351

                                                     Date:

		Unit cost	£ p
180	fillets lemon sole		
2 kg	peeled prawns		
10 × 2 kg	pkts jumbo scampi		
12 kg	fillet smoked haddock		
30 kg	headless whole cod		
	(regret no kippers)		

Delivery date:

Received by:

2 The delivery note is often made out in duplicate, one of the signed copies being taken back by the delivery person.

3 Some suppliers use invoices as delivery notes.

Stock records – cards and files

It is essential to have a system of consolidating the various aspects of stores operation and control. Stock record cards and files can offer an efficient way of doing this. Single stock record cards are simple to use but time-consuming to make up. The details are easy to see at a glance and give information regarding dates, receipts, issues and stock in hand, together with its value. Figure 56 is an example of this type of stock card.

Figure 57 shows a bin card which gives more information. As with the stock card it is kept in the stores or store office and is made up each time a transaction takes place, either the receipt of a delivery or the issue of stock to a department. It shows both the cost of issues and the value of stock in hand.

A perpetual stock file can give relevant information concerning the complete stock of the store in a single easily available form. It consists of a loose-leaf file containing a form for each item. The forms are held by ring binders and arranged so that the name of each item is immediately visible on opening the book. The name of the commodity is written on one of the forms and inserted in the file in alphabetical order or in groups according to kind, e.g. flour, baking powder, dried milk, custard powder, cornflour, canned fruit, vegetables. Each day's transactions are entered and the balance should agree with the actual amount in the stores. When one of the forms is filled up a new one can be clipped in. This type of multiple stock sheet is useful for calculating kitchen percentages, provided, of course, that accurate records are kept. They are also used for stocktaking at the end of the trading period. Figure 58 is an example of this type of stock sheet.

Figure 56   Example of a stock record card

STOCK RECORD							
Item: Salad oil					Minimum stock: 10 litres Maximum stock: 50 litres		
Date	Stock	Additions	Issues	Balance	Unit price	Value £	p
15.2.19_ _	30	30	10	50	120p	60	00
22.2.19_ _	50	00	10	40		48	00
29.2.19_ _	40	00	10	30		36	00
5.3.19_ _	30	30	10	50	125p	62	50

Figure 57   Example of a bin card

Item: Spaghetti									Minimum stock: 10 pkts Maximum stock: 50 pkts		

Unit   500 g packs

Price: 25p   Supplier: Greenleighs

	Received				Issued				In hand		
Date	Quantity	Value £	p	Quantity	Value £		p	Quantity	Value £		p
Jan 30								32	8		00
Jan 30				10	2		50	22	5		50
Feb 3				10	2		50	12	3		00
Feb 6	40	10	00					52	13		00
Feb 8				6	1		50	46	11		50
Feb 9				8	2		00	38	9		50

Figure 58   Example of a loose leaf from a perpetual stock file

Item: Butter		Code No. 28		Unit 500 g	Min. stock 80			Max. stock 140		

Date 19_ _	Department issued to	Quantity			Unit price £ p	Value					
		Issued	Received	Balance		Issues £ p	Received £ p	Balance £ p			
June 1 Kitchen		5		50	2 00	10 00		100 00			
June 2 Stillroom		4	20	66		8 00	40 00	132 00			
June 3 Kitchen		6		60		12 00		120 00			
June 3 Pastry		4		56		8 00		112 00			
June 3 Dining Room		2		54		4 00		108 00			
June 4 Kitchen		6		48		12 00		96 00			
June 4 Stillroom		4		44		8 00		88 00			

Stocktaking and valuation

Regular stocktaking of the contents of store and cellar will ensure that these departments are being operated efficiently and that the goods on the stock sheets are actually in hand. Stocktaking can assist in increasing the profitability of a business because:

1 it helps in formulating buying policy
2 it pinpoints any weaknesses in pricing policy
3 it assists in forecasting
4 it draws attention to overstocking
5 it ensures that goods received have been invoiced and accounted for
6 it is a necessary part of budgetary control.

The best system will be a simple one that is tailored to the size of the business. It should not take an undue length of time to carry out and any possible error of calculation should be eliminated, or at least reduced to a minimum. Good staff like to know that stocktaking is carried and will not mistrust it, even though it may sometimes take the form of a spot check. Stocktaking shows store and cellar staff that management is interested in their affairs and wants them to be cost-conscious.

It is possible to put all this stock and inventory control into a microcomputer system which will rationalise and possibly reduce unit stock levels, thus improving storage efficiency. The routine clerical functions would be reduced by basing inventory control on minimum stock levels and average usage data, to produce pre-costed re-ordering lists.

Security of stock and stores premises

It is very important to keep stocks of food, drink, cleaning materials and small equipment safe so that no losses occur. Responsibility for the security of stocks and the premises where they are kept must be given to somebody of integrity who will not allow any dishonesty or permit any unauthorised person on the premises. Arrangements for the handling of stores keys must ensure that they are not accessible to people who are not entitled to use them. All refrigerators and cupboards must be kept locked. Strict and regular stocktaking, together with random spot checks on desirable goods at all issuing points, will make pilfering impossible, even to an employee who considers that a share of the firm's property is a perk of the job.

Stores issuing

Stock held in the stores or cellar may be issued only on presentation of an authentic requisition signed or countersigned by an authorised person. No unsigned checks should be honoured and no stores issued on the promise of a requisition to come later. Only when standard issues are in operation can stores be issued automatically without a covering requisition.

It is the responsibility of the stores or cellar assistant to issue only goods as intended, to get someone to counter-check them, and to deliver only to the appropriate section or person authorised to collect them. The person receiving the goods should also check them for correctness.

As goods are issued so the amounts should be deducted from bin cards or entered on the file as in Figure 58. Each requisition will be costed by the stores-person so that at the end of each day's business the total value of issues is known. The value of perishable items ordered for the day's menus has to be added in, even though they may not have gone through the stores. These figures are required in order to arrive at the kitchen profit percentage.

A deadline is needed for the submission of requisitions beyond which the stores are closed. This is for stores staff to attend to routine clerical and other duties.

Requisitions

Requisitions originate from the various departments and sections of the establishment such as the kitchen, stillroom, dining-room and dispense bar. In a large kitchen each chef de partie will look at the menu for the following day and decide the kind and amount of goods required to produce the estimated number of dishes. He or she will then write out a list, submit it to the head chef or sous chef for approval, and receive the issue first thing in the morning. The head or sous chef countersigning the requisition will be experienced enough to judge whether all the items are actually required and have the authority to delete or diminish any item. All the signed requisitions are sent to the stores and the orders are made up and distributed as required.

Figure 59 shows an example of a requisition from the fish section, listing the day's stores required to carry out the cooking of fish as determined by the menu. It is for use in conjunction with the items supplied from the larder; the fish itself will have been ordered through the normal ordering system.

Figure 59   Sample requisition form

UNIVERSAL HOTEL		Kitchen requisition No. 26			
Fish section		Date			
Please supply:		Unit	Price	£	p
2 kg	unsalted butter	500 g			
60	eggs	dozen			
4 litres	cream	litre			
10 litres	milk	litre			

Larder issues

Raw commodities are prepared in the larder and fish larder before they are despatched to the kitchen sections for cooking, and the chefs in charge of these two preparation sections (which are often combined) have to ensure they hold sufficient stock to cater for the expected business of the day.

The control over this system of issuing is the twice-daily stocktaking list of all meat, poultry, game, fish, shellfish, and other important items such as smoked salmon, caviar and foie gras. It is drawn up at the close of business after each meal and shows the stock in hand from the previous sheet, the day's deliveries, and the amounts issued to the kitchen. This list is handed to the head chef who can quickly check that the issues match the day's business. Control is made by comparing the issues with the number of portions sold.

Payment of accounts

Every catering establishment relies on its suppliers to provide prompt delivery of goods, and in return the suppliers of commodities need prompt and regular payment of their accounts. The establishment should therefore pass accounts for payment as soon as possible, once they have been checked as being correct. The temptation to delay payment of accounts until the last possible moment so that money can remain in the deposit account accruing interest should not override the requirement to pay within a reasonable length of time after receipt of the invoice. Persistently bad payers risk not being allowed credit facilities and may be made to pay in cash for every delivery. Non-payment can cause a supplier to use a firm of debt-recovery agents which will pay out a percentage of all the money owed, thus providing the necessary cash flow for the supplier to continue in business while the debts are collected.

Figure 60 shows a typical invoice. Some firms issue a monthly statement showing dates of orders, order numbers, amounts due, any credits allowed, and amount outstanding at the end of each month. An invoice is a business document that states the price of goods as sold, the terms of payment and the discount if any; it should be compared with the monthly statement before payment is made. Where goods are delivered incorrectly and have to be returned to the supplier, they should not be deducted from the delivery note and invoice but accounted for by a supplier's credit note. The amount will appear on the monthly statement.

Electronic control

In practice, all of the procedures outlined in this chapter would be carried out on a computer programmed to deal with every transaction in all sections of the food and beverage operation. Only a very small-scale operator would carry out these

Figure 60   Example of an invoice

INVOICE	James Fish Suppliers

To: Universal Hotel
　　Pondtown Road
　　Stornfold

HULL

No.   6070

Date:

Product code	Quantity	Item	Unit cost	Total £ p
10052	20 kg	Lemon sole fillets	£2.05	41. 00
10053	6 kg	Herrings	£1.90	11. 40
13055	20 kg	Whole salmon	£4.10	82. 00
14122	30 kg	Whole cod	£3.75	102. 50

procedures manually, but a sound knowledge of the principles is essential to every manager and owner who wants to keep a human touch to the job.

Barcoding

The checkout system used in shops and stores of all kinds, where a scanner shines a thin infra-red beam on the bar code of every item purchased, can be used in the large-scale distribution of meals. These can be at ambient, chilled or frozen temperature, packed in individual or multi-portion packs for use in hospitals, schools, factory canteens, in-flight food production centres and other outlets. The barcode identifies the item, its individual price, total price, time and date of distribution, and can provide management with details of the current stock position of all goods, their value and date of production. The barcode system was developed by Joseph Woodland in the late 1960s.

Electronic Data Interchange

Electronic Data Interchange (EDI) is a link that can be set up between the purchasing officer of an establishment and a supplier of materials for the routine ordering and invoicing of certain supplies. This system eliminates the traditional way of telephoning the order through and also makes the use of a fax machine unnecessary. There are no paper invoices and therefore no expenditure on headed order forms, envelopes and postage stamps. The system rejects any incorrect orders and out-of-line ordering procedures and gives much greater control than traditional systems of obtaining supplies.

Further reading

Coltman, M. M. (1997) *Hospitality Management Accounting*. John Wiley & Sons

Compton, H. and Jessop, D. (1995) *Dictionary of Purchasing and Supply*. Tudor Business

Gadde, L. and Hakan, H. (1994) *Professional Purchasing*. International Thomson Business Press

Stefanelli, J. (1997) *Purchasing, Selection and Procurement for the Hospitality Industry*. Wiley

Woods, F. and Lightowlers, P. (1985) *Purchasing, Costing and Finance in the Hotel & Catering Industry*. Addison Wesley Longman

12 Production and distribution I
Organisation and operation

Organisation; Types of authority relationships; The role of management; The kitchen; Kitchen organisation; Kitchen staff; Kitchen routine; Productivity; Continuous production techniques; The dining-room; Dining-room staff; Methods of food and beverage service; Routine of the dining-room; The bars; Ancillary areas.

A catering operation supplies three elements – food, drink and service. In the main, food is produced on the premises from raw materials then served directly or distributed to service points for sale to consumers. Drink is usually dispensed in much the same form as it is purchased, except for hot beverages which are made on the premises. The third element, service, stems from the first two and depends on the skill and personality of staff. The activities surrounding these three elements take place in the main areas of the operation – the kitchen, dining-room and bars. These areas exist as separate units each with a person in charge, but since they are so closely related it is essential to have a person in overall charge to coordinate the entire operation. This person supervises the whole organisation and the routine operation of the three areas, and is responsible for the work of every member of staff in the catering department.

Organisation

Organisation in this sense means the distribution of tasks necessary to achieve the set objectives to members of staff, so that each can contribute to the success of the enterprise. This involves:

1 assessing the component parts of the operation
2 determining how these can best be done, without duplication of effort and in the most efficient and economical manner
3 assigning the individual tasks which make up the total operation to specific persons or teams
4 defining how the various tasks can be accomplished with minimum effort but maximum efficiency; this may include financial budgets and the need to follow company codes of ethical practice, for example when purchasing materials

5 ensuring that every member of staff clearly understands their responsibilities and accountability; this is particularly important in an enterprise which is organised into departments, as without a clearly defined structure of authority a subordinate may be unaware of limits on decision making which could lead to conflict.

Types of authority relationships

Line management authority

In a line management organisation, lines of authority are clearly defined and there is a direct subordinate/superior relationship. The various aspects of authority rank from the top of the hierarchy down the line, with each member of staff knowing who they are responsible to and who is accountable to them. The advantages of this are:

1 job descriptions can be precise
2 decision making is quick
3 clear lines of responsibility are shown
4 problem areas are easy to identify

Functional authority

In a functional authority organisation, each specialist function is under a professionally qualified and experienced head whose parameters of operation would be laid down by the board of directors or general manager. There are specialists in charge of such areas as sales and marketing, purchasing, accounting and control, and personnel. In each individual unit of the company, specific areas would be the responsibility of the particular heads of department actually working there, the advantage being that each is a specialist and has complete authority over an area. At head office level there may be an executive or adviser who decides the general policy for the entire company, but in this case there must be a clearly defined structure to avoid any possible duplication of effort.

Line and staff authority

This type of organisation appears to combine the advantages of both previous styles, as it operates on functional lines together with a line management approach. It retains central control with specialists having no direct control over individual managers or departmental heads, but helping in an advisory capacity to establish a framework of operations. A major drawback of this type of organisation is that it can be used only by large groups which can afford to employ the necessary range of specialists.

The role of management

The role of management should be easy to define because of the known framework in which each manager works, but in practice it is ambiguous. The catering industry has a reputation for having old-fashioned ideas on how to run its business. Established practices usually prevent any new methods being introduced. Old hands take pride in sticking to traditional ways and will not undergo any development training to improve their efficiency. The result of this is that the very people who could make a worthwhile contribution to better food and beverage operations, for example head chefs, are seldom promoted to the post of food and beverage manager, so their specialist knowledge does not become available to bring about changes in established practices.

Is the head chef or head waiter a manager or a head of department? In the organisation of a large establishment they are actually managers in charge of major departments that can be virtually self-contained. But where a combination of line and staff organisation is in use and central control is exerted, a head chef may be given authority to place orders with nominated suppliers under contractual agreement negotiated by head office. In such instances structural guidelines are given rather than explicit statements which have to be followed to the letter.

The managerial task

The major responsibilities of the line or functional manager are to:

1 interpret the objectives of the company, or in some cases to determine the objectives
2 plan how these objectives can be achieved
3 organise and establish the framework in which these objectives can be achieved efficiently
4 monitor, control and coordinate progress towards the achievement of the objectives.

These responsibilities apply to the people in charge of the main departments of a catering operation. In the following pages we attempt to show how the techniques of management are related to the practical organisation of the kitchen, dining-room, bars and their ancillary departments.

The kitchen

The kitchen is the department where food as a raw material is processed into dishes by a team of cooks working under a head cook or head chef. The head chef's responsibility is to allocate the workload between the various kitchen sections and to see that the results are of the expected standard. He or she organises the kitchen on specialisms by assigning particular tasks to specialists in those tasks. This is known as the 'partie' system in which the team of cooks of various grades is divided into separate sections, each dealing with a particular aspect of cookery and supplying certain sections of the menu. The term kitchen brigade is sometimes used to describe the full staff of a kitchen. All kitchens of whatever size and in any type of catering operation run on this system, albeit modified or adapted where necessary. It leads to efficient operation and better results when compared with moving staff from one task to another during the course of the daily routine. It functions well in all situations from a fast-food unit to a continuous production cook-freeze or cook-chill operation.

Figure 61 shows the kitchen brigade in its most extensive form. It can be modified by combining some of the parties according to the type and amount of business done as well as the physical space available in a particular kitchen.

The kitchen of a small establishment could be staffed as shown in Figure 62. Here the head chef might run the sauce, roast and fish section until service time then take over on the hotplate to supervise the service, leaving the commis to dish up the food to order. In the absence of the head chef, the sauce, roast and fish chef would take over the running of the kitchen in the capacity of sous chef. If administrative duties were found to occupy a lot of time, a senior chef would be needed to run the partie, while the head chef advised and assisted whenever possible.

The kitchen of a large-scale establishment, such as a hospital or factory, might be staffed as shown in Figure 63. There will be less emphasis on specialisms, with every member of staff being capable of carrying out any of the necessary duties. The head cook or kitchen superintendent would probably run the section, producing main meals and carrying out administrative duties delegated by the caterer. The assistant cooks could move from one section to another on a rota so as to ensure all-round experience.

Kitchen organisation

The first step in kitchen organisation is to establish the scope, size and nature of the operation. Normally there will be policy guidelines on the objectives, nature and standard of the operation. More luxurious establishments will charge higher prices and be run on classical lines, offering mainly à la Carte dishes with perhaps a Table d'Hôte menu at lunchtime. A busy establishment of this kind, serving say 200 dinners, could well require 30 staff in the kitchen.

The head chef needs to break down the overall task into its components, grouping these in an orderly sequence of self-contained sections:

1 the production of a work schedule which indicates exactly what has to be produced for any one meal in accordance with the menu
2 the purchase of materials according to the requirements by means of the agreed procedures
3 the issue of these materials for processing
4 the preparation of meals

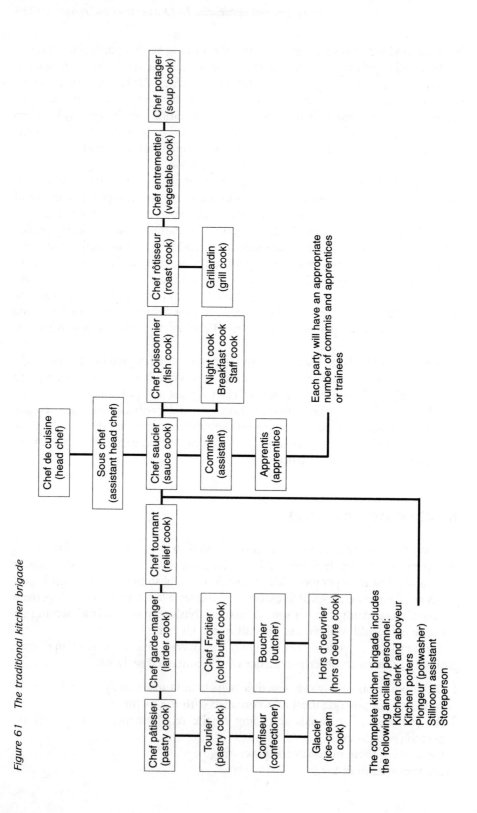

Figure 61   The traditional kitchen brigade

Figure 62   The kitchen staff of a small establishment

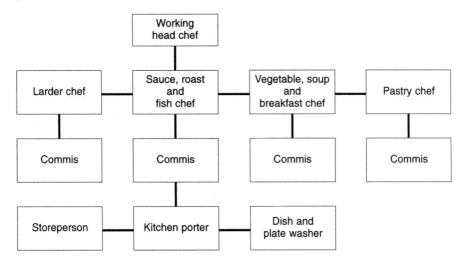

Figure 63   The kitchen staff of a large-scale establishment

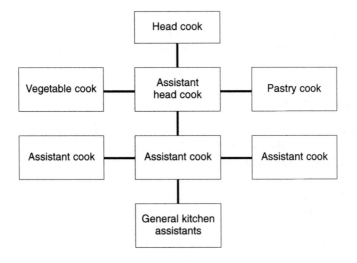

5 the distribution of meals to customers
6 the organisation of the ancillary support services of washing up and cleaning
7 the staffing of the kitchen groups and supportive services.

Once these components have been identified, thought must be given to their actual location to enable the progression of activities to proceed in a logical sequence. From these the levels of manning can also be determined.

The sequence of operations in a kitchen of any size is shown in Figure 64. Areas 1–8 usually come under the control of the head chef. He or she allocates

Figure 64   The sequence of operations

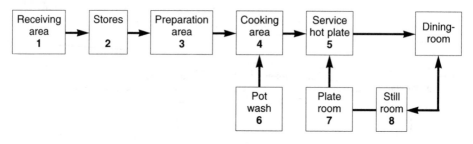

the number of staff required to operate each area, basing it on experience or by an allowance of manpower per customer served, according to the type of operation.

Kitchen staff

The following details cover all the staff who might be employed in the kitchen of a large organisation and give an outline of the duties and responsibilities of each. As previously indicated, the actual names, grades and numbers of staff are determined by the operation and can be scaled down to suit all types and sizes of kitchen.

Head chef (chef de cuisine)

The head chef holds one of the most important positions in a catering establishment. The success of the establishment and its reputation depend to a great extent on his or her knowledge. The head chef is responsible for producing or advising on menus which will satisfy customers and at the same time provide a satisfactory financial return for the business. To do this effectively he or she has to keep abreast of changes in taste and fashion as they arise, which can mean interpreting and adapting traditional recipes to the specific needs of the clientele. The head chef determines the quality and quantity of materials required and must communicate these by means of purchasing specifications to the storekeeper who places the orders. When compiling menus he or she must take care to allocate the work evenly amongst the sections of the kitchen and must interpret and communicate desired standards to the staff. The head chef is ultimately responsible for the correct preparation, presentation and quality of all dishes, both hot and cold, which are served to customers. To ensure this is carried out successfully, he or she must:

1 keep up to date with information on seasonal availability so that menus are fresh and interesting with a suitable variety of items
2 note customers' complaints and take immediate action to rectify them, at the same time bringing this to the notice of staff

3 ensure that there is no unnecessary waste and that regular stocktaking is carried out
4 maintain the desired kitchen percentage of profit and be good at interpreting figures
5 produce the annual budget for the department and operate within it
6 be a good disciplinarian and maintain a code of conduct for staff that is ethical
7 keep calm under stress
8 maintain good standards of safety and hygiene
9 see that apprentices and trainees receive proper tuition
10 maintain good relationships with staff and with other heads of department and management.

Assistant head chef (sous chef)

A large busy kitchen will need more than one senior chef to carry out the volume of work, the most senior acting as the immediate subordinate to the head chef. If banqueting is part of the operation there will be one sous chef specifically for this; others could be related to the early and late shifts and all will participate in the service on the hotplate. A good sous chef needs to have expert knowledge of all sectors of the kitchen. The main duties of the sous chef are to:

1 relieve the head chef when absent and assist in day-to-day administration and organisation of the kitchen
2 countersign stores requisitions
3 take charge of banqueting work
4 arrange duty rotas, days off and holidays
5 act as staff manager to the kitchen
6 maintain good staff relationships.

Sauce cook (chef saucier)

It is generally recognised that the sauce cook is the most senior chef de partie, and it follows that the sauce section has great demands placed on it in terms of expertise and volume of work. The sauce cook is responsible for:

1 the production of all main meat dishes that are cooked by boiling, stewing, praising, poêling and shallow frying, together with their garnishes
2 the preparation of most hot sauces.

Larder cook (chef garde manger)

The larder is the kitchen storeroom and distribution point for all main perishable commodities. A good larder cook must ensure that all items are properly stored and used fresh and that all usable leftover dishes are reissued to avoid waste. In a large busy kitchen the larder cook is assisted by a butcher to deal with meat, a fishmonger to prepare raw fish, someone to prepare cold buffet work, and others to prepare hors-d'oeuvres, salads, the cheese board and fruit baskets. The larder cook is responsible for:

1 preparing and cutting meat
2 preparing poultry and game according to requirements
3 cleaning and preparing fish
4 sending raw prepared commodities for cooking to the correct partie at the right time and in the right quantities
5 preparing hors-d'oeuvres
6 preparing items for cocktail parties and receptions such as canapés, sandwiches and fillings for bouchées
7 preparing and decorating aspic jellies and chaudfroid for use in cold buffet items; also galantines, cold pies and pâtés
8 preparing simple and composed salads together with the necessary dressings and cold sauces
9 preparing the cheese board and fruit baskets
10 ensuring the correct storage and control of all items held in the cold store, and drawing up the daily stock sheets showing goods received, issued and in stock
11 advising the head chef on suitable items for the menu.

Pastry cook (chef pâtissier)

The pastry department of a large kitchen often runs as a separate entity under the overall direction of a chef who is responsible directly to the head chef. This is because of the specialist nature of the work. The staff do not usually move to other parties, unlike those in the main kitchen. In a large busy pastry department there are specialists for the preparation of basic pastes used in making pastries and sweet dishes; others are responsible for making ice-cream, sweets and presentation pieces in sugar, gum paste and nougat. The pastry cook is responsible for:

1 preparing, cooking and serving all hot and cold sweets on the menu, including ice-cream
2 preparing cakes and pastries for afternoon teas and receptions
3 preparing petits fours
4 baking, icing and decorating birthday and wedding cakes
5 preparing centrepieces in nougat and chocolate
6 preparing flan cases, vols-au-vent and barquettes for filling with hot or cold mixtures in the main kitchen or larder
7 covering pies and puddings
8 making hot soufflés, sometimes including savoury ones.

Fish cook (chef poissonier)

The cooking of fish and its accompanying sauces demands a high degree of skill, together with a certain feeling for delicacy and elegance. A good palate and a degree of finesse are the two most important attributes required by this job. The fish cook is responsible for:

1 cooking and presenting all hot fish and shellfish dishes except those that are deep fried or grilled
2 cooking fish and shellfish for cold presentation by the larder
3 preparing all hot fish sauces plus others such as Hollandaise and Béchamel.

Roast cook (chef rôtisseur)

The roast cook's work is based on three methods of cookery – roasting, grilling and deep frying. It covers a very wide range of items, including fish, meat, poultry, game, potatoes and vegetables. The roast cook is also responsible for the production of gravies and some of the sauces that accompany these dishes as well as the savouries. This job demands sound practical knowledge and experience in one of the basic cooking techniques, namely roasting. In large kitchens a member of this section is responsible as grill cook for all grilled items of food.

Vegetable cook (chef entremettier)

The vegetable cook's responsibility is for the preparation of all vegetables and potatoes on the menu and others that are served as a garnish with a main dish. Savoury soufflés are often made to order by this section. Although the position does not enjoy the same status as the sauce cook, the job calls for a high degree of organisation and attention to detail. Because of the amount of work involved in this section, it is usually well staffed with assistants. The description chef entremettier, which may appear illogical when applied to the vegetable cook, dates from the time when vegetables were served as a dish in their own right and were sandwiched between two other more important courses. In the nineteenth century this course was referred to as entremets and comprised a selection of sweet and vegetable dishes. Today the word entremets refers solely to the sweet course.

Soup chef (chef potager)

The soup cook is responsible for the preparation of special stocks for soups and others for general kitchen use. He or she is also responsible for the egg and farinaceous dishes that feature on the day's menu – usually only for lunch – and receives the sauces to accompany them from either the sauce or fish cook. Only a large busy kitchen would warrant a separate soup section, otherwise the work is part of the vegetable cook's responsibilities.

Relief cook (chef tournant)

A relief cook is usually employed only in a large busy kitchen that is open seven days a week. The role is to act as relief for the other chefs de partie when they take their day off during the week or at holiday time. This chef needs to know the work of each section, except perhaps that of the pastry and larder where the first commis usually takes over.

Breakfast cook

The breakfast cook usually works to a fixed menu that seldom changes since it covers most customers' requirements. Cooking breakfasts calls for a high degree of organisation and speed to satisfy customers. Because of the level of culinary skills and experience required, it does not rank as a separate partie. The breakfast cook usually assists on the vegetable section when the breakfast service ends.

Night cook (chef de nuit)

A night cook is engaged in an all-night restaurant or hotel offering night-time room service. Wide experience is required since a night cook usually works alone and may be called on to produce quite elaborate dishes. Usually the bulk of the work consists of making sandwiches, serving staff suppers and preparing early breakfasts.

Assistant cook

Commis are assistants who work under the orders of the chefs de partie. They are graded as first, second, and third commis according to length of service and ability, with the first commis being the direct assistant to the chef de partie and responsible for directing much of the work of the other commis. The term demi-chef is sometimes used to denote the first commis of each major partie.

In addition to the above there are staff employed in the ancillary departments of the kitchen who are dealt with later in this Chapter.

Equal opportunities

At one time hardly any female staff worked in professional kitchens. Those who were employed worked mainly in the stillroom or vegetable preparation area. The main kitchen was an all-male enclave where only strong men able to withstand the heat and throw the heavy saucepans around could survive.

College catering courses attracted many female students who attained high standards and, although most of them took jobs in the cost sector of the industry, some were accepted as commis in high-class kitchens, particularly in the pastry and hors-d'oeuvre sections.

Equal opportunity means that females must now be given access to jobs in the kitchen and dining-room and gain promotion according to their capabilities. This means that a woman could be promoted to head chef or head waiter to run the brigade of a large establishment. Applications from women must be given equal consideration to those from men and be selected on their competence and experience. The catering industry employs a large number of female staff who are entitled to the same rates of pay as male employees. Part-time female employees must be paid the full rate and be offered participation in a company pension scheme and share options.

Kitchen routine

It is very difficult to describe a pattern of routine which applies to all kitchens, as the routine varies according to factors such as the type of business, the menu, and the prices charged. The common elements are:

- ordering, storage and distribution of commodities for their preparation and cooking according to the envisaged numbers of customers
- serving prepared food directly to the customer or service staff
- cleaning and hygiene of kitchens and ancillary departments
- cleaning and maintenance of equipment.

However, it is useful to look at some associated factors and to detail some of the problems peculiar to them.

The length of the working day and the number of days worked each week depend on the type of business. In many instances, such as a hospital, the kitchen never closes and there is always someone on duty day and night every day of the year. In a school the kitchen would be open only from 10 a.m. to 3 p.m., Monday to Friday. The dining-room connected to every kitchen has to be open at mealtimes to serve the food, unless the kitchen is one that runs on continuous production lines and deep freezes or chills the meals; here production and distribution are totally divorced.

The routine of any kitchen is based on the menu and the expected number of meals to be prepared. The number of portions of each dish to be produced can be estimated from records of numbers sold and the comparative popularity of dishes. In institutional catering the number of consumers is usually fairly steady. The big question is, how many portions of each menu choice should be produced so that those who come at the last sitting are not disappointed because some dishes are sold out? There is no easy answer to this, but general opinion is that it is better to run out than be left with a lot of cooked food which may have to be used in rechauffé dishes.

In many establishments a combined à la Carte and Table d'Hôte menu is used on which any special dishes of the day and seasonal items can also be featured. This conventional type of operation can be quite complicated and requires good organisation with full cooperation between the kitchen and dining-room staff. An analysis of such an operation would reveal the following requirements:

- the staff of the kitchen must be seen as a whole, with each section working in close cooperation with the others to ensure smooth running
- every member of staff must conscientously fulfil a role in the organisation
- production must be able to meet demand, even though the forecast of business may be incorrect
- resources of materials and equipment must be at such a level that they can meet all possible demands
- the problem of over-production and subsequent utilisation must be overcome
- some spare capacity of staff may be needed to meet any extraordinary demands of business.

An à la Carte operation raises the problem of keeping sufficient stock of perishable items in perfect condition so that customers receive fresh food that has been cooked to order. If some food has to be used up before it starts to deteriorate, it should be sold off at a lower price on the Table d'Hôte menu. Its profitability as a possible à la Carte dish is of course lost.

Productivity

In an à la Carte system where only a certain amount of preparation is carried out beforehand and where all or most of the food is cooked as required, it is difficult to bring productivity to a desirable standard. This is because standing about or wasting time is inherent in the system. Much of the work will come in a rush over a short period of time, passing from one section of the kitchen to another as the various courses of the meal are served.

It is useful to distinguish between the terms production and productivity. Production refers to the transformation of an item from its raw state to a finished product. The production cycle is shown in Figure 65. Productivity refers to the ability of a firm to produce goods efficiently. It can be explained as follows.

1 Productivity results when a higher output is achieved from the same input, e.g. more portions are obtained from the same weight because of less shrinkage.
2 Productivity results when a higher output is achieved from a lower input, e.g. when fewer staff hours are needed to produce the same number of meals of a similar quality.

Figure 65   Production cycle

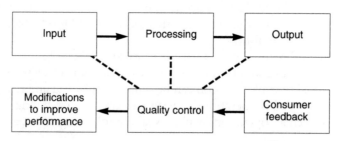

3 Productivity results when a slight increase in input produces a considerable increase in output, e.g. a larger capacity deep fryer may increase the number of items considerably whilst still using the same number of staff hours.

Thus in order to remain competitive an organisation must strive continuously to improve productivity. In catering, attempts to improve the use of resources in the kitchen have met with little success and only batch production on a short-run system has achieved good results and the necessary customer satisfaction. Most manufacturing industries operate on a long-run basis of continuous production which permits maximum use of resources. This is achieved mainly by using a capital-intensive method of production rather than labour-intensive methods. By its nature, catering is a labour-intensive industry and any move away from this will need to be prompted by some form of technological innovation.

It has been estimated that only 35–40 per cent of a cook's time is actually spent on preparing and cooking food, the remaining working hours being taken up with routine chores. Obviously a method of continuous production would save much wasted time and increase productivity; also the resources of space, equipment, labour and energy would be more fully utilised by such a system. It would show great savings, in sharp contrast to those obtained in traditional methods of food production. It is recognised that the partie system can be wasteful and cause higher prices, because even when every partie works continuously they do not always reach peak efficiency at the same time. Inevitably some wasted time and capacity is built into this system. The big troughs in the daily routine have traditionally been offset by having staff work on split duties, but this system, although still used, is not popular and enlightened employers offer straight shifts which helps with recruitment.

Another important factor is the non-utilisation of parts of the kitchen area during off-peak periods, which means that business rates are being paid on under-used premises. Efficiency in all these areas could be improved by the introduction of a process of continuous production. Technology might well provide the way, although many long cherished traditional rituals and attitudes would have to change.

Continuous production techniques

The systems that provide continuous production are cook-freeze and cook-chill. They function by concentrating on the production of one single item at a time and doing it on a large scale. The item is produced according to a rigid formula which covers all the various aspects of buying, issuing, cooking, packaging and preserving – on a large scale like this, there is no room for costly errors. The kitchens must be planned to allow for a good flow line of operations and the fixed equipment must be of a capacity to contain the number of portions being cooked. A small number of staff can cope with large numbers of portions and the facilities are in use throughout the day, meaning that production costs per dish can be very low. Continuous production systems are discussed further in Chapter 14.

The dining-room

There are many different kinds of dining-room and several names to describe them according to type and use. Names such as canteen, cafeteria, dining hall, dining-room, messroom and refectory indicate large eating places, possibly for use by residents; while names such as bistro, buttery, café, carvery, chophouse, coffee shop, diner, grillroom, pizza parlour, restaurant and trattoria indicate small-scale establishments, each supplying a specific need with a wide range of foods from snacks to full meals.

There are dining-rooms and restaurants that cater for every individual taste. Some have music from a pianist, a palm-court orchestra, danceband or tapes. Most are licensed to sell alcoholic drink with meals. Some restaurants serve only one kind of food, e.g. chicken or burgers. Some specialise in food of particular countries, e.g. Chinese, Indian, Japanese or Thai, or particular beliefs, e.g. kosher, vegan or vegetarian. Restaurant and pub chains offer their clientele a similar range of food, drink and decor in every branch. They often have a theme which gives people an impression of what to expect on the menu and bar tariff.

When people go out to dinner they choose a restaurant where they think the food and drink will be to their liking and suit their pocket, where they will not be kept waiting before being served, and where they find the atmosphere congenial. The decor may be outlandishly opulent or bland and minimalist. For example, a fast-food outlet will be clinically clean and bright, as the philosophy is to encourage a quick turnover of customers. In complete contrast, a luxury restaurant will have a restful background, encouraging customers to stay as long as they like and hopefully spend more money.

Staff play a part in creating an atmosphere in a pub or restaurant. Employees of a fast-food unit provide quick service in a lively but relatively informal manner. Colourful and well-designed uniforms add to the mood of the place. In contrast, the tranquil atmosphere of a high-class restaurant is complemented by unruffled and meticulous staff dressed in conventional clothing.

Dining-room staff

Just as there are many different kinds of dining-room, so there are several different ways of staffing them, usually according to the type of service offered and the prices charged. The traditional hierarchy of a luxury restaurant, shown in Figure 66, sets the pattern and can be modified according to requirements.

Restaurant manager

A restaurant manager in charge of the entire food service operation requires a wide knowledge of all aspects of catering, an ability with languages, an interest in current affairs, tact and diplomacy in dealing with customers, and a strong personality and pleasing appearance that reflect the style of the establishment and

Figure 66   Traditional staffing structure of a dining-room

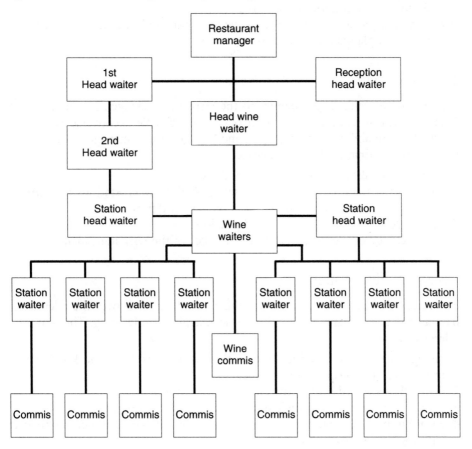

satisfy customers' expectations. Until fairly recently it was not uncommon for a restaurant manager to create a loyal clientele who would follow if he or she moved to a new establishment. There was often a special rapport between manager and customer which suggests that personality has as much pulling power as sumptuous surroundings. A restaurant manager is responsible for:

1 setting standards of service in all areas, including the bars and reception or foyer
2 carrying out internal training in all aspects of food and beverage service
3 organising an efficient system of table reservations to make proper use of space by combining customers' comfort with maximum occupancy
4 organising staff rotas to cover days off, sickness and holidays
5 arranging any special displays
6 instructing staff about dishes on the menu and service procedures for them
7 demonstrating specialised service techniques including flambé and guéridon work

8 receiving clients on their arrival, monitoring their satisfaction during the meal, and bidding them goodbye on leaving

9 supervising the smooth running of the operation and dealing with any problems or complaints that may arise.

First head waiter

The first head waiter is the deputy to the restaurant manager. He or she must have a wide knowledge and experience of catering, be able to converse easily with guests, have an ability with languages, and be a good staff manager. The responsibilities of the first head waiter include:

1 assisting the restaurant manager in all duties

2 allocating waiters to stations and rotating staff between stations in order to build up their confidence and ensure evenness of duties

3 carrying out specialised carving and guéridon work

4 taking charge of the restaurant in the absence of the restaurant manager.

Reception head waiter

The reception head waiter should be able to converse well over the telephone, have an ability with languages and have clear, legible handwriting. The responsibilities include:

1 taking reservations, entering them in the reservations diary, and keeping this in a correct and proper state of order

2 instructing selected staff in the taking of reservations

3 conducting customers to their reserved table and assisting in seating

4 ensuring that the restaurant is 'dressed' correctly and that customers are treated with the deference due to them.

Section or station head waiter

This person should have good organising ability and be able to maintain a good relationship with subordinate staff. There could be several section head waiters in a large establishment, each responsible for:

1 the smooth running of a section of the dining-room, comprising up to four stations

2 ensuring that the section is adequately staffed and briefed

3 seeing that the area is clean and tidy

4 seeing that the tables are correctly laid and the stations stocked

5 receiving guests from the reception head waiter and, after assisting them to their seats, explaining the menu, suggesting dishes and wine and taking the order

6 supervising the section during the service and dealing with any incidents or complaints.

Station waiter

A station waiter is known as a chef de rang and works under the supervision of the station head waiter. He or she is in charge of the service of a specific area of the room containing 4–6 tables, seating up to 20 customers. Responsibilities include:

1 helping to seat customers and offering them the menu
2 taking the order and sending a commis water to collect the dishes
3 serving the dishes to customers, remembering what each person ordered and in the correct order of protocol
4 ensuring customers are not kept waiting too long before being served
5 presenting the bill, taking the money to the cashier, and returning with the receipted bill and any change
6 clearing and relaying the table.

Commis waiter

The commis waiter is responsible for clearing the station and laying the tables. Duties include:

1 assisting with general preparations, e.g. filling cruets, fetching laundry, etc.
2 fetching food from the kitchen
3 clearing the table of dirties and taking soiled crockery and cutlery to be washed up
4 assisting with the easier parts of the service, e.g. serving coffee under the supervision of the station waiter.

In some restaurants an aspiring commis water may be given a small station to look after under the title of demi-chef de rang. This role is midway between a commis and a station waiter.

A young trainee waiter is sometimes known as a commis débarrasseur. With a foot on the bottom rung of the ladder, he or she must be of smart appearance, alert and have the ability to get on well with people, even though the duties at this stage are concerned only with cleaning up, taking out dirty dishes, bringing in clean plates and perhaps clearing the table.

Wine-waiting staff

The service of drink in a high-class restaurant is operated by separate waiting staff with a sound knowledge of wine and other drinks and their service. These members of staff are called wine waiters and they often wear a badge depicting a bunch of grapes to indicate their role; they may wear the insignia of the Guild of Sommeliers, their own professional body, and often wear a different colour jacket from ordinary waiters.

The head wine waiter is in charge of all wine-waiting staff and is responsible for the service of wine, spirits and soft drinks in the dining-room. The responsibilities involve:

1 taking the customers' orders for all drinks except those dispensed by the still-room
2 knowing the wine list intimately, being able to describe to customers the characteristic of each in proper terms and advising which wines go best with which food
3 knowing about other drinks such as aperitifs, cocktails, non-alcoholic beverages, liqueurs and beers
4 knowing when a wine is in poor condition and why
5 suggesting additions to the wine list
6 being able to open bottles correctly and to decant fine wines and vintage port
7 ensuring that wines are served at the correct temperature, in the correct type of glass
8 instructing wine waiters and commis in their duties
9 ensuring that close contact is maintained with the cellar regarding prompt delivery, adequate stock levels and adjacent sites
10 ensuring the correct functioning of the dispense bar and its efficient control, although in some circumstances this responsibility may be that of the head bartender
11 ensuring that this section makes a significant contribution to the profitability of the operation.

Wine waiters carry out the service of wine for a number of stations, working in liaison with the food waiters but coming under the jurisdiction of the head wine waiter.

In addition there are a number of commis wine waiters whose duties would be mainly concerned with bringing the right kind of glasses for different wines.

There are a number of ancillary staff connected with the dining-room and they are dealt with later in this chapter.

Job prospects for waiting staff

The catering industry employs a very large number of people for the sole purpose of serving food and drink to customers. At catering colleges the skills of serving at table are learnt by students as part of a general course, but few choose to follow a career in the dining-room.

There are many advantages to this type of work. A waiter usually works in the pleasant surroundings of a dining-room and in close contact with the public. The prospects for promotion are good and it is an honourable and lucrative vocation. Among the drawbacks are the need to work unsocial hours, to be on one's feet all the time, to wear a uniform, to take pride in one's appearance and to bottle up all emotions.

The success of any catering business depends as much on the quality of service as on the food served and is judged by the ability of those who do the serving. Many head waiters start their career as commis débarrasseurs and gradually work their way to the top by means of their personality and social and technical skills. It is the head waiter's knowledge of food and wine and their charm and strength of character that make the reputation of a dining-room, which is after all the place where the money is made in the catering business.

Methods of food and beverage service

The quality of the food produced must be matched by that of the service, no matter what form it takes. Whether in a cafeteria, a help-yourself buffet or a dining-room using plate service or guéridon service, the customer must be given full satisfaction.

The job of being a food server is often looked on as a menial one, because apart from keeping the customer happy there is no tangible evidence that anything has been produced. In fact there is a great art in serving food correctly and fine manual skills are required for this job. The laying of a table must not be looked upon as a daily chore but as an orderly routine which requires a measure of dexterity. Staff engaged in the service of food, whether behind a counter or handing things at table, must be considerate and polite.

The type of service offered by an eating place will vary according to its status, which in turn is determined by the kind of customers who patronise it. The customers' needs have to be satisfied according to their expectations of quality service.

Basically there are two main forms of food service – direct service in which the customer goes to the food, as in a cafeteria, school-meal service or fast-food outlet, and indirect service where food is taken to the customer on a plate or served from dishes. The following gives details of the most widely used methods of service.

Plate service

This method of service used to be associated with very modest establishments and unskilled staff. It is now more widely used, having been adopted by high-class establishments. Here the food is arranged on the plate in an artistic and predetermined manner, ready to set before the customer. At a slightly higher level the main item of food is placed on the plate and the vegetables in a dish; all the server has to do is to place the prepared plate in front of the customer with the dish of vegetables near at hand on the table. This method became popular in the United States in the 1920s and was commonly used in many good establishments. It was not until the 1950s that caterers in the UK began to question the need to employ highly skilled staff merely to place a plate of food in front of customers. Plate service should not be considered an inferior form of serving food, as a good deal of thought is needed to get it right. It is better to use this method than to let unskilled staff spoil the work of the cooks by serving it in a careless manner.

An upmarket version of plate service is widely used in high-class restaurants where chefs plate the main course in the kitchen in an artistic manner and cover it with a domed silver cover. Waiters put the plates in front of the customers and a sufficient number of them stand and await a signal from their station waiter before removing the covers with a flourish.

Self-service

Self-service became popular during the Second World War when there was a shortage of labour in the catering industry. It is now the most widely used method, not only in industrial and institutional catering, but also in fast-food operations and all other places where quick service is essential. It is a direct form of service with no one intervening between server and consumer. Customers go to the counter to help themselves or to select what they want, and the counter hand places it on the plate.

This form of service can be combined with plate service, where guests are expected to serve themselves one of the courses. An example of this is a carvery: the first and third courses are served on a plate, but for the second course customers go to the counter and carve the joint, or have it carved by the chef, and help themselves to vegetables. A prestigious form of self-service is used for buffets, balls, wedding receptions and cocktail parties. A display of hot and cold food is prepared to which guests help themselves, often assisted by a number of staff who carve and portion some of the items.

Self-service is not an inferior form of service. It satisfies a simple but functional need and it requires that food be presented neatly in identifiable portions in a manner which will allow large numbers to obtain their requirements quickly. Figure 67 shows how a self-service operation might be staffed.

Figure 67   Staffing structure of a self-service operation

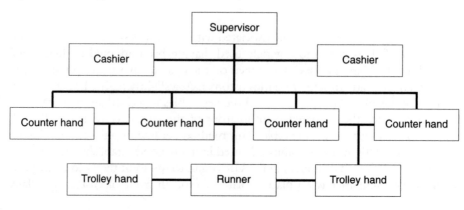

Silver service

This method of service costs more to operate than the others, mainly because it requires an adequate number of skilled staff to serve the food and expensive equipment on which to display it. The staffing structure for this kind of service is shown in Figure 66 (page 265). The number of staff of each rank will depend on the estimated number of customers likely to patronise the restaurant. It is also affected by the size of the room, the prices charged (which are a reflection of the standard of the establishment), and to some extent the distance between the dining-room and various service points. Figure 66 shows only two stations; in reality the number of stations would depend on the size of the room and the level of service offered. The diagram indicates that each station would be staffed by a head waiter, four station waiters and four commis, but in addition there could well be a number of assistants for clearing. The number of tables and seats to each station can vary from 8 to 18, again according to the standard of service and therefore the prices charged. The most favoured stations where important regular customers are seated would have fewer seats so that the service is more attentive than elsewhere in the room.

The equipment needed for silver service must be made of stainless steel or electroplated nickel silver (EPNS). It should be of good quality and kept highly polished. In many instances silverware is used only for underdishes and covers, with the actual food presented on other kinds of dishes of the correct size and shape. The waiter presents the dish for the customer's approval, then transfers the food dextrously on to the plate previously placed on the table in front of the guest.

Guéridon service

This is similar to silver service except that most of the work is done from a trolley or side table with a lamp on it to ensure the food is hot. This arrangement of trolley or table and lamp is called the guéridon. The guéridon is positioned close to the diners so that the service is more direct, giving them more visual contact with the food. This service is quite smooth as the waiter can use both hands to arrange the items on the plate, avoiding any delay. In many dining-rooms at lunchtime one of the main dishes, usually the roast, is served from a heated carving trolley which is wheeled to the table for the meat to be carved by a trancheur in view of the client. Otherwise the carving of small items of meat or poultry is carried out by the station head waiter on the guéridon.

Flambé service

Most à la Carte menus feature a small number of dishes that can be cooked by a waiter in front of the guest. They are dishes that can be cooked fairly quickly over a lamp using uncomplicated recipes. Dextrous skills and a touch of showmanship are required for this style of service. Flambé dishes use spirit or liqueur as a flavouring, which can be ignited to impressive effect. These dishes command a premium price because of their individual treatment and the cost of the spirit or liqueur.

The lamp is fuelled by a gas cylinder or methylated spirit and can be dangerous if untrained staff are allowed to do this kind of work. It must not be carried out near curtains or furnishing drapes, and the flames must be left to die out before taking the pan to the table to serve the contents on to the customer's plate. It is advisable to take out liability insurance for all flambé work of food and drink.

Family service

This form of service is used on formal occasions, for example when royalty is present at a function or at high table in a university. It is the same as silver service except that guests are proffered the dish containing the food and help themselves to what they want, using the serving spoon and fork. The term also applies to dishes of meat, vegetables and potatoes sent in bulk to table for portioning on to plates by the host before being handed round by waiting staff.

Routine of the dining-room

The daily routine of the dining-room starts long before the actual service of the meal. The room has to be cleaned, tables laid, glasses polished, cruets filled, table napkins folded, lamps maintained, and many other duties carried out to ensure that when the service begins all preparations have been completed.

The form of routine varies considerably from one dining-room to another and the following details will not necessarily apply to all. This is because there are many patterns of operation, brought about by company policy, type of business, prices charged, staff employed, hours of opening, and whether the dining-room is open for breakfast and for other meals throughout the day.

There are three common activities that apply to all kinds of dining-rooms where more than one mealtime per day is offered. These are:

1 the preparation period, leading to
2 the service period, followed by
3 the post-service clearing time with advance preparation for the next meal.

The way in which these stages are operated and the times at which they take place differ from place to place, but in each case it is important that they are carried out in an efficient manner with attention to detail, though it may be looked on as a daily chore.

Figure 68 gives an outline of the daily routine and sequence of activities which take place in the average high-class commercial establishment.

Figure 68   Sequence of dining-room activities

Receiving bookings for specific dates and times	Preparing for bookings and chance arrivals	Accommodating the customer and taking the order	Recording the order in the system and exchanging order for goods	Serving of food and drink. Clearing and preparation for next meal
1 Informing kitchen of number of bookings, special menus, special customers' preferences and special parties	1 Arranging tables in keeping with bookings	1 Organising the customers' reception	1 Using the appropriate order form and ensuring the accuracy, clarity and legibility of orders	1 Serving the tables in correct time sequence, avoiding long intervals between courses
2 Informing head waiter of extra staffing needs	2 Distributing stations to cope with numbers	2 Taking customers to reserved tables	2 Transferring the order to the recording point – cash desk or register	2 Serving food and wine at the correct temperatures and presenting the food for maximum effect
3 Informing laundry room of linen requirements	3 Manning the stations	3 Serving drinks prior to taking orders for meal	3 Taking the order to the kitchen, ensuring that all items are available	3 Ensuring that customers have the correct implements and accompaniments for each course, and clearing as required during the meal
4 Ordering flower decorations	4 Informing head waiters of special menus and requests	4 Taking orders	4 Revising customer's order in the event of non-availability of any item	4 Ensuring that the customer is billed correctly at the end of the meal and that cash is paid in
5 Informing cellar of unusual wine requests	5 Allocating specific tables to customers	5 Advising customers of possible waiting times for special dishes	5 Collecting items at the appropriate time	5 Seeing the customer away
6 Informing uniformed attendants of special customers	6 Checking table; sideboard and trolley preparations			6 Clearing and preparing for the next meal
	7 Changing into uniform for service			

The bars

The service of drink is a very important and profitable part of a licensed catering establishment and quite often the bar is the first place the customer encounters on entering a restaurant. The bar should make an impact on the customer by the way it is decorated and furnished and through the personality of the barperson, so that each guest immediately feels at ease and has a sense of security and belonging.

The barperson needs not only a considerable knowledge of all types of drinks and their service, but also the kind of personality that makes him or her popular with guests. A pleasant and helpful nature, a good memory for names and faces, honesty and trustworthiness, and skill at mixing drinks are essential attributes. The duties and responsibilities of a barperson include:

1 stocking up all drinks required in the bar
2 arranging the bar in an attractive manner, including such things as nuts, crisps and olives
3 maintaining close contact with the cellar
4 ensuring that the bar is run according to the licensing laws and other regulations
5 keeping the bar in a state of good hygiene
6 seeing that all the necessary equipment is at hand and is in good condition
7 knowing the price of each drink; ensuring that money is handled correctly
8 maintaining tight security over stocks and premises
9 supervising the work of assistant bartenders
10 serving drinks at table where necessary.

The dispense bar is usually behind the scenes and does not therefore need any special presentation because customers do not see it. The personality of the dispense barperson does not have to be the same as one who is always in contact with the public, unless it is the policy to change staff from one bar to another. In this case, all barpersons need to be selected on their smartness, pleasant disposition and ability to get on well with people. The dispense bar of a residential establishment is usually open longer than the other bars.

The duties of the dispense barperson would be similar to those of the general barstaff. Orders must be dealt with quickly so that drinks can be brought or sent to the customer as soon as possible, ensuring that nothing is issued without a proper requisition.

Details about the control of stocks of drink in bars and cellars and of cash received are included in Chapter 15.

Ancillary areas

These areas are the stores, stillroom, dishwash and potwash, all of which play an important role in the total catering operation. The staff who work in these areas often come under the jurisdiction of the chef, even though in some cases the work done in the stillroom and dishwash is more closely connected with the dining-room than with the kitchen. The work of the potwash and dishwash areas is largely unskilled and repetitive, but provided there is a reliable person in charge, efficiency and some degree of job satisfaction can be obtained. It must be stressed that the work done in all the ancillary areas is essential to the smooth and efficient running of the whole operation.

The stores

The importance of a well-managed and organised stores cannot be over-emphasised. The reputation of the establishment rests upon the correct handling and storage of commodities. The quality, quantity and availability to the kitchen of food for cooking is a prime responsibility of the stores. Not having this quality and quantity available at the right time can have a disastrous effect on the well-ordered operation of the kitchen and can lead to frustration, bad tempers and a general lowering of the standard of cooked dishes. The storeperson needs to be technically skilled, highly knowledgeable, honest and trustworthy. The duties and responsibilities of the storeperson include:

1 ordering commodities as instructed and to stated stock levels
2 receipt and safekeeping of goods
3 protecting foods from contamination and spoilage
4 issuing stores in accordance with requisitions in correct rotation and at the right time
5 keeping records as instructed
6 safeguarding stock and premises
7 stocktaking as instructed
8 making sure the head chef or person responsible knows about any goods that need to be used quickly.

The stillroom

Service from the stillroom is almost entirely to the waiting staff who go there to collect the adjuncts to the meal such as rolls, toast, butter and the beverages such as tea, coffee and fruit juice. The staff come under the orders of the head chef and the cost of running it and of the goods used in it are part of kitchen costings. It is usual to have a head stillroom person in charge, two if there are two shifts, and a sufficient number of semi-skilled staff to do the routine work of making tea and toast to order and such things as making butter pats, serving coffee, and squeezing oranges for juice. In some restaurants the cheese board and fruit basket are prepared here. In a large-scale establishment the beverage counter is the stillroom. The responsibilities of the head stillroom person include:

1 maintaining an adequate stock of fresh beverages in readiness to serve
2 ordering supplies of commodities from the stores

3 ensuring that beverages served are of the desired quality
4 issuing goods only against a waiter's check
5 making out the duty rosters to ensure the department is always adequately staffed
6 maintaining a good standard of hygiene.

The installation of press-button coffee-making machines, hot-water dispensers and automatic toasters means that it is now possible to operate a stillroom with no permanent staff and only one person to look in occasionally.

The dishwashing area

In a large establishment there can be several sections in this area, each dealing with a separate category of items, namely crockery, cutlery and silverware, and glassware. If housed separately there could be a chargehand in each who works under the direction of a person who is in overall charge.

In a large-scale industrial situation where only crockery and cutlery are handled it is usual to do all the washing up of dining-room equipment in one room, using a dishwashing machine that is capable of dealing with large numbers of a restricted range of utensils.

The number of staff required to work in these areas depends on the size of the establishment, the amount of business done, the length of the working day, and the number of hours of duty worked by staff. In the commercial sector it may be necessary to have two shifts or for staff to work on split duties. Some establishments in the welfare sector serve a midday meal only which means that part-time staff can be employed.

A dishwashing machine of a size and capacity to suit the operation helps to lighten the burden of the work in this area and makes hand washing unnecessary.

The potwash

This area is sometimes referred to as the scullery or plonge and is situated in or close to the kitchen, whereas the dishwashing area is more usually adjacent to the dining-room. Scullery staff clean all the kitchen utensils either by hand, mechanical scourer or potwashing machine and according to the volume of work. Mechanical aids and detergents have made it easier for them to carry out this work and to take pride in the results. The duties of the scullery staff include:

1 keeping the supply of pans and other kitchen utensils constantly available by washing them up as soon as possible
2 ensuring that utensils are thoroughly cleaned and polished
3 knowing how to clean the different metals used for pans
4 withdrawing from use any utensils which need repairing or refurbishing
5 keeping the area in a clean and orderly condition.

The Waldorf Astoria in New York

The famous Waldorf Astoria Hotel on 5th Avenue in New York City had its own railway siding in the hotel's basement where guests could alight instead of at Grand Central Station. A lift took them up to reception and straight to their apartments. The hotel had its own private hospital for guests who were taken ill whilst staying there. There were six different kitchens serving the various sections of the hotel, with 200 chefs to cook the meals, 500 waiters to serve them, and 100 people to wash up afterwards.

Oscar of the Waldorf was a famous character who attracted high society to come and be seen in the restaurant. He worked as restaurant manager, just as he had done at Delmonicos which was New York's most well-known restaurant until it closed in 1923.

Other ancillary staff

In addition to the staff of the potwash and dishwashing areas, there are others who carry out general cleaning duties. Kitchen porters clean the fixed equipment and other items installed in the kitchen, and keep the floor and walls of the department in a hygienic condition. Some of the tasks they carry out have to be done daily, but there should also be a planned programme of cleaning and maintenance for jobs that need to be done periodically. There may be a need to employ a person as a dining-room porter whose job is to keep the customer amenities area and staff facilities in a clean condition.

A stores porter, who works under the order of the storekeeper, does the lifting, fetching and carrying of goods, possibly making up the requisitions and delivering them but also keeping the stores and surrounding areas clean. This person may also have to keep the rubbish areas in good order. Some establishments find it desirable to use the services of a firm of industrial cleaners to clean all the areas rather than employing the staff themselves. The advantage is that the cleaning contractor can send in the team at a time when the whole area is otherwise closed, thus allowing them to do a thorough job without interruption.

Customers' toilets and cloakrooms

In a large establishment cloakroom attendants are required to run each of these areas, one for the female side and one for the male side. Their duties include:

1 taking charge of customers' outdoor apparel, issuing a chit for it, safeguarding it and returning it against presentation of the duplicate chit
2 keeping the toilets and wash rooms in a state of perfect hygiene
3 maintaining supplies of soap, towels and toilet rolls
4 offering simple first aid for such things as headaches or migraine.

In smaller establishments it may not be necessary to staff these areas permanently as an attendant could look in occasionally to check that all is in order and there are sufficient toiletries. Coin-in-slot lockers could take care of outdoor wear.

Further reading

Cracknell, H. and Nobis, G. (1989) *Mastering Restaurant Service*. Macmillan*
Dawson, S. (1996) *Analysing Organisations*. Macmillan
Denney, G. (ed.) (1994) *Hotel Management and Operations*. Van Nostrand Reinhold
Irons, K. (1997) *The World of Super Service*. Addison Wesley
Powers, T. (1999) *Introduction to the Hospitality Industry*. John Wiley
Wood, R. (1994) *Organisational Behaviour for Hospitality Management*. Butterworth-Heinemann

*Out of print but available in many libraries.

13 Production and distribution II
Specialised operations

Industrial catering; Hospital catering; Catering in educational institutes; Catering for the elderly; Leisure catering; Catering for travellers; Catering for the armed forces; Catering in prisons; Food in public houses; Members' clubs; Banqueting; On-location catering; Vending; Fast-food chains.

This chapter looks at a number of significant parts of the catering industry which may not have such an illustrious image as the grand hotels but are perhaps of greater value to the community. It covers most aspects of the cost sector, such as looking after the sick and elderly, pupils at school and students in colleges, plus prisoners and the armed forces. In addition several commercial operations such as motorway service areas, leisure centres, holiday camps and clubs are dealt with. The organisation of banquets and on-location catering are covered, giving glimpses of the operation and highlighting possible problems connected to this important part of the industry.

Industrial catering

This is the sector where people working in factories, office blocks, government and local council buildings and many other parts of the cost sector are fed during working hours. There are two main forms of operation. The first and largest is where a catering contractor is engaged to feed the workforce. The second is where the firm employs its own staff to run its own canteen or restaurant and carries out its own catering facilities. The entire sector has over 20,000 outlets which serve some 600 million meals a year, which equals 8 per cent of all meals eaten outside the home.

Firms of catering contractors operate locally, nationally and internationally. Each is judged on its reputation for keeping its customers satisfied by providing good food and service at economical prices. A feature of this sector is that its customers are the same people every day. They see the same faces and surroundings and if the menu cycle is a short one, can tell which day of the week it is by the dishes on sale. The monotony must be broken by sales promotions such as seasonal specialities, chef's special dishes, featuring the cuisine of another country, or healthy-eating menus. Outside competition must be fought by making the on-site restaurant more attractive than pubs or cafés.

The British Hospitality Association Contract Catering Survey gave the following figures for 1994:

	Contractor-operated units
Business and industry	7,473
State education	4,603
Independent schools	579
Hospitals	459
Local authority buildings	295
Ministry and defence	267
Oil rigs, building sites, training	263
Public catering	1,062
Total	15,001

The number of staff employed was 113,606, with a wages bill of £925 million which represented 43 per cent of total turnover. The total revenue of the contract catering section was £2.18 billion.

In-house catering is the name given to the other side of industrial catering where a firm directly manages the feeding facilities for its employees. It installs and equips the premises, buys the food and drink, pays the wages of catering staff and sets the prices. It may subsidise the operation to recover only food costs. It is looked upon as a form of welfare or reward to staff.

The commercial sector and the cost sector have to market their products and make use of the tools of marketing outlined in Chapter 3. One of the ways of increasing take-up of meals is to copy popular high-street quick-service empires. The cost of opening a branch of one of the well-known brand names could amount to £15,000. Staff of an authentic brand outlet have to be trained to do their job, using designated equipment and commodities. Even though it is sited in a firm's canteen, a royalty will be payable for use of the brand name.

Acquired Rights Directive

The Acquired Rights Directive is a piece of legislation under which a change of ownership of an establishment – whether the whole or only part of the undertaking, whether taken over by a sale or transfer, and whether with or without a break in the operation – must not be prejudicial to the staff originally employed.

Staff must retain their existing employment rights and the continuation of their jobs with the new owners, and the consent of the existing trade union must be obtained before the changeover takes place. No staff may be dismissed as a cause of the transfer.

This Directive applies to commercial and cost sector catering businesses where the same sort of business continues to operate. Staff must be transferred to the new employer on their previous terms and pay, and all staff must be kept on the payroll. The Directive applies, for example, when a staff dining-room that was run directly by the firm is given to a catering contractor to run at a profit.

TUPE

This abbreviation, which means Transfer of Undertaking Protection of Employment, is closely connected with the Acquired Rights Directive. It is legislation backed by the EU to safeguard the jobs of all staff on the payroll at a time when a business is taken over by a new contractor who has bid successfully for the catering rights of any kind of firm.

Hospital catering

This is one of the few areas of cost sector catering where meals are supplied free of charge. The three meals supplied daily to patients in hospital play a large part in their recovery. The standard of catering affects the reputation of the hospital.

Hospital kitchens are open every day of the year and staff work in shifts where meals are prepared in the traditional way. There are a number of service systems using frozen, chilled or ambient foods in bulk or individual packs. Each patient's choice is assembled on a tray and put into a trolley which keeps the meal hot or cool according to what was ordered. It is then sent to the ward where it is served by a member of the catering staff or a ward orderly. Patients tick their choice on the day's menu and the total number of portions ordered is read by a machine. This governs the issue of commodities for producing meals and prevents overproduction.

Many hospitals now use contractors to run the catering, cleaning, laundry, security and other services. Compulsory Competitive Tendering legislation opened hospitals and many government and local authority establishments to contractors who may bid to operate the business against the in-house team already running it. The in-house team has to put in a competitive bid and abide by the regulations imposed by the hospital authority. The contract goes to the lowest bid, all things being equal.

Direct Service Organisation

Direct Service Organisation (DSO) is the title given to in-house catering and other forms of local authority services where the authority maintains control over these ancillary services. Under the Compulsory Competitive Tendering (CCT) legislation, all council services must be put out to tender. If the present operator under the council's wing wishes to continue it has to make a bid for the business by submitting a tender giving details of proposed standards, costs, charges, etc. At present about three-quarters of services are held by DSOs, with a quarter in the hands of contractors who bid and took these services from local authorities.

All services for schools, hospitals, old people's homes, etc. must be run at nil-subsidy. Private contractors have to make their profit by bulk buying, keen pricing and greater efficiency without downgrading quality, reducing their staff numbers or lowering wages. Some DSOs form their own collective buying agency with food and equipment suppliers as a means of cutting their costs. Compulsory Competitive Tendering was introduced to enable private firms to compete for government work and to create greater efficiency in all branches of local authority services. It was expected to cut costs by reducing over-staffing.

Catering in educational institutes

This part of cost sector catering covers the country's schools, colleges, universities and many private academic institutes. The Local Government Act 1988 made it compulsory for services, including catering, to be put out to tender. This means that contract caterers can bid to run the school meals service of a local authority against the service given under the authority's control. If the contractor wins, it will offer a service which is good for business and produces a profit. This applies to state-funded colleges and universities, and the bursars of many public schools and private colleges find that handing catering to a contractor saves them a lot of headaches.

Obviously the food served must meet popular demand and turnover is all-important. Schools find it profitable to offer ethnic and vegetarian dishes and the kinds of food sold in quick-serve restaurants under brand names. Giving the pupils choice makes it impossible to calculate nutritional intake; caterers put on promotions to encourage healthy eating.

Colleges and universities have seen the advantage of breaking refectories into food halls where, instead of one long serving counter for everything, there are smaller ones for each dish. This could include Chinese, Indian, Italian and Thai food, baked potatoes, burgers, a cold buffet, fried chicken, grills, a hot dish of the day, pastas, pizzas, sandwiches, seafood, vegetarian, wholefood and other eateries, plus a coffee shop, breakfast bar and patisserie. Preparatory work can be done in the main kitchen and sent to each serving point.

College and university halls of residence and catering facilities have to be marketed for conference and holiday business during vacations. Buying consortiums consisting of a number of institutions in an area can negotiate keen prices with suppliers of goods.

School meals

Local councils run the school meals service in the UK either directly by employing their own staff, usually in the form of a company, or indirectly through a private firm of contract caterers. Each enterprise has to put in a bid stating how it intends to run the service, what standards it will achieve, the prices it will charge, staff costs and numbers, nutritional value of meals, conditions of service, trade union recognition, and any subsidy. Local councils are required to seek the most efficient way of delivering the school meals service, usually for all the schools under local authority control. The Government holds reserve powers that satisfy auditors in providing a cost-effective service.

The traditional school meal pattern of a set two-course meal of meat, two vegetables and sweet disappeared long ago. School canteens now offer a wider range of dishes rather than set meals, with many snacks and bought-in goods set out on a self-selection counter. The choice of food rests with the pupils and depends on the amount they are prepared to pay for a meal.

Compulsory standards for school meals were abolished in the UK in 1970, but there may well be a need to reinstate them. In contrast every state school in France stops work for an hour while all its pupils sit down to a daily three-course lunch consisting of soup or appetiser, meat or fish dish with a garnish and vegetables, ending with a 'healthy' sweet such as yoghurt or fromage frais. There is no choice, but pupils are not forced to eat anything they don't like. The school authorities and teachers have to ensure the meal is eaten properly as a social occasion where the communal meal is regarded as an important part of the curriculum.

Catering for the elderly

The increased longevity of people has created the need for old people's homes and nursing homes for those who cannot look after themselves. Most homes are run as businesses under private or company ownership. Local councils and charities also operate old people's homes as well as warden-supervised flats or houses and day centres.

Elderly people capable of looking after themselves are encouraged to live at home or in sheltered accommodation with a resident warden on call. Social services departments will provide home help and meals to those who cannot care for themselves. The meals-on-wheels delivery service is run largely by the food-service arm of the Women's Royal Voluntary Service (WRVS) which delivers hot meals to people who are housebound. Some councils deliver a week's supply of frozen meals to be put in a hired compact freezer and a steam oven in which to store and regenerate meals as required. Others send meals in polycarbonate, heated outer containers containing a latent heat accumulator which keeps food piping hot for two hours. Customers serve food on to their own plates and return the container. This system also works for cold meals.

Privately owned homes for the elderly are inspected by local social services staff to ensure that occupants are well looked after and properly fed.

Day centres are operated by local authorities or charitable and welfare organisations. They serve refreshments and cooked lunches at reasonable prices, either cooked on the premises or delivered from a central kitchen in frozen, chilled or ambient form. Customers are encouraged to participate in various activities including remedial instruction and therapy.

Leisure catering

Catering in some form is included both as an amenity and a source of profit in all kinds of leisure and sports centres. This may range from a restaurant serving meals cooked to order and drinks at a bar to confectionery, snacks and drinks from vending machines. Fans at football or rugby matches can obtain food and drink to their liking, whether hot dogs, burgers, sandwiches and tea, or high-class meals in the director's suite. Meals of various kinds are supplied to spectators at cricket matches, bowling alleys, and ice or roller skating rinks. Members of golf, polo and tennis clubs can eat and drink at a high standard in their own clubs.

Bingo halls offer members snacks and drinks during breaks in sessions. Punters at racecourses can spend their winnings or drown their sorrows at losing in a range of catering outlets from a high-class restaurant to bookmaker's sandwiches from a snackbar.

Holiday centres form an important part of the catering industry. Holiday-makers can choose from full-board or self-catering accommodation and enjoy being waited on or trying out the various kinds of restaurants and bars on site. Meals are mainly traditional to satisfy average tastes, with options from cold buffet or salad bar, omelette, burger, pizza, vegetarian, Chinese, Indian, Italian, Mexican and stir-fry counters, as well as children's menus featuring chicken nuggets, fish fingers, chips and beans.

Catering for travellers

In the car

Motorway service stations cater for motorists and passengers on the move who need to pull in for something to eat and drink and stretch their legs. The food and drink can be a snack and beverage or a full meal. This important section of the industry requires high managerial qualities to keep it functioning efficiently for 24 hours per day throughout the year. Service stations are sited in isolated places where there can be problems with supplies and transporting staff to and from the nearest urban area. There might be as many as three shifts to cover the day, and there must be enough staff on duty to deal with any unexpected rush of customers.

Many motorway service stations offer accommodation with all the facilities of a hotel or motel; all supply motor fuel.

On the train

Catering is available on train journeys lasting longer than one hour. The firm responsible for this in the UK is called ERC. It handles more than 1,000 trains daily and is the fourth largest caterer in Europe. It stems from OBS services which was a management buyout of British Rail's on-board catering services. The company is now owned by Rail Gourmet, a branch of the Swiss Air Group.

The main means of selling food and drink to rail passengers is from a hi-tec trolley serving hot pizzas, filled rolls and baguettes, pastries, sandwiches, tea, coffee and other drinks, all sold under the Prego brand name.

The familiar buffet car is now known as the Prego Café. It sells hot dishes including breakfast, soups and snacks, salads and drinks, and cooked food. These can be eaten in the seating area of the buffet car or served in the dining car.

The Eurostar train runs through the Channel tunnel to Paris or Brussels. The first-class rail ticket includes a meal brought to the passenger's seat. The meals are prepared at main terminus depots for finishing on the train.

Pullman railway carriages

In 1858 George Pullman gave his name to luxury railway coaches and sleeping cars which he leased to American railroad companies. Soon whole trains of Pullman carriages operated in many countries including Great Britain. They offered comfortable seats and quality meals cooked on board and served by stewards in dining cars. Today the trans-Europe Orient Express uses these Pullman coaches on its exciting journeys. They include sleeping coaches with en-suite facilities and attendants, bars and dining cars serving gourmet meals.

At sea

Catering on board ship stems from the days when ships were the only form of international transport. There were many steamship companies with passenger ships that catered for every grade of traveller from steerage to luxury cabin class. On long voyages meals played an important part and their quality was a deciding point when choosing which ship to travel on. Nowadays luxury liners are, in effect, floating hotels offering the delights of cruising, including four- or five-course meals with wine, captain's champagne party, cabaret, cinema, discotheques, casino, deck games, late-night buffets and sight-seeing trips ashore.

Senior staff may be nationals, but often stewards and cooks are foreign. A large cruise ship could carry as many as 500 catering crew consisting of bartenders, bakers, cellarpersons, chefs, kitchen porters, plongeurs, dishwashers, silver cleaners, storehands and stewards who serve in cabins, public rooms, bars and restaurants. Tours of duty do not allow days off at sea; stewards normally wait at table for two sittings three times a day.

Ferries run services to other countries and islands on regular sailings. They aim to give an agreeable voyage with plenty of opportunities for eating and drinking. Catering staff are firstly merchant sailors and secondly cooks and stewards. On-board catering outlets include self-service cafeterias, plate and silver-service restaurants, snack bars, brand name quick-food outlets, licensed bars and a good-class restaurant for lorry drivers. There must also be a crew's mess. Some ferry companies use catering contractors to run these retail outlets.

Plate 8   The Burren Buttery, Irish Ferries

In the air

In-flight and airport catering includes refreshment and meals served during a flight and facilities for passengers and visitors at airports. This is a large and important section of the catering industry. British Airways, for example, produces 25,000 meals a day at Heathrow Airport, London, for its own passengers. First-class and business-class passengers have a choice of menus of expensive foods and fine wines, all easily digestible, expertly served on expensive crockery with quality cutlery and glassware. At the other end of a plane, set meals are trayed for ease and speed of serving and clearing. Meals are usually freshly cooked, blast-chilled and kept on board in insulated trolleys at 5°C until meal-times when they are reheated to 70°C for service. Airlines spend about 4 per cent of turnover on in-flight meals.

Airline catering contractors supply meals to companies which do not run their own commissariat. One of these may cater for as many as 100 airlines, each having different requirements. On return journeys the food may be produced to specification by local suppliers. Each airline will provide the kind of meals enjoyed in its country, but meals for the special needs of passengers of different religions or races will also be served. Airlines are gradually questioning the need to provide meals which really only have a comforting effect and help relieve the monotony of a long flight. Snacks may replace full meals on many airlines and passengers may only be served a full meal if at least 70 per cent of flying time is during a normal meal time.

Airport catering includes a range of restaurants, coffee shops, snack bars, patisseries, fast-food outlets, oyster stalls, licensed bars and, of course, vending machines. Firms bid to rent prime locations to gain very good, round-the-clock business.

Catering for the armed forces

All branches of Her Majesty's Forces offer good career prospects, and personnel are much sought after on their return to civilian life.

The Army has been served at home and abroad, in peace and war, by the Army Catering Corps which is now part of the Royal Logistic Corps. This is made up of the army's bakers, cooks and slaughterers. Recruits are soldiers first and cooks second. They are trained at base depot to NVQ Level 2 then sent to put their acquired skills to use in a regiment. They return to train for advancement and promotion and learn field cookery under combat conditions. Alongside this, much of the Army's catering is now done by catering contractors who run the officers' and the men's messes at base depots using civilian workers.

The Royal Navy runs a school to teach sailors how to become cooks and stewards in the galleys and messes of battleships. They must prepare satisfying meals for the ship's crew to keep them strong and healthy and boost their morale. The requirement is for large-scale production for the sailors' mess, officers' wardroom and captain's dining-room, and also for high-class buffets when paying courtesy visits to foreign ports when local dignitaries are invited aboard, all this from the precious space allocated to galley and bakery. Many naval bases are catered for by contractors who employ civilian workers. The Royal Marine's catering personnel are trained to the same high standard as the other armed forces. They serve on warships and on land and have to cook under field conditions during emergencies and on manoeuvres.

The Royal Air Force is as proud of its culinary traditions as the other armed forces. All branches of the services are keen competitors at Salons Culinaires and are honoured by their successes, none more so than the cooks of the Royal Air Force. High standards are set at its training base.

The NAAFI is the official trading organisation for all branches of Her Majesty's Forces. It was founded in the 1920s as the Navy, Army and Airforce Institute to run canteens for personnel and to supply messes with drinks and other goods. It now runs supermarkets and shops for the forces and their families in many parts of the world. It is a commercial enterprise which supplies its services on a profit basis.

Catering in prisons

In this branch of the cost sector each prison is given the freedom to plan the catering according to its own needs, running it on an average cost per person of less than £1.50 per day. Each prison can write its own menus based on prisoners' choices of two hot and one snack meal per day. Civilian cooks are employed to work with prisoners under the management of a prison catering officer. It is possible for prisoners to learn how to cook in preparation for a chef's job when they gain their release.

Food in public houses

The quantity and quality of food served in public houses has increased sharply since the Licensing Act 1988 relaxed opening times. Much of this has been achieved by the efforts of pub landladies who were encouraged to develop what is known as the 'dry' side. The average amount of income from food is about 30 per cent of turnover on a traditional public house, but can be as high as 70 per cent in a very dedicated or upmarket pub where skilled catering staff are employed. It is estimated that some four million meals are eaten each day in the UK's 39,000 public houses. There are several chains of new-style public houses where the food is as important as the drink and the interior decoration. Some have the ambience of an old-fashioned tavern with a saloon bar and table service. Some have a similar theme and menu in all branches; some feature entertainment; others offer reduced prices to the over 50s, have smoking areas, serve cask-brewed beers and feature guest beers – there is no end to the market choices they offer.

Members' clubs

This division of the catering industry borders the profit and cost sectors. There are nearly 17,000 clubs of various kinds in the UK, some in the business for profit, others covering or subsidising costs. They range from working men's clubs to exclusive members' clubs in the St James district of central London and in most other cities. Some attract politicians, ex-public schoolboys, forces personnel or people connected with the art world or entertainment; others may be gaming clubs or masonic lodges. Only members and their guests are eligible. Some clubs serve only food and drink at levels which suit their image; others have short-stay residential accommodation, possibly with room service. A restaurant or members' dining-room, lounge, library, billiard room, bar room, health centre and swimming pool are amenities commonly found in members' clubs.

Club staff, who used to be classed as servants, consist of porters, bartenders, steward, sommeliers and cooks. One of the best-known chefs of all time, Alexis Soyer, worked at the Reform Club in Pall Mall for 12 years.

Banqueting

A banquet is a gathering of people who meet together to partake of a special meal. The food and drink is usually the same for everyone except for a person who is a vegetarian or on a strict diet. Th total event includes the reception before the meal when canapés or hot hors-d'oeuvre and aperitifs are served, the Grace, the toasts, speeches, and possibly some awards. There can be a top table for distinguished guests and officials of the organisation and a master of ceremonies when it is a formal affair.

A banquet can be a luncheon or dinner meal and for any occasion, such as the anniversary of a person or club, annual reunion, ladies' night, wedding feast, end of conference, birthday celebration or other feast. The table plan can be formal in long rows or less formal at separate tables.

A banqueting room can be a lucrative source of extra income through the banqueting season which lasts from October to May. Only a nucleus of staff is required with extras brought in as part-time waiting staff. There will be a banqueting manager to organise the business and make out a booking form as shown in Figure 69. The client will choose the menu and wines from priced lists and decide on the full programme from available amenities or extra items.

A popular banqueting venue might have a banqueting kitchen with its own staff. Otherwise the food will be cooked in the main kitchen then sent to the banqueting servery for retention under safe storage conditions. The food can be presented in services of ten portions on silver dishes or on individual plates to be regenerated in a hot air oven and sauced and covered with lids at the moment of serving.

Caterers who specialise in banqueting may employ a sales manager and staff to market the facilities by advertising and visiting potential customers. They can sell

Figure 69   Simplified banquet booking form

Noble Hotel BANQUET DEPARTMENT

Function: Wedding Breakfast   No. of covers: 125 adults / 20 children
Date: Saturday 17th June 20_ _
Organiser: Mr J. A. Holmes
Firm/Society:
Address: 17 Welbeck Road, Strathfield
Telephone No.: Office: 0135 640750   Home: 01272 527960
Room: Ballroom

Menu	Time of arrival	1300
Melon ball cocktail with	Departure	2100
Cointreau	Toastmaster	✓
—	Orchestra/disco	disco
Chicken breast en croûte	Cabaret	✗
Runner beans	Changing rooms	✓
New potatoes	Floral arrangements	Hotel florist
—	Microphone	✗
Baked Alaska	Seating plan	✓
—	Cash bar	✓
Coffee and Mints	Menu cards	✓
—	Place cards	✗
Wines	Service charge	15%
Buck's Fizz on arrival	VAT	17.5%
Bin 22 Bernkasteler Riesling		
Bin 36 Vinprom Haskovo		
Bulgarian		
Champagne de Venoge NV		

---

the banqueting facilities by outlining room capacities and showing photographs of the department, discussing the number of courses and accompanying wines, and quoting their prices. If the customer wants to see the set-up, the visitor should be offered some hospitality whilst discussing the proposed function with the manager. Relevant information from the booking form must be passed to every department that will have any contact with the event. This could be the car park, porter's lodge, bar and cellar, kitchen, plateroom, housekeeping, entertainment department and toastmaster.

Grosvenor House Hotel

The Great Room at Grosvenor House, the Granada Hotel in Park Lane, is the largest banqueting room in London and probably in Europe. This room was originally an ice-skating rink before its conversion, and can seat 1,600 for a banquet and several thousand for an awards ceremony, cocktail party, lecture or wedding reception. It has its own kitchen and ancillary departments. The hotel, which was designed by Sir Edward Lutyens and opened in 1928, has a further 25 smaller dining-rooms for banqueting use.

The biggest banquet?

Possibly the greatest number of people ever catered for at a single banquet was the 7,554 freemasons who sat down to lunch at long lines of tables at Olympia in Kensington, London, in 1925. J. Lyons & Co held the catering rights for this exhibition hall and they mustered 200 'nippy' waitresses to serve the food and wine of the following cold meal. It took 700 chefs and kitchen staff to cook and dress it.

Menu	Wine
Hors-d'Oeuvre Suédoise	Amontillado Sherry
Darne de Saumon Ravigote	Sauternes
Ravier de Concombre	
Côtelette d'Agneau Victoria	Mumm Cordon Rouge 1913
Poulet et Jambon froid	
Salade Mimosa	
Boute de Niege Plombiere	
Gâteau Mascotte	
	Courvoisier VVO
Café	Liqueur Brandy

Lyons was a well-known outdoor caterer for such events as this and did the catering for Royal garden parties, Wimbledon tennis, and very many banquets of all sizes and standards.

Receptions

Receptions are carried out by the banqueting department. They are mainly stand-up social gatherings which bring invited guests together to celebrate a particular event. This kind of function used to be called a cocktail party and is similar to a cheese and wine party. They are informal events which do not last very long and get their message across very quickly.

Guests are crowded fairly close together and the few chairs made available are for use by elderly and disabled guests. Food and drink will be either laid out on a buffet table and bar or brought from the kitchen and offered around by waiting staff. The range of food and drink can be limited to sandwiches and sausage rolls, crisps and chipolatas or include more exotic attereaux, filled fresh parmesan and smoked salmon cornets and caviar-filled bouchées. Drinks can be red or white wine, champagne, sherry or mixed drinks such as gin and tonic or popular cocktails. It all depends on the agreed price per person which includes room hire, service, food and estimated amount of drink, and wage costs of, for example, a master of ceremonies or commissionaire on duty at the door.

Kosher catering

Kosher catering comes into the sphere of banqueting because when people of the Jewish faith attend a function in a hotel or restaurant the catering must be carried out under strictly kosher conditions. Some catering establishments are approved by the Kashrus Commission to do banquets for Jewish customers. There are a number of kosher catering firms which use approved facilities in good hotels and banqueting rooms and run the function themselves. The rules governing these events are so complicated that a rabbi has to be present in the kitchen and restaurant to check that every thing is done correctly.

One major restriction is that meat and milk may not be consumed in the same meal. Separate equipment for cooking, serving and eating must be kept for meals that include meat and for meals that include milk in any form. A Jewish institute has to have two completely separate kitchens, one for food containing meat and the other for food containing milk, and nothing may be switched from one to the other. Worn working surfaces in the kitchen will have to be covered with pristine tablecloths before work can commence. Before the banquet can begin, the presiding rabbi has to fill in a card confirming that all food was prepared according to religious laws and present it to the host.

On-location catering

This branch of the commercial sector is also called outdoor catering; it is recognised as being more challenging than a conventional catering business carried out on dedicated premises. On-location means transporting all the kitchen and dining-room equipment to a place where a meal is to be prepared and served to a number of people. The firm of outdoor caterers has to provide the food and drink and the staff to prepare and serve it, clear up leaving the place as it was before they arrived, and transport staff and equipment back to base.

These functions take place in many different locations: indoors in a person's home or outside in a marquee for a birthday party or wedding breakfast; at an agricultural or other kind of show over a number of days where everything is sold for cash; in a village hall; on a river boat; in the grounds of a school; or in the canteen of a factory. Services of electricity or gas, water, security of goods, disposal of rubbish, hire of furniture and floral arrangements all need to be laid on.

When planning on-location catering, it is important that the catering firm knows exactly what will be required. The following checklist highlights the information needed:

1 The name, address and telephone number of the organiser.
2 The type of function – for example a banquet, buffet, catering for a race meeting, reception or tea.
3 The number of persons to be catered for – this can have a bearing on the menu and equipment as well as the number of staff required.
4 The date and time of the function – how long it will take to set up and dismantle the facilities required; whether it is for several days.
5 The exact address of the function and the kind of site to be used.
6 The distance of the site from the caterer's central depot – mileage and travelling home have to be taken into account when quoting for the job.
7 The price to be charged per person.
8 How payment is to be made – whether cash is to be taken at any points or whether the entire bill will be paid by the organiser.
9 The menu – whether it is to be a full meal served by waiting staff, a cold meal served from a buffet, or a combination of menus to suit the particular occasion. The preparation of cold buffets can usually be done better at base than in the confines of a hot marquee on site.
10 The availability of water, gas and electricity supplies – when catering for a hot meal, some caterers prefer to cook on site because of the regulations concerning transportation of hot food. Some like to do the washing up on site rather than returning dirty dishes to base. Toilet, washing and clockroom facilities may be required. Any problems regarding hygiene will be dealt with by the environmental health officer on his or her daily visit.
11 The size and decoration of marquees if needed, and the furniture required – whether the site is likely to become muddy soon after people start walking on it so requiring some form of covering. Space allocation per guest and for food preparation area and bar.
12 The grades of staff required and the number of each – the manager in overall charge, head chef, head waiter, bartenders, waiters and extras or this function only may be recruited locally or through a private employment agency. Details regarding staff transport facilities, staff changing rooms, uniforms, meals on duty and method of payment all require decisions.
13 The security of the premises and equipment – if set up overnight, this may require the services of guards. It may be necessary to insure the function against loss or weather conditions which could cause the failure of the event.
14 Bars – it is usual to serve drinks at outdoor functions, either as an integral

part of the meal or on sale for cash. Accordingly it may be necessary to set up bars, nominate staff, decide on prices to be charged, install cash tills and bar tariffs, and so on. Security of stock and reconciliation of takings with quantity sold are important factors. It may be necessary to obtain a licence for the sale of alcoholic drinks.

15 The equipment required: kitchen – stoves, boilers, pans, ovens, canisters of liquid gas, tables, chopping boards, serving dishes, covers; dining-room – cutlery, crockery and glassware in their required numbers, tables, tablecloths, serviettes and tea towels, cruets, ashtrays, baths for cooling white wines, cutlery baskets, floral decorations; bar – glasses, jugs, optics, and all the paraphernalia of bar service.

16 Commodities – this will include all the necessary foodstuffs and drink required for the particular function.

17 Arrangements for disposal of rubbish – this may be done by the local council or privately, but it is essential to clear up thoroughly and to leave the site as it was found. On some jobs the outdoor catering company will pay a concession fee to the organiser to cover the food or bars, or both.

Alfresco cooking

A barbecue is a very popular way of grilling and serving meals in the open air in warm weather. Customers like to watch their food being cooked by this primitive method, and the range of suitable items is extensive. A successful barbecue requires efficient organisation, and close attention must be given to the following details:

- The weather forecast should be considered, especially the wind direction.
- The barbecue should be sited close to the source of supply of foods.
- If not purpose-built, the barbecue must be set on a level surface.
- A fire extinguisher, buckets of sand and water, and a fire blanket must be at hand.
- If liquid petroleum gas is used, the supply pipe must be checked for leaks.
- Do not use petrol or any other inflammable liquid to light or boost the fire.
- Do not let children go too close to the barbecue.
- Have all the necessary dishes and utensils to hand. Use oven gloves, long-handled tongs, a basting brush, a grill-cleaning brush and a stainless-steel turner.
- The selected fuel should be glowing red before beginning to cook the food.
- Prepare food in the kitchen. Keep a selection on display covered with clingfilm and replenish items as necessary.
- Pre-cook large, thick items, and dry off any marinated items.

- Use flat metal skewers or soaked bamboo skewers for kebabs.
- Defrost frozen foods before cooking them.
- Do not pierce foods with a fork while cooking as the juices will run out.
- Place lidded waste bins around the area.
- Observe the Food Hygiene (General) Regulations 1970 and the Health and Safety at Work Act 1974.

Vending

Vending machines can fulfil a need in many establishments provided they are carefully sited, properly serviced on a preventative basis with faults quickly rectified, subject to quality-control procedures, and kept filled. Vending machines for beverages, snacks and meals offer a service at any time and can serve remote sites. There is no need for fixed break times, they save labour costs, give exact portion control, and can be more profitable than a conventional service. The only disadvantages are the loss of personal service and social contact, their inability to cope with masses of people all at once, and that sometimes they break down. Staff have to be trained to keep machines clean and to refill them on a regular basis. Control is easy because the meter reading will indicate the number of sales made of each item in the machine over a set period; the ingredient cost and the number of portions per pack can be compared with takings to show the gross profit. The time taken by the operators to look after the machine and the rental or leasing cost and maintenance charges are known.

Vending machines for the sale of meals to heat in a microwave oven can form the total cafeteria service for a small number of customers, or can be an addition to a traditional service counter. Chilled or frozen meals on plates are placed in the refrigerated vending machine and when the correct money is placed in the slot for a particular meal, it unlocks. The meal is put into the adjacent microwave oven, the time token attached to the plate inserted, and when the oven door is closed the microwave operates for a time related to the meal. Together with a hot and cold beverage vending machine, such a micro-vending unit serves a very useful purpose after the main servery has closed and for night duty staff.

In hotels, vending machines can replace room service. Guests obtain their requirements from a bank of machines in the foyer or on each floor, selling miniatures of alcohol, chilled soft drinks and mixers, all kinds of snack items, confectionery and hot drinks. The machines are designed to blend in with the decor of the hotel. They are operated by guests swiping the card which identifies them and acts as the key to their room through the machine. This then delivers the required items and automatically charges them to the account under that room number. Guests' children can use these machines with their own cards that operate only for low-priced items, thus preventing them from obtaining alcohol.

These machines can be filled and serviced by a vending contractor, or by a member of staff under the food and beverage manager. They cannot make mistakes and everything gets paid for, reducing the possibility of pilferage.

Fast-food chains

In city centres, town and village high streets, shopping malls, outpatient departments, leisure centres, college refectories, train stations and many other prime sites we find the familiar shopfront of one of the major quick-service or fast-food firms.

The spread of the national and international fast-food chains is remarkable and sees no end. It is very obvious that they supply the public with food it likes. Their food and drink is appetising, piquant and easy to eat without the need for cutlery, either sitting on a stool or walking down the street.

This important part of the commercial sector had a turnover of £4 billion in 1992 which is increasing rapidly. Their prices are competitive because the overheads are low as there is no requirement for skilled staff. There is a Level 2 NVQ course in Preparing and Serving Food – Quick Service for these employees.

Standards of hygiene are exemplary. Staff are invariably polite and efficient even in those outlets that stay open all day and night. Full-time employees can see a possible career structure in addition to bonus and award payments.

The objective of these restaurants is to offer a popular choice of quickly prepared snack-type meals and drinks which can be eaten either standing, sitting or taken away. Eating utensils are disposable and in effect this is a called-order type of catering loosely based on à la Carte service.

The history of McDonald's

Minced and shaped beef in the form of hamburgers has become a staple food of young people of many countries. For example, McDonald's – the world's most famous purveyor of fast food – sold £500 million of burgers in its 526 outlets in 1993 and serves one million customers per day.

The first restaurant of this particular chain opened in 1940 in San Bernardino, a small town near Los Angeles. It was an instant success and the two owners, Mack and Dick McDonald, found that a limited menu of low-priced products cooked on what they called the Speedie Service System brought in good profits from a quick turnover.

In 1958 Ray Kroc, who sold catering equipment, negotiated a franchise agreement with the brothers and opened his first McDonald's restaurant in Des Plaines, Illinois. He went on to found the McDonald Corporation that now controls the worldwide chain. The first McDonald's is now a museum with waxwork figures cooking and eating the burgers.

Ray Kroc died in 1984, but the chain he founded continues apace with a wider menu and a programme for opening up to 1,200 new outlets a year all over the world to meet the demand. There are now outlets in supermarkets, hospitals and cross-channel ferries.

Further reading

Ashley, S. (1993) *Catering for Large Numbers*. Butterworth-Heinemann

Ashley, S. and Anderson, S. (1996) *The Concise Theory of Catering*. Macmillan Education Australia

Dittmer, R. and Griffin, S. (1997) *The Dimension of the Hospitality Industry*. John Wiley & Sons

Montgomery, R. and Strick, S. (1994) *Meetings, Conventions and Expositions*. John Wiley & Sons

Sargent, M. and Lyle, T. (1994) *Successful Pubs and Inns*. Butterworth-Heinemann

Thuries, Y. (1997) *Buffet Cocktails and Receptions*. Van Nostrand Reinhold

14 Production and distribution III
Catering systems

Definition of catering systems; Types of systems; The sequence of operation; Continuous production systems; Food service systems; Brand name systems.

The aim of every commercial catering business is to give its customers full satisfaction, thus keeping the place busy and bringing a good return on the money invested. This also applies to the cost sector except that there is a smaller profit or the business breaks even.

To achieve this aim, all the resources of the business must be used to their full extent. This means that each component part of the kitchen and dining-room must make a measurable contribution to the end result. Every member of staff and each item of equipment must play a full part during the working day.

Normal kitchen and dining-room routine is to spend the morning cooking the food and getting the room ready for lunch, leading to a peak period of one and a half to two hours of serving customers. The same routine is then followed to serve dinner. There may be one shift of staff for each meal or a split duty system where staff cook and serve both meals. In both cases there are gaps in the daily routine when staff are not fully occupied, so the introduction of a catering system could help fulfil the aims of most catering businesses by bringing about greater efficiency and full use of resources.

Definition of catering systems

A system is an interacting series of activities that together form a unified whole. The individual activities can be termed subsystems, especially those important but ancillary ones such as publicity and advertising, and research and development. Each must be assessed as to its value to the whole system. In effect, each segment of the catering cycle can be called a subsystem.

- The system must be seen as a whole rather than a series of unconnected parts or separate sections.
- The objective must be clearly defined and show the targets to be attained in order to meet consumer demands.
- The input and output are the beginning and end of a system. Goods are received and manpower transforms the goods into output in the form of meals.

- The system should be monitored to ensure that each stage of the operation is working effectively. Improvements should be carried out to increase efficiency, and the dishes produced must meet customers' expectations.

Types of systems

Any kind of eating place can implement a system to suit its particular need. An establishment which operates on conventional lines could buy ready prepared high-class dishes that can be regenerated and given a personal touch of embellishment. This could lead to lower labour costs, less expenditure on fuel and equipment, and a saving on storage and working space.

Open and closed systems

A system can be classified as open when the input and output are not fixed. The open system is not evenly balanced like the closed system where what goes in comes out. Here commodities await selection by a customer who chooses them from the à la Carte menu. Perishable items may not get used during a particular mealtime, so have to be kept fresh until ordered. The route of the open system can never be direct, and even when a product is ordered it can be prepared in many different ways.

A closed system is where there is a known number of people to be fed at any one meal. There can be some choice of courses, but the total number of meals produced exactly corresponds with the known number of customers. All food will be cooked at the same time and kept ready throughout the meal period.

Short-run and long-run systems

The short-run system is used by an establishment where food is only cooked for a firm order, in other words on the à la Carte pattern. The long-run or continuous system refers to the mass production of meals, such as the cook-freeze and cook-chill systems explained on page 301.

The sequence of operation

The sequence of any system follows the pattern shown in Figure 70, the main point of which is quality control. A system will give complete satisfaction to customers, staff and management if it operates according to a rigid plan of operation with strong control throughout.

Every kind of system must follow this pattern. The quality-control point ensures that standards are constantly maintained. It is at this point that samples

Figure 70   The sequence of a system

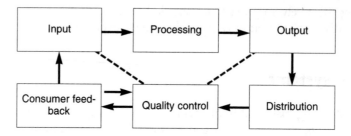

of food are taken for laboratory checking on their safety, calorific value and acceptability.

In the operation of a large-scale cook-freeze or cook-chill system producing a large number of portions of a particular dish, the first step is to order the right quantity of ingredients. These are prepared by members of the kitchen staff who then cook them, pack and label the finished product, and place them into the freezing or chilling unit prior to storage and distribution to centres where they will be regenerated and served.

Continuous production systems

Organisation

The organisation of a large-scale unit would be headed by a production manager and, if the operation warrants them, a personnel manager and an accountant. A salesperson could bring in additional business to use capacity to the full. Other senior staff might be a purchasing officer, a research and development officer and laboratory technicians. A head cook with a brigade of cooks, packers and cleaners would carry out the practical work. Figure 71 shows how the personnel and sections are related.

Work and method study

The work schedule must be planned to ensure a continuous flow of goods going along the system without any obstruction. A flow diagram can show the direction of goods and where each member of staff should be stationed according to their particular input. The diagram should explain the what, where, why and when of every action and how long each takes to carry out.

Production resources

The resources of an organisation include the equipment and staff required to produce the goods. Maximum use must be made of the resources available.

Figure 71   Organisation of a continuous production system

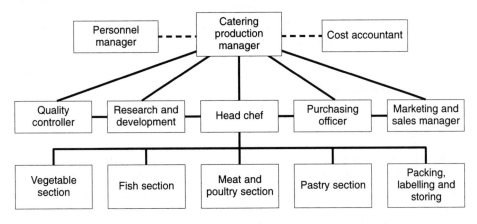

Equipment should be multi-purpose where possible and kept in good condition. Although staff must be given specific duties, they should be adaptable and capable of taking over when required. A continuous production system must never lose its momentum.

Cook-freeze system

As meals are produced, packed and labelled, they are put in or passed through a fast-freezing unit to reduce the temperature from hot to –18°C. The food is then stored in a deep freezer at –20°C in readiness for distribution to service points on demand.

Under this system the preparation and cooking operations are separated and peaks and troughs of production are eliminated. Costs of production are reduced and control can be more efficient. Prepared dishes can be single or multi-packs in foil dishes or inside plastic bags. Information on the label should include name of dish, date of manufacture, sell-by date, regeneration methods, and storage and regeneration temperatures and times.

Cook-chill system

Meals are prepared in the normal, large-scale way, using only high-quality and suitable ingredients. Production units should be purpose-built with suitable equipment for large-scale operations and individual portioning. Good hygiene standards must be maintained from start to finish.

Containers for single portion meals are made of cardboard and plastic laminates, foil or reusable ceramic or stainless steel with airtight and watertight lids. Multi-packs must be capable of holding up to 3 kg, which means that foil cannot be used. Ceramic or stainless-steel containers are recommended. Food is cooked, portioned and lidded whilst still hot, then put into or through a chiller to reduce the temperature rapidly to 3°C. It must be stored at that temperature for a maximum of 5 days. It can then be regenerated, portioned from the multi-packs into individual servings on plates, being monitored throughout the process. The food should be distributed in refrigerated trolleys or vans or in insulated boxes especially designed to keep food at the required low temperature.

Sous-vide system

Under this system, meals are prepared by a large-scale production method then placed into laminated plastic pouches, vacuum sealed, and chilled and stored at 4°C until required, for a period of 21 days. Raw ingredients can be prepared and packaged for cooking in the pouch. Sous-vide foods have a longer life than those prepared by the cook-chill system. Meals are regenerated in a combi-oven, pressure steamer or pan of boiling water, and individual portions can be reheated in 3–4 minutes. Cold items are ready to serve.

Skill-less cookery

The industrialisation of food production in the form of prepared meals is now well established. These dishes are cooked to perfection in food factories and sold in frozen, chilled, sous-vide or ambient form in single or multiple portion packs at prices that still give those caterers who use them a good margin of profit.

The economic advantages of using ready meals and partly prepared ingredients are that unskilled staff can be employed to serve them in accordance with the instructions on the packet, and could even add a few embellishments to give a home-made look. This cuts the cost of staff wages and reduces the number of staff and the amount of time needed to run a traditional kitchen. With no preparation carried out in the kitchen, the premises will be much more hygienic and the number of items of cooking equipment will be reduced.

The deskilling of catering staff by the use of prepared meals is, however, likely to lead to a uniformity of taste and quality across a wide range of eating places. Initially it could have a demoralising effect upon staff because the routine will be fairly monotonous and there will be no opportunity to create new dishes or make variations to classical ones.

Long ago there was an abundance of cheap labour and every item in the kitchen was prepared from scratch. Now all the chores are done at source and the cooks simply put the food on a plate or dish and call it their own handiwork.

Food service systems

There are a number of firms which produce customised service systems for large-scale production units. They can be used for serving hot and cold plated meals or for transporting bulk meals to be portioned in a hospital ward or school refectory. To serve plated meals, the containers of freshly cooked or regenerated foods are brought to appropriate sections of a conveyor belt. Serving trays, cutlery, crockery, glassware and cards showing each customer's choice of dishes are assembled and as each tray moves along, staff portion the food on to each plate by reference to menu cards.

The filled trays are placed into heated trolleys which are then taken to the central point for issue to customers. Microchip monitors enable hot and cold dishes to be stored in the same trolley. Hot meals are kept at the desirable safe temperature with no chance of drying out, and cold foods are protected by insulated hoods which keep them chilled. New equipment such as combi-ovens and pressure steamers, pressure frying units and microwave ovens make it possible to reheat prepared meals to order, thus eliminating overproduction or the formation of queues of customers.

Serving counters can be used to form self-service or cafeteria service systems to suit the particular operation. The service area can be designed so that customers move along one counter choosing the desired food and drink for a complete meal and paying at a cash desk, or different counters may serve main dishes, sweets, beverages or sundries. Counters can also be divided up to serve snack-type meals such as pizzas, pasta, baked potatoes, salads, vegetarian and ethnic foods.

Plate 9   Food service system, Victor Manufacturing

Brand name systems

A fast-food or quick-service restaurant which runs as a unit of a large national or international company usually offers a limited-choice menu of popular dishes that can be cooked quickly. The holding company may operate all its branches or franchise some to individuals or companies. Every unit is run according to the formula laid down by the company which probably has a trademark name and logo. Ingredients and methods used must comply with the company formula, though there may be some flexibility of prices charged in different locations. High standards of hygiene must be maintained.

Further reading

Knight, B. and Kotschevar, L. (1989) *Quantity Food Production*. 2nd Edition. John Wiley & Sons

Light, N. and Walker, A. (1990) *Cook Chill Catering: Technology and Management*. Kluwer Academic Publishers

15 Control of costs and revenue

Costing; Catering costs; Control of materials; Control of food costs; Control of alcoholic beverages; Pricing by the gross profit method; Pricing by the unitary control method; Control of labour costs; Control of overheads; Control of revenue; Departmental control; Analysis of sales.

The main purpose of financial control is to ensure that an enterprise operates within its budget and, in the case of a commercial undertaking, produces a profit to ensure its further progress and development. Each department must make its contribution towards the financial objectives of the enterprise and every activity that takes place must project the image of the enterprise and seek to enhance it.

The techniques used to ensure financial control include forecasting the amount of business that will be done over a period of time, issuing budgets for each part of the operation, and having cost control systems in place to monitor results.

Costing

In order to control the financial aspect of a catering enterprise, it is necessary to know the exact cost of every item bought, produced and served so that its value and its cost to the customer can be assessed. This should enable the customer to receive fair value for money whilst at the same time generating sufficient profit to keep the business financially solvent. Costing is thus a means of control and a technique to ensure the prosperity of a firm in both its own and the customers' interests. Costing must, however, be the servant and not the master of the control system as it might otherwise exert an adverse effect on sales. Cheaper items such as a serving of fruit juice can bear a mark-up of, say, 250 per cent, whereas items which are expensive to buy, such as caviar, could not be given such a heavy mark-up as they would never sell. It is necessary to know what charges are incurred in the production and service of food and drink to customers and it is essential to ensure that costs are passed on in the prices charged.

Catering costs

There are two broad categories of costs used in the operation of a catering enterprise; the first is usually known as the fixed costs or direct costs, and the other as the variable or indirect costs, but it is advisable not to categorise them too rigidly as sometimes a more flexible classification may produce a better profit. In fact it is possible to put some from both the fixed and variable lists into a third category and label it semi-variable costs, as in practice all three have similar characteristics in terms of flexibility and inflexibility.

Fixed costs

Under this heading is generally included loan repayment or interest charges, rent, business rates, local authority charges, water and sewerage, insurance, legal services, advertising costs, maintenance costs, depreciation and replacement, and net profit which must be at least comparable to the investment.

LOAN REPAYMENT AND INTEREST

The direct purchase of premises is better than renting since over a period of time inflation reduces the initial proportion of the purchasing cost. If a loan is secured for seven years at the current rate of interest, the interest paid is approximately the same as the capital loan repayment. Over a ten-year period there would be a smaller capital loan repayment per annum, but a total higher interest paid.

Figure 72 illustrates how a loan taken out for various periods of time can be repaid, showing the difference in total repayments.

RENT

The cost of renting premises depends on the location and value of the property. Rent is charged for a fixed period with reviews at set intervals. Renting means that the capital requirement is considerably lessened, which offers many advantages over the short-term but disadvantages over the long-term in that the premises never belong to the operator. The charges increase as the value of the property increases. The owner will want to increase the rent of a successful business since it, in turn, has increased the value of the property.

Figure 72   Loan repayment figures

Amount of loan: £200,000 Rate of interest: 7½% per annum, constant			
No. of years	**10**	**15**	**20**
Capital loan repayment	£20,000 × 10 = 200,000	£13,333 × 15 = 200,000	£10,000 × 20 = 200,000
Interest	£7,500 × 10 = 75,000	£10,000 × 15 = 150,000	£15,000 × 20 = 300,000
Total repayments	£275,000	£350,000	£500,000

BUSINESS RATES

The rateable value of property varies according to its locality. High-street properties are charged higher rates than those elsewhere. The amount is calculated by multiplying the business's 1995 rateable value with the Government's national rate in the pound. The resultant figure may then have to be adjusted to reflect any transitional arrangements or relief applicable to the particular circumstances of the property.

ADVERTISING

The amount of money spent on advertising may not amount to more than 1 per cent of turnover, although most restaurateurs recognise the need to keep the public aware of the existence of the business. A budget allowance should be made for advertising, but feedback of information is necessary to see how effective various means of advertising are.

MAINTENANCE AND REPAIRS

It is usually impossible to predict exactly how much the cost of maintenance and repairs is going to be in any trading period, so a specific sum should be set aside for this. The amount is expressed as a percentage of turnover, probably of the order of $2\frac{1}{2}$ per cent. If the establishment is not big enough to have its own works department or to employ a maintenance engineer, it should follow a planned programme of maintenance and set up a maintenance contract for all expensive and frequently used equipment.

DEPRECIATION AND REPLACEMENT

Utensils and other equipment wear out after a time and need to be replaced, so an allowance of up to $2\frac{1}{2}$ per cent of turnover should be allocated to this. The usual life of fixed equipment and machinery can be estimated and it is necessary to make an allowance for replacement of obsolete items.

NET PROFIT

It is accepted that the net profit of a commercial undertaking is a fixed cost, since without any profit the business could not survive. The precise amount of net profit to be expected is related to the amount of capital invested. The enterprise should yield at least the same gain as if the capital had been invested in bonds, stocks or shares, or in a deposit account, after the payment of the owner's salary. It should be remembered that a catering business tends to be capital intensive and may need premises in a prime location. If it has been purchased by the owner its periodic revaluation will be a form of profit or loss.

The influence of turnover on fixed costs

Each place allocated for the use of a customer in the dining-room costs a certain amount of money to provide and maintain. There is the cost of setting up and equipping the room, which as part of the capital expenditure is recouped over a certain number of years. There are also the daily running costs of the room. By adding these together then dividing by the seating capacity and the number of days the establishment operates, the cost of providing each seat can be calculated. This basic cost has to be recovered from each client who uses the seat.

The occupancy rate will obviously have an effect upon the amount to be recouped from each occupant of the seat, since if the chair is occupied by several customers during the two main meal periods the cost to each would be less than if occupied once only. Thus if the recurring cost is £3 per chair per day and it was used by four customers, the charge for each would be 75p. This suggests that there is a great advantage to be gained from maximising turnover rather than under-using the resources. In general this fixed cost per seat is incorporated into the price of the meals and is reflected in the gross profit and the kitchen percentage.

Variable costs

These are the costs involved in the production of items for sale, including food and drink as well as labour and energy. They are called variable costs because they show the direct relationship of increased expenditure to additional business.

Semi-variable costs

Some of the headings from the foregoing lists can be put into this third category because their costs can fluctuate during the financial year. They would include energy, maintenance, and repair and renewal of equipment. Every establishment uses energy regardless of the volume of business; staff have to be kept on duty even at quiet periods, and staff meals provided even if the customers' dining-room is empty.

The three categories of costs can be seen, then, in the following light:– fixed costs tend to remain static over a trading period; variable costs have a fixed nature up to a certain rate of usage; and semi-variable costs have a tendency to move in the same direction as the variable ones. In this industry, the greater the number of customers served at any one mealtime, the lower the cost per head.

Control of materials

A large proportion of the expenditure of any catering establishment is for materials, including food and drink. The control of materials begins when goods are ordered and continues through the storage and preparation stages. In the preparation stage there are two methods of control – the unitary method and the gross profit method.

Unitary method of control

Each item of material is classed as a unit, so making it possible to control it by count from the time it arrives to when it is sold. This method is much used in fast-food operations and can be used with a cyclical Table d'Hôte menu. It is not suitable for a high-class establishment as it tends to restrict choice of foods and methods of cooking and finishing; in these places the gross profit system is widely used.

Gross profit method of control

Under this method the person responsible for the production and finishing of dishes will have received materials to a certain value into the kitchen. The chef is then expected to achieve a return of monies through sales which will be sufficient to recover the original value of these materials plus a gross profit to pay the fixed and variable costs. This means having to add a figure of 50–300 per cent or, in other words, multiplying the materials cost by $1\frac{1}{2}$ to 4 times its value to arrive at the selling price. These percentages are not expressed as an addition on sales but as a fraction of sales returns which represent 100 per cent of revenue.

Budgetary control

In some large-scale catering establishments there is a system whereby a total sum of money is allocated to run the operation over the year to cover the cost of food and service for the expected number of customers and at a certain standard. The total sum is divided into the various costs and may not be exceeded; for example, in a hospital where the cost is, say, £2 per day per patient which includes breakfast, a two-course luncheon and an evening meal.

Control of food costs

The problem of keeping strict control over costs by constraint over the usage of materials can be solved by determining the exact number of customers expected on any day at any meal and by reference to records of past business and other local factors. It is also necessary to forecast fairly accurately the numbers of each item customers will be likely to choose from the day's menu. Figures can be obtained by keeping a record of menu item popularity. Together these will help to prevent overproduction and balance supply and demand.

Records of purchases, performance and sales, together with a cyclical menu and standardised recipes, can all help in solving the problem of how many portions to produce. They are important in establishing a streamlined organisation which prevents the chances of over- or underproduction. The head chef instructs his or her assistants as to the number of portions to be produced, and a check on numbers as they are being sold will prevent customers being disappointed by being told a dish is 'off' after having ordered it. With some menu items it is possible to cook more portions if there is an unexpected demand, especially if the cooking process is not a long one.

In estimating the number of portions there are to be sold, it is necessary to evaluate how much of the original amount issued is likely to be lost in the transformatory process from raw to cooked stages. The following calculation shows what weight of raw meat should be ordered from the butcher to serve 100 portions of roast rib of beef, allowing 100 g cooked weight per person:

Total amount of cooked weight required	100×100 g = 10,000 g = 10 kg
Add bones and carved trimmings	250 g
Allow for cooking loss	3,000 g
Allow for preparation loss	270 g
Amount of raw weight required	13,530 g = $13\frac{1}{2}$ kg

For the economic roasting of meat, a combi-type oven helps to prevent excessive cooking losses by the injection of vapour into the oven. This can be controlled to give an authentic roast taste and flavour and cuts weight loss and shrinkage. Computerised control gives the required degree of heat and time of cooking and an internal probe shows the temperature at the centre of the joint, so there is no need to estimate or guess if the meat is properly cooked.

Control of alcoholic beverages

The main difference between the control of food commodities and the control of drink lies in the fact that many foodstuffs are of a highly perishable nature in contrast to drink which, in general, stores quite well. Not all foods lend themselves to unitary control, whereas drink is practically all bought in unitary form. All that is required is to know the range of drinks offered for sale, predict the demand for each, and set up an operation that establishes stock levels and re-ordering procedures. The stock levels are set to ensure continuity of supply to cover the normal demand plus a reserve to meet any sudden unexpected demand.

To find out how much of each drink to keep in stock it is necessary to know how many are likely to be sold each day and how often delivery can be made by the supplier, and to add on an amount for a buffer stock to cover any sudden demand. The total value of stock in hand should not exceed the period allowed for payment which is normally 28 days.

The control of wine is quite straightforward and each sale can be accounted for through the checking system used. Beer and soft drinks are also easy to control. Other drinks are sold by the measure and yield a certain number of portions per bottle according to contents, as shown in Figure 73. Outage refers to the number of portions obtained from the full bottle.

Figure 73   Alcohol drinks – outage per bottle

	Measure	No. per 1 litre bottle	No. per 70 cl bottle
Gin, rum, vodka, whisky	25 ml	40	28
	30 ml	33+	23
	35 ml	28+	20
Liqueurs	30 ml		23
Fortified wines	45 ml	22	16+

Figure 74   Sales and related costs

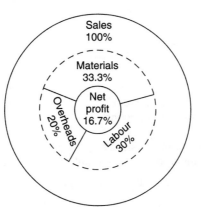

Pricing by the gross profit method

The gross profit method of costing is the one most widely used because it fulfils a twofold function: its simple formula makes it easy to calculate the correct selling price, and it ensures that all costs are recovered from every sale, including the element of profit.

Figure 74 shows in a simple form how the elements of cost are related to sales. Sales are obviously 100 per cent of revenue. Costs – materials, labour and the overheads previously mentioned – represent a percentage of sales. When the costs are subtracted from the sales what is left is the net profit.

The materials are basically the food and drink, with cigars and cigarettes kept separate – the profit from the latter is usually 10 per cent which is below that for food and drink. The proportion ascribed to labour includes wages and necessary expenses associated with employment such as National Insurance contributions, pensions, uniforms and welfare costs, and meals on duty. The overheads consist of all the other fixed or semi-variable costs. However, to arrive at the figure for gross profit there is only one figure to consider, which is the difference between the sales and the cost of materials, as shown in Figure 75.

So to arrive at the figure for gross profit, all that is necessary is to deduct the cost of materials from the sales. The cost of materials over a trading period is arrived at as in the following example:

Figure 75   Sales and related gross profit

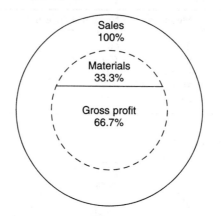

	£
Value of opening stock	5,000
+ purchases during period	20,000
− value of closing stock	2,500
∴ the cost of materials used equals	22,500
Sales during the period equal	67,500

The materials cost percentage can thus be expressed as:

$$\frac{\text{Materials}}{\text{Sales}} \times 100 = \text{Materials cost \%}$$

Using the above figures, £22,500 for materials and £67,500 for sales during the same period, the materials percentage becomes:

$$\frac{22,500}{67,500} \times \frac{100}{1} = 33.3\%$$

which gives the following percentages:

Sales (takings)	= £67,500 = 100%
Materials (goods consumed)	= £22,500 = 33.3%
Gross profit	= £45,000 = 66.7%

The gross profit percentage representing the kitchen's contribution to the profitability of the business is commonly referred to as the kitchen percentage, and this is the figure which shows chefs how efficiently they are running the kitchen. The figures used to arrive at the kitchen percentage must be the cost and sales of food only. Those for drink would be calculated separately. The formula used for arriving at the kitchen percentage is:

$$\frac{\text{Gross profit}}{\text{Sales}} \times \frac{100}{1} = \text{Gross profit \% for the kitchen}$$

Using the same figures as before but related to the costs and sales of food only, the kitchen percentage becomes:

$$\frac{\text{(Gross profit)}}{\text{(Sales)}} \quad \frac{45,000}{67,500} \times \frac{100}{1} = 66.6\%$$

Another way of expressing gross profit is the difference between sales revenue and the cost of materials as in the following example:

	£
Sales	20,000
− Cost of materials	6,600
∴ gross profit	13,400

To arrive at the figure for net profit it is necessary to deduct from the gross profit the cost of labour and other overheads as previously defined.

Costing dishes

To calculate the cost of a dish accurately before including it on the menu, the recipe must be defined precisely. For example, a Supreme of Chicken Marechal might have a food cost when cooked and garnished of £2.50, which at different gross profits would be:

$$2.50 \times \frac{100}{40} = £6.25 \text{ (gross profit 60\%)}$$

$$2.50 \times \frac{100}{33.3} = £7.50 \text{ (gross profit 66.7\%)}$$

$$2.50 \times \frac{100}{30} = £8.35 \text{ (gross profit 70\%)}$$

The quick way to do each of these is to multiply by $2\frac{1}{2}$, 3 and $3\frac{1}{3}$. It is usual to round the figures up to the nearest 5p to give the selling price. A full Table d'Hôte menu can be costed to give the total selling price per meal in a similar manner.

For this system of costing to be an effective means of control, it is inadvisable to set a different rate of gross profit for different courses as this would create differing results in the expected return. This applies particularly to drinks as they cannot be separated into various percentage returns unless sales are recorded separately, and variance from expected percentages would occur as drinking patterns change with the seasons. To suggest that beer should yield a lower profit than spirits has some merit, but the results in terms of control become unsatisfactory. The average gross return on bar sales is approximately 50 per cent as anything higher would have a detrimental effect on sales. The pricing of wine is a different matter and according to quality it can yield a gross profit of 50–75 per cent, bearing in mind that there is no processing but simply storage and service.

The pricing of wine

With a mark-up of 50 per cent, a bottle of wine that cost £2 to buy can be sold for £6, but a fine wine that costs £10 would be listed at £30 which may put off prospective customers. It may be advisable to add gross profit on a pro rata scale applied in reverse as follows – 50 per cent gross profit on wines costing up to £5 per bottle, 40 per cent on those up to £10, and only 30 per cent on fine wines that cost the firm £20 per bottle.

It is not necessary to control wine by the gross profit method, however, since it is so easy to do it in unit form which also gives flexibility of pricing.

Limitations of the gross profit method of pricing

Although this method of pricing is a useful tool of management, it must be understood that as a tool of costing it can prove inflexible if complete accuracy is required. In the wrong hands it can cause serious damage to a firm's turnover. One of the hallmarks of good business practice is that it should be both adaptable and flexible – with this system it cannot be so. The accurate and formal application of the gross profit system may be the reason for the disappearance of some of the more expensive items from menus, leading to the conformity of dishes that is noticeable in many catering establishments.

The following examples illustrate this statement, but first it is necessary to pose the question 'Should a restaurateur expect bigger profits from customers with more sophisticated tastes?' and 'Why should a person wanting an expensive first course pay as much as four times more for the rental of the chair than the one who selects a cheaper one?' This is asked in the knowledge that the restaurateur will not settle the account with the suppliers until well after the foodstuffs are used and will not be charged any interest on the credit allowed.

EXAMPLE 1

Smoked Scotch Salmon

	£
1 portion of 70 g @ £8.50 per 500 g	1.20
Brown bread and butter	0.10
Lemon, cress	0.05
Cost price	1.35
Selling price @ 65% gross profit	3.85
Gross profit	2.50

Florida Cocktail

	£
1 grapefruit	0.25
1/2 orange	0.15
Sugar	0.02
Cherry	0.03
Cost price	0.45
Selling price @ 65% gross profit	1.30
Gross profit	0.85

In this example the cheaper course is the most labour intensive of the two and yet the profit is only a third of that for the expensive item.

The next example shows how inflation can have an effect upon costing and, in turn, competitiveness, because of the method of pricing used.

EXAMPLE 2

Grilled Entrecôte Steak

	£
200 g sirloin @ £12.80 per kg	2.56
Garnish	0.24
Total cost	2.80
Selling price @ 66.7% gross profit	8.40

The following year the sirloin and garnish may have increased in price by 10 per cent and therefore the calculation will be:

200 g sirloin @ £14.08 per kg	2.82
Garnish	0.26
Total cost	3.08
Selling price @ 66.7% gross profit	9.25

The result of inflation shows a rise in the selling price of the steak, which could have an adverse effect upon demand – the higher the price, the lower the demand.

Pricing by the unitary control method

In an establishment that operates on a restricted menu, such as a steak house or fast-food snack bar, this method permits total food control by numbers which means that everything is done by count, as shown in Figure 76.

The left-hand side of the stock sheet is completed from the purchasing records and the right from sales records or waiter's checks. Rather than having various percentage mark-ups for different items, a single charge may be made per item sold according to course, e.g. first courses £1, main course £3, dessert £1.50, thus creating conditions where every customer pays the same amount per chair rent. This is a simple but successful method of operation, except that it offers little flexibility and caterers become totally dependent upon portion control lines, for which they probably pay more than if they prepared them on site.

Figure 76 Unitary control stock sheet

Stock sheet for week ending 23.7.__

Steaks	A Opening stock	B Purchases M T W T F	Total A + B	Less closing stock	Total usage	Daily usage M T W T F
Sirloin 180 g	24	40 50	114	24	90	10 6 18 26 30
Sirloin 250 g	20	30 50	100	23	77	7 6 14 18 32
Rump 180 g	30	30 50	110	26	84	8 7 16 19 34
Rump 250 g	34	30 50	114	42	72	7 7 12 16 30
Porterhouse 550 g	10	20 20	50	7	43	2 6 10 10 15

Control of labour costs

In many catering establishments the cost of labour is higher than materials. This may not always be apparent, however, since the major part of labour costs are generated by the kitchen and dining-room and may become diffused in the total labour costs of the establishment whereby the total figure in proportion becomes more acceptable. The cost of serving drinks, for example, may be only $7\frac{1}{2}$ per cent of sale as against labour costs for the kitchen of, say, 35 per cent, but this brings down the average to a more acceptable 21 per cent, assuming that both sales are equal.

The first task in the control of labour should be to draw a baseline in relation to turnover of customers and the proposed standard of service. Judging the standard against another similar unit may be helpful in deciding on numbers of personnel. It is important that standards are set for each member of staff, including managerial, supervisory, skilled and unskilled operatives. Where figures for business turnover exist, the best way to obtain a clear perspective is to allocate a specific time to each section in relation to customer numbers, as shown in Figure 77. This example relates to a high-class dining-room with 200 seats which is open for only five days per week and serves 400 customers per day. The table shows the number of staff employed; the total number of hours worked per week; and the time devoted to each customer as a percentage of the total and in minutes.

Having set the correct hourly staffing level, the next stage would be to include the wages paid plus employer contributions and staff meals, to arrive at the total cost of labour for this establishment.

By establishing staffing levels, turnover analysis will indicate clearly when staff hours increase disproportionately to customer usage. By taking the average labour expense per hour, the baseline would clearly indicate how much each customer should pay in charges to cover labour expenses on the average daily usage. Assuming a labour cost of £6 per hour, the customer should contribute that amount in the bill. It is important to see that labour costs are kept under control

Figure 77   Staff, time and customer ratio

	Number of staff	Total hours per week	% time devoted to each customer	Minutes devoted to each customer
Manager	1	40	2	1.2
Assistant managers	2	80	4	2.4
Chefs	20	800	40	24.0
Waiters	20	800	40	24.0
Storekeepers	2	80	4	2.4
Stillroom hands	2	80	4	2.4
Dishwash hands	2	80	4	2.4
General porter	1	40	2	1.2
Total	**50**	**2,000**	**100**	**60.0**

by ensuring that the time allocated per cover or cost per hour does not increase, otherwise the figures budgeted become meaningless and there is less net profit at the end. The figures given so far are representative of a high-class restaurant, but a similar formula is used to establish a baseline for other forms of business. For large-scale preparation and cafeteria service the amount allocated per customer may be decreased to 10 minutes or less of labour hours per customer.

Having established a baseline for control of labour costs, it is necessary to ensure that service periods are not allowed to extend with the result that over-time has to be worked. Labour-saving equipment can help to lessen the burden on staff, allowing them to operate at full efficiency. The use of a proportion of convenience foods will reduce labour requirements by cutting out a lot of preparation work. The application of work-study techniques in production practice and the ideal siting of equipment can also contribute to the effective use of labour.

Control of overheads

The cost of overheads continues to rise all the time and must therefore be looked at regularly to try to keep it in check. The following points are given as examples of where savings may be made.

Staff can make savings in the use of energy by turning on equipment only shortly before it is required and off again when no longer required. Management must make staff aware of this: a weekly target showing how much less has been used than the previous week, an example of what a particular item of equipment costs to run per hour, and information on the need to conserve sources of energy for future generations are all useful deterrents against waste.

A regular programme of maintenance and repair will save money as minor faults are less costly to put right before they deteriorate further. Staff should be encouraged to report defects as soon as they occur.

Laundry charges can be reduced by using slip cloths over tablecloths and by forbidding the misuse of table napkins, waiter's cloths and teacloths.

Control of revenue

After ensuring that control is maintained all along the line, the final point is reached when the correct amount of money is received for all goods supplied to consumers and is paid into the accounts of the business. There are several methods of revenue control available – manual, mechanical or electronic installations according to the needs of the establishment. The traditional system of the waiter writing out the customer's order in numbered triplicate – top copy, bottom copy and flimsy copy – and going through the process as illustrated in Figure 78 is being replaced in many establishments by more sophisticated ordering systems that also act as a means of control.

Figure 78   *Triplicate checking method*

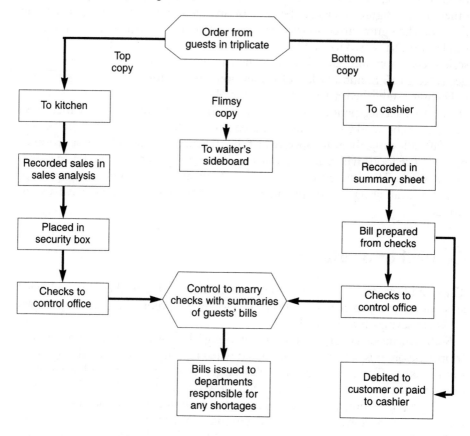

The waiter billing machine

Various billing machines have been introduced to replace the traditional system of waiter's checks. A machine can remove the need to employ a restaurant cashier and offers a quick analysis of goods sold by means of a memory system. With one such machine, the waiter notes down the customer's order on a pad, goes to the machine to insert a coded key and enters the order by pressing numbered buttons for each item. This appears in the kitchen in printed form to be announced, and when everything is dished up the waiter's number is flashed on a screen in the dining-room informing him or her that the food can be collected. This system means that waiting staff do not have to run backwards and forwards between dining-room and kitchen unnecessarily.

The waiter then prints out the customer's bill which provides an easy-to-read list of each item ordered, its cost and the total to be paid plus VAT and service charge. At the conclusion of the service an assistant manager will press each waiter's key to see how much each one has taken and the total business for that session. The total is broken down under food, wine, spirits and any other relevant heading. One of the advantages of such a system is that, as the ordering terminals and screen are very compact, they can be placed in between stations so that they can be used by several waiters. They work very successfully in fast-food, pay-as-you-leave, drive-in and other similar operations, but may require further sophistication before they can be used in every class of waiter service establishment.

A similar system can be used in the control of sales and revenue in the bar. A microprocessor connected to the optics and beer engines will record every sale. The monitor is housed in an office away from the bar where usage and income can be checked at the end of each service period and, indeed, at any time in between. When an empty spirit bottle is replaced by a new one this is shown.

It is possible to put all control on to a computer. From a bank of dishes with their recipes, a complete menu cycle can be programmed giving the precise amount of ingredients to be issued for a given number of portions. It can also show the nutritional value and the cost of a meal. Microprocessors can handle hundreds of recipes with up to 30 ingredients in each, as well as all other information necessary for the efficient operation and control of the kitchen.

Departmental control

The aim of departmental control should be to provide management with information showing how each part of the enterprise is fulfilling its role in achieving the anticipated revenue return, so contributing effectively to its overall success. Norms for each department are not easy to establish, since it is inevitable that one may contribute to the success of another; for example, a lounge bar obtains much of its income from dining-room customers. Yet the fact remains that in the catering industry the profit comes only from the public areas and each square metre must contribute towards it.

The exact method of control varies from one place to another, but certain data must be provided to ensure that profitability is maintained and constantly improved. The data needed by management include:

- daily takings
- average spending per customer
- occupancy rate of the room per meal, per day and per week
- average spend per customer on food and on drink
- takings for à la Carte meals, for Table d'Hôte meals, and for drinks.

This information can then be extended to provide weekly, monthly and annual reports so that performance can be monitored on an ongoing basis. This will allow areas of low revenue or excessive expenditure to be pinpointed. Quiet periods and low operating performance can be isolated so that extra resources can be allocated there to promote profitability.

Analysis of sales

Part of the control of revenue comes from an analysis or summary sheet of each day's business. This is produced by cashiers or computers who record the actual sales of food and drink as taken from waiter's orders. When completed the form is forwarded to the office to be reconciled with the checks received from the kitchen and those from the cashier. This control over the day's business can show how profitable the kitchen or bar has been as well as the sales of each separate department.

From this sheet a daily report giving comparisons of business done can be compiled, but not all the information provided by the summary sheet is necessary to monitor the economic performance of the establishment. All that is required is the essential information about how the unit operates within its stated objectives. An example is shown in Figure 79. It is based on a 110-seater dining-room.

This information is prepared for management perusal each day to provide details of the number of customers served and the occupancy rate. Occupancy rate is calculated by dividing the number of users by the number of available seats. Although the figures in Figure 79 appear to be very satisfactory, the

Figure 79　Daily comparisons of business

	Monday 15th February 20_ _	Same day last week	Same day last year
Takings (£)			
Total	5,000	4,800	4,000
Lunch			
Table d'Hôte	448	396	500
à la Carte	802	804	500
Drinks	416	400	334
Dinner			
Table d'Hôte	830	800	800
à la Carte	1,640	1,600	1,200
Drinks	834	800	666
Average spend (£)			
Lunch			
Food	15.62	14.10	11.10
Drink	5.60	4.70	3.70
Dinner			
Food	25.00	24.00	20.00
Drink	8.36	8.18	6.66
Number of covers			
Lunch	80	85	90
Dinner	100	100	100
Occupancy rate (%)			
Lunch	93	77	82
Dinner	91	91	91

Figure 80   *Weekly comparison with last year's business*

Week ending 10th May 20_ _

	Monday		Tuesday		Wednesday		Thursday		Friday		Saturday	
	This year	Last year	This year	Last year	This year	Last year	This year	Last year	This year	Last year	This year	Last year
Total												
No. of covers	165	160	170	165	175	180	170	165	200	200	220	220
Takings (£)	3,000	2,400	3,200	2,800	3,600	3,200	3,600	3,200	5,000	4,000	5,600	4,600
Food (£)	2,000	1,600	2,200	1,800	2,400	2,200	2,400	2,400	3,600	2,800	4,000	3,400
Drink (£)	1,000	800	1,000	1,000	1,200	1,000	1,200	800	1,400	1,200	1,600	1,200
Lunch												
No. of covers	75	80	80	80	80	85	80	85	90	90	90	95
Food (£)	665	540	740	400	800	740	800	800	1,200	1,100	1,400	1,200
Drink (£)	300	260	300	200	400	300	400	266	460	400	540	400
Dinner												
No. of covers	90	80	90	85	95	95	90	80	120	110	130	125
Food (£)	1,334	1,160	1,460	1,200	1,600	1,460	1,600	1,600	2,400	1,700	2,600	2,200
Drink (£)	700	540	700	700	800	700	800	534	940	800	1,060	800

Total takings for the week:
This year £24,000
Last year £20,200

occupancy rate points to a low level of business at lunchtime, which calls for action. A manager might plot the occupancy rate of the dining-room in the form of a graph so that he or she can keep a constant check on the progress of the business.

Figure 80 shows a weekly report which highlights the days of the week when business is slack. This situation might be improved by means of various marketing methods, such as an advertisement offering a special attraction. A close look at this report shows that despite the increased takings, which could be due to inflation or to higher prices charged, the business performance has not increased very much at dinner and the takings for lunch are down from the previous year. In an establishment that has several dining-rooms, a comparison between the performance of each one can be made.

A trading report to show the profitability of the operation should be kept separate from the business reports as too much information presented at a glance could lose its essential impact. A trading report can be produced weekly, monthly or annually, and its format can vary according to the needs of the company. A sample monthly report is shown in Figure 81.

The purpose of these reports is to provide the manager with sufficient information to take effective decisions in order to maintain the desired business performance. Where a business incorporates several units, each possessing a clear identity, it becomes important to collect relevant statistics on each so as to point out any differences in their performance. This could also be useful in a large establishment with several function rooms.

Figure 82 is an example of another important report, showing occupancy figures over a period of time. It could be an exercise to stimulate a manager to

Figure 81   Monthly trading report – dining-room and bar

Month ending June 30th 20_ _

	No. of covers	Sales £	Average selling price £	Materials cost £	% sales	Gross profit %	Labour costs £	% sales	Operating profit %
Dining-room									
Food	20,000	60,000	6.00	20,000	33.3	66.7	20,000	33.3	33.3
Drink		20,000	2.00	10,000	50.0	50.0	2,000	10.0	40.0
Bar									
Drink		10,000	5.00	5,000	50.0	50.0	2,000	20.0	30.0
Food	4,000	6,000	3.00	2,000	33.3	66.7	2,000	33.3	33.3
Total	24,000	96,000		37,000			26,000		

Figure 82   Monthly occupancy report

Month ending 31st March 20_ _

	Seating capacity	Optimum capacity per day	Optimum capacity per month	Actual users	Capacity usage %
Restaurant	150	300	7,800	5,200	66
Grill room	100	200	5,200	5,800	111
Coffee shop	80	400	10,400	10,000	96
Banqueting Suite A	100	200	5,200	1,200	23
Banqueting Suite B	300	600	15,600	4,800	30

improve business performance. The spare capacity here is highlighted and action is required in some areas, as only the grill room is operating to capacity.

The last of these forms of control of a business's performance is the yearly report which can be presented in various ways but should give the information shown in Figure 83. It should be noted that this is not a financial statement but a managerial report. For this reason VAT, service charges and cigarette sales are excluded since the main purpose of this report is to indicate salient points and too much detail would only detract from its relevance. In this example it can be seen that only the banqueting suites have had an unfavourable trading period as compared to the previous year. Unfavourable trends can be given emphasis by the use of either coloured or bold type.

The report can be used for setting up operating budgets. In addition, management has the responsibility of taking action to bring all the areas within a desirable course of action. A computer will be used to provide this information, giving updated trading comparisons with previous periods and producing an annual comparison at the end of each month. This applies equally to the cost sector and the commercial sector.

Figure 83   *Yearly trading report*

YEARLY TRADING REPORT

Year ending 31st December 20__

	No. of covers	Revenue (excl. VAT) £	Materials cost £	%	Labour costs £	%	Operating profit £	%
Restaurant								
Food	30,000	600,000	200,000	33.3	200,000	33.3	200,000	33.3
Drink		180,000	96,000	50.0	18,000	10.0	72,000	40.0
Grill room								
Food	35,500	375,000	125,000	33.3	100,000	26.6	150,000	40.0
Drink		142,000	70,000	49.2	14,200	10.0	57,800	40.7
Coffeeshop								
Sales	60,000	240,000	96,000	40.2	70,000	29.1	74,000	30.8
Banqueting								
Suite A								
Food	3,500	105,000	35,000	33.3	40,000	38.5	30,000	28.6
Drink		28,000	14,000	50.0	2,500	8.9	11,500	41.0
Suite B								
Food	15,000	300,000	120,000	40.0	100,000	33.3	80,000	26.6
Drink		90,000	45,000	50.0	9,000	10.0	36,000	40.0
Totals	144,000	2,060,000	795,000		553,700		711,300	

	£	%
Administration	120,000	5.82
Heating and energy	103,000	5.00
Repairs and maintenance	50,000	2.42
Replacements	41,000	2.00
Advertising	25,000	1.21
Total	339,200	
Net profit before fixed costs	372,100	

Year ending 31st December 20__

	No. of covers	Revenue (excl. VAT) £	Materials cost £	%	Labour costs £	%	Operating profit £	%
Restaurant								
Food	25,000	450,000	160,000	35.5	180,000	40.0	110,000	24.4
Drink		150,000	75,000	50.0	15,000	10.0	60,000	40.0
Grill room								
Food	35,000	350,000	115,000	32.8	90,000	25.7	145,000	41.4
Drink		135,000	72,500	53.7	13,800	10.2	48,700	38.0
Coffeeshop								
Sales	50,000	190,000	67,000	35.3	62,000	32.6	61,000	32.1
Banqueting								
Suite A								
Food	5,000	135,000	45,000	33.3	38,000	28.1	52,000	38.5
Drink		35,000	17,500	50.0	3,600	10.3	13,900	39.7
Suite B								
Food	14,000	250,000	75,000	30.0	81,000	32.4	94,000	37.6
Drink		70,000	36,000	51.4	7,000	10.0	27,000	38.5
Totals	129,000	1,765,000	663,200		490,400		611,500	

	£	%
Administration	112,000	6.34
Heating and energy	98,000	5.55
Repairs and maintenance	44,000	2.49
Replacements	30,000	1.70
Advertising	24,000	1.35
Total	308,000	
Net profit before fixed costs	303,600	

Further reading

Berry, A. J. *et al.* (1995) *Management Control: Themes, Issues and Practices.* Macmillan

Boardman, R. (1990) *Hotel and Catering Accounts.* Butterworth-Heinemann

Dittmer, R. and Griffin, S. (1994) *Principles of Food, Beverage and Labour Cost Control.* 5th Edition. John Wiley & Sons

Harris, P. (1992) *Profit Planning.* Butterworth-Heinemann

Harris, P. and Hazard, P. (1992) *Managerial Accounting in the Hospitality Industry*, Volumes 1 and 2. Stanley Thornes

Kotas, R. and Jayawardena, C. (1994) *Profitable Food and Beverage Management.* Hodder and Stoughton

O'Connor, P. (1999) *Using Computers in Hospitality.* 2nd Edition. Cassell

Powers, T. and J. M. (1991) *Food Service Operations: Planning and Control.* Krieger

Smith, J. (1990) *Practical Computing: A Guide for Hotel and Catering Students.* Butterworth-Heinemann

16 Monitoring consumer satisfaction

Application of consumer satisfaction; Customer loyalty; Customer questionnaires; Product evaluation procedures; Food leftovers; Quality control; Budgetary control.

Implicit in each segment of the catering cycle that we outlined in Chapter 2 is the need for a systematic approach to the entire operation. Each stage of the cycle should include ways of feeding back information about the working of the operation to enable modifications to be made. No segment should be allowed to deviate from the original policy unless consent is given in the light of a change of strategy. The operation has to be monitored at every stage, from the identification of demand to when the customer leaves the dining-room having consumed a satisfying meal.

The purpose of monitoring the level of customers' satisfaction with the intended standards of food, drink and service is to detect and eliminate any imperfections. Any business which fails to find out customers' views of its products may find that it is operating with false confidence that everything is alright.

If a restaurant is popular because of the quality and price of its food and it is always full, it may not see the need to ask customers if they are satisfied. If the enterprise sees no reason to listen to its customers and therefore makes no changes, there is a risk of them changing to a rival establishment which offers innovatory dishes at a cheaper price.

Application of consumer satisfaction

In the past caterers did not go out of their way to obtain any feedback from customers about the food they had eaten. There was less competition and overheads were low, for example waiting staff were paid a low basic wage which was made up by shares of the tronc which contained the gratuities paid by customers in the form of tips. Typically the proprietor or head waiter would walk through the dining-room at meal times and pause at a table to ask customers if everything was to their satisfaction, not really wanting to hear the opinions expressed. Complaints would be brushed aside by the offer of a free brandy or liqueur or deduction from the bill rather than eliciting an explanation or apology.

Complaints were not wanted and would be quickly forgotten. No one took the blame. Shortage of skilled and qualified staff, high staff turnover, the need for more training, team work and multi-skilled personnel have long been an excuse for customer dissatisfaction which the catering industry still faces.

Complaints handled promptly and properly can be of advantage and value to the enterprise. If a complaint is dealt with properly, the complainant will gain a feeling of importance which may lead him or her to becoming a loyal and regular client who will champion the business to friends, colleagues and relatives because the problem was well handled.

The person who handles customers' complaints must take immediate action and show concern about the incident. Evidence must be taken from everyone connected with it. A decision to accept or reject the complaint should ideally be taken immediately and the reasons why given. If no decision can be reached at the time, the customer must be told what steps will be taken. The affair must be handled diplomatically, voiced in a low tone and strictly confined. Notes must be taken at the time and written up in a complaints book, recording the name of the aggrieved customer, the cause of the complaint, when and how it was dealt with, and what steps were taken to prevent it reoccurring. If necessary this information should be sent to head office for a decision and a suitable reply.

Complaints about food are not a common occurrence because British people feel uneasy about voicing them. Instead they bottle them up and take their business elsewhere, so the manager should almost encourage guests to make complaints or at least get them to discuss the food and drink they are consuming and obtain their views on it. For each customer who makes a complaint, there could be a dozen who do not and leave the restaurant feeling aggrieved and harbouring their resentment. They will tell others of their complaint and discourage them from patronising the place, so causing a drop in business and reputation.

Solving a complaint, especially one that arises frequently, can eradicate it entirely. In other words, criticism can help increase customer loyalty and bear out the saying 'the customer is always right'.

It is best that a customer makes the complaint at the time it arises rather than taking it to the trading standards department of the local authority, to the local or national office of a catering trades association, or to the editor of a local newspaper. In the cost sector a complaint and suggestions book should be made available to customers to voice their approval, disapproval or opinion of the food and service.

Customer loyalty

It costs the restaurant business four times more to bring a new customer on to its premises than to retain an existing one, so customer loyalty must be valued and encouraged. This can be shown by members of the waiting staff in the way they greet customers on arrival, serving the meal well and bidding farewell on departure. When a customer books a table, the reception head waiter has to evaluate the customer's standing and allocate a table that befits the person's status. It should be remembered that in a very high-class restaurant a regular customer is someone who dines there, say, six times a year. Advertising agencies divide the population of a country into traditional socio-demographic groups. A restaurateur will find the statistics related to these groups of great value in assessing the spending power of customers. A loyalty scheme is a way of keeping customers from taking their custom away by offering priority bookings and advance notice of gourmet dinners cooked by well-known visiting chefs. Points can be awarded for each visit or amount paid on the bill, to be exchanged for a personal gift, free meal, two meals for the price of one, or other incentives and rewards. Details of customers, including their social status, likes and dislikes, can be kept on the restaurant's database.

Customer questionnaires

When designing a questionnaire to obtain customers' views on a restaurant, each question must provide an answer to each component part of the operation. Questionnaires may be sent or given to clients to fill out themselves, or filled in by an interviewer on the spot – there will be a different design and wording for both kinds. Every question must be clearly phrased so that it can be answered with a single tick or in a few words. It would be advantageous for questions to be asked at the end of the meal whilst the event is fresh in the customer's mind.

The format of questionnaires

To make them authoritative, questionnaires should get straight to the point, be precise, and not take too long to complete. The first part should gain a profile of the interviewee since no names, addresses or signatures will normally be required. This information will be useful later, as the completed answers can be sorted into age, gender and social groups. Younger customers are more likely to express a need for innovative products and suave service as against their elders who prefer to continue with established standards. Figure 84 shows a possible outline of a questionnaire.

A more concise questionnaire can be used to yield yes or no answers as shown in Figure 85. A short questionnaire is easier for customers to answer as well as being quick to collate.

It should be remembered that the task of collating the answers can be a daunting one and that not all the information gained can be acted upon. At least this method of obtaining feedback from customers helps those who are reluctant to complain verbally.

Evaluation of questionnaires

To gain full value from questionnaires, the results must be promptly analysed and acted upon. The results can be divided into three categories: standard, psychological and physiological.

Figure 84   Customer questionnaire

Customer questionnaire	CONFIDENTIAL

1 Which age group do you belong to?

Tick here

Under 20	☐
20–29	☐
30–39	☐
40–50	☐
Above 50	☐

2 Are you male? ☐
      female? ☐

3 What is your occupation? _____

4 How often do you eat out in restaurants?

daily	☐
weekly	☐
monthly	☐
rarely	☐

5 What would you say is a reasonable price to pay for a 3-course meal, including coffee?

up to £10.00	☐
between £10.00 and £15.00	☐
between £15.00 and £20.00	☐

6 Do you normally take wine with your meal?

yes	☐
no	☐

7 How do you rate the car parking facilities and customer amenities?

Car parking

good	☐
adequate	☐
poor	☐

Cloakroom

good	☐
adequate	☐
poor	☐

Toilets

good	☐
adequate	☐
poor	☐

Customer questionnaire (continued)   **CONFIDENTIAL**

Tick here

8 How do you find the atmosphere of the dining-room?

        warm and welcoming   ☐
        pleasant and relaxing   ☐
        noisy and irritating   ☐

9 How would you describe the menu language?

        clear and informative   ☐
        muddled with technical jargon ☐

10 Did you book a table beforehand?

        yes   ☐
        no   ☐

11 When you arrived at the dining-room was the head waiter at the door to greet you?

        yes   ☐
        no   ☐

12 Rate how the head waiter received you by circling the most appropriate number below

        most cordially   5   4   3   2   1   unpleasantly

13 Were you kept waiting for your table?

        yes   ☐
        no   ☐

14 If so, for how long?

        10 minutes   ☐
        20 minutes   ☐
        30 minutes   ☐

15 How do you value the menu choice?

        excellent   5   4   3   2   1   very unsatisfactory

16 How do you value the wine list?

        excellent   5   4   3   2   1   very unsatisfactory

17 Please indicate in terms of value for money if the portions of food you received were

        very generous   ☐
        generous   ☐
        satisfactory   ☐
        just sufficient   ☐
        insufficient   ☐

Figure 85   Short questionnaire

	Please tick	
	Yes	No
Did you enjoy your visit to our establishment?	☐	☐
Was the price reasonable?	☐	☐
Was a good choice provided?	☐	☐
Was the quality good?	☐	☐
Was the service efficient?	☐	☐
Would you recommend us to your friends?	☐	☐

Standard comments or complaints are associated with:
- the facilities of the restaurant, including its decor and atmosphere
- the style and standard of service
- the quality of the food and drink served
- the customer's interpretation of value for money.

Psychological comments or complaints are connected to:
- courtesy, such as apologising if the customer has been kept waiting
- the customer's welcome on entering the restaurant
- undue delay in serving the courses
- the waiter confusing the order
- unfamiliar food colours and shapes, leading to loss of appetite
- the clatter of cutlery and crockery; loud music in the background
- fear of fire if several guéridon lamps are in use.

Physiological comments or complaints are related to:
- over- or under-heating the room
- lack of air-conditioning
- food that is too hot or too cold
- unusual combinations of ingredients, not in keeping with the name of the dish
- incorrect sequence of courses.

By separating the replies to the questionnaires under the above headings, it is possible to pinpoint the causes of complaints. These can then be brought to the attention of the staff who can help eradicate them.

Product evaluation procedures

New products are usually tried out by a panel of tasters before being included in the menu. The panel should include customers – their views are just as important as those of experts in food tasting. Members of the panel should be chosen

Figure 86   Marking sheet for a new product

Please circle the statement which most closely related to the product you have just tasted.	
Like exceedingly	9
Like considerably	8
Like moderately	7
Like slightly	6
Neither like or dislike	5
Dislike slightly	4
Dislike partially	3
Dislike considerably	2
Dislike intensely	1

to cover every aspect of the dish, including gastronomic, ethnic and health considerations.

The panel has to predict customer reaction to the dish under blind-tasting conditions and in realistic surroundings, assessing the product for colour, texture, flavour and aroma. Figure 86 shows how it is possible to grade the overall impression of a dish.

Food leftovers

Plate waste must be monitored regularly by looking at the dirties as they arrive in the dishwashing section from the restaurant. The waiter will have scraped the debris on to one plate when clearing them from the table, and this residue must be checked to see if it is mostly edible food and not chicken or cutlet bones, skin or stones. If it is food there must be a reason why customers have not eaten it. A large amount of plate waste could indicate that:

- portion control is not being practised
- items are not sufficiently trimmed of indigestible matter
- inferior quality ingredients are being used
- the meal combination was incongruous
- a hot meal was tepid to the taste.

While there is no accounting for customers' taste, a chef's self-respect is offended by excessive plate waste and he or she will want to find the reason for it and see that it only happens on rare occasions.

Chefs must keep an eye on the way food is prepared in all sections of the kitchen. Preparation losses must be kept to a minimum and should not exceed an average of 10 per cent of any commodity, whether peeling potatoes, cutting and trimming an entrecôte or filleting a sole. The amount of waste is an indication of, firstly, the quality of the food purchased and, secondly, the skill of the staff doing the preparation. The amount of wastage should be investigated at each stage of the cooking cycle, from delivery to plate waste. Deliveries must be checked for quantity and quality. Correct storage of perishables and non-perishables is essential to prevent anything being kept beyond its sell-by date. Wastage during the cooking process, such as shrinkage of meat caused by cooking at a high temperature, the prolonged boiling of green vegetables resulting in loss of vitamin and mineral content, and a deep fryer being kept at high temperature throughout the service period so shortening its useful life, can all be avoided thus reducing costs of materials, energy and equipment. Other examples of needless food waste include making too much toast for breakfast or serving too much sauce – always consider the actual needs of the customers.

Quality control

The use of questionnaires to ascertain customers' opinions and attempts to limit the wastage of food in the kitchen can be backed up by quality control, or total quality management (TQM) as it is often called. This will assist by monitoring every stage of the operation from the managerial point of view. Chapter 17 shows how quality control can be implemented throughout a catering business, whether in the commercial or the cost sector, through the ISO 9000 accreditations.

The most important function of the person in charge of any business is to plan and control it. But the standard to which the business operates should be one which benefits customers rather than the manager. Customers buy what they can afford within a quality interpretation of value for money. Most success stories in catering are those which introduced a total package based on a simple but popular item of food, or on a stylish, trendy combination of food, drink and service in a congenial atmosphere. Success was ensured because the price was viewed as good value by most people and yielded a high level of profit. This requires a continuous check to see that consumer product interpretation does not change over a period of time. If it does, the system will need to be adapted or altered. Standards are therefore set by the consumer. Management must maintain a framework which ensures that the internal organisation does not conflict with this precept, that what is provided must also be what the consumer wants and is willing to pay for. This calls for an ability on the part of management to set precise working procedures which assist in achieving the aims.

Internal targets of production, revenue and costs can be set for every part of the operation, based on previous performance or that of similar establishments. They must be closely monitored to ensure they are realistic. Once proven correct, they can form the norm to be achieved. The set objectives become the measure of performance at which the unit should operate. This form of operational and managerial technique is known as Management by Objectives. It is measured strictly by numbers, with precise target figures being set for each aspect of the operation's budgetary control.

Budgetary control

The budget is an organised operational plan which monitors and regulates the activities of a business in financial terms. Many claims are made for budgetary control, for example that it sets standards on which an individual performance can be measured, that it ensures best use of production resources, that it maximises profitability, that it controls expenditure and promotes cost consciousness, and that a budget co-ordinates business activities. There is a good deal of truth in all these claims, but what is certain is that a budget maintains an awareness of the need to achieve good results and within TQM it can pinpoint problematic areas in financial terms. It gives the people who plan and implement it a total perspective of the organisation's needs and shows them the interdependence of its commercial activities.

Planning an operational budget

In multi-unit organisations the planning of operational budgets is carried out in the accounting department at head office. In individual units the budget should be planned by a committee composed of management and departmental heads, such as the food and beverage manager, head chef and head waiter. The pattern of planning is generally as follows:

1 Ascertain from previous records the level of business and possible income.
2 Determine the period to be covered by the budget.
3 Outline the commitments and expectations for the forthcoming period and deal with:
   • any variations from targets set in the previous year
   • any areas requiring consideration, such as wage increases
   • market interpretation
   • possible changes in practices, such as methods of service or portion size
   • impending increases in the price of fuel, maintenance contracts, rates, etc.
   • any other useful information relating to the matter.
4 Give members of the committee a brief period in which to submit the budget requirements of their department.
5 Discuss the budget and set a precise target for each department.

The total budget should then be compiled by the general manager and an accountant and the final version presented to the committee. Once approval for it has been received a period for reviewing performance will be set.

From the main operating budget figure, a number of more detailed specialised budgets can be constructed as required. For example, a sales budget may be drawn up to show the desirable return from any specific area such as dining-room or bar, the desirable sales mix of food and drink, the nature of food sales in relation to mealtimes, and ideal figures for lunch and dinner. The idea can be extended to cover any specific area such as labour, purchases or maintenance. The budget is used as a device to monitor the financial progress or otherwise of the

Figure 87   Budget for a commercial establishment

Projected budget for year ending 31.12.20_ _

	Jan	Feb	Mar	Apr	May	June	Jul	Aug	Sept	Oct	Nov	Dec	Totals
Sales													
Food	12,000	12,400	13,000	15,000	16,000	17,000	22,000	22,000	18,000	17,000	14,000	16,000	194,400
Beverages	6,000	6,200	6,400	7,500	8,000	8,500	12,000	14,000	9,000	8,000	7,000	8,000	100,600
Total	18,000	18,600	19,400	22,500	24,000	25,500	34,000	36,000	27,000	25,000	21,000	24,000	295,000
Cost of sales													
Food	4,000	4,200	4,400	5,000	5,400	5,700	7,400	7,400	6,000	5,400	4,800	5,200	64,900
Beverages	3,000	3,100	3,200	3,750	4,000	4,300	6,000	7,000	4,500	4,000	3,500	4,000	50,350
Total	7,000	7,300	7,600	8,750	9,400	10,000	13,400	14,400	11,100	9,400	8,300	9,200	115,250
Gross profit	11,000	11,300	11,800	13,750	14,600	15,500	20,600	21,600	16,500	15,600	13,700	14,800	179,750
Controllable expenses													
Administration	1,800	1,800	1,800	1,800	1,800	1,800	1,800	1,800	1,800	1,800	1,800	1,800	21,600
Labour	4,000	4,000	4,400	5,000	6,000	6,000	8,000	8,000	7,000	6,000	5,000	6,000	69,400
Heat and energy	1,200	1,200	1,000	1,000	1,000	1,200	1,400	1,400	1,200	1,200	1,200	1,200	14,200
Repair and maintenance	600	600	600	600	600	600	600	600	600	600	600	600	7,200
Cleaning materials	400	400	400	600	600	600	600	600	600	600	600	600	6,600
Advertising	400	400	400	200	200	200	200	200	200	400	400	400	3,600
Printing and stationery	200	200	200	200	200	200	200	200	200	200	200	200	2,400
Telephone and miscellaneous	200	200	200	200	200	200	200	200	200	200	200	200	2,400
Total	8,800	8,800	9,000	9,600	10,600	10,800	13,000	13,000	11,800	11,000	10,000	11,000	127,000
Operating profit	2,200	2,500	2,800	4,150	4,000	4,700	7,600	8,600	4,700	4,600	2,700	3,800	52,350

operation and to adjust relevant factors to emerging situations. This could include adjusting the number of staff employed at periods when business is quiet and increasing it at busy times, or spending more money on advertising at quiet periods and less when business is good. In effect a budget is a form of financial quality control which assists in maintaining a desirable return on investment and ensuring the operating health of the enterprise. An example of a budget for a commercial undertaking is given in Figure 87.

Budgets do not only apply to the commercial sector, they are also extremely important in the cost and welfare sector. Hospital caterers will be given a budget of a specific amount per person for food and drink and for labour costs and must keep within it. Industrial caterers should know the value of subsidies they will receive and be able to forecast income from sales for the financial year, and from this to establish an operating budget to guide the operation to a break-even point in the end.

Further reading

Baron, S. and Harris, K. (1995) *Services: Marketing Text and Cases*. Macmillan

Bergman, B. and Klefsjö, B. (1994) *Quality from Customer Needs to Customer Satisfaction*. McGraw-Hill

Gunter, B. and Furnham, A. (1992) *Consumer Profiles*. International Thomson Business Press

Lashley, C. (1997) *Empowering Service Excellence: Beyond the Quick Fix*. Cassell

Watson, J. (1997) *Managing Quality in Customer Care*. Butterworth-Heinemann

Wearne, N. and Morrison, A. (1996) *Hospitality Marketing*. Butterworth-Heinemann

17 Quality management

Quality concepts; Defining quality; The perceptual gap; Quality control; Official dimensions of quality.

This chapter outlines the methods of implementing quality control over the entire catering operation. Quality management must start at the top with the manager who sets the standards to be achieved by every member of staff of the department. Each action or process must be defined in clear, precise instructions.

Quality concepts

It is not easy to decide what constitutes perfect quality. One person's idea of what the highest standards of perfection should be may be very different from that of another member of staff. The surest way of achieving the required quality is to draw up a quality specification for each item and demand strict adherence to it.

In the manufacturing industry it is possible to lay down precise product codes of practice and to operate machines which perform to exact specifications. The British Standards Institute (BSI) was established early in the century to specify optimum quality standards and to devise rigid codes of practice for carrying out tasks. Manufacturers of all kinds of goods could adopt these standards voluntarily and obtain BSI approval of their products.

In some cases compliance with British Standards is obligatory. Testing and Certification Services BS 5750 are dealt with later in this chapter.

Defining quality

One definition of quality is that the product has a distinguishing characteristic which shows a superior standard of excellence as compared with a lesser product. This means that dishes must be judged on their appearance as well as their taste. The following points are aspects of quality:

- the dishes suit the tastes of a cross-section of the customers
- the dishes are appropriate to the kind of meal and the occasion
- the food is fit for human consumption and is produced in compliance with legislation
- the standard size portions give value for money

- the food is prepared and served to retain its nutritional value
- the dishes have a degree of originality but are true to their names and menu descriptions
- the meals contain a proper balance of taste, texture, seasoning and aroma
- the dishes are neatly and artistically arranged to make them visually attractive
- the dishes are served at the correct temperature and to the correct standard.

The perceptual gap

Perception is the process of detecting and interpreting information from the external world. The knowledge is stored, processed and used as required. It helps us make sense of daily occurrences and how to deal with them.

Waiting staff have to make use of their perception when dealing with customers and take action to prevent any barrier building up between them and their customers. Quality of service is judged by the way that staff in the restaurant look, speak, behave and dress and how knowledgeable they are about food and drink and the finer points of service. The lack of any of these attributes could cause a gap to form between server and consumer which could prevent the latter from enjoying the meal and the former from getting job satisfaction. Waiters should try to put themselves in the place of the customer and imagine what it is like to be kept waiting to be served.

Figure 88 shows the perceptual gap that exists between the producer, who evaluates a dish according to its quality and what it cost to produce, and the customer, who evaluates a dish according to its look, smell, taste and value for money. It is important that efforts are made to bridge the gap to ensure customer satisfaction. This can only be achieved through empathy or adopting the perspective of the other party.

Quality control

Quality control is used by manufacturers to ensure that products meet approved specifications regarding reliability, performance and safety standards. It should

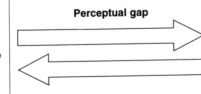

Producer perception	Perceptual gap	Customer perception
Product – intrinsic quality, service and delivery are projected to the customer by the provider		Customer evaluation of quality in relation to the perceived value and level of satisfaction prior to the delivery of the product

Figure 88   Perceptual differences

also cover the packaging, storage, delivery and after-sales service as well as manufacturers' guarantees. Any defective article must be discarded or possibly sold cheaply as a 'second'. Quality control must be in place throughout the entire manufacturing or production process.

The main use of quality control in the catering industry is for aspects of hygiene and health in cook-freeze and cook-chill production units which produce meals on a large scale. The control must extend from the purchase of ingredients to the regeneration of the meals at the ultimate destination. Ideally, quality control should be implicit in all kitchens and services. Statistical sampling is an inherent part of the process.

Quality assurance is an aspect of quality control which sets out to ensure that the quality of products on sale meets the needs of customers. It means serving meals which fulfil customer expectations at the price level of a particular establishment.

The restaurant of a luxury hotel will have a large menu and wine list filled with expensive dishes and wines to meet its customers' requirements of gourmet food and skilled service. At the other extreme a small restaurant tucked away in a back street can fulfil its customers' requirements from a very limited list of food and drink and operate as successfully as the much grander hotel restaurant. Each gives good-quality food of its kind in relation to the charges it makes.

Quality assurance has been a major factor in the success of some of the UK's biggest food retailers who in the annual reports and accounts make mention of the research they carry out for new products and commitment to quality assurance of all their goods. No compromise in quality is allowed in the drive to expand their choice of dishes.

Quality assurance concentrates on the actual product. Total quality management or TQM considers not only the finished product but all areas of the establishment, so that quality becomes everybody's responsibility, from the most junior member of staff to the most senior manager. In this way an organisation develops a framework enabling quality to be achieved at all levels.

This highlights the need to train staff of all grades in order to develop their awareness of quality standards and to give them a sense of involvement. Staff must be encouraged to put forward new ideas that could improve the operation of the business. A working party consisting of departmental heads and members of the workforce should meet regularly to establish goals and how they may be achieved, with the aim of promoting a culture which will encourage all to work to their highest possible standards.

Official dimensions of quality

BS 5750

In the UK the most thorough way of achieving quality assurance is by gaining the BS 5750, the British Standard for firms. This scheme is administered by the

National Accreditation Council of Certification Bodies. Firms which implement the highest possible level of quality control as specified by the NAC can apply for accreditation. A quality manual has to be drawn up by the firm to show how each and every procedure within the operation, in this case food, drink and service or provision of accommodation, is carried out. The accreditation body will study the quality manual and if it meets the required standard will visit and inspect the firm. Members of the body will check that all work is carried out in accordance with the submitted manual and, if satisfied, grant accreditation. The accreditation body will revisit the firm on subsequent occasions to ensure that standards are constantly maintained.

A small-scale catering firm may find it too costly to try for BS 5750, but can benefit by using suppliers and contractors who have gained accreditation.

ISO 9000

ISO 9000 is the international accreditation for quality standards. The organisation is a federation of national standard bodies from 91 countries, including the British Standards Institute. The International Organisation for Standards (ISO) began its work in 1976 by developing a series of standards of quality management systems. The European parliament has issued directions which require companies producing specific goods to gain approved quality systems.

The ISO 9000 is the most comprehensive quality system; it lays down 20 standards which have to be attained to gain accreditation. In relation to our food examples, the following quality standards need to be established:

1 A policy statement must be produced which specifies the organisation's objectives in relation to quality, management and individual responsibilities.
2 Products and services will be provided in relation to the consumer expectation of satisfaction. Every item produced must comply with present legal regulations.
3 Product specifications should be drawn up to ensure that all commodities, including water, are safe and of the required quality.
4 The environment in which food is processed should meet legal safety and hygiene standards. Processing equipment must be capable of producing goods which meet the required standards.
5 The premises must conform to legal requirements on lighting, heating, ventilation and noise levels. Premises must also be kept in a hygienic condition at all times.
6 Staff working in all areas of the production unit must maintain a high standard of personal hygiene.
7 Production methods should be specified and yield consistent results.
8 Purchasing must be strictly related to need and the requirements clearly stated.
9 All goods must be inspected on delivery for quantity and quality.
10 Recipe manuals should include instructions on safe cooking practices and packaging.

11 Control procedures should be specified, with clear instructions for management intervention.

12 Samples of cooked food should be tested for safety and quality. Records must be kept of production to simplify the tracing and isolation of possible contaminated batches.

13 The production manual should specify the post-processing treatment, including portioning and cooling of food, to meet legal safety requirements.

14 The equipment used in food production and product testing, such as oven thermostats, temperature probes and incubators, must be checked at regular intervals to ensure optimum performance.

15 A precise method for stock rotation must be implemented. Specific delivery instructions must also be provided, including the care of temperatures during transportation.

16 An instruction manual must be compiled for the end user to ensure the product is used safely and in its optimum condition, including regeneration methods, storage methods, use-by-dates, etc.

17 Quality control at the holding stage should be implemented. The flavour and appearance can be damaged and nutritional values lost by prolonged storage at serving temperatures. The optimum holding temperature is 65–70°C.

18 The principle of work study can be used to determine if the service could be run more efficiently.

19 Staff training is an important part of quality improvement. Staff must be aware of the quality expectations and of the dangers associated with food contamination.

20 Customer feedback on the products and services should be obtained to ensure that the operation meets the stated objectives.

Further reading

Dale, B. (1999) *Managing Quality*. 3rd Edition. Blackwell
East, J. (1993) *Managing Quality in the Catering Industry*. Croner
Lockwood, A. *et al.* (1996) *Quality Management in Hospitality*. Cassell
Kolarik, W. J. (1995) *Creating Quality Concepts, Systems, Strategy*. McGraw-Hill
Teare, R. *et al.* (1993) *Achieving Quality Performance*. Cassell
Van der Wagen, L. (1995) *Building Quality Service*. Butterworth-Heinemann

18 Personnel, training and education

Training: the historical background; Methods of staff training; National Vocational Qualifications (NVQs); General National Vocational Qualifications (GNVQs); Modern Apprenticeships; Higher National Diplomas; HCIMA courses; Catering degree courses; International qualifications; Staff management.

Human resources play a very important part in most industries, but none so conspicuously as the catering industry which is closely associated with the tourist industry and constitutes an integral part of its commercial sector. Together catering and tourism earn several billion pounds sterling in foreign exchange for the benefit of the UK balance of payments each year.

Catering has to compete with other service industries to attract the best available staff. The industry does not actually manufacture anything (in the context of durable products), but provides services to the public by supplying accommodation, food and drink away from home. To do this it requires as many as 2.5 million employees, which is almost 9 per cent of the working population of the UK.

In many cases staff have to be on duty to provide these services throughout the day on every day of the year. The number of 9 a.m. to 5 p.m. jobs is very limited, and these are mainly in the cost or welfare sector. Hours of duty and working conditions, whether in front of or behind the scenes, are not always congenial as service is demanded from early morning to late at night, at weekends and on Bank Holidays. In many departments the work is heavy and tiring, which could exclude the employment of elderly people and even female workers.

It is estimated that the industry needs to recruit at least 64,000 people annually as replacements for those who leave or retire from their jobs. It is an industry which encompasses a total of 122,000 establishments of which 86 per cent are small businesses earning about £5,000 per week each. The total turnover of 17,500 firms in the commercial restaurant sector amounted to £38 billion in 1992.

Staff turnover

The Wages Council for the catering industry was in operation from 1909 until its abolition in 1993. During this time it set minimum wage levels for all grades of catering staff and acted as a safety net for workers' rights. Catering staff now have no alternative but to accept the terms and conditions offered by employers. The Council was abolished so that wages can be allowed to fluctuate depending on the economic environment, enabling firms to be more competitive. For example, during a recession employers have to cut their costs, which they may do by cutting wages, hours of work, or actual jobs – or all three.

Competition among establishments does not necessarily create better conditions or higher salaries. The image of the catering industry to outsiders is that employers are not in general very fair to their staff, a situation that is likely to get worse now that deregulation has taken place. This could mean that it will be more difficult to attract good people into the industry and then to keep them. Turnover of staff is estimated at 30 per cent of the total number of employees, both full- and part-time. There is a continuous need for good induction and training to reduce this number and so improve the image of the catering industry.

Training: the historical background

In 1902 local education authorities were given money by the government to set up colleges that would offer technical courses, mainly for people who wished to become better qualified and skilled at their daily jobs. Daytime and evening classes were offered on a voluntary basis until the 1944 Education Act made it compulsory for young people under the age of 18 who were in work to attend day-release classes in their chosen subject.

The City and Guilds has been involved in technical education since it was founded in 1878. It published syllabuses and gave approval to technical colleges to offer courses. At the end of the second World War it made an enormous contribution to the post-war expansion of technical training which eventually led to the provision of courses for the catering industry in nearly 250 colleges in the UK. It now operates the National Vocational Qualification (NVQ) schemes in conjunction with the Hotel and Catering Training Company, the NVQ Council, and the Hotel and Catering International Management Association.

The Government White Paper on Education and Training for the 21st Century came into effect in 1993 and made all colleges of further education and sixth-form colleges independent of their local education authorities. Instead they came under the authority of the Further Education Funding Council. The Council assesses the work carried out in all colleges and keeps a close watch on the financial framework of each to ensure that their public funds are properly managed and they are run on a commercial basis. All examination schemes are run subject to the Council's quality assessment.

Teaching staff are employed and paid by the college through its governing body which sees that they are involved in curriculum development as well as marketing their department's facilities. College departments can offer their own courses such as diplomas in professional cookery or specialised chef courses, usually on a three- or four-year sandwich or part-time basis, with periods of paid employment in good hotels or restaurants. Some of these courses are operated with the approval and support of professional associations such as the Académie Culinaire de France.

Methods of staff training

Many firms carry out on-the-job training for their own particular operation by utilising the skills and knowledge of their own supervisory members of staff who are capable of giving instruction on the company's methods and policies. Some firms have a philosophy of encouraging staff to become more accomplished by positive encouragement and the prospect of incentives to staff who show a willingness to increase their capabilities. It is possible to build up an ethos of continuous learning by keeping a library of textbooks and trade journals in the staff recreation room. Some establishments will give support to staff wishing to participate in national and local Salons Culinaire, whilst others will give staff time off work with pay to study at college or pay fees for distance learning schemes. Senior staff may be sent on a visit or tour of other establishments in other countries where they can gather ideas for new techniques and new dishes.

There are several commercial firms of trainers who offer their own tailor-made courses to various grades of staff employed in a catering business. Such courses aim to increase the capabilities of all members of staff from kitchen porter to middle-rank manager. They are on the client's premises or at the training firm's own school. The aims are to widen the horizons of each member of staff, to give them a deeper understanding of their importance in the team, to help them take pride in their job, to boost their morale, and of course to make them more effective at their job. The courses are conducted by experienced trainers who are capable of drawing out better results from staff, whether new recruits or long-serving hands taking a refresher course.

National Vocational Qualifications (NVQs)

Training for the catering industry is based on what is known as the NVQ system. This has replaced the well-respected City and Guilds courses which have been the benchmark of qualified staff for the past 50 years. Since 1992 craft courses have been run as industry-based National Vocational Qualifications, where training is meant to be undertaken in the workplace with time spent at a local college of further education.

Figure 89   A sample unit from NVQ Catering and Hospitality (Food Preparation and Presentation), Level 2

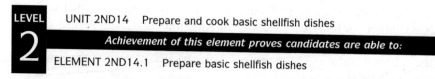

LEVEL 2

UNIT 2ND14   Prepare and cook basic shellfish dishes

Achievement of this element proves candidates are able to:

ELEMENT 2ND14.1   Prepare basic shellfish dishes

Performance criteria

Assessment shows the element has been achieved because:

1 Preparation areas and suitable equipment are hygienic and ready for use.

2 **Shellfish** are of the type, quality and quantity required.

3 Any **problems** identified with the quality of **shellfish** or **other ingredients** are reported promptly to the appropriate person.

4 **Shellfish** is correctly prepared using the appropriate **preparation methods** and combined with **other ingredients** ready for cooking.

5 Shellfish dishes not for immediate use are stored correctly.

6 Preparation areas and equipment are cleaned correctly after use.

7 All work is prioritised and carried out in an organised and efficient manner in line with appropriate organisational procedures and **legal requirements**.

Range

List of situations to which the element applies:

A Shellfish relates to **PC2,3,4**

• crab
• prawns
• shrimps
• scampi
• mussels
• oysters

B Problems relates to **PC3**

• in terms of freshness
• in terms of quantity

C Other ingredients relates to **PC3,4**

• dairy products
• eggs
• fruit
• vegetables
• breadcrumbs

D Preparation methods relates to **PC4**

• trimming
• shelling
• debearding
• scraping/cleaning
• coating

E Legal requirements relates to **PC7**

• current relevant legislation relating to hygienic and safe working practices when preparing basic shellfish dishes

Continues Element:

ELEMENT 2ND14.1 Prepare basic shellfish dishes

Underpinning knowledge

List of essential knowledge needed to achieve this element

Health and safety

- What safe working practices should be followed when preparing basic shellfish dishes.

Food hygiene

- Why it is important to keep preparation areas and equipment hygienic when preparing basic shellfish dishes.
- What the main contamination threats are when preparing and storing basic shellfish dishes.
- Why time and temperature are important when preparing basic shellfish dishes.
- Why prepared shellfish should be stored at the required safe temperature before cooking.

Product knowledge

- What quality points to look for in shellfish.
- What basic preparation methods are suitable for different types of shellfish.

Health catering practices

- Which products could be used to substitute high fat ingredients when preparing basic shellfish dishes.
- Which fats/oils can contribute to healthy catering practices
- Why increasing the fibre content of basic shellfish dishes can contribute to healthy catering practices.

Assessment of performance

Collecting evidence of competence:

- Competence must be assessed to cover:
  - all the performance criteria
  - all of the range based on the relevant performance criteria
  - the underpinning knowledge
  either in the workplace or realistic work environment
- Competence must be demonstrated consistently over a period of time
- The methods of assessment shown below must be used.

Evidence requirements

Part one **and** part two must be covered but not necessarily separately.

Part One – *Evidence to cover performance criteria & range*

Option 1 – Using a combination of performance and supplementary evidence as follows:
a) By performance evidence in the form of observation to cover performance criteria 1,2,4,6 and a minimum of:
    3 from the range of A
    3 from the range of C
    3 from the range of D

and

b) By **either** performance evidence in the form of observation **or** supplementary evidence in the form of questioning[§] and/or witness testimony to cover the rest of the performance criteria.

and

c) By supplementary evidence in the form of questioning[§] and/or witness testimony to cover the rest of the range
[§]Questioning can be oral, written or using visual aids.

or **Option 2**: Totally through performance evidence in the form of observation.
or **Option 3**: Totally or partly using suitable evidence of prior achievement. This evidence must be authentic and prove current competence.

Part Two – *Evidence to cover underpinning knowledge*

This must be assessed using questioning which may be oral, written or using visual aids.

Under the NVQ system students concentrate on a single operation or dish, getting to know all about it by collecting data on it and compiling a portfolio of work.

Course subjects are based on employers' needs and are done to their particular standard. Trainees are given guidance by on-the-job trainers who assess the results and by an external assessor who may be present to check that the performance is of an acceptable standard. This combination of paid employment and regular training is available to everyone regardless of age and previous experience. There are no final practical or theoretical examinations or time limits imposed.

Each NVQ is made up of a number of units which put together lead to the award of the certificate. An example of a unit for Level 2 is shown in Figure 89. The training must be carried out at the workplace or an authorised centre run by an agent approved by the awarding body. The external assessor also views the diary kept by the candidate which shows all classes attended and skills acquired and includes the observations of the trainer in the workplace plus the college lecturer's view of the level of competence attained.

Level 1 covers the work done by a commis cook, call-order cook, fast-food cook, counterhand, room attendant, reception porter and catering assistant. Level 2 leads to chef de partie, chef de rang, bar person, receptionist or silver-service waiter status. Level 3 is head of department level such as head waiter, head housekeeper or head chef and does not include craft examinations. It is the equivalent of 2 A levels and on a par with a two-year full-time course. There are two higher levels: 4 which is entirely theoretical and is the equivalent of an ordinary degree, and 5 which is equivalent to a Masters degree.

The NVQ programmes in the hotel and catering industry seem to be amongst the most successful. A considerable amount of their success is due to the work of the Hospitality Training Foundation (winners of the National Training Award 1995) in developing and providing study materials for the various levels of the NVQ. It is expected that by the turn of the century some 50 per cent of the total workforce in catering will be qualified to NVQ Level 3. In Scotland these qualifications are distinguished as SVQs.

General National Vocational Qualifications (GNVQs)

These are vocational qualifications for school leavers of 16+ years who either want to stay at their school for a further year of study or attend a sixth-form college or a college of further education as an alternative to studying for A level examinations. Schools and colleges have to obtain the NVQ Council's approval.

As with NVQs, there is no final examination and no time limit for the subject. A GNVQ course incorporates the skills of the chosen subject, numeracy, communication, problem-solving, and some industrial experience. Figure 90 shows how NVQs and GNVQs compare with academic courses.

Figure 90   Equivalence of qualifications

Level	NVQ	GNVQ	Academic
5	Professional	–	Higher education Masters degree
	Management		
4	Higher technical	–	Higher education first degree
	Junior management		
3	Technician	Advanced	2 A levels
	Supervisor		
2	Craft	Intermedicate	5 GCSEs at grades A–C
1	Foundation	Foundation	GCSE grades D and E

Modern Apprenticeships

The Government has provided funds to run a new apprenticeship scheme for a number of crafts, including catering, for young people of 16–19 years of age. These are three-stage programmes designed for people who wish to become chefs, food servers, wine waiters, housekeepers or public-house keepers. This form of apprenticeship is not indentured but applicants must be prepared to sign a pledge to agree the terms and conditions and to complete the full programme. A Modern Apprenticeship can also lead to the attainment of NVQ Level 3 in the chosen field.

Higher National Diplomas

These are full-time or sandwich-type courses for applicants with two A levels who wish to acquire the competence and skills needed to achieve head of department status. These courses usually include practical work in the type of establishment considered for a subsequent career. They are well regarded by employers because they know the course produces people who are not afraid to roll up their sleeves and tackle any kind of task in an emergency and can inspire staff by their practical ability.

HCIMA courses

The Hotel and Catering International Management Association is the UK's professional body for all sectors of the catering industry and has members in several other countries. One of its objectives is to prepare managers for the industry by offering syllabuses and examinations to be run by a number of colleges as full-time, sandwich, part-time, day-release or distance learning (home-based) courses.

The professional certificate is for prospective supervisors or line managers. The professional diploma is an advanced course for students who aspire to senior management level. Each embraces syllabuses for food and beverage studies, accommodation, human resources, marketing and finance, plus an in-depth project of the student's choice.

Catering degree courses

These advanced courses are offered at no less than 30 universities in the UK, some on traditional lines, others on a modular basis which allows undergraduates to select a number of disciplines in accordance with their prospective employment and ambitions, thus giving them a broader outlook. The core subject is compulsory and consists of several modules such as food and beverage operations, accommodation, economics, finance, marketing, personnel, and social aspects of the hospitality industry. Each module is individually assessed and progress through the course is made by accumulating a number of points – 27 for a pass at honours level and 23 for an ordinary degree.

Courses normally include one year's industrial practice. This period of industrial release can be done in a foreign country where students can work alongside nationals of that country and students from other countries and colleges also on industrial release. This gives students a thorough insight into how foreign catering establishments are run and the opportunity to learn the language. Colleges and universities in the UK have forged links with similar establishments abroad with the idea of promoting an exchange of students.

Students who have completed an HND course are permitted to enrol for the second stage of a degree course and students who have attained Level 3 of a GNVQ are eligible to apply to a university for a degree course.

International qualifications

At present there is a considerable difference between countries in relation to the type and award of catering qualifications. There is, however, a major movement in Europe initiated principally by the Eurhodip Association towards a convergence of awards.

Catering education in France is under the influence and control of the French Ministry of National Education which ensures that every college follows the same syllabus and attains a specific standard. This can be seen in the standard practical textbooks *Travaux Pratiques de Cuisine*, *Travaux Pratiques de Restaurant*, *Sciences Appliqués a l'Alimentation*, and others published in French by Editions BPI in Paris.

The Certificat d'Aptitude Professional, or CAP as it is better known, is the general craft course equivalent to NVQ Level 2 or CG 706/2; the Brevet Technicien Hôtellier is equivalent to the National Diploma and BTEC courses;

and the Brevet Technicien Superieur is equivalent to the Higher National Diploma. There is also the Brevet d'Etudes Professionelles, known as the Baccalauréat, which is the advanced cookery course, the equivalent of the former CG 706/3.

It is perfectly possible for a British student to apply to attend a French catering college if they have some knowledge of the language and the necessary finances, and equally French nationals can apply to study in UK colleges. At present there are no government-sponsored first degrees in France for the study of hospitality management, although such a programme of study is offered in Paris by Cornell/Essec, a subsidiary of the American Cornell University, comprising topics compatible with a hospitality degree programme in the UK.

Hotel and catering education, like any post-secondary qualification in most European countries, is controlled by the individual governments and in general they all demonstrate a strong affinity with the French model. Within the EU and neighbouring countries in what is loosely described as Continental Europe, the hotel and catering business is still considered a craft trade even at managerial level. Consequently it is believed that the nature and level of hotel and catering work does not require degree-level programmes of studies.

In general these hotel and catering courses involve a three-year post junior/secondary vocational programme of studies, which is the normal alternative route to the more academic studies in preparation for higher education. The courses consist of a certificate of craft qualification in cookery, waiting or reception work. Successful candidates from these courses may elect to continue their studies for a further two years which will give them an Expert/Technician Diploma in Hotel Operations. This is equivalent to the BTEC Diploma in the UK. In a number of countries the diploma consists of a three-year post-craft study, which would be equivalent to a Higher National Diploma in the UK.

As in France, alternatives to these national courses exist in many parts of Europe. They are provided by private hotel schools with strict entrance requirements, such as those in Lausanne and the Hague. Up to the mid 1980s they offered diplomas in hotel management, but now offer recognised degree programmes. The Schiller International University operates on the American credit system and offers first degrees and postgraduate degree-level courses in a number of centres in Europe.

In the United States of America, the country which led the first boom in the service industries, degree programmes in hotel management have a long history. The first courses were offered as far back as 1922 at Cornell University, and now they are available on a number of campuses throughout the country. In general these courses all cover the same subjects of accounting, economics, food and beverage production and service, food science, gastronomy, housekeeping, interior design, languages, law, personnel management, planning, marketing and product development. There are also many colleges offering tourism at several levels.

Staff management

Human resources are essential to the success of every catering business, but selecting the right kind of staff who are good at customer service can be difficult. The personnel officer or manager of a catering business must know the qualities to look for when recruiting new staff. Staff must be selected on their capabilities or potential for the particular post. Those who have to deal directly with customers must possess the necessary social skills as well as the practical skills of the job.

Employees working at the front of the house, which includes waiting and reception, should be selected for their personality, appearance on duty, stance and body language, use of eye contact, facial expression, composure and manner of speech. The intuition of the personnel manager can be backed up by a psychometric test and the candidate's references from school, college or previous employer, as well as the keenness of the applicant to get the job.

A manpower programme based on the Modern Apprenticeships Scheme or the NVQ system can help to ensure a constant supply of qualified staff. Contact with local schools, colleges and youth clubs can be useful as a means of recruiting staff for full-time or casual work. The manager may find it useful to keep the establishment in the public eye by acting as public relations officer which will stimulate appreciation by the local population.

Further reading

Boella, M. (1996) *Human Resource Management in the Hospitality Industry.* Stanley Thornes

Bratton, J. and Gold, J. (1999) *Human Resource Management Theory and Practice.* Macmillan

Brewester, C. and Harris, H. (1998) *International HRM Contemporary Issues in Europe.* Routledge

Goldsmith, A. (1997) *Human Resource Management in Hospitality Services.* International Thomson Business Press

Hayter, R. (1990) *Careers in Hotel Catering and Tourism.* Butterworth-Heinemann

Maxwell, G. (1997) *Managing Human Resources in Hospitality.* Cassell

Riley, M. (1996) *Human Resource Management.* Butterworth-Heinemann

Appendix: Genetically modified (GM) foods

Biotechnology is using genetic engineering to modify traditional agricultural and horticultural produce. Present-day scientists have the technology to identify genes within species of fruits and vegetables which have particular desirable traits. They can then transfer a copy of the genes to the living cells of plants in order to make a new substance or to perform a new function. This is done with the intent of improving the all-round quality of the chosen produce. It is believed that with appropriate modification, existing species could taste better, be more nutritious, have a longer shelf-life, and generally be more acceptable.

To an extent, farmers have been doing something like this throughout the ages. Both in the past and today farmers identify that a certain crop is growing hardier, is more prolific and disease-resistant, so they keep its seeds for future sowing to reap any possible benefits from it.

The first genetically engineered products were tomatoes. The Food and Drugs Administration in the United States approved the growing of genetically modified tomatoes in 1994, and they are on sale nationwide. The American public accept them knowing they will be fresh and edible for at least ten days, even though they were picked at full maturity, therefore with their fullest flavour.

In this country the government and firms in the GM food industry have encountered many obstacles in their small-scale trials, which are mainly of maize and soya. There has been much debate and publicity, to the extent that the general public is waiting to see more trialing and testing done, so as to be reassured on possible adverse consequences. Potential growers have to obtain government permission to plant these products on their land, and the resultant produce then has to be labelled. If processed, the product is monitored so that the user will know if even small traces of it are contained in any foodstuffs.

New labelling laws require caterers to declare on their menus if any of the ingredients used in a dish contain genetically modified produce. Caterers will have to obtain a written assurance from the supplier as to whether a particular product contains any GM maize or soya. Only in this way can caterers cover themselves legally. The government is committed to ensuring that customers can make an infomed choice; but to be on the safe side, caterers may well refrain from using any such ingredients.

The agriculture industry is always seeking to improve its productivity, and, through the use of chemical fertilisers and plant-breeding techniques in this century alone, has increased the grain harvest five-fold. It is estimated that there are 800 million people in this world who go hungry and are malnourished; a number estimated to double in the twenty-first century. Further increases in production may be thwarted by the decreased amount of water available for irrigation, but it is known that biotechnology can improve yields further, and the use of GM food may become a necessity of life.

Index